CW00952130

THE CELESTIAL HUNTER

BY ROBERTO CALASSO

THE CELESTIAL HUNTER

ROBERTO CALASSO

TRANSLATED FROM THE ITALIAN
BY RICHARD DIXON

ALLEN LANE
an imprint of
PENGUIN BOOKS

ALLEN LANE

UK | USA | Canada | Ireland | Australia
India | New Zealand | South Africa

Allen Lane is part of the Penguin Random House group of companies
whose addresses can be found at global.penguinrandomhouse.com.

First published in Italian as *Il Cacciatore Celeste* by Adelphi Edizione, Italy 2016
English translation first published by Farrar, Straus and Giroux 2020
This edition first published by Allen Lane 2020
001

Copyright © Adelphi Edizioni S.p.A Milano, 2016
Translation copyright © Richard Dixon, 2020

The moral right of the author and the translator has been asserted

Printed and bound in Great Britain by Clays Ltd, Elcograf S.p.A.

A CIP catalogue record for this book is available from the British Library

ISBN: 978-0-241-29674-5

What is god, or not god, or in between?

—EURIPIDES, *HELEN*

CONTENTS

I

IN THE TIME
OF THE
GREAT RAVEN

In the time of the Great Raven even the invisible was visible. And it continually transformed itself. Animals, at that time, were not necessarily animals. They might happen to be animals, but sometimes they were humans, gods, lords of a species, demons, ancestors. And humans weren't necessarily humans but could also be the transient form of something else. There were no tricks for recognizing those that appeared. They had to be already known, as one knows a friend or an adversary. Everything, from spiders to the dead, occurred within a single flow of forms. It was the realm of metamorphosis.

The change was continual, as later happened only in the cavity of the mind. Things, animals, humans: distinctions never clear cut, always temporary. When a vast part of what existed withdrew into the invisible, this didn't mean it stopped happening. But it became easier to think it wasn't happening.

How could the invisible return to being visible? By animating the drum. The stretched skin of a dead animal was the steed, it was the journey, the gilded whirlwind. It led to the place where the grasses roar, where the rushes moan, where not even a needle could pierce the gray thickness.

When hunting began, it was not a man who chased an animal. It was a being that chased another being. No one could say with certainty who each of them were. The animal being chased could be a man transformed or a god or simply an animal or a spirit or a dead being. And, one day, humans added another invention to the many others: they began to surround themselves with animals that adapted to humans, whereas for a very long time it had been humans that had imitated animals. They became settled—and already somewhat staid.

Why so much hesitation before setting off to hunt the bear? Because the bear could also be a man. People had to be careful when talking, since the bear could hear everything said about it, even when it was far away. Even when it retired into its den, even when it was asleep, the bear carried on following what was happening in the world. "The earth is the ear of a bear," people said. When they met to plan the hunt, the bear was never named. And generally, if the bear were mentioned, it was never called by its name: it was "Old Man," "Old Black Man," "Grandfather," "Cousin," "Worthy Old Man," "Black Beast," "Uncle." Those preparing for the hunt avoided saying anything. Cautious, wrapped in concentration, they knew the slightest sound could ruin the enterprise. If the bear appears unexpectedly in the forest, it's a good idea to step aside, take off one's hat, and say: "Go on your way, most honorable one." Otherwise one tries to kill it. The whole of the bear is valuable. Its body is medicine. When they managed to kill it, they ran off immediately. Then they would return to the scene, as if by chance, as though they were taking a stroll. And they would discover to their great surprise that someone unknown had killed the bear.

The first divine being whose name it was forbidden to mention was the bear. In this respect monotheism was not an innovation but a revival, a hardening. The novelty was the prohibition on images.

Knowing that the bear understood everything they said, they would talk with it before attacking, or immediately after. "It wasn't us," some would say. They would thank the bear for allowing itself to be killed. Often they would apologize. Some would add: "I'm poor, this is why I'm hunting you." Some would sing as they killed the bear, so that the bear, while dying, could say: "I like that song."

They would hang the bear's skull in the branches of a tree, sometimes with tobacco between its teeth. Sometimes decorated with red stripes. They attached ribbons to it, wrapped the bones in a bundle, and hung them from another tree. If one bone was lost, the spirit of the bear would hold the hunter responsible. Its nose ended up in some secret place in the woods.

When they captured one of the bear's cubs they would put it in a cage. It was often nursed by the hunter's wife. In this way it grew up, until one day the cage was opened and "the dear little divine thing" was invited to the feast at which it would be sacrificed. Everyone would dance around the bear and clap their hands. The woman who had nursed it would cry. Then a hunter would say a few words to the bear: "O thou divine one, thou wast sent into the world for us to hunt. O thou precious little divinity, we worship thee: pray hear our prayer. We have nourished thee and brought thee up with a deal of pain and trouble, all because we love thee so. Now, as thou hast grown big, we are about to send thee to thy father and mother. When thou comest to them please speak well of us, and tell them how kind we have been; please come back to us again and we will sacrifice thee." Then they would kill it.

The oldest thought, the thought that for the first time felt no need to be presented as a story, took the form of *aphorisms on hunting*. Like a murmur, between tents and fires, transmitted like nursery rhymes:

"Wild animals are similar to human beings, only more
    sacred."
"Hunting is pure. Wild animals love people who are pure."
"How could I hunt, if before it I had not done a drawing?"
"The biggest danger in life is that the food of humans is all
    made of souls."
"The soul of the bear is a miniature bear that is found in its
    head."
"The bear can talk, but prefers to remain silent."
"Those who talk to the bear, calling it by name, make it gentle
    and harmless."

"An inept man who sacrifices takes more wild animals than an
able hunter who doesn't sacrifice."
"Animals that are hunted are like women who flirt."
"Female animals seduce the hunters."
"Every hunt is a hunt for souls."

In the beginning it wasn't even clear what hunting was for. Like
an actor who tries to enter the role of a character, they were trying to become predators. But certain animals ran faster. Others
were forbidding and circumspect. And then, what was killing?
Not much different from being killed. If the man became the bear,
when he was killing it he was attacking himself. And all the more
obscure was the relationship between killing and eating. Those
who eat are making something disappear. This is even more mysterious than killing. Where does it go when it disappears? It goes
into the invisible. Which eventually teems with presences. There is
nothing more alive than absence. What, then, is to be done about
all those beings? Perhaps they need to be helped on their way to
absence, to be accompanied for part of their journey. Killing was
like saying good-bye. And, like every good-bye, it required certain
gestures, certain words. They began to celebrate sacrifices.

Hunting starts as an inevitable act and ends as a gratuitous act.
It elaborates a sequence of ritual practices that precede the act (the
killing) and follow it. The act can only be encompassed in time, as
the prey is encompassed in space. But the course of the hunt itself
is unnamable and uncontrollable, like intercourse. No one knows
what will happen between hunter and prey when they face each
other. But what is certain, prior to the hunt the hunter performs
acts of devotion. And after the hunt he feels the need to offload a
feeling of guilt. He welcomes the dead animal into his hut like a
noble guest. In front of the bear that has just been cut into pieces,
the hunter murmurs a prayer of vertiginous sweetness: "Allow me
to kill you even in the future."

The prey has to be brought into focus: the isolating gaze reduces the field of vision to one point. It is a knowledge that proceeds through successive gaps, carving figures out from a background. Circumscribing them, it isolates them like a target. Indeed, the gesture of carving them out is already the gesture that attacks them. Otherwise the figure is not born. Myths, each time, are a superimposition of severed outlines. By pushing this way of knowledge each time to the extreme, by accumulating outlines, the backdrop from which they had been torn once again begins to form. This is the knowledge of the hunter.

With pastoralism and agriculture, the animal was just an animal, forever separated from man. For hunters, on the contrary, the animal was yet another being, neither animal nor human, hunted by beings who were neither animals nor humans. When that event took place which was *the* event of every history before history, when the separation took place from something called animal by something that would be called man, no one thought wisdom—old and new wisdom—could be found anywhere other than in someone who shared the two forms of life. Among the caves and forests of Mount Pelion, Chiron the Centaur became the source of wisdom, the one who more than any other could teach justice, astronomy, medicine, and hunting: almost everything that could be taught at that time.

For the heroes raised by Chiron, hunting was the first element of *paideía*. But that "education," that first proof of *areté*, of the "virtue" that would then be so frequently evoked, took place entirely outside the bounds of society. And it had no use. The hunting practiced by the heroes did not serve to nurture the community. It was a bloody and solitary exercise, practiced *for no further purpose*. In the hunt, the animal turns against itself and tries to kill itself. The great hunters, before being protagonists in many tales of metamorphosis, were themselves the result of a metamorphosis. Apollo, before killing the wolf or mice, was a wolf and a mouse. Artemis, before killing bears, had been a bear. The pathos of hunting, the complicity between hunter and prey, goes back to the beginning, when the hunter was himself the animal, when Apollo was the general of an army of mice and head of a pack of wolves. The foundation of hunting was a discovery of logic: the working of negation. This founding and intoxicating discovery needed to be perpetually confirmed, repeated. While the life of the city pulsated, it was matched by another parallel life in the mountains. Tireless and solitary, Apollo and Artemis, and Dionysus, too, carried on hunting. The energy that their gestures unleashed was the necessary allusion, the framework hidden behind market trading, families at sleep, laboring in the fields. None of all that constituted city life could have existed without those hunts, those mountain ambushes, without those arrows shot, and that blood. It might be said that society had never felt itself sufficiently alive, and perhaps real, without that parallel and superfluous, roaming life of the hunter gods lost in the woods. Like the monk's prayer, the silent pursuit of the hunter gods held up the walls that enclosed the city: indeed, it was that hunting that encircled it, like a perpetual whirlwind.

Men became metaphysical animals during the hunt. Agriculture would give only one key element to thought: rhythm, the alternation between blossoming and withering. But the burden of society on man would be much increased. The great cities are heirs to those places where reserves of food were kept for the first time in tall jars in storehouses. Hunters could have no idea about reserves. They had no inventories, nor records.

The paleoanthropologist Jean Clottes found himself at Rocky Hill, in central California, in front of a cave wall decorated with pictures. He had been taken there by Hector, a Yokut Indian, the spiritual guardian of the site. Clottes concentrated on a figure that brought to mind a shaman with his drum. "It's a bear," said Hector. Surprised, the paleoanthropologist replied: "Really? I would have thought it was a man." "It's the same thing," said Hector. And he fell silent.

One of the signs of detachment from the animal came when a group of men disguised themselves as a pack of wolves: finally interchangeable, equal, like the spokes of a wheel. The intoxication was twofold and simultaneous: the intoxication of the hunted animal that turns into a predator—an intoxication of power and of metamorphosis, while still closed inside the animal circle; and the intoxication of the being that finds its equal, its substitute, its equivalent—an intoxication of knowledge, which does not reveal itself in any visible sign but marks a gap that will, from then on, be unbridgeable. The first equals were the wolves and the dead. That pack of beings that each looked like a duplication of the other took a decisive step toward abstraction: from that moment the world was branded with the mark of identity. It was their invisible banner. Its empire is revealed in a multiple, roaming, ubiquitous figure.

In order to be separated from animal continuity, the first stratagem was the mask, camouflage. That pack of wolves that roamed the forest consisted of the first men, the first who felt so irremediably human that they sought to disguise themselves as wolves. When man became man alone, a last curtain could hide him from the world: a mask of silk or velvet that left his mouth exposed. In French it is called a *loup*: because certain wolves carry the shape of a mask on their face, as if they were inviting man to imitate them, disguising himself as a wolf.

With no drum there is no shaman. But only the shaman knows how to animate the drum. At first the drum is bare, an animal skin stretched and held by a hoop of wood. As time passes, it is decorated with metallic appendages, small resonant hanging figures. It becomes overloaded, more and more. The wooden part is cut from a trunk of birch or larch. The metallic appendages: it's better for them to be old. Even better if they come from other shamans. The first sound of the drum is like the humming of a swarm of insects and a distant roar of thunder. When it is animated, it becomes a horse, then an eagle. If two shamans fight each other, blood drips from the drum of the loser. When the shaman dies they hang his drum from the branches of the nearest tree.

The shaman was obliged to operate in a world that others shunned. There, if he fought with another shaman, he would rally multitudes of familiar spirits. He had a fiery gaze that he would often conceal with a fringed hat. The shaman's drum was like the hunter's bow. The bow allowed the hunter to transform himself into an animal that strikes in a flash, with a fatal blow. The drum was the lake into which the shaman sank in order to enter a world that others did not see. First of all, the tree trunk had to be found from which the hoop of the drum was made. And the shaman animated the drum by telling the story of that tree. Even the skin of the drum spoke. It told how it had lived, until the time when a hunter had shot it. The drum is the tree and animal that were killed. The shaman became that tree and that animal. At this point the drum would begin to guide the shaman. It was a feather, a steed. The shaman held on to the drum as he would the mane of a horse.

There are three worlds, and humans are normally in the middle world. Shamans are in all three. Sometimes their heads are in one world, but their feet are in another. In all three worlds there is the same amount of life, grass, wild animals, leaves. The spirits are sometimes smaller than mosquitoes. At other times, if seen from afar, they look like mountains.

For people to hunt, they first had to imitate. To dance the step of the partridge, of the bear, of the leopard, of the crane, of the sable. To become predators, they had to take on the gestures of the predator and the prey. In this way imitation led to killing. And hidden within killing was imitation. The prey was attracted and entranced because it heard itself being called in its own language. At that moment the hunter struck. Hunter and shaman are the beings most akin to each other. They often speak the same secret language, which is then the language of animals. The shaman summons them so that they will protect and help him, the hunter summons them to draw them closer and kill them. Both activities are sacred—and each illuminates the other. At the point where they meet, there is a deep mergence. Éveline Lot-Falck preferred to go no further: "To what extent the language of the hunter mixes with that of the shaman is difficult to say. A part of the vocabulary [. . .] is probably common to the hunter and the shaman—and could have been taught by the latter to the former. It remains to be known to what extent the shaman can claim the monopoly over this science." Though he is essential for the success of the enterprise, the shaman does not take part in the hunt, nor is he present. Likewise he obtains no advantage. His role is knowledge.

The word *shaman* appeared for the first time, in Russian, in *The Life of the Archpriest Avvakum*, written between 1672 and 1673. But the word is Tungusic—and comes from a vast, desolate, remote part of Siberia. Its origin is much disputed. "Some have sought to trace the word back to the Chinese *sha-men*, others to the Pali *samana*, a transcription of the Sanskrit *sramana*." Finally, Berthold Laufer traced the word to the Turkish *kam*. Éveline Lot-Falck recalled that Paul Pelliot had found the word in a Jurchen document of 1130 (and the Jurchen were ancestors of the Tungusic people). On further research he found that "in Tungusic there are three other series of terms expressing the action of shamanizing, the first linked to the idea of praying to fire, the second to that of speech, and the third to the idea of sacred power." Lot-Falck then identified various terms for the act of shamanizing in other Turkic, Altaic, and Mongolic languages. There were many connections to further meanings. But the short conclusion of her research was this: "The etymology that emerges for the Tungusic and Jakut terms emphasizes the idea of movement, of bodily agitation. All observers of shamanism have therefore been rightly struck by this gestural activity that gives shamanism its name."

Habent sua fata verba, words have their destiny, as Proust's Professor Brichot might have said. Originating in a tiny and faraway population, the word *shaman* became the universal key for a sort of religious Esperanto. And all in a few decades, starting from Mircea Eliade's *Shamanism: Archaic Techniques of Ecstasy*, published in 1951. Evidently the world no longer had words to describe a journey that was both physical and psychic, a state—which would be called "shamanizing"—in which the bounds between visible and invisible tend to cancel each other out, where the word and the sound of the drum, the movement of the body and the challenge of the mind, overlap and merge together. The need for this word, and its absence, must have been so great that its expansion was irresistible and indiscriminate. In recent years there was a leaflet going around in California that read: "Shamanic Finance Is: Integrating Money with Spirit." In the end, it has become difficult to say what is *not* shamanic. As for shamans, they have either disappeared or manage not to be recognized.

Some regarded Siberian shamans as poor lunatics afflicted by a mysterious illness called "Arctic hysteria," which becomes more acute the farther north one goes. Others thought they were the only people capable of curing illnesses, because they knew, because they had seen the other world that opens up behind that world which for others is the only existing one, and they were the only ones able to deal with spirits and with the dead. Those doubts didn't apply only to Siberian shamans. They could be applied, with appropriate transpositions and modifications, to Empedocles or to Saint Paul. Or to Nietzsche.

Siberian shamans can be distinguished from others *that know*, in other parts of the world, first of all because their visible world is reduced to the minimum. There are no cities, nor kingdoms, nor riches, nor trade. Only the taiga, animals, intense cold. To gain access to the invisible, they had first to *dress*, to put on the few tangible objects that can have power. The clothing of Siberian shamans could weigh as much as sixty-five pounds. But those who wore it could move with a lightness of step.

The *Rgveda* refers to long-haired *muni*, who rode the wind, wrapped in "filthy red rags." They let "the gods enter them," they looked down from above on two oceans, to the east and west, they understood the minds of nymphs, and of genies, and of wild animals. From a cup they drank a substance about which we know nothing, except that it could have been a drug or a poison. It was called *viṣá*, it came from the god Rudra and they passed it to Rudra. This was the first appearance of ascetics, of *yogin*, of *sādhus*, who have emerged constantly in India, from Vedic times till today.

Ecstasy and *possession* are words that carry positive or negative connotations according to place and time. Both indicate *metamorphic* knowledge, the knowledge that transforms the person who knows at the moment at which he knows. The common assumption: a permeable mind, subject to the ebb and flow of elements that may at first sight seem extraneous but are also capable of establishing themselves as permanent guests. Yet where there is an I that is equipped with watertight compartments and is the supposed master of its own boundaries, ecstasy and possession can no longer enter. At the same time, the area that is knowable—or merely open to investigation—is vastly restricted. Many were proud of this, but it is not clear why. Apart from one reason: they had a more tranquil life, less prone to disturbance, as though they had been blinkered—and this seemed to them to be part of the natural order of things.

Apollo flies to the Hyperboreans carried by white swans, in the same way that Abaris reaches Greece from the Hyperboreans riding a golden arrow. Shamanic journeys. Apollo: god of light, of meter, of wolves and mice.

The sky was the place of the past. Lying on their backs, staring into the night at those tremulous pinpricks, they discovered what had happened: a dark and indifferent canvas, tarnished with minuscule flecks of light. This was all that remained, among multitudes of events, of actions, of beings. This was all that had been chosen to keep a meaning, a form that lit up again every night. From whatever place they observed the sky, they came across the Hunter. The hunter was the trial of memory. The sky, the first mnemotechnical order. Its vault became the house of the past, an unsullied museum. Indispensable stories glimmered each night—or remained temporarily concealed behind a veil of cloud. And the surface of the cave was another sky, just as the sky itself was the inner face of the vast cosmic cavern. To be able to hunt, one has to draw.

One day, a day that lasted not less than twenty-five thousand years, the men of the Upper Paleolithic period began to draw. Draw what? The question of choice didn't even arise: the only possible objects were animals. Animals were power in movement, which attacked or had to be attacked. This wasn't magic, as moderns might have naïvely imagined. People transformed themselves into an animal: by transforming themselves, they escaped from the animal. The animal and those who drew it belonged to the same continuum of forms. That was the moment in which the pressure of powers imposed the severest aesthetic discipline: the line, to be effective, had to be *right*. Ingres would have approved of them. If the line wasn't right, the power was not evoked. Sometimes, deep in the bowels of the rock where only one person could squeeze by, the person drawing found himself in the first camera obscura and observed the wonder of the form that emerged from his barely visible hands.

For a long time they preferred to draw the most majestic and fearsome animals, which were only rarely hunted. Drawing them was the first step toward imitating and curtailing their power. On the other hand, the human figures drawn on the rocks were for a long time marginal and casual. The most usual, immediate, and understandable way for men to represent themselves was by drawing themselves as *composite animals*, surrounded by other animals. It took many years before Greek statuary, after various meanders and byways, came to represent the human figure *alone*—and, above all, naked.

Along with animals, geometry had emerged. Countless figures drawn with animals or that stood alone on the rocky walls. All have held their secret. But all had one shared characteristic: that of being the *negation* of the world as it manifested itself, just like the first wall that stood perfectly perpendicular to the ground. They were another world, which could be inferred only by joining together various small luminous dots in the sky.

We cannot say much for sure about the people who lived during the Magdalenian period and drew on rock walls in the Dordogne. Apart from this: they drew with amazing confidence, rarely achieved again for thousands of years. Suddenly—and everywhere: in Egypt, in northern Spain, in France, in England: at Creswell, the last limit before the ice. Why did it happen? It would be rash to say. But if drawing is an act of intelligence, then the intelligence of the Magdalenian people must have been very high. And they must perhaps have had something in common with the whalers who, before they set sail, waited to see a whale in their dreams. If it didn't appear to them, they could never encounter it in reality.

Magdalenian man, for thousands of years, always used two basic signs, one vertical and the other curved: the javelin and the wound. A javelin was the weapon with which the world was struck without physical contact: a single stroke, the simplest mark. A wound was a circle, a blood-coated ring.

If the constellation is an arbitrary place to which stories are attached, not unlike the way meanings are attached to sounds, it will not be easy to explain why whenever people, not only in Greece but in Persia, in Mesopotamia, in India, in China, in Australia, and even in Surinam, looked into the same segment of sky over thousands of years, they saw the exploits of a Celestial Hunter that they never grew tired of contemplating.

The invisible is the place of the gods, the dead, ancestors, the whole of the past. It doesn't necessarily require a cult, but it seeps into every crevice of the mind. Like a metal string, it need not vibrate, it can remain inert. If it vibrates, the intensity can be convulsive. The invisible is not to be sought far away. Indeed, it might even be too close to be found. The invisible ends up in each person's head. Where it is even more difficult to distinguish, protected by a bone case. And mixes with everything else in an amalgam that can smother it.

Until the invention of writing it was impossible to fix in story form what was going on. But "of all the needs of the human soul, none is more vital than the past." And so the sacrifice, at least in some of its forms (the Buphonia in Athens, the *soma* ceremonies in Vedic India), came to recall and rekindle the past. For several thousand years, in the multiplicity of its forms, those rites encapsulated what had taken place between man and animals—and what was continuing to take place between man and the invisible. No story could have been as effective, as eloquent as those sequences of gestures. Killer and adorer: these two characteristics were inescapable results after something that had lasted hundreds of thousands of years. With such characteristics a form had to be composed—and this form was the sacrifice. The Mass, too, is the remembrance of a past day. And every sacrifice is the remembrance of a day that lasted the length of remote eras. Killing wasn't enough, there had to be adoration. Adoration wasn't enough, it had to be remembered that there was killing.

This is what Aua the Inuit told Knud Rasmussen: "Even though everything was ready for me at the time when I was in my mother's womb, I tried vainly to become a summoner of spirits with the help of others. I never succeeded. I visited many famous shamans and offered them great gifts, which they immediately passed to others. For, if they had kept them, their children would be dead. Then I sought solitude and soon I felt very sad. In a strange way, I could burst into tears and become unhappy, without understanding the reason for it. Then suddenly everything changed, and I felt a great inexplicable joy, a joy so strong that I couldn't control it. I had to burst into song, into a powerful song, that allowed only this word: *Joy! Joy! Joy!* And in the middle of this mysterious, overwhelming rapture I became a shaman, without knowing how. But that was it, I could see and hear in a completely new way. Every true summoner of spirits has to feel a radiation from inside their body, inside their head or in their brain, something that irradiates like fire, that gives the power of sight to eyes closed in the darkness, to see things hidden or the future, or even other people's secrets. I felt I now possessed that marvelous capacity."

The vocation of the man of knowledge was a call. It came from a world of mighty beings, whom others could not perceive. That call acted as a seduction, an enticement into the invisible—and at the same time an invitation to combat. The man of knowledge acquired his wisdom during the course of this combat or was defeated. He was then a poor, sick being. And he knew that almost all forms of sickness were a theft of souls. But, if he emerged victorious from the invisible combat, then he could be the one who summoned the spirits, just as they had once summoned him. He would be the one who drew them in solitude, who gathered them around him, he would be the one who made them act. This was the deal that had to be transacted in his life. But first his body had to be remade. His physical unity had to be taken apart, organ by organ. His heart, lungs, liver, eyes: nothing could be used as it was. Knowledge implies a cutting up, a division of elements, a change in their substance. Quartz crystals were positioned in key places, the joints articulated once again after the heap of bones had been wrapped in birch bark. It was a torture that took place in solitude, throughout the world. But the scene was crowded with presences: the dead shamans flocked around the being that had to become one of them. With long knives they separated his flesh from his bones. But that was not enough. The flesh had to be cooked, to be seasoned, to make it perfect. The dead shamans worked away in silent frenzy. They sometimes made the new chosen one stand upright like a pole, then they moved away and pierced him with arrows. Then they approached again, removed the bones from his body, and began counting them, like moneylenders. If there wasn't the right number, the chosen one became a scrap of junk to be thrown away. He had no true vocation. He was a wretch. Often the candidate's head was fixed to the top of a hut. From there he could see how the remainder of his corpse was cut to pieces. It was essential that the future shaman remained conscious and could see, moment by moment, what was happening. The candidate could one day become a shaman only if he had this capacity for contemplation. It was also said that a true shaman had to let himself be cut to pieces at least three times. He also had to see how his bones were cleaned and polished. Dead shamans were greedy. Sometimes, when they had thrown some organ of the aspiring shaman onto the trails of evil, which are countless, and lead off in many directions, they demanded a ransom for the return of the organ: they demanded the death of a relative or perhaps just some serious illness. It was a risky time for anyone related to the aspiring shaman, who suffered in silence. On one occasion ten people died when the bones in the skull of an aspiring shaman had been ransomed. Sometimes the shamans grew tired of the spirits. And the spirits grew tired of the shamans. Then they changed paths and they would sometimes no longer meet.

To be a shaman was *another life*, which involved the offering and dividing up of one's own body, in much the same way as animals suffered when sacrificed. Shamans indeed were no more than the last of those animals. Every shaman had an animal mother who reemerged and came to him two or three days before he died. If the shaman allowed certain spirits to chew his flesh, those spirits were later obliged to answer to him. They could no longer act as if they were deaf. The shaman had become flesh of their flesh. Antonin Artaud is the only modern writer to have described and depicted what happened in such cases.

Every thought is measured with the dead. Henry James's *The Altar of the Dead* came from a "small fancy": he imagined "a man whose noble and beautiful religion is the worship of the Dead." He "is struck with the way they are forgotten, are unhallowed— unhonoured, neglected, shoved out of sight; allowed to become so much more dead, even, than the fate that has overtaken them has made them. He is struck with the rudeness, the coldness, that surrounds their memory."

At Sungir, just over 100 miles east of Moscow, a 27,000-year-old site was excavated. The finds included the tomb of two adolescents: a boy covered by strings of beads, 4,903 in all, and a belt around his waist with over 250 canine teeth from arctic foxes. Beside the corpse, various ivory objects, including a lance too heavy to be used. The girl was covered with 5,274 beads.

Architecture, according to Adolf Loos, originated with these burials. Ornamentation, which Loos deplored, also appeared alongside the dead. Or, at least, we encounter it for the first time in the dead. It wasn't done for show. But to accompany them to the "icy, savage climate" that would otherwise surround their memory. Those unknown people of Sungir, who lived tens of thousands of years before Henry James, knew this well.

Simulacra, amulets, idols, talismans, fetishes, in every form and material: between the taiga and the tundra they called them *šajtan*. The same word meant "demon" for Muslims, "satan" for Christians. They transported them piled on great sleds. The women could not approach. The reindeer that pulled those sleds were sacred. They couldn't be used for any work, nor sold, nor killed. But other reindeer were killed and their blood smeared over each *šajtan*.

The Soviet authorities demanded that the drums be handed over. When the people handed them over they felt defenseless, exposed to attack from the spirits. They feared being strangled by them. Some tried to substitute the drums with branches, bows and arrows, whips, hats. Even saucepan lids and ladles. Some drew drums on pieces of fabric and banged them in silence. Or they used cloth remnants without drawings and let them flutter in the air.

Éveline Lot-Falck, the most congenial historian of Siberian hunters, wrote soberly and precisely. She, no less than they, went straight to the point, to the essential: "Nothing must recall daily life from which the hunter has broken away. In the forest there is no place for any domestic object. Through a fiction of language, they adapt to the places, they merge into the surroundings. The hunter's intentions are wrapped in the indispensable mystery of the success of his projects. [. . .] Thus covered by many prohibitions, having broken his attachments with ordinary life, with secular life, to enter into the domain of the hunt, with his camouflaged identity, protected by his anonymity like a shield, the hunter sets out to confront the mysterious forces of the forest. [. . .] When he is in the forest, in the domain of the ancient ancestral powers, the hunter escapes the jurisdiction of the official church and avoids revealing his quality as Orthodox, Buddhist, or Muslim." In comparison with the forest, all other beliefs are something recent, artificial. Their obsessive humming liturgies are left suspended on the edge of the forest—and of its silence.

It was difficult to come back from hunting. Like the woman's body on the man, the forest left a fragrant trace on the hunter. Some chewed alder bark so as not to be contaminated by the sickness of the forest. Those who had killed a bear could not be honored for their deed unless they had spent three days in a tent prepared for the occasion. Slowly, cautiously the hunters managed to "untie the bonds they had forged, to dissociate from that domain into which they had penetrated, where they had managed to remain and from which they leave as though from another world, with the fear of being pursued." That fear of retaliation wasn't just the persistent feeling of certain Siberian hunters. Anyone who has crossed or continues to cross the boundary with the visible—especially if the invisible itself is not recognized as such—will live in the state of one who expects to be attacked at any moment. And of one who knows very well from where the attack will come—even if he is sometimes the only one to know it.

The hunter prepared for his expedition as though for a dance. The body had to be pure, scented. There was a different scent for every animal to be hunted. Any involvement in sex before the hunt was forbidden. For hunting *was* sex. And the animals were jealous, they noticed immediately. From his first steps, the hunter began a long courtship.

When two shamans met, it was never clear what would happen. They could sit beside each other, on a bench, quietly exchanging words or silently gazing into emptiness. But neither could be trusted. Each was tied by an invisible leather thong to a reindeer that was often very far away. And when the reindeer roamed in the tundra the lace stretched ever farther, for miles and miles. The two shamans' reindeer could also meet—and even fight fierce duels, without witnesses. Meanwhile the two shamans would sit chewing tobacco on the bench and exchange an occasional word. The reindeer would continue attacking each other. If one of them was knocked down, the shaman who was attached to it felt his thong being pulled. He would stand and go off in silence. Soon he would be dead. There was also talk of a "river of misery and ruin" whose banks had to be strengthened with the bodies of the shaman's relatives, which were used as posts. "For the life of the shaman is redeemed by his relatives."

To cure a sick person, the shaman Narzalé received the sickness himself. To lance the sickness, he lanced himself. The sick person recovered. Then the shaman left, in just the same way as he arrived. News about him soon came. It was said that Narzalé had gone to gather wood in the forest and a bear had torn him apart. And what had happened was explained thus: "The bear had torn him apart because he had given his soul for the sick person. He had said: You, *katcha* [spirit of illness], take my soul in place of the sick person. That's why he died. Otherwise why would a bear have left his den, in winter, to tear him apart?" Éveline Lot-Falck concluded that "the narrator and those involved do not show excessive surprise or gratitude especially because, among such populations, there is an economy of words and of outward display, and then because

Narzalé has done what few shamans do, after all, he had simply carried out his obligations and his mission."

There was a man with a nervous illness, kept in a bolted room. His family spent five years searching for a shaman who could cure him. Eventually the shaman Küstäch arrived. A drunkard appeared and left, insulting him. The shaman was unperturbed, concerned only about his familiar spirits. At a certain point he said: "When the most powerful of my familiar spirits descends on me, immediately undo the bolt." This is what happened. The sick man hurled himself upon the shaman, who gripped his chest, bent back, and blew into his face. The sick man fainted. The shaman touched his forehead with the drumsticks and said: "Get up. And now, do you want to drink some tea? Shall we sit at a table?" They sat and drank tea.

Shamans live in a large tree, a larch, which has many levels. The most powerful shamans nest on the higher levels, the others lower down. Shamans throughout the world are brought up in that tree. Their teacher is the raven, who moves from branch to branch. When a shaman is defeated by another shaman, he returns to shelter in the tree where he grew up. Sometimes, one shaman who is fighting another shaman tries to destroy his adversary's nest. Shamans never die a natural death. They are always overcome in a struggle with another shaman, who swallows them up.

The khan Ögödei ordered a chair to be placed on the highest point of the hill. From there he could survey an expanse that vanished in the western haze. A boundless hunting territory. And, as he fixed his gaze upon the distance, animals of all species came out from their dens and hiding places and moved toward the foot of the hill, looking up, toward Ögödei's throne. A lament could then be heard rising from the earth. The voices of all the animals joined together, similar to the voices of those who begged for justice.

They used to say the universe is made essentially of hexagonal rock crystals, also—and especially—where it is darker and more shapeless, in the spaces that open up beyond the Milky Way. Those same hexagonal crystals are alveoli in the brain, where images emerged. And the central commissure of the encephalon, two entwined serpents, is to be found in the Milky Way.

Others say the Milky Way is the place of visions and the passageway between sky and earth, but also a terrible place, since all diseases converge there. And it is like a vast mass of waste. Vultures hide there, since there they can find nourishment. So the Milky Way is a place of great danger. Anyone who ventures there must be aware of this.

"*Todos los adornos son escrituras*," "all decoration is writing," said Bonifacio Bautista Aragón, guardian of Mitla, close to the city of Oaxaca. His house, a small dark hovel, stood to one side of the ruins. He came out when summoned by a visitor, who was standing by a pink wall filled with decorations. Which were "in the heart of the wall," added Bonifacio. But then he went back to that phrase about the *adornos*. Few visitors understood this, he added, to himself: "*Los modernos se creen . . .*" The *moderns* thought they were decorations, like cotillions at carnival time. The moderns believe many things that are not so. Then Bonifacio repeated his phrase: "*Todos los adornos son escrituras.*" It didn't matter that he had never deciphered those writings. His task was to repeat that phrase.

The Lord of the Animals is sly and lecherous. He spies on women and follows young girls along the river in the form of a lizard. As he watches he lashes the air with his tail. If he manages to possess them in their sleep they often wake in a daze—and soon they die of consumption. Then for quite some time, all around, there is a strange confusion.

The Lord of the Animals is curious and jealous about anything to do with sex. He stares from the cracks in the walls. With the hunters he negotiates the number of animals he will allow to be killed. And in exchange he asks for the souls of the dead, to be housed in vast storerooms in the mountains.

The Lord of the Animals follows every step of the hunters, who never feel alone. They know they are being watched. Sometimes they stop at a tree and carve images in its bark. A snail, a flute. Always to distract the Lord of the Animals, who is captivated by those signs. The hunter then moves on, free for a while.

There wasn't just one Lord of the Animals. Various lords were known, who ruled different parts of the forest. They appeared as "composite images of animal and human, of prey and predator," similar at times to a feathered man, an ominous Papageno. If too many animals were killed in the hunt or the rules were not observed, they would express their anger with yellowy lights at dusk and a continual roar of thunder. The heads of the animals killed in the hunt had to be hung from the trees of the forest. Otherwise it would be the Lord of the Animals who would start hunting the men. This is how Patakuru described it: "The game hunted by the lord of the forest are the humans. His aspect is like that of humans. He is like us. As big as us. Some are male, others are female. The male lord of the forest screws women and screws men. Because he appears deceptively as man or as woman. He or she appears as our husband or as our wife, just like evil hawks. If we screw her or he screws us, we are as good as dead. If you have/are screwed, you don't know it anymore. You forget what happened, but then you die. Only certain spirit familiars of the shamans can discover what happened and cure us so that we do not die."

Killing involved a continuous risk of retaliation. The Lord of the Animals would always prey on humans, in the same way that humans had hunted prey in his realm. It was enough to attack in *their* mind, in certain particular and vulnerable places. The Lord of the Animals then began the hunt, getting wild pigs and cassowaries to follow him, in the same way that humans went hunting with their dogs. This was the balance, this was the law. That is why hunting was not enough, there had to be sacrifice.

Who could the hunter befriend? Mai-kaffo, for example. In ancient times, Mai-kaffo was the chief of the buffaloes. But he wasn't a buffalo. Mai-kaffo was part buffalo and part human. He was part bird and part antelope. He had horns. He lived in woodland, in a tamarind tree. A hunter met him and began talking. The hunter said: "We have no medicines against the spirits." Mai-kaffo said: "Don't worry. The buffaloes belong to me." One day the hunter brought honey for Mai-kaffo. "How strange," said Mai-kaffo, "the woodland belongs to me, no one can take honey without my knowing about it." The hunter told a story about how the honey had been obtained. "It's good, though," said Mai-kaffo with his mouth full of honey. "You've brought me something good. You're a friend. I'll give you a buffalo. You can kill it." And so the hunter killed the buffalo and carried it to the village. The hunter was then honored. Every so often he called Mai-kaffo, sacrificing an animal with black skin, as his friend liked it. Mai-kaffo then appeared in the village, with his son Mekirabo. Mai-kaffo and the hunter talked long, particularly about medicine. Meanwhile Mekirabo went off into the tent with the hunter's wife and made love with her.

Suddenly a female deer appeared. Behind her was a stretch of water, the vast Maeotian Swamp, which until then had seemed an ocean. The doe watched the hunters, calmly. Then it turned toward the swamp and began to run. When it was too far from the hunters, it stopped. It rubbed its muzzle against the shrubs and the frozen mud. The hunters approached it in this way several times. And each time, as soon as they came close, the doe resumed its gentle canter, turning its head back for a moment, as if to beckon them. Hunor and Magor rode and rode, thinking only of the doe. They forgot the others. Looking back, they found themselves alone. They said nothing and carried on riding. That swamp which, as children, they had been told had no limits and continued into the sky, now appeared to them like an icy leaden gray plain that merged with the horizon. At times the doe was a small black moving dot, at times it was so close that they thought they could stroke it. They never lost sight of it. Nor did they notice that they were no longer riding on ice, but on fresh soft ground, different from the steppe where they had grown up. Night fell and the doe kept more and more of a distance. They saw the black dot blend with the black immensity around them. The doe had vanished. But they carried on riding. And soon they thought they had entered a dream. They recognized a glimmer of fires in the darkness. They saw moving shadows. Hidden behind a tent, still saddled on their horses, they watched the scene. Men and women were dancing around fires. They were captivated by the sound of the music. At the center were two old men, standing still. Hunor and Magor caught sight of two girls flitting about like lizards, women of another race, taller and paler than those they had known until then. The two girls seemed to be leading the dance. They followed them for a long time with their eyes, as they had followed the doe. The fire flashed on their thin ankles and bare feet when they were exposed now and then among their long, dark, pleated clothing.

Then Hunor and Magor burst into the circle and the dancers saw two demons seize the two girls by the waist. They vanished into the night, clutching those two damp bodies to their muskrat coats. When they returned to their people, crossing the boundless swamp as though it were the last confine of the steppe, they said they had finally found the land, the land their people had always been searching for, which they had heard whispered about since their childhood, the land that was good for animals and for food. And so it happened that the Huns advanced toward Europe.

The animal is both prey and a guide, like the doe for the Huns. The hunter who follows the animal, keeping his eye on one single point, fails to notice he is venturing into the unknown. This is how discovery is made: by following the call of another being that is constantly escaping, remaining always in view, but can never be reached. Whereas that which is discovered is already around, already behind—and is almost no longer visible.

There are two kinds of prey: that which is killed (and the site of the killing becomes the foundation site), and that which vanishes (and causes the hunters to be killed). Every so often the animal guide wants to be reached, agrees to become prey. That's how it must be, if the city is to be founded. The city is the place where the animal guide is brought down. Ephesus was founded by one who had obeyed these words of the oracle: "A wild boar will indicate the way." And in that place where the wild boar fell, struck by a javelin, "today there stands the temple of Athena." That place today is Ephesus.

One who writes is following the animal guide. In his work he attacks it—and kills it: in that place where it is killed, the work appears. Or otherwise he discovers that the animal guide has disappeared. And the animal becomes the emblem on a standard. The difference between those works in which the animal guide is killed and those in which it vanishes: in Balzac, the animal is killed. In Baudelaire, it advances as the emblem on the standard. A book is written when there is something specific that has to be discovered. The writer doesn't know what it is, nor where it is, but knows it has to be found. The hunt then begins. The writing begins.

Standards first emerged in Egypt, the place of remote things. The Egyptians, having been defeated several times for a certain lack of order among their troops, "had the idea of carrying standards before the various ranks. As a result, it is said, the commanders fashioned the images of the animals that they worship today and carried them fixed to their lances, so that each knew where his place was." The animals serve to establish "good order," which is so valuable in battle. But not only this. The men looked upon the animals as the order they had broken—and to which at times, in moments of anxiety, they would have liked to return. Or which at least they would have liked to summon in aid, to be protected by them.

Thus, "intending to demonstrate their gratitude, they began the custom of not killing any of the animals whose image they had fashioned, but of awarding them respect and devotion as cult objects." Consequently the animals on the standards were often wild animals, not used for sacrifice, not edible.

The Piceni tribes were so named because "a woodpecker [Latin: *picus*] showed their forefathers the way." When they went to war, to be seen "on their standards was the woodpecker." They weren't of course the only ones. Eagles, wolves, bulls, horses, or wild boar could be seen on the standards of the Roman troops in Republican times.

Then Marius, during his second consulship, ordered a reform: the only animal at the head of the legions was to be the eagle. "The other standards were left in the camps." It would be said that Marius had foreshadowed the Empire, which was precisely this: a single animal. But previously there had been many animals—and many would be reintroduced. The disintegration of the Roman Empire was heralded, accompanied, and followed by the appearance of other animals on Barbarian standards: wild boars for the Gauls, ravens for the Normans, snakes for the Lombards, dragons for the Franks, lions for the Saxons, bulls for the Cimbrians. A standard is what goes *ahead*, if only one step ahead. The troops that follow it, its loyal followers, are the hunters, who at one time followed the tracks of the animal guide without ever reaching it. But that pursuit gave form to their life, it was their life. There is no more intimate relationship than that between the standard and the warrior. Now the pursuit continues, even if the standard is only a little way ahead and its loyal followers are no longer hunters but soldiers. When they were defeated, the animal on the standard remained "*quietissimus totoque corpore demissus*," "completely still and with its whole body prostrate." But when they won, the standard fluttered in the breeze. The raven spread its wings once again, and soared into the air.

II

THE MISTRESS OF THE ANIMALS

The Mistress of the Animals, unearthed in countless statuettes throughout Europe, was conspicuous in her immobility. Her vast buttocks, heavy chest, legs joined, scarcely concealed how she had once been a tree. Whereas now she could only be lodged, with her legs together, in the cavity of a tree trunk. Animals, all animals, all things born: they were her followers. The goddess watched over them, motionless. She supported creatures just as a mighty trunk supports even the farthest branches. Everything was a seething circle around her. All were part of her foliage.

Suddenly the goddess stretched out one arm, then the other. Her hands closed in a firm clasp around the necks of two panthers—or two water birds. Or they grasped the hoofs of two deer—or two lions—and tossed them in the air. She appeared as a majestic scarecrow. Another moment followed, the most mysterious, one that nobody dared describe, the hiatus in the life of the goddess: when she took her first step, which was immediately a run. She kept away from the city and its people. She sought out solitary and inaccessible places, places flattened by the sky. Or swamps with rustling reeds. Or clearings in the forest, untrodden by human feet. She was the goddess of the intact. She ran and chased the invisible beast. Even the mighty bull bowed down before her. All animals were afraid of her running. All knew that the goddess's arrow would have reached them. But, when she stopped to rest, a young fawn would emerge from the thicket and lick her hands.

The Mistress of the Animals was the support for a mobile wardrobe: nature. Animals clung to the goddess's cloak and remained entangled in it. In her effigy at Ephesus, all but her face, her outstretched arms, and the tips of her toes were hidden by a heavy layer of clothing. And her skin was black with oil that dripped from orifices anointed with nard. From that enforced immobility, from those ponderous images, she slipped away, as though divesting herself with an agile gesture and abandoning a sheath, Artemis, the nimblest goddess, who chases and strikes, while a short chiton flutters above her knee.

Once having abandoned her Asiatic covering, no longer oppressed by animal protomes and by those heavy bull testicles which for many years were mistaken for numerous breasts, half naked and shimmering under her taut skin, Artemis, while she ran, summoned another who was the other, the reverse side of nature, of which she had grown tired. Another who, like her, knew how to strike at nature but to whom nature could never glue itself. Another who was familiar above all with detachment. Artemis would never have touched him. Contact between them would be a perennial and invisible superimposition. She evoked a twin: Apollo.

Artemis ran like a male—and the keenest desire that men had for a woman was the desire for Artemis who runs. Artemis ran like a male as long as she knew she could be seen. But she entered the water like a woman, for then no one could see her, apart from her maidservants and hunting companions. The pool of water at the center of the *locus amoenus* is the secret place par excellence, the place where the goddess returns to sink into the humidity of her body, the place where she accepts that her unperishable profile is partially canceled in the flow from which it sprang. Her female companions then look at Artemis—and this is the secret that they alone share. But who are those companions? They are Artemis refracted and multiplied, delicately varied, scattered. Artemis shows herself not only to her companions, but also to her animals. And so Actaeon placed a deerskin over his head and shoulders. Horns emerged from behind the mossy mass, like branches among the leaves. His offense was certainly not that of wanting to rape the goddess—which would have been most unseemly—but of wanting to look at her through the eyes of an animal. There is no offense more serious than this, which obliged the goddess to remember the remote time when she herself was an animal, the miraculous doe that escaped. But goddesses, even more than gods, don't like being forced to remember.

Eros is a "wondrous hunter," "*thēreutès deinós.*" This was what Diotima told Socrates. And at the same time Eros "spends his life philosophizing." From Plato onward, hunting and knowledge are ideas that chase and overlap each other. Implied in the connection is a certain deadly characteristic of knowledge, which in reaching its object can kill it. But the opposite idea is also implicit: that the hunter, having once reached the prey, can be blissfully contaminated by it, until he himself becomes prey. And so the hunter Actaeon becomes prey to his gaze and lets himself be torn apart by his own dogs, who want only to obey him. This is how Giordano Bruno described what happened next: "Since the ultimate and final purpose of this chase is to arrive at the capture of that fugitive and wild prey, for which the predator becomes the prey, the hunter becomes the thing hunted; for in all other kinds of chase done for particular things, the hunter comes to capture the other things for himself, absorbing these through the mouth of his own intelligence; but in that divine and universal chase he comes to understand to such an extent that he remains necessarily included, absorbed, united. Hence from common, ordinary, civil, and popular he becomes wild as a stag and an inhabitant of the desert; he lives godlike beneath that tall forest, lives in the unadorned chambers of mountain caverns, where he beholds the sources of the great rivers, where he vegetates intact and pure from ordinary forms of greed, where divinity converses more freely, a state to which many men have aspired longing to taste the celestial life while on earth, and with one voice have said: *Ecce elongavi fugiens, et mansi in solitudine.* Thus the dogs, thoughts of divine things, devour this Actaeon, making him dead to the people, to the multitude, unbound from the knots of troubled senses, free from the carnal prison of matter; whence he no longer sees his Diana as if through orifices and through windows, but having pushed down the walls, he has a complete view of the whole horizon."

The discovery of hunting, of what hunting involved once it was separated from every dietary purpose, and caught in the pureness and hardness of its action, in the repeated scenario of a human that chases and an animal being chased, of an arrow shot and a wound that opens, such a discovery ought to absorb a divine creature totally in itself, to distract it from its ecumenical sovereignty over every animal and vegetable form. To pass from the maximum extension to the maximum intensity. From the surface of the earth to the point of the arrow. This was Artemis. Having folded back her wings, cast off her opulent and Asiatic garments, abandoned every frontal fixity, she darted among the trees without snapping branches—and always returned to exercising that violent activity that served no purpose. The gods do not feed on blood, nor were humans ever able to eat or sacrifice Artemis's prey. The hunt is a tautology, the self-affirming exercise. And, buried in its past, we encounter negation: the animal that negates itself. Tautology, negation: is it not perhaps the circle of thought? Artemis, enchanted, no longer wished to leave that circle. But that circle came close to other circles. Sometimes, on coming close to each other, they caught fire. Never was erotic desire so whetted as around Artemis, as in Artemis, who denied sex—and abhorred contact. While she denied it, she extolled it. Artemis was the same as her twin, Apollo, in everything, except sex: "*solusque dabat discrimina sexus.*" So she sought to negate sex, to abolish that sole dividing line to make herself identical to her sole lover, her unnamable lover: Apollo— and to detach herself, along with him, from all the rest.

Apollo rose up from his mother's hands. An archer's bow was protruding from Leto's arms. The tiny god leaned out, like over a parapet. Artemis, nestling in the other hollow of Leto's arms, watched her brother. Then she looked ahead and saw an immense mountain, speckled yellow and green. The mountain slowly swelled up and then shrank. It was a pulsating mountain. Leto continued climbing, with difficulty. The speckles drew closer. Apollo's torso was taut, shiny. In the silence he pointed an arrow. It was the first gesture of his life. Artemis saw these gestures for the first time and was already familiar with them. The arrow quivered in the air, the only sound. Artemis saw it hurtle into a small, delicate, central speckle. The mountain gasped. For a moment it seemed destined to expand and burst, swallowing them up. Then it shrank. A new color appeared close to the point where the arrow had stuck. An opaque, black liquid slowly trickled out. Death. While higher up, at the point where the coils, now immobile, of the serpent left an open cleft in the mountain, water began to gush forth, clear and perpetual. One day it became known as the Castalian Spring.

Eros and hunting are incompatible since they resemble each other too much. They are incest. They are an exposure once again of the whole surface of the body, and of the mind, to nature, to the danger of being reabsorbed by it. But if that exposure is twofold, if hunting and eros coexist, the tension ends in paralysis and falls into ruin. This is why the first and most highly charged erotic stories are those about male and female hunters. This is why they are stories about impossible love that always end in disaster.

It has always been asked why incest is forbidden. And the more detailed and persuasive the explanations, the more ambiguous and elusive the question seems to be. Why should feelings so precisely comply, at all times and in all places, with the need to respect the rules of kinship? Or perhaps the rules of kinship themselves refer to something else that isn't named but which tirelessly nourishes the sentiment that assures respect for the prohibition? And what is the *other* unnamed thing? Communality with animals. This state of perpetual guilt, this metamorphic lack of distinction, gives rise to the ban on all that is too intimate. In the time of the Great Raven, when man was hunted and went hunting, when he was not just man but an animal or a spirit or a god and he hunted another being of equally uncertain and changeable nature, at that time animal incest reigned. From that time, every other time had to become detached, if it was to be the time for a history of mankind.

But when, for cruel sport, for pure pleasure, Artemis takes her bow and goes off hunting, we are once again enveloped in the aura of incest, we once again sense the violation of a prohibition that no one would otherwise dare to violate. And something that is just a maxim—that hunting is incest—still lingers in the air, for no apparent reason.

People maintained their kinship with the animal by wearing its skin. The hero wore the skin of the animal that he himself had killed. He never abandoned it, in the same way that Athena never appeared without her aegis embossed with the head of Medusa. And the head of Heracles appeared between the jaws of the Nemean lion. The expression of Heracles and of Athena was always double. Together with that mobile expression on their face was the fixed expression of death that they carried with them. But for many unknown others it was enough to wrap an animal skin around themselves. The skin of a wolf, bear, panther, lynx. Impregnated with sweat and dust, they guaranteed an untrammeled promiscuity. *Scortum*, "skin," "leather," is the most common way of saying "whore." Contact with the skin of a dead animal made it possible to communicate with all other animal species. It was the lingua franca of metamorphosis. All of this could be disapproved only by those who were inventing a humanity with a clear, irreversible profile. In the same way that they used *scortum* to describe that part of the female body "that suffers the insult of coitus," similarly they thought of anyone adhering to another skin as a common prostitute. They knew that those flayed scraps were evidence of an enduring promiscuity with the realm of the spirits.

At Sparta, boys were *wolves*; in Athens, young girls were *she-bears*. The textbooks repeatedly suggest that youth initiation served as an introduction to the city's order. On the contrary, it harked back to a point of the past, to a state of commingling with the animal from which humans had detached themselves by becoming wolves and bears—and then becoming the ones who killed wolves and bears. The initiation was an invitation to remember. One day, at a certain age, history would be studied. But now they had to discover what had happened before all history: that humans, for a time, had become wolves and she-bears.

At Sparta, it was the citizen's duty to go hunting; in Athens, the decision was left to individual choice. State hunting dogs were available for everyone at Sparta. And children were given little to eat so that they were forced to hunt. And yet the material utility of hunting was secondary. Hunting began only after praises had been sung to Artemis.

Why does Artemis, the most beautiful of all, the goddess swathed in an erotic aura, so much so that Aura is one of her names and one of her guises, immediately want, as her first childish desire, virginity? Virginity is the sign of separation, of unbridgeable distance. The world cannot burst in upon Artemis, whereas it is Artemis that shoots her arrows on the world. And nor does Artemis want to conquer the world, which already belongs to her, as the queen of wild beasts, of the swamps and of unviolated places. Artemis wants only to transfix the world, she chooses from time to time a fragment of it, a body in flight. From far away she reaches it—and in blood she brings it back to herself. Whoever strikes, knows. The mind detaches itself from its natural tangle, observes the world, watches it, detaches a part of it in turn, and rejoins itself to that part in the most intimate bond, death, which snatches the breath from its prey and isolates it forever. This way of knowledge, which then became the usual way of knowledge, was in the beginning an immense exertion, a bending of nature against itself. History in the end attributed this gesture to Apollo. But it was his twin sister, Artemis, born just before him, who acted as its midwife. It was Artemis who placed that action obsessively, repeatedly, tirelessly, at the center of their life. She didn't even need to label that action with the word *knowledge*. For her it was hunting, merely hunting. For Apollo, hunting became knowledge. The darker past, now pushed back toward the steppe, was once again the focus of attention, but with a twist of meaning so abrupt that memory might seem to have been lopped away. Artemis shook off her garments heavy with animal remains and slipped into a chiton that rose above her knee. It was no longer a question of wearing nature, but of penetrating it from afar. Artemis's body, which no one had seen until then, more than naked was exposed, while she ran, ignoring all around her that wasn't prey.

Artemis left to her twin brother, Apollo, the privileges of knowledge that declares its own name. In her sanctuaries there were no stern priests, masters of hypothetical syllogism, but young girl-bears and torturers of strangers or adolescents covered with blood from being whipped. This didn't mean, though, that thought was absent. It was merely covered by an opaque curtain. Iphigenia, Artemis's favorite who most resembled her, railed furiously against "the sophistries of the goddess."

That relations between Artemis and Apollo were not just those of brother and sister was perfectly clear to Herophile, the oldest of the Sibyls of Delphi and the "first woman to chant oracles." The people of Delos remembered one of her hymns, in which Herophile said she was also Artemis, and as such "wife and sometimes sister and then daughter" of Apollo. When Herophile composed that hymn she was "delirious and possessed by the god," but her ravings were accurate: she had also foretold that "Helen would be brought up in Sparta to be the ruin of Asia and of Europe, and that for her sake the Greeks would capture Troy."

It is a god's first wish to have many names. Young Artemis declared this when she was still sitting on the knee of her father, Zeus. The claim to eternal virginity is associated with *polyōnymíē*, the "capacity to be called by many names." If only to contend and compete with her twin, Apollo. Every name is a portion of what it is, over which the god's sovereignty extends. Which is an absolute singular, but demands to be called each time by the right name, by just one of his many appellatives. This is a perennial concern of the devout polytheist: to identify not only each individual god, but the right name with which to invoke him on a certain occasion, in a certain place. A concern unknown to those who follow the religions of the Book.

Hypostases, epicleses, appellatives: none of the other Greek divinities have accumulated such a number around themselves. For Artemis, names become like the various animals she carries fixed to her simulacrum in Ephesus. Scholars shake their heads: what keeps her stories together? How can the many-breasted, immobile Asiatic mother become the young virgin who runs into the woods wearing her short chiton? Artemis was never a mother, nor did she have many breasts. This is the oldest of the misconceptions that surround her. She was never *multimammia*, as the Christian writers described her. If anything, she could be mistaken for a young male, one of those who pursued Apollo or whom Apollo had pursued.

Hunting, as Artemis understood it, was a model for gratuitous action that could not be reduced to any kind of purpose. The animal hunted was not then sacrificed—nor even eaten. Certainly not by Artemis, who ate other foods. Nor by her followers, who were never portrayed feasting. Bathing was their only shared activity, apart from hunting. And this because hunting created impurity, it mixed together sweat, dust, and blood.

Purity appears with hunting and with Artemis: *hagné*, "pure," the goddess par excellence invoked with this word (only Persephone has the right to the same title in Homer). But what is purity? Distinction, separation. The hunter washes before he goes off hunting so as to separate himself from what he doesn't want to be, from what blends him with the world. The menstruating woman is not pure because her blood keeps her in enforced contact with the outside. Pure is that which stands out against a background, which has a profile, which can thus become a target. The wild animal loves pure men because those men, at one time, were themselves prey. From the moment when man sharpens the tip of an arrow, purity is imposed. Artemis advances, "proud of having slaughtered wild beasts." There is no purity unless it is accompanied by a trail of blood. So Artemis cannot be separated from her bathing, which washes away those traces—and every trace.

Hagnós: a Greek category that has no equivalent in modern languages. "Saint" and "sacred" are tolerable approximations to *hágios* and *hierós*. If *hagnós* is translated as "pure," it merely prolongs the uncertainty. How does *hagnós* differ from *katharós*, which usually describes purity? Jean Rudhardt has established several points: "*Hagnós*, more frequent than *hágios*, is also used for sanctuaries, sacred woods, and rituals. Moreover it qualifies certain offerings and certain objects of worship; it is applied to light, to the ether, to fire; it is used especially for men and for gods." It indicates a state from which one falls by shedding blood: there is no *hagnòs phónos*, whereas there is a *hágios phónos*. And yet Artemis kills and at the same time she is *hagné*. Perhaps because "one needs to be *hagnós* . . . to carry a certain concentration of power." Wilamowitz translated *hagnós* as "chaste," thinking of Hippolytus. A misleading translation. *Hagnós* implies a "detachment." And reverence in front of the unknown. The quality corresponding to *hagnós* is called *hagneía*: without it, no act of worship can be effective.

Artemis and Dionysus: members of the same family, like all gods, but distant. She a virgin, he promiscuous. Their paths rarely cross. And only in desolate places. Both had a retinue to follow them. Boisterous, that of Dionysus. Rustling and all female, that of Artemis. What did they have in common? The extreme—and communality with animals. The extreme implies a chance intensification of emotions, of actions—sudden, wounding. To look at certain statuettes of Artemis or Dionysus could bring madness, even if these were only simulacra. This happened to Astrabacus and Alopecus, who found a statuette of Artemis in a thicket of reeds, thrown there by Orestes. From the Crimea to Sparta, no longer bathed by blood, it had lost none of its power. It happened to Eurypylus, who at the burning of Troy opened a chest left there as a curse by Cassandra. That chest concealed an image of Dionysus that no one was supposed to see.

Artemis encountered Dionysus in the bull and in water. On various coins found at Amphipolis, Artemis is riding a bull and lets a veil billow out over her head, like a sail, holding it with her hands. In a mutilated statue in the British Museum she is standing, nimbly, on a bull, of which only the head remains. This is Artemis Tauropolos. The women of Argus invoked Dionysus as a bull that emerges from the waters. Artemis bathing was not just Artemis stopping to wash after the hunt. It was the return to the figure of Artemis Lousiatis and Limnaia, to the goddess of that which flows and runs away. It is no surprise that documents of the Athenian officials who administered the sanctuary at Delos refer to "a purple garment decorated with gold, made by the Athenians using the revenues of Apollo," a garment that had originally clothed a statue of Artemis and then one of Dionysus.

Apollo, Artemis, Dionysus, the three guides for the flock of predators: the nymph, the breeze that makes garments billow, only appears around them, only behind them. *Nýmphai* means those who are "swelling." While the juices of life began to saturate children's limbs and raised domes and curtains of flesh on their bodies, a goddess—Artemis—abducted them. How many were in her retinue? According to Callimachus, she asked her father, Zeus, for eighty. But for Virgil there were "a hundred for the forests and a hundred for the springs."

They lived 9,720 years, forever young, full-breasted, hair neatly plaited, they followed the destiny neither of mortals nor of immortals. They divided their love between men and gods, sometimes attracting, sometimes shunning. They carried "the gift of life," says Aeschylus, but also madness when they planted themselves in the mind of a man who had seen them bathing naked. They lived in the trees or immersed in springs or in fragrant grottoes. But most of all, like a militia, they accompanied the three predators— Apollo, Artemis, and Dionysus. The highest erotic and aesthetic abstraction was to be found in their retinue. Wet nurses and huntresses, prophetesses and musicians, dancers and priestesses. To look at, they resembled the most beautiful of women or gods. But their element was neither human nor celestial. This omnipresent tribe, roving, multiform yet always the same, was the swathing daemonic cloud, the plurality of forces and figures that mediate between extremes. It was the mental liquid that holds together all that happens. *Cumatilis*, "resembling the waves," was how their color was described. They were the stuff stories are made of.

In the Sanctuary of Artemis Orthia there was no difference between the two adorers and the goddess, either in their facial features or the shape of their bodies, as though the goddess were reflected in two mirrors. But Artemis was clasping in each hand the tail of a lion, and wings sprouted from her shoulders, while the adorers were holding a crown.

There is no hint of the moral in Artemis. She is ruthless in her punishment and in her demands, but appeals to no law. Those who offend her—and it's hard not to offend her—already know why they offend her. Unlike her twin brother, Apollo, Artemis passes no judgments. Nor does she seem to involve herself with the council of the gods, even though she is present at certain crucial moments, as in the rape of Kore. She played no part in city life, but cities would still always build temples and sanctuaries to her.

Artemis the pure is also the most ruthless. "Her personality retains more traces of savagery than that of any other Greek divinity," observed Lewis Farnell. There is also some doubt about her chastity. Cyrene, the nymph with whom Apollo had intercourse in the form of a wolf, was an ancient form of Artemis, as if the two twins had had a previous sexual, violent, and happy life. And Cyrene was not alone. Since Artemis had a great capacity to divide herself in hypostases, she sent her emissaries to have intercourse with Apollo: the prophetess Herophile, and Chrysothemis, who with Apollo begat Parthenos. It is said also that Callisto, a follower of Artemis, begat Arcas not with Zeus but with Apollo.

The Sanctuary of Artemis Laphria dominated Patras from its highest point. The statue of the goddess, in gold and ivory, came from Calydon. It showed her as an Amazon and a huntress, with her right breast bare. The festival of the goddess was celebrated each year, in spring, preceded by a magnificent procession that ended with the virgin priestess on a chariot pulled by deer. The whole population took part.

There were wooden logs still green, in a circle, around the altar. And dry logs stacked on the altar. They sprinkled earth on its steps. Onto the altar they threw "live, edible birds, and every other kind of victim." Also "wild boar and deer and gazelles." "Wolf cubs and bear cubs" as well—and fully grown animals. And also the fruit of cultivated trees. "After which they set the wood alight." At this point Pausanias saw a bear and other animals trying to escape from the flames. But "those who had thrown them there dragged them back to the pyre." He observed then that no one remembered anyone ever having been injured by the animals.

Nobody, ancient or modern, has managed to explain why Artemis Laphria demanded this holocaust. Nor is its name clear: some people associated it with a certain Laphrio, who had erected the statue of the goddess in Calydon; others thought that Laphria derived from *elaphróteron*, "milder," in that the goddess is said to have shown herself milder in her anger toward Oeneus, whose land she had let the Calydonian Boar ravage. But it is difficult to see why a rigorous and all-embracing holocaust could be a sign of mildness.

With Artemis one enters each time into the thorniest metaphysics of myth. The Patrai sacrifice involved animals that the goddess both protected and hunted, decreeing the extermination of all. The ceremony had no functional purpose. There was no food to be shared: the animals had to be burned alive, with no exception. No more and no less was required. And these were wild animals, which in Vedic India were excluded from the sacrifice. At the same time they were the animals that Artemis had more to do with. If seen from a distance, in the mythical landscape of Greece, that rite could appear like a perpetual farewell to a whole epoch, a very long epoch, compared with which the splendors of agriculture seemed like a recent intrusion: the age of hunting, now reduced to ashes.

The Greeks entrusted the legacy of the bear to Artemis. Young Athenian girls between the ages of five and ten, dressed in saffron, were taken to the goddess's sanctuary at Brauron, on the northern coast of Attica. They were called "she-bears."

For mathematicians, "singularities" are certain elements—for example, functions—that "diverge" (so they say) beyond a given point. If they are asked why they use that verb, they reply that a function of such a kind "tends to infinity." Something similar happened with the Olympians. Hermes and Artemis appeared as a young, agile, vigorous young man with a pointed beard, and as a huntress of noble beauty. One might encounter them among passersby wandering the streets, some of whom could even seem like their distant relatives. But anyone who followed them would soon be lost. As happens with certain mathematical singularities, he would be close to "an infinitely sharp point somewhere on a smooth surface." Or he would be forced to witness the delicate moment in which the god became inhuman.

When the *pólis* was established, when it submitted to the recurrent return of the fruits of the earth, when the communities began to abandon themselves to the power of trade, there remained nevertheless a nostalgia for another life: certainly poorer in its elements, much more repetitive, obsessive. And yet irreducible: hunting. Now that it was no longer necessary for survival, since domestic animals were killed for meat, hunting was needed to satisfy another imperious call.

The young, handsome Hippolytus scorned the city and its powers, did not eat meat, but devoted himself obsessively to hunting. He was the reverse of the civilized man who no longer hunts but continues to eat the meat of domestic animals. Hunting, for Hippolytus, was an exercise. Every exercise was a form of hunting. And the prey, the arrow, the bow, could now be both visible and invisible. Artemis is protectress and sovereign where there is a tension, a target, a distance. But what happens when distance is removed through contact? Then the stories began about Artemis and about her lovers who were spurned—and sometimes killed.

The Greeks were not like the Yakuts, for whom hunting was an activity of vital importance. Killing the odd hare, fawn, or an occasional doe certainly didn't alter the economic system, which was fundamentally agricultural. Hunting then, as many centuries later in Europe, was already primarily an amusement, a sport. But why are Greek myths so often stories about hunting, and why is their central character a hunter or a huntress, or both? There were numerous myths about Artemis, and hunting—her favorite and almost exclusive occupation—appeared in each of them. Apollo also had to preside over the divination, over the Muses, he had to visit the Hyperboreans. Artemis meanwhile hunted—or rested between one hunting expedition and the next, surrounded by her followers. She seems to have had no other interest or pursuit. In Artemis's hunting the Greeks identified two actions in their purest state: preying and killing. Taken in themselves, detached from any setting that was not the forest, those actions formed the basis of endless ideas and stories. And, in the cruel clarity of their outline, they could be entrusted only to the noble protection of a goddess that was *hagnḗ*, "pure."

If the gods cannot eat meat, why would they have to hunt? Do they act in this way purely for the pleasure of killing? Or purely for the pleasure of striking? Striking is the action that distinguishes the gods. Killing is just a variation of it. Indeed, striking gives an aesthetic justification to killing—and at the same time establishes it at the center of existence. If there had been no hunting by the gods, killing would have been protected and sealed only by sacrifice. But hunting released it from ritual obligations. And that game perpetually repeated, but through impulse and whim, had preceded sacrifice and its fixity. It was something solemn, definitive, it was the game to which the divinities of detachment—Artemis, Apollo, Athena—immediately laid claim. But Athena preferred war and the action of the wise weaver. Whereas the twins born to Leto stormed in among the branches, their minds fixed on one point: the target.

Artemis was never interested in hunting as a civilizing activity that sought to exterminate wild beasts and monsters, rebalancing the excessive power of nature. Indeed, she was against it. Hunting, for her, was a monotonous and invincible game that started all over again each time. The hunter's feet retraced her steps, his arm slipped the arrow out of its quiver, his knees bent into the ambush position. The hunting ground was the geometrical locus for what was not development. It began from nothing and returned to nothing. Its features were few in number and could not be more: daybreak, paths untrodden, the chase, the midday rest, the arrow shot, bathing in the spring, blood.

It was not in the *pólis* or in the village or in the palace that the game was played out with what had preceded every *pólis*, every village, every palace. What had once been there would one day be called *nature*. But at the beginning it was simply forest, a place untamed, intact. And a life there went on parallel to that of the community. A story of individuals who roamed about stalking prey. Or fighting each other. Or desiring each other. There are so many Greek stories about hunting that we might suppose they couldn't do without it. They provided the setting that articulated and regulated relations with the animal world, with that dark entity that had gone before, and from which all community life had detached itself. But the significant point was that in such stories the animals appeared not because they represented something that was to be eaten, but simply because they were something that was killed.

Pure killing—animals and hunters killing each other—was the essential axis around which the stories revolved.

If all that happens in myth is then repeated in history, the birth of the individual took place in a forest, when the hunter appeared. He was the first self-sufficient being, who has no need to communicate except through his art. This is the first solitary profile, detached from any tribe, that we come across in nature. In the background: animals and plants.

Hunters do not conquer, build, govern, celebrate. They hunt— and are interested in nothing else. At most, like Orion, they may claim that they will exterminate all wild beasts. And with this they already go beyond simple hunting. By this route, through Heracles, we arrive at the city founder–hero: Theseus. Otherwise, the only interference can be erotic. Daphne shuns Apollo because *all* she wants to do is hunt.

For a long time hunting was central to all that happened: something violent and intimate, something of an intimacy that involved all humans and animals. Something that had to be short-lasting, like a convulsion. Something that took lengthy preparation, involving a series of gestures: which brought about, created an imbalance that would have to be redressed by other gestures. And one day that thing that had been central became an ornament, relegated to the frame. Hunting became entertainment for kings and queens: they would amuse themselves in their parks, with a retinue of slaves and dignitaries. But for Artemis hunting was the axis around which everything spun. It had no purpose, fed no tribe—nor did it even feed the huntress. It was the activity par excellence, which obscured everything else.

Hunting is a state. The hunter is in the hunt in the same way that he might be in a cloud. And those who enter the hunt don't leave it, except through death. Sometimes not even through death, since the hunt continues in a simulacrum fixed onto the vault of the sky. And it continues in the underworld, where Orion, the

Celestial Hunter, still roams with his club, chasing prey, as in the sky, where he continues to chase the Pleiades.

In the time of Artemis, a hunter was the self-sufficient individual. And, as Aristotle observed, he can only be "animal or god." Consequently the state of the hunter naturally wavers between extremes: Actaeon can return to being a deer, in the same way that Orion can be abducted by Eos into a divine life.

Artemisian hunting was incestuous, presupposing a communality, an extreme intimacy between the hunter and the animal being hunted. Killing was the ultimate sign of a primordial affinity that did not allow the separate existence of either the animal or the human, but recognized only the perpetual oscillation between forms.

Hunting and sex: opposites that overlap. Everything that was said about hunting described sex. Everything that was said about sex described hunting. But they were incompatible: to mix sex and hunting brought disaster. During hunting, a triangular desire developed. The hunter, the rival, the prey. Apollo and Artemis, with Orion. Eos and Artemis, with Orion. Orion was sometimes the rival, sometimes the prey.

To deal firmly with the Olympians, nothing less than a goddess was needed. Calypso called them *schétlioi*, "heartless," because they wouldn't allow her to remain forever with Odysseus. And Apollo had used the same word when Hera and Athena did not flinch at the sight of Hector's mangled body, which Achilles had dragged through the dust at sunrise each morning, around the tomb of Patroclus. And this all because Paris had preferred Aphrodite, who had offered him "lust that brings suffering." In both cases the motive was jealousy—and Calypso dared to add that the gods were "more jealous than anyone else." They would not tolerate goddesses "going to bed with men." There's no other way of putting it: *eunázesthai*, the verb used by Calypso, means "share the *euné,*" the "bed." Among the many famous relationships between goddesses and men, the first example that Calypso chose was that of Eos and Orion, as if all cases that followed took it as a model.

Orion was an immoderate hunter. All he did was hunt, which could become a work of reclamation or extermination. At Chios, the island of snakes and of the grapevine, he promised Oenopion to clear it of those pernicious animals. He acted in this case as a civilizing hero. But on other occasions Orion sought to exterminate animals and killed them "*amenti corde,*" "with frenzied mind." And thus he infringed a rule that went before him, that included him, and was not to be broken. At any moment, and whatever he was doing, Orion wavered between benevolence and malevolence.

Corinna, Pindar's teacher and rival, said that Orion was "the most devoted" among men. The moderns take a very different view. In the twentieth century, Fontenrose found him rather "dimwitted"; and in the Romantic period K. O. Müller wrote that, apparently, "for people in ancient times it was very natural to regard Orion as a powerful giant, but also as an impudent and stupid fellow." But Orion's adventures are to be measured on an astral scale. Without batting an eye, Lévi-Strauss explained: "Scholars of prehistory consider that the American Indians arrived from the Old World during the Middle Paleolithic period, and we could accept that the mythology of Orion dates back to an equally ancient period, and has come with them."

Orion was not a giant but was *pelórios,* a word that indicates something immense and awe-inspiring. In Aeschylus it is said that "the powers of the first ages" were *pelória.* And Achilles is also *pelórios,* as is everything overwhelming and uncontainable. Waves and armor too. But most of all, Orion was extremely handsome. When Odysseus saw Otus and Ephialtes in Hades, he said that never had any beings appeared on earth who were "taller and more handsome, apart from noble Orion." Whom Odysseus had been able to see soon after, while on the meadow of asphodels, hunting the wild creatures "that he himself had killed on the barren hills." On earth, as in Hades, or in the sky, where he shone each night, Orion could do nothing other than this: hunt.

The birth of Orion comes in two versions, which couldn't be more distant and incompatible. And the same is true for every episode of his life, about which only tiny fragments survive. And yet it must have been a very old story and universally known if Calypso sought to give it first place among the disastrous loves between goddesses and mortals.

But "though fifth-century Hellenes knew the constellation by his name, the hero Orion had by then faded into the background, eclipsed by Heracles, Theseus, Perseus, and other heroes." The tragedians ignored him, except in a satirical drama by Sophocles, *Kēdalíōn*, of which almost nothing remains.

The two versions of the birth of Orion have only one feature in common: his father—or one of his fathers—Poseidon. Who is said to have produced Orion with Minos's daughter Euryale. About whom nothing can be said, except that she was a sister of Phaedra and Ariadne. Those two bold and ill-fated princesses were his aunts.

The second version is a perennial scandal. K. O. Müller wasn't the only one to describe it as the "repugnant legend of the procreation of Orion, which one would very gladly expel from this cycle of myths that is otherwise so beautiful." Even Ovid, who is certainly not squeamish, having reached the crucial point of the story, holds back: "*pudor est ulteriora loqui*," "I'm ashamed to go any further." He described what had happened one day, toward the end of the afternoon, close to Tanagra. Three men were walking on the plain. Two were grown-up and well built, the third a sharp-featured young man. Zeus, Poseidon, and the psychopomp Hermes, standing in for the third brother, Hades. As we know, Hades likes to avoid being seen on earth.

An old farmer was sitting in front of a small house. He said: "The road is still long and our door is open to guests." The gods followed him, disguising themselves. Smoky walls, fire almost out. The old man tried to rekindle it. There were two cooking pots, with beans and cabbage. They came to the boil. The old man poured the first glass of wine for Poseidon. His hand trembled. Poseidon said: "Now it's Zeus's turn." When he heard that name, the old man turned pale.

When he recovered, he had no second thoughts. He sacrificed his only ox, which he used for plowing his small field. While the meat roasted, the three gods reclined on low beds, on mattresses stuffed with river sedge and covered with linen. He began to pass around a wine that the old man had laid up many years before. It was now warm. Zeus said: "If you have a wish, say it. You shall have all." The old man replied that he was alone. His beloved wife, a love of his youth, had died. One day he had told her she would be his only woman. He wanted to keep his word. But now he wished for a son. The three gods nodded. Then they got up and stood around the hide of the ox that Hermes had skinned and laid out as a bloodstained rug. They spilled their seed onto the ox hide. Then they buried it. Ten months later Orion was born.

Ovid's version of the birth of Orion is, according to Otto Gruppe, a "parody." In the story told in the *Fasti*, the three gods urinate on the ox hide and so give birth to Orion. But the Greeks and the Romans knew well that no being could be born from urine. Whereas they had accepted that Erichthonius, supreme guardian of Athens, was born from a cloth soaked with the sperm of Hephaestus that Athena, in fury, had thrown to the ground. Hephaestus, in a moment of aberration, had seduced her in his workshop and his sperm had fallen on one of the goddess's thighs. Disgusted, Athena's only thought was to wipe herself and to get rid of the damp cloth. From it, Gaia would one day give birth to the boy whom Athena would cherish no less than a son.

Beyond the Mediterranean and the Khyber Pass, under a distant sky, other gods gave birth to Vasiṣṭha, one of the Saptarṣis, the

Seven Seers who then went to live in Ursa Major. They were Mitra and Varuṇa, earthly and celestial dominion. Unlike Zeus, Poseidon, and Hermes, we do not know what they looked like. And Varuṇa can be described as the most mysterious of all the gods.

We are not told when or why—the Ṛgveda generally refrains from giving such details—Mitra and Varuṇa summoned a female phantom, Urvaśī, the most beautiful of the Apsaras, the celestial nymphs. In the same way that Zeus, Poseidon, and Hermes had spilled their seed onto the hide of the ox that had just been skinned, Mitra and Varuṇ let it fall into a jug, kumbha, from which Vasiṣṭha would be born, who would then be called kumbhayoni, "he-who-has-had-a-pot-as-a-womb." That jug, the Ṛgveda says, was the "mind of Urvaśī." Compared with the legalistic crudeness of Ovid's version of the birth of Orion, written in pure Quirite style, here we find a story that is far more articulated and subtle. Mitra and Varuṇa did not forgo the presence of a woman to give birth to a being. Indeed, they wanted to be captivated by the irresistible phantom of an Apsara in order to spill their seed "in sight and in proximity of Urvaśī."

Hunting and sex made up the whole of Orion's life. There is no sign of any other activity. Or of any other passion. Apart from momentary arrogance. "I will wipe out all wild beasts," he said one day—and Artemis was offended. "I can shoot my bow better than you," he one day told his hunting companion, who was offended once again. And for Artemis no word of offense was empty. Orion once dared to lift the hem of her chiton, which was already short. And another time he had struck Upi, one of her Hyperborean followers, and it was as if he had struck Artemis herself. And yet she still went hunting with Orion.

"Pallidus in Side silvis errabat Orion," "Orion wandered pallid in the forest, searching for Side": this is how Ovid described Orion, the handsome and at times sad lover, searching for Side, his wife-pomegranate (which is what her name means), swallowed

up in Hades because she had dared to rival Hera in beauty. But this appearance of Orion had to be covered and blotted out by that of the brutal exterminator of wild beasts. Ovid's line was therefore corrupted, from copyist to copyist, and instead of Side was the word *lynxes*, as though it were a hunting scene. But there was an inconsistency. Why should the hunter Orion have displayed the pallid appearance of a lover ("*Palleat omnis amans*," according to Ovid)? And finally Nicolaas Heinsius came to the rescue with his *editio nova* of Ovid, Amsterdam, 1658. It was he who brought back the name of Side. *Salus ex philologis.*

The arrow eliminates physical contact. The virginity of Artemis: the avoidance of contact. The place where things do not touch—the mind—becomes supreme. Those killed by the arrows of Artemis: Tityos, giant son of Zeus, when he tried to rape her mother, Leto; Coronis, a king's daughter, whom her brother Apollo, loved; six daughters of Niobe; Actaeon, hunter; Callisto, huntress, whom Zeus loved. With Otus and Ephialtes, Artemis devised a stratagem: she darted about in the form of a deer, and the two mighty hunters shot and killed each other as they tried to hit the escaping deer.

All kinds of injustices and misdemeanors are attributed to the gods—and first of all "*fabulas illas turpiculas*," "certain dirty stories," as Christian August Lobeck wrote. But ancient writers never mention a practice that was repeatedly adopted: calling for each other's help as assassins to kill someone, especially women. Thus Dionysus appeals to Artemis to shoot Ariadne; thus Artemis kills Coronis at Apollo's wish; thus Hera persuades Artemis to shoot her arrow at Callisto. Artemis is the favorite assassin; with her bow she never misses her target.

Something dark and despicable is at work, as though the gods had lost their courage at the moment of killing—and needed a fellow accomplice. Humans are just the same when it comes to the crucial moment of the sacrifice. But the gods often resort to using a god-assassin at the end of a love story. It might be said that certain ominous events are unbearable even for the gods and impede the action. But it doesn't stop them signaling for the accomplice to go ahead.

In only one instance did Artemis kill unintentionally. It happened with Orion, the Celestial Hunter. Artemis loved him, though they had clashed several times. According to Istros, it even seemed as though she wished to marry him. Apollo was not pleased. One day Orion had plunged his majestic body into the sea and only his head was visible, far away. Apollo, out of spite, challenged his sister to shoot at the small black point that could be seen in the splendor of the glassy and shimmering waters. Artemis accepted: for her, the bow was thought itself. With the first arrow she pierced Orion's head. After a while, the waves propelled that great lifeless corpse to the shore.

It was Artemis who transported Orion into the sky, with his dog, who became Sirius and was called Canis Major, "the brightest star but sinister, bringing much fever to poor mortals," we read in Homer. Catasterization signals an end to the era of metamorphosis. When someone can no longer be transformed, but has to be saved, he is cast into a star. In the world of Zeus, these are the cases where there is no other way out. So it could be said that life on earth was *constellated* with stories suspended, attached to the vault of the sky. For the Vedic people, what took place in space among Sirius, Orion, Aldebaran, and the Pleiades was the scene that preceded every other scene and coincided with the manifestation of that which appears. Between Rudra, Prajāpati, Uṣas, and the Devas, astonished spectators, was the space where all that was essential to know took place.

For the Greeks of the classical age, Orion was associated with a story split into disparate and scalene fragments, between which were vast blanks. Writers warily avoided it. They didn't even allow Orion the privilege of becoming a character, as though his story were too remote. But, after every kind of inversion, transposition, and disguise, the story remained the same: the story of the Celestial Hunter.

III

THE GOLD-TIPPED
JAVELIN

Procris came ashore from an Athenian ship at Crete, alone and confused among merchants, goats, and craftsmen. The daughter of a king, a young woman in search of adventure, she was fleeing from the scandal of a double adultery. Her arrival couldn't have escaped the notice of King Minos, who would lay his hands on young girls newly arrived from the continent before they were offered to his son-in-law, the Minotaur. According to the stories that went around, Procris was very beautiful, had shared her father's bed, was a huntress and the wife of Cephalus, a hunter who had been abducted by a goddess and had occupied the place that many previous lovers had taken in her bed. It was also said that Procris had betrayed Cephalus, giving herself to a stranger laden with gifts.

Minos didn't search out Procris straightaway. He was told she had left the city, heading for the mountains. One day she reappeared. Minos didn't need to seduce her. Procris, with her clear and direct gaze, made him understand she was available. She behaved like a woman of the port just as much as a queen. Minos decided to confess to her the trouble that was afflicting him. He felt he had to tell her since he had realized she was the daughter of the king of Athens. His lust for women, he said, had been punished some time ago. Not only was his radiant consort Pasiphaë cheating on him with a bull, but she had placed a wicked spell on him, to stop his amorous escapades. When he had intercourse with a woman, the thalassocrat continued, he could never enjoy sex in peace because each time he would discharge serpents, scorpions, and centipedes into the vagina of his casual bedfellow. Procris didn't seem at all shocked. All he had to do, she said in a practical tone, was obtain a goat's bladder. Having found one, she placed it in her vagina and invited Minos to bed.

The love affair between Minos and Procris lasted a long time. Meanwhile, Minos's passion, his obsession for Procris, grew. He looked for no other women than she, protected always by the goat's bladder. Each day, with uneasy wonder, Minos became increasingly aware of something in Procris that greatly resembled the only woman who had escaped him, the woman he had most desired, she too a traveler and a huntress: Britomartis. He had pursued her in vain through all the gorges of Crete for nine uninterrupted months. And when, in his mad pursuit, they had reached a sheer cliff over the sea and Minos's hand was about to seize the hem of her chiton, Britomartis had thrown herself into the void, plunging into the waters. Minos never found out that Britomartis had been saved and protected by fishermen who had pulled her out of the sea in their nets. He went off, distraught, telling himself he had never managed to touch her. And yet the image of that woman had stayed etched in his mind more than any other. He still went looking for her. Now she seemed to have reappeared— and not only had she not escaped, but she waited for his visits with a lover's patience and received inside her the countless poisonous beasts that Minos's body produced. What more tender intimacy could he imagine than Procris's gesture of getting out of bed each time and emptying scorpions and centipedes into a tub?

But at the same time Minos felt that something separated him from Procris, as if that goat's bladder were the fragment of an invisible curtain. Maybe he had never touched her, maybe the story of Britomartis was happening all over again. How could he win over someone who was already giving herself so totally? In his somber mind, Minos thought of offering Procris an unparalleled gift. He knew that Procris loved wealth, but he didn't want to treat her like one of his many concubines. What is there beyond wealth? A gift from a god. One day he came to Procris holding a javelin and followed by a dog. "This dog, called Laelaps," he said, "and this gold-tipped javelin were a gift from Zeus to my mother, Europa, when he left her alone on this island. Nothing can escape either one or the other. Laelaps will always catch in its teeth the prey it is chasing. You are a huntress: now they will help you when you go hunting alone." Procris was thrilled. But she touched the javelin and stroked the dog thinking about something else, about something Minos knew nothing about.

Then she let it pass. "I, too, have a divine gift for you," his lover said. From a chest where she kept her traveling clothes she took out an herb that Minos had never seen. "Look," she said. "Now we can do without that goat's bladder so often filled with scorpions inside me. Besides, this remedy also comes from your family. You remember how the giant Picolous tried to drive your sister-in-law Circe from his island? This root grew from the black blood of Picolous. But Helios has bleached its flower. If you use it, you will no longer discharge snakes. So you can go into your wife's bed and even make her pregnant, unless you want the earth to be scattered with bastards born from your nymphs: whereas the Palace of Knossos has no heirs, except for that young man with the head of a bull, who isn't even your son." Minos failed to realize at the time that the miraculous herb was a farewell gift. The following day, Procris was gone. His informers reported that she had taken ship for Athens.

Minos had paid regular visits to Procris over a long period. They were never seen outside her room so as not to tempt the fury of Pasiphaë. They talked and talked, then curled up together on the bed. Minos, the most regal of kings, the first to have taken control of the seas, the only king to have sought the advice not of a minister but of Zeus his father, now revealed the secrets of his family and of his realm to that fearless Athenian girl, who lived in solitude on his island for no other reason than their vain and wondrous encounters. Procris also told him about her own life. About her love, as a young child, for her father, Erechtheus. About her love, as a girl, for Cephalus, for his stunning beauty, and the promise they had made never to be unfaithful to each other. About the love she had always had for hunting. Procris also had a few secrets to tell. She hid nothing, except for one story about which she would never breathe a word to anyone. It had happened in Crete, before her meeting with Minos. When she set foot on the island, she was neither an adventuress or a fugitive but a princess trying to reach her goddess. She had left the port immediately and started to wander the mountains, looking for Artemis.

Artemis watched Procris, and from her small and perfect mouth that Praxiteles would try to imitate she proffered these words: "I know you are mine, I know you are me, even if for your whole life you have done what I condemn. You have offered your body on every occasion—and with greater pleasure whenever the occasion was unlawful, with greatest pleasure if just for a gold crown. You are a daughter of the city, who celebrates its mysteries between four walls. You are a king's daughter—and you cannot hide yourself among my nymphs. But, above all, you are a huntress. This is your beginning, this will be your end. I am the one who sent you into the city as my secret messenger, I am the one who left you to shame yourself so naturally, I am the one who wanted, through you, to keep a hold on Cephalus, the most handsome of hunters. And Cephalus will never know that his fate has always been governed by me. Eos by then was exasperating him, with her sweet arms, with the softness of her pillows, with the obsessive chirruping of her cicada—and Cephalus thought, smitten by nostalgia, of the young girl he had left in Athens, thin and nervous, his cheeky playmate. He thought of Procris—and, through you, he worshipped me. So now I will not welcome you into my chorus, I will not allow you—as you would like—to abandon your life as a lost woman among men, I will reject you as though you were unworthy of me. But I'll entrust you with what is most precious: see this javelin, see this dog. This gold-tipped javelin will one day be called 'Procris's javelin,' for it never misses a target; this dog is called Laelaps, it's a tornado and no prey can ever escape from it. But don't think I'm offering you some ordinary fairy gift, which serves only to increase your powers. This dog looks like an ordinary dog: but on its tongue you will recognize a star, and another on its forehead. This dog is a star, it is Sirius, more powerful than the gods. The sky and the earth obey this dog: it is thanks to him that they are not consumed by an immense fire. You, who will be remembered only as jealous and adulterous, who seem to spend your life in a woeful circle of passions, you will once again be my secret messenger. This dog and this javelin will be of no use to you, except for a subtle amorous revenge, but they will save the world when you hand them over to your husband, lover, brother." While Artemis was speaking, Procris felt a stabbing pain pass through her like a wedge. But at the same time she felt an infusion of bliss greater than any other she had ever felt. She recognized herself in Artemis, as if she had willfully obeyed her, without knowing it, in all the meanders of her life. And yet now she saw her for the first time, for the first time she heard her—and it would be the last time. Procris had always felt that the realms of jealousy and adultery were not, in her case, governed by Aphrodite, but by that other goddess, who scorned and ignored them in front of everyone. She needed to return to those realms, accompanied by Laelaps and the javelin. Procris bowed in silence and vanished into the forest.

Procris boarded the ship back to Athens dressed as a boy: hair trimmed short, the bordered chlamys of a hunter, a petasos thrown back over her shoulders. She held a javelin tightly in her hand and was followed by a dog. Having arrived, she headed for Thorai, below Mount Hymettus. She passed the house where she had lived happily with Cephalus. She didn't even stop, and began climbing the slopes of the mountain. She was looking for the footpaths Cephalus used to tread. And at last she found him. He was resting under a pine tree, in a clearing. They spoke like two hunters who don't know each other and can talk only about hunting. Procris let Laelaps run off: each time he sped back with the prey. Three times she shot her javelin much farther than that of Cephalus. And each time it struck an animal. Cephalus watched the dog and the javelin with the same amazement and concentration he'd experienced as a child, when Procris used to hide her fine toys from him. Procris approached him and said: "They can be yours, if you let me take you." Cephalus agreed and stretched out on the grass, waiting for his unknown lover to take the initiative. Then Procris bared her breast and her manner became cheeky: "You recognize this, at least?" Cephalus understood straightaway, but didn't say a word. Procris had now sat down: "Remember, we were children and I secretly left my father's bed to play with you. Then came the marriage, and we were so excited and silly that we promised never to be unfaithful to each other. Then you started going off hunting—and you didn't want me to go with you, perhaps you were afraid I was better than you. One day you went off on a journey that took eight years. I got to hear that Eos had taken you and was offering you her bed. When Pteleon came to woo me, I yielded out of spite—and not just because I was attracted by the gold crown he wanted to give me. You surprised us: it was you who had arranged for me to meet Pteleon, so that I would fall into the trap. But now I want to tell you: on that occasion I felt an intense pleasure that no one—neither my father, nor you—had given me before. It was the pleasure you experience only with the first man who happens to pass—and then he vanishes. Everyone in Athens knew about our affair and they laughed. So I took ship for Crete. This dog and this javelin were given to me there, twice: by a goddess and by the most powerful king. But for me their only purpose was to show that you don't need a goddess to be unfaithful to me. The first boy you come across on Mount Hymettus is enough." Cephalus then stroked Procris's naked breast and smiled. They went back to their old house, both feeling they could be no better off with anyone else in the world.

When Cephalus had been abducted by Eos, for some time he had been overcome with terror. Then he thought he was destined for a life of perpetual bliss. And finally he was gripped once again by terror and a desperate urge to escape. This happened because once, while Eos was traveling in the sky, he had discovered a tiny scroll, on the shelf where he saw small bottles and jars that his abductor used for her makeup, lined up like soldiers. So Cephalus read these words:

"Eos awoke one day in a shell deep in the ocean. She stretched her arms straight out, with a lazy gesture. And felt the thrill of indeterminate strength, ready to take over everything. When she stretched her fingers, strips of pink light furrowed the leaden celestial vault. Then, between one finger and the next, a glow emerged, and the outline of her hands abandoned over the sky became lost in a single radiant beam. It was dawn.

"At that moment, Eos was already putting on her makeup. Then she turned westward and, from a balcony of cloud, displayed her bare breast to the world. In the silence, wearing a saffron robe, she climbed onto a chariot drawn by four white horses and went off for her ride, for her hunt. She looked down at the earth and especially at the most rugged mountains, in search of lovers. She liked hunters in particular. Tithonus was one of them, one of many. Eos knew that, for every man, her passage was wondrous, but also fatal. Each new day wore out their time, helped them to die away. She surprised handsome and lonely youths, such as Cephalus or Cleitus. She snatched them away on her chariot, bundling them into her arms. But soon she had to abandon her lovers, since Aphrodite had condemned her to constantly renew them.

"From Zeus she asked—and obtained—endless life for Tithonus. But she forgot to ask for endless youth. She flew with him to the land of the Ethiopians and, for several years, she thought they would live together forever. Now each morning she woke in the same bed with the same man—and before him she put on her dancer's makeup. But one day she realized Tithonus was growing old. Like all the daughters of the Titans, it was difficult for Eos to distinguish between her mind and what the rest of her was made of: above all, light and time. To articulate a thought was an exertion, a rare and unnatural task. So she hadn't known how to formulate what she should have asked for Tithonus. What was youth, other than existence itself? It didn't need to be named.

"As she watched this man wither away beside her, she felt a loss of heart, a dangerous and unfamiliar sensation. Tithonus the hunter had grown smaller, his body shriveled. And his voice altered during their long conversations. There was something stubborn, gentle, and desperate about him. Eos realized she could no longer share her bed with such a body. She took him in her arms, like a sick child, and laid him in another room. Each evening, on her return, she served him with human food mixed with other food unknown to humans. Tithonus no longer spoke. At night, behind the walls, Eos could hear a steady, inarticulate sound, the only sound that reached her. One day she opened the door of his room and saw the bed empty. Then, in the semidarkness, she heard the voice of Tithonus once more. She looked down—and recognized an insect slowly approaching her soft foot: a cicada. She picked it up and shut it in a cage. Then she placed it beside the bed where she continued to receive her lovers. Beside him Tithonus now saw, like a landscape of boulders and tree trunks, the line of scent bottles and tiny boxes that Eos kept for her makeup. Each morning, Eos fed him lovingly with leaves and ambrosia. The chirrup of the cicada accompanied her in her sleep."

That evening, when Eos returned, Cephalus asked if he could go back onto the earth. His beloved agreed.

Now that Procris had given him Laelaps and the javelin, he went out each morning, impatient to go off hunting. Procris let him go. She then went off hunting alone elsewhere. One day an eager hunter told her he had met Cephalus on Mount Hymettus. He was propped against the trunk of a pine tree, motionless, and was calling: "Aura, Aura, come to me." Or: "Nephele, Nephele, come to me." "He is calling the breeze or a protective mist," said the hunter—and the eternal euhemerist spoke in him. But Procris had turned white. Having grown up with fables, she had fought with fables and knew they could not be overcome. "These are women, worse even than women," she muttered to herself. Shut in her room, certain painful stories came back to mind. Aura was a nymph, whom Dionysus had possessed in her sleep. And who was this Nephele? Might she be another name for Eos, might Cephalus's first hated lover be hiding in that dawn mist? Might Cephalus be yearning to be abducted once again, even if his beard had grown wiry with age? And wasn't Nephele also the name given to the image of Hera, on whom the cruel and lustful Ixion had thrown himself? And weren't the Centaurs born from her? Can an image then also give birth? But what is an image made of, if not breeze and mist? Might it be true that images are no less powerful than those from which they emanate? Procris felt pangs of jealousy returning more painfully than ever. But this time she foresaw that the whirl of betrayals was about to come to an end.

She was no longer the confident woman she had thought she was, but the desperate girl, lonely and furious in her own house. She put on her high hunting sandals and went off once again to look for Cephalus. In the same clearing that the hunter had described to her, propped against the same pine, Cephalus was calling Nephele, calling Aura. His voice was like that of another, as if a ghost lived inside him. Procris crouched down behind a bush and watched him. And, without realizing, she let out a groan that was not hers, as if some other ghost inside her were speaking as well. Laelaps immediately pricked his ears and headed toward the bush. Cephalus looked about, took hold of the javelin. Procris felt the leaves stir and the point of javelin pierce her breast. "I've been killed," she thought. She saw Laelaps licking her feet and Cephalus, who was bending lovingly over her. Then she died.

With Procris's bloodstained corpse in his arms, Cephalus went to Erechtheus. The incestuous father looked silently at his daughter. Into her grave he would plant a spear, a gesture that indicated a violent death waiting for redress. For the Athenians, the involuntary nature of a killing was no mitigation, nor did it cancel out a wrong, indeed it made it more subtle, more solemn. For someone killed by mistake there is a further significance, which goes beyond the mean fallacy of the killer. But what was the significance of Procris? Always to be the model for every comedy or melodrama or drama of unfaithful lovers, up to *Così fan tutte* and beyond? Or was there something more mysterious, glorious, and secret in her? Odysseus would have already glimpsed her in Hades, between Phaedra and Ariadne. Why did that Athenian girl go around with such illustrious and ill-fated figures? The Areopagus considered all this when it was convened to pass judgment on Cephalus. Its sentence: perpetual banishment from Athens. Shouldering Procris's javelin and followed by Laelaps, Cephalus set off alone in the direction of Thebes.

When Erechtheus thrust his lance into the grave of Procris, everyone thought of the ancient law about murder. The body of Procris was stabbed a second time, as if the first of her lovers, her father, were wishing to emphasize the death that her second lover, Cephalus, had inflicted. Erechtheus wasn't thinking about the husband assassin. He was thinking about the history of Athens, of its salvation, shrouded from the beginning in a cloud of maidens who had been sacrificed or had killed themselves—but the one and the other cause of death merged together. First the daughters of Cecrops, the first king of Athens: the maidens of the dew, who threw themselves to their death beneath the Acropolis—Aglaurus, Herse, and Pandrosus. Then his own daughters: Protogeneia, Pandora, Creusa, Orithyia, Chthonia. And now Procris. They had been struck down by the word of the oracle. Erechtheus had consulted the oracle of Delphi to know what he should do for Athens to win its bitter war with the Eleusinians. "Sacrifice your daughter for the city" was the answer. Scholars of antiquity and mythology disagree, as always, over which daughter this was. One anonymous source suggests Procris was the chosen one. But they were all chosen ones, since they had sworn not to live beyond their sister's sacrifice. So they were all sacrificed, but each differently. We know that Orithyia was abducted by Boreas; and Creusa raped by Apollo in a cave of the Acropolis. And Procris? Her name already means "the chosen one," but one lexicographer tells us that *prókris* was a type of fig. And "figs," *sykaî*, was the name given to incestuous women.

By enticing his daughter into his bed, Erechtheus had chosen to enclose Procris within a wall of forbidden love and infidelity, so that she might eventually reach that death which, for the fact of being involuntary and accidental, heightened the sacrifice, transforming it into its opposite. Incest had served to delay the sacrifice.

In this way Procris would die not as an ignorant virgin, but as a romantic heroine, like an Alexandrian adolescent who had experienced the whole cycle of passions. Few knew that Procris had had a daughter by Erechtheus: they called her Aglaurus, in memory of one of the daughters of Cecrops who had killed herself. At Salamis there was a ceremony in honor of that maiden of the dew: "Pushed by youths, the man who was to be immolated ran three times around the altar. Then the priest struck him in the throat with a spear, after which he had him completely burned on the pyre." In the silent language of ritual, that spear corresponded to the spear that Erechtheus had planted on the grave of Procris. It was the javelin that killed her—and at the same time the spear that demanded revenge and honor for her.

From the moment when the heirs of Cadmus were banished from the city, the people of Thebes had been afflicted by a scourge sent by Zeus. Hidden among the bushes of Teumessos, a thin and hungry fox was lying in wait and systematically killing whoever it came across. The meagerness of the animal made the sentence even more difficult to escape. That fox was like the tiny infection that soon devastates a vast body, perhaps the whole land. The Thebans, in their desolation, decided to respond to those repeated attacks with repeated ceremonies. Each month they exposed a young child outside the gates of the city. They knew the fox would soon come down from Teumessos and would devour it. But the evil that had been lodged in the Teumessian fox could not be mitigated. The evil lay in its destiny never to be caught. It would carry on killing with the same patient regularity with which the sun rises.

Amphitryon then asked Cephalus for help. He had heard talk of Procris's dog and its miraculous power: why not unleash one animal against the other, the animal that cannot be caught and the animal that cannot fail to catch anything? It was an incompatibility to be entrusted to Zeus, an expert in incompatibilities. If Cephalus helped the Thebans, Amphitryon added, then the Thebans would purify him of the killing of Procris.

And so Cephalus unleashed Laelaps. It ran up to Teumessos, to face the fox. Zeus watched the scene. Those two small, lean, and ferocious animals, he thought, were the epitome of the world. Laelaps was Sirius, the celestial dog, around which was arranged the workings of the spheres. What a tangle of circumstances, what tortuous adventures to make it reach that mountain in Boeotia, where it would finally reveal its cosmic nature. In the beginning it was a golden dog that Zeus had left to guard Europa, still lying on her back, intoxicated on the bough of the plane tree at Gortyn where Zeus, in the form of an eagle, had possessed her. Then Europa had given it to her beloved son Minos. She was the only one not to be frightened by its dark look, for she knew where it came from: it was the look of Hades. Minos would then give it to Procris, his favorite among many lovers. And it was simply the repetition of a gift, for Procris had already received that dog from Artemis, from her goddess. She was the figure of salvation, Zeus thought. The whole of Procris's tangled life, which seemed absorbed in amorous torments and delights and nothing else, had provided an excuse for her to return from Crete one day, disguised as a young hunter, with that dog—and for her then to give it to the only one she loved: Cephalus. Procris would never know this, but it was thanks only to her that Greece, then the world, would not be slowly torn apart by the Teumessian fox.

Zeus looked down on the two incompatible animals as they ran: he turned the fox to stone and dissolved the dog into the air, sending it back to its place in the sky, where Sirius shines brighter than any other star. That chase could only be suspended—and one day it would be resumed, for the whole time that Zeus maintained his realm.

Not much is known about Cephalus after the Teumessian fox had been turned to stone. He moved west, farther away from Athens, following Amphitryon, like a noble wanderer, in his war against the Teleboans. He wanted to forget being a hunter and a lover. He was looking for death and obscurity. But his careless audacity made him famous, no less than his story, which everyone recounted, and would recount for centuries, since Pausanias could still refer to the "story of Procris, that everyone sings." He knew nothing and wanted to know nothing about his enemies. In vain: in the evening, in tents, warriors were constantly talking about him. He heard it said many times that such a war was pointless, because the enemy king—called Pterelaus—had a strand of golden hair that gave him immortality. Cephalus thought: "All I want to do is die— and I can't. Pterelaus can't die." He felt a strange sympathy for that man whom he imagined to be unhappy because of his invulner- ability. He knew nothing more about him. He asked his comrades for more details. They told him casually that Pterelaus was the son of Deioneus. Cephalus was startled. His own father was called Deioneus. Was he perhaps fighting against an unknown brother?

He heard other stories about Pterelaus: they said he had taken his daughter Althaea as a lover. And they said another daughter, Comaetho, appeared for no reason on the terraces of the walls. Cephalus, who always jumped ahead of everyone else, recognized her one day. He stared at her, as if they were alone in a room— and that look, to his horror, reopened the wound of memory. Then everything happened fast: Comaetho surprised her father in his sleep and plucked out the golden hair. Soon after, Pterelaus was killed by Amphitryon in a duel. It was rumored in the camps that Comaetho had carried out that salutary misdeed out of love for Cephalus. Comaetho was also killed, with contempt. The warriors scattered and Cephalus was once again alone. "I am accompanied only by betrayal," he thought.

He desired nothing more in the world. His life had been a tan- gle of women, of which nothing was left. Not even a child. Why? He wanted to ask the oracle. And the answer was that he had to have intercourse with the first female he met. Locked in his gloom, Cephalus wandered off again in the mountains. He came across a she-bear. "A good chance to get myself killed," thought the hunter. And he approached it, defenseless. But the she-bear stroked one of his arms with its paw. Cephalus realized the she-bear was cling- ing to him like a woman. Stretched out on the grass, intermingled with the fur of that great and very tender animal, Cephalus found his last moments of elation. The she-bear wrapped itself around him, drowned him in a spell. Their bodies moved with the sleepy certainty of a past familiarity. A single thought passed, now and then, through his mind: he remembered Procris and what she had told him about the pleasure given by strangers. Then he lost his senses. When he awoke, he no longer saw the she-bear, who had become Procris. She gave birth to Arcesius, father of Laertes, whose son was Odysseus. When Odysseus the hero recognized her among the famous women in Hades, he didn't know that Procris was blood of his blood.

Alone once again, Cephalus continued wandering. On the island of Lefkada he climbed up to a tall sheer cliff overlooking the sea. From that point "it was an ancient tradition for the inhabitants of Lefkada each year, during the sacrifice in honor of Apollo, to keep evil away by throwing off a criminal: they would tie him to birds of every kind, so that by flapping their wings they would lighten the fall; and many men, who gathered in a small circle in small fishing boats beneath the rock, would try as far as they could to save the man who had been thrown off, pulling him on board and carrying him beyond the boundaries." Cephalus looked around. There was absolute solitude. Not a boat in the sea. He then hurled himself from the cliff, with a sense of relief. But he wasn't saved like Britomartis. People said he had killed himself for love of Pterelaus.

In Hades, Procris represented the novel. Daughter of the king of Athens, in love with a youth who came from a small Attic port, she lived during a period of warfare, when the Athenians called themselves Athenians for the first time. What she wove within her, from her childhood, was a web of emotions: one day they would be called feelings. She mixed with royalty and with goddesses, but her story, from beginning to end, was totally private. Only a gust of wind separated her from Anna Karenina, or a character from

Schnitzler. This is also why—or especially why?—Homer wanted to name her. And Polygnotus, in his *léschē* at Delphi, depicted Procris and Clymene, another of Cephalus's women, who turned their backs on each other, still filled with jealousy and recrimination even in the underworld. The art of those Greeks encapsulated not just the past, but was already unraveling, thread by thread, the tangle that would be called literature.

Cephalus and Procris are now dead. Their story remains suspended, still to be understood. Why were these perfect lovers not destined for a happy and ordinary life? Why did they constantly and endlessly betray each other, having sworn never to be unfaithful? What was the cause of their perpetual unrest? And why, of all the stories of mutual betrayal, has no other survived so long? They were two hunters.

IV

THE BRIEF AGE OF
HEROES

There were fifty men and one woman. Among them, the most celebrated heroes. They set sail on the *Argo*, the ship Eratosthenes described as "the first ship equipped and endowed with speech, the first to cross the hitherto unnavigable sea." They had to capture the Golden Fleece, which hung from the topmost branches of an oak, protected by a dragon in the remote kingdom of Colchis. It was the test to which Jason was subjected by King Pelias, who was convinced it was tantamount to a sentence of death. But other heroes gathered from all parts of Greece to run the same risk.

To capture the Golden Fleece, to hunt the Calydonian Boar, to fight the Trojan War: three times—and only those three times—did the heroes gather for an expedition. For the remains of an animal, to kill an animal, to win back a woman. No other reason could be sufficient for the heroes to act together. There were three patterns of events. In the first, a monster was killed. In the second, a powerful animal was hunted. In the third, men killed one another. First kill the monster, then hunt, then kill one another. It was the epitome of all that had happened since primordial times.

Jason is the man who did not want to become king. This was his intention from the start. When he appeared before Pelias, who had usurped his father's throne, he fell immediately into his first trap, as if on purpose. "What quest is impossible?" he was asked. To capture the Golden Fleece, said Jason, recklessly—or even "by chance." Did he speak *by chance* at the meeting that would determine his entire life? This itself was strange. And Jason immediately accepted the impossible quest. It was always better than fighting for the throne. Jason harbored a doubt over everything relating to royalty. And yet he was the one to lead the expedition to recapture the talisman of royalty—which, at the end of his adventure, wasn't even of any use. When Jason returned to Iolcos, the

Golden Fleece was mentioned no more. No one seemed interested in it. There were other concerns. The cruel king Pelias still ruled. It hadn't been enough for him to depose Jason's father. He had had him killed by forcing him to drink bull's blood. An atrocious and unprecedented death. But that wasn't all: Pelias had also killed Jason's infant brother Promachus. He wanted to be safe on all sides. And Jason didn't seem to worry him so much. A rumor spread that the Argonauts had all died. A plausible rumor, much welcomed.

Jason had to make a long, painstaking tour of Greece to recruit the Argonauts. There had to be no fewer than fifty, almost all of divine origin, "born from the blood of the Blessed." He had to go as far as Arcadia, the land most rugged and alien to the sea. His mission there was the opposite: not to persuade but to dissuade. He knew the huntress Atalanta wanted nothing more than to join up with the Argonauts. Jason always began by using a tone of reason. No, he said, he didn't think it appropriate for a lone woman, and of radiant beauty, to board the same ship as fifty men on a quest that everyone considered hopeless. She would be the cause of disagreements. He explained that he "was afraid of terrible arguments over love." Atalanta listened to Jason in silence and took hold of a javelin. It was the gift she had prepared for her guest.

Apollonius of Rhodes doesn't include Atalanta on the list of Argonauts who assembled at Iolcos. But according to Diodorus Siculus, when the angry king Aeëtes and his bodyguard reached the Argonauts on the shore, where they were making frantic preparations for setting off again, Iphitos was killed in the fight and "the leader Jason, Laertes, Atalanta, and the sons of Thespius" were wounded. Atalanta was therefore with the Argonauts, was one of them, equal to them. It was Medea who healed their wounds, in just a few days, with her herbs and concoctions.

On the *Argo*, Meleager and Atalanta watched each other, spied on each other. Each day, each moment. But only they knew about it. None of the other Argonauts were aware. Each day Meleager and Atalanta felt a growing tension that drew them together and which they never showed. All was deferred. Now they had to take part in the capture of the Golden Fleece, which didn't much matter to them. But they felt that, for them, there would be another fateful appointment: the hunt for the Calydonian Boar.

Pelion: a mountain that dropped into the sea, clad entirely by forest, like a fleece. A dark green mass with patches of emerald. On its promontory, among the rocks, the Argonauts sighted three figures that waved to them, the last image before the open sea. A woman of austere beauty; a Centaur; a blond child. Philyra, Chiron, Achilles. Philyra had been caught by Rhea in Cronus's embrace, in the final spasm. Cronus had got up straightaway, transformed into a horse, and trotted into the distance. He wanted to avoid matrimonial conflict. Chiron, the first of the Centaurs, was born from his seed. And young Achilles was entrusted to Chiron, to be taught everything essential.

Chiron, Philyra: Jason watched them as they grew smaller and smaller into a dot, lost against the last outline of Mount Pelion. The other Argonauts watched, but none of them knew that Chiron, Philyra, and the forests of Pelion had been Jason's whole world for twenty years. Then one day he left them and turned up in Iolcos, "holding two javelins, a wondrous man," according to Pindar. Who added: "His splendid locks of hair had not been cut away, but flowed shining down his back." He walked straight on and stopped in the center of the square. It was the first city square he had seen. "No one knew him; everyone admired him."

Jason now thought of that tiny figure, with blond hair too, whom he had glimpsed between Chiron and Philyra, as if in some already prepared space. It had to be another link in the cycle of heroes. But first the Argonauts had to close their link. Now all that surrounded them was the sea.

Nothing is achieved without a sacrifice. And so, before boarding, the Argonauts performed a blood sacrifice. Two oxen were led to the altar. Then Heracles "with his club, struck one of the oxen in the middle of the head, at the front, and the animal fell to the ground." After him, Ancaeus struck the other ox on the neck with his two-bladed ax. Killing the animal was a privilege that went to the hero who was heaviest (to such an extent that at one point it was feared the *Argo* would be unable to carry him). And it was the deed that has most weight.

When they landed on an island inhabited only by women eager for foreign men, having killed all their husbands and banished all men from Lemnos, the Argonauts were in no doubt. They agreed straightaway to remain there and to live "secluded." Their vocation for glorious deeds was not inescapable, if to achieve it required arrows that came from the most improbable master of sarcasm: Heracles. In the end they sailed on, reluctantly. None more reluctant than Jason, who said farewell to his lover Hypsipyle with these revealing words: "For me it is enough to dwell in my native land, with the consent of Pelias. May it please the gods to relieve me from my tasks." Never as in this confession have we come so close to the hero's secret. Not just Jason's but that of heroes in general: the deep desire to be freed from the tasks they had to carry out, this obligation devised by the gods, perhaps for their pleasure alone. In saying farewell to his lover, the hero would often resort to noble lies. But not Jason: on the contrary, this was the moment when he could say in the simplest terms what he could never say again. And he was "moved."

Greek darkness was enameled, dark blue rather than black. *Kyáneos* was the word for it. And the color was so significant that the clashing rocks through which the Argonauts had to pass were called *Kyáneai*, the Blues. *Kýanos* is the blue enamel that is found already described for Mycenaean artifacts. Dark blue is the color of Poseidon's hair. Or the mourning peplos of Demeter and Thetis. Plato explains that *kyanoûn* was produced by mixing black and white with *lamprón*, the "bright." The feet of a table can also be blue, or the bow of a ship, or clouds. As well as the eyebrows of Zeus.

Was Phineus a blind seer who helped the Argonauts and obtained help from the Argonauts—or was he an enemy of the Argonauts, and blinded by them? The first version is told by Apollonius of Rhodes, the other by Aeschylus and Sophocles. How do we choose? One had to find some way of accepting both. The most difficult aspect, in the history of the heroes, relates to monsters. Every hero has to kill a monster. Jason, too, a reluctant hero, has to kill the enormous dragon, as long as the *Argo*, coiled around the tree where the Golden Fleece hung from the topmost branches. But few dare to admit that, for every hero who kills the monster, in the shadow there is the monster who kills the hero. A clear instance was provided by Jason himself. In a *kýlix* by Douris, of around 480 B.C.E., the hero can be seen emerging from the jaws of the dragon. The body is intact, perfectly relaxed, like that of a sleeping man being regurgitated. Athena watches the scene, deep in thought. Jason is naked, and he shows no signs of injury, even though the dragon is holding him between two full sets of small, sharp teeth. The dragon is returning him to the world—and the goddess alone is able to witness the scene. Jason regurgitated by the dragon appears only in the *kýlix* by Douris. That image is essential in reconstructing the secret life of Jason, where words provide no help.

According to the careful calculations of Hermann Fränkel, Medea must have been not much older than fifteen when the Argonauts arrived. How could she be recognized? That was obvious. Like her sister Circe, like all the daughters of the Sun, "she gave off a distant sparkle, as though emitting a golden splendor."

The heroes' quest was merely a pretext: this is what Medea dreamed, immediately after having seen Jason. The stranger had come *for her*: "She reckoned that, if the stranger had accepted the contest, it was not out of a desire to take away the ram's fleece." She was the one he wanted to take, as "lawful wife." The fifty heroes, the ship that speaks, the flying ram, the clashing rocks, the Harpies: everything dissolved into the dream of Medea. Once the myth had sunk, what remained was amorous mythomania. Only two figures were left on stage: the stranger and Medea. This was already Racine.

The ram with the Golden Fleece had saved Phrixus and Helle from death just as they were about to be sacrificed. It had demonstrated a wondrous and unprecedented ability to rescue them from all danger, flying them hundreds of miles when no man was capable of flying. Suspended in the air, it had spoken words of consolation to Phrixus when his sister had fallen into the sea that separates Europe from Asia. After so many exploits, once they had landed in Colchis, a distant and unknown land, the ram might have expected to be worshipped like an Egyptian god. Instead, it immediately asked Phrixus to kill it, in sacrifice. The man whom the ram had saved from sacrifice had to become its sacrificer. There was no way of escaping from the motions of sacrifice. King Aeëtes was pleased to accept the ram's wondrous remains and gave his daughter Chalciope to the stranger Phrixus. Nor was there any need for gifts. The gift was the Golden Fleece.

Between Homer's epic and Apollonius of Rhodes's *Argonautica* there is a divinatory reversal: in the *Iliad* and in the *Odyssey* the raptors that have seized their prey are a sign of favor and victory. In the *Argonautica*, the "timid dove" that escapes from the claws of the falcon and falls into Jason's lap signifies the benevolence of the gods and Aphrodite's favor: the Argonauts will save themselves only thanks to the help of Medea. But, looking further ahead, Aphrodite's favor turns out to be disastrous. The "gentle bird" that has now escaped from the predator will one day kill her children.

Jason performs the tasks required and never fails to fulfill the duties of the hero, though "not desiring them." But he cannot take credit for the capture of the Golden Fleece. Apollonius of Rhodes was very clear: "Jason took the fleece to Iolcos thanks to Medea's love." It's as though the hero were a necessary puppet, moved by external forces. Having once completed his tasks, the hero is reduced to an empty carcass. And no one seemed to have been less of a hero than Jason. Having reached the kingdom of the cruel Aeëtes, who systematically killed strangers as soon as they approached, Jason tried to persuade him, with suitable words, to hand over the Golden Fleece to a group of strangers. An orator's vain hope. As he listened to Jason's words, Aeëtes pondered whether to kill him there and then.

The Argonauts soon realized they were on dark and hostile soil. Once off the boat, they proceeded to a flat land that carried the name of Circe. There were tamarisks and willows, at the top of which were "corpses suspended from ropes." Those bodies ravaged by the elements, wrapped in ox hides, hung at the threshold of a shamanic kingdom. In her eyes, said Princess Chalciope, Medea's sister, "the desire for Greece" was no more than "an ominous infatuation." Did her sons want to go back to Orchomenus, to claim the legacy of Athamas. Orchomenus? And where might Orchomenus be?

Sometimes the gods preferred to take control of what was going on, dismissing men as irrelevant. Even heroes—or indeed, especially heroes—whom they prized most among living beings. The *Argo* was sailing toward Scylla and Charybdis on its tortuous return journey. The Argonauts had already managed to pass through the Blue Rocks, the clashing rocks, on their route to Colchis. And this thanks only to Phineus, the soothsayer who—unfortunately for him—"had no qualms even about revealing accurately to men the sacred thought of Zeus." But now the ordeal was repeated. To pass from one world to the other they had to sail between rocks in perpetual movement, rocks that crush. Or by a bridge that is like a razor blade.

This time the gods felt they no longer needed to put the Argonauts to the test. They had already captured the Golden Fleece. All they had to do now was survive, to get back to their kingdoms and live out their days. At most, they would meet up again to hunt a prodigious wild boar. Not only out of need, but for old times' sake.

Hera knew she couldn't act alone. She asked Thetis, the only female whom Zeus had loved in vain. He had kept away from her body when told their son would be "greater than his father." And Zeus intended to reign forever. But Hera didn't believe it was the only reason for their unconsummated love. She thought Thetis hadn't yielded to Zeus partly out of consideration for her consort. The only woman, the only goddess who had had such consideration. And so Hera, who had no friends, considered her almost a friend.

And now among the Argonauts who were about to be wrecked on the roaring rocks there was also Peleus, the mortal with whom Thetis would eventually be joined. No one else could offer so much help. For Thetis was also the sea. As in an agreement among friends, Hera asked Thetis to take the place of the Argonauts. By themselves they would not be saved. Thetis agreed.

They saw her surface from the waters and climb onto the stern of the *Argo*. Like a weathered sailor she took the helm, ignoring the Argonauts, who were following her, astonished. But her skill wouldn't have been enough. They then saw emerging against the dark and confused background, among foam and vapor, groups of nimble young white-skinned women, lashed by the wind. They moved as though they were in a meadow rather than among rocks and waves. They were the Nereids. Playing. From one shore to the other, they tossed the ship and its cargo of heroes like a ball. Instead of sailing, the ship now flew. High up, like a clear patch among the rocks, a male figure could be seen, leaning on a mighty hammer: Hephaestus. But there were other witnesses too. Higher still, now silhouetted in the sky, was the one who controlled events: Hera herself. And to her breast she was holding Athena, the goddess she could consider neither as her daughter nor as one of the countless illegitimate children that Zeus had scattered over the earth. The cold, luminous eyes of the two goddesses were staring down at the scene. They, too, had no idea whether the gamble would pay off.

With "great dismay," Apollonius of Rhodes had to acknowledge that "diseases and wounds are not the only paths to death." One can also kill just with the mind, "from afar."

The moment had come to describe how Medea had brought down Talos, the bronze giant, who hurled rocks into the sea to prevent the Argonauts from docking at Crete. It was then that Medea decided to act. Holding her hand, Jason took her to the bridge of the ship. First the enchantress drew her purple peplos to her face. Her radiant eyes were still exposed. She murmured words that no one understood. She addressed the "swift hounds of Hades, who roam everywhere hunting out the living." But this was just the start. She then formed a "mischievous thought" and turned to look at the metallic giant who was watching them from the land. Medea's eyes sent out impalpable "simulacra," *eídōla*, that went and lodged themselves in Talos's immense body.

At first nothing happened. A heavy silence reigned. Talos then started running again and throwing boulders into the waters. As he was running, a sharp stone wounded him close to the ankle. It was his single, tiny vulnerable point, the lost-wax hole. From there, a liquid began to flow, which looked like molten lead. Talos collapsed like a house of cards. The Argonauts could then land that night in Crete. They immediately built a sanctuary for the Minoan Athena. As soon as they touched land, wherever they were, the heroes were careful to perform a sacrifice or establish a holy place.

But when they resumed their voyage, they thought once more about Medea, about her "mischievous thought." It was a grim night, of the kind that sailors call "sepulchral." There was a heavy pall of darkness. The moon and stars could not be seen, yet there was no mist. The Argonauts wondered whether they were sailing in Hades or in the sea. A "black chaos" opened up in the sky. Tears ran down Jason's cheeks. He cried out to Apollo—and continued until he saw the shape of a golden bow emerging in the darkness.

Pelias had been cruel throughout his life. And even at the end, as an old man, he showed excessive cruelty and malice. He was clubbed to death by three of his daughters (Alcestis abstained), who then cut him into pieces, which they threw into a boiling cauldron. He was supposed to emerge from it whole. As diligent disciples, they were applying the formula proposed by Medea to rejuvenate their father. But Medea took no part in the operation. She said she had to pray to the Moon. She climbed onto the palace terraces and lit a fire. It was the agreed signal for Jason and his men, who stormed and occupied the palace, with much bloodshed.

When he returned to Iolcos with the Golden Fleece, Jason found himself in a similar situation to when he had left. Indeed, worse. His family had been exterminated. And Jason was still the legitimate heir who couldn't assert his claim. In the end, he had Pelias out of the way only because Medea had practiced her arts. But even then he didn't become king. It was as though he had never wanted to take advantage of his victories. During the ten years he would spend in Corinth with Medea and their children, he was happy to be treated as an honored guest. But with no specific role. And where was the Golden Fleece? Once again, no one mentioned it.

Even if, according to Homer, the story of the Argonauts was "on everyone's lips," the surviving accounts are full of gaps and omissions. Neither Pindar nor Apollonius of Rhodes, nor even the austere chronicles of Apollodorus and Diodorus Siculus, tell us why it was so important to capture the Golden Fleece or why the most glorious Greek heroes had immediately obeyed the herald who called them to Iolcos, and had then set off on that quest. And nothing is said about what happened to the Golden Fleece once it was retaken. The only use to which it was put, so far as we know, was that of the soft bright cover on Jason and Medea's couch during the first wedding night in the cave of the Phaeacians. The decision to use it was made out of expedience and necessity. If Medea had remained a virgin another day, Alcinous would have delivered her up to her violent father, Aeëtes, who would have taken her back to Colchis. But even on that night the Golden Fleece was no more than an ornament.

Otherwise, during the four tumultuous months of the return journey, the Golden Fleece was left hanging on the rigging on the *Argo*'s bridge. The heroes didn't even guard it. And there were other misfortunes after the *Argo*'s return to Iolcos, but no further mention of the Golden Fleece. If it had been a talisman of sovereignty, that sovereignty was no longer exercised. Jason made no objection when he was banished, together with Medea, to Corinth. In the end, the question of him becoming king was no longer raised.

There was a period when the divine had not only to be recognized, but flowed in certain beings. These were the "children of the gods," born because Zeus—or Poseidon or Aphrodite or Thetis—had "mingled in sexual union" with mortal women or men. It was a brief and anomalous period. It lasted few generations and was an age associated not with a metal but with the blood of those who were called *heroes*. A name that Homer extended to everyone, including those with no name, who fought beneath the walls of Troy.

The map and the family tree of that period were contained in the *Catalogue of Women*, a poem that in ancient times was generally attributed to Hesiod. Only a few eloquent fragments of it survive. Human beings were divided into various families, each of which originated from one of Zeus's sexual forays. The end was marked by the return of the Greek warriors from Troy. This is how the cycle came to a close. What preceded it was a bewildering sequence of convulsions linked to generic names—Titans, Giants, Hecatoncheires. What followed is the history of mankind alone, where it would be hard to find a story line as dense with significance and enigma. And where it would lack the mesh that holds

together all the strands like those of a single family, however rami-
fied. This is the mesh that allows each mythical strand to reverberate in all the others. Whereas the strands of novels remain forever
isolated. Even if the stories of people in power, or in love, or in
adversity, each time share some common trait. But their nobility
lies in the isolation of each individual case.

If Zeus had been merely just, there would have been no commingling with the divine. His father, Cronus, could not have been
just, since that word didn't even exist at that time. A god then could
only be exact. Exactness was his supreme virtue. So no one talks
about the justice of Cronus. Whereas people talk about the justice of Zeus, who continually breached it. Zeus claimed the privilege of arbitrary will. He isolated a woman, found his way around
her, often deceitfully, took advantage of her. One by one, through
arbitrary will, he built human history part by part. In this way,
humanity could finally escape from the rigid and anonymous repetition of nature. And in the meantime a highly ambiguous tribe
emerged, that of the heroes. Through their ancestry, the heroes are
part of the divine, and are therefore entitled to assume some ves-
tige of that arbitrary will. But they can never be sure whether the
arbitrary will that they practice belongs to the divine or to another
part of their ancestry, which is human. The mark of their privilege would then become a simple violation of order—and would be
open to punishment. This is the insurmountable perplexity about
the heroes.

Zeus's passion was for the visible, for the existence of outlines
in the light. That was the wonder the Orphics attributed to Phanes.
Now, once he had come to reign, Zeus tried to repeat it. An immense radiant light—and countless bodies, objects, bathed by the
light. A golden chain kept them tied, but it was almost to prevent
the figures from bursting out, wandering forth. Zeus kept an eye
on measures. But he wasn't the one who set them. Measure belonged to the reign of his father, to Cronus. Zeus liked to fix his attention elsewhere: on metamorphosis, on the capacity of forms to

live many lives, swiftly and smoothly. Figures appeared and disappeared on the earth in a flash. They obeyed in a trice, encountered deceit. They sought only that which appears—and they were sated by it. The gods also only sought that which appears. They expected earthly figures to exist, more than to worship them. A little sacrificial smoke was enough. Whereas they had no greater dislike than for that which avoided the glory of appearance. To be sure that people understood this, the twelve Olympians often appeared on the earth and on the sea. In this way people knew what splendor can be. Likewise the people who lived during those years were captivated by the visible, in which the gods also occasionally played a part. For the heroes, this seemed a desirable life: radiant, intense, brief, like a duel. A life that brimmed with force—and often ended in the intoxication of force. But as soon as life ended and the last breath came out of the nostrils, a long and monotonous unhappiness began. There was no darkness and unconsciousness, but a faint glow, which hurt the eyes, and a great weariness through which ran memories of another life, of the life in the light. It was a state similar to that of someone who is tired and cannot sleep. In that larval shade everyone yearned for just one thing: blood. And this ubiquitous greed linked the shadows to a flock of animals ready to rip one another apart. If the shadows didn't throw themselves onto the other shadows it was only because they wouldn't have found blood there.

According to Hesiod, humans are fallen beings, even though they belong to the same stock as the gods. There are two stories about their fall—one brusque and linked to a single act, the other spread over time. In the first version, Prometheus steals fire from Olympus, and Zeus responds by giving Pandora to the humans. The fall that follows is immediate and irremediable.

In the other version, which Hesiod calls *lógos*, "discourse" (and, as M. L. West observes, is "the earliest example of the word in the singular"), but is just as much *mŷthos*, to the annoyance of moderns, who want to keep the two words well apart, mankind declines over a succession of ages. But it is not a gradual and straightforward fall, as progress would one day be envisaged, though in the opposite direction. Indeed, it takes an unpredictable, tortuous, and irregular path. There isn't always a deterioration. On the contrary, the age of heroes, which precedes the Iron Age, "is more just, and better," than the grim Bronze Age. Names and stories appear for the first time. It isn't necessary to be a warrior to have a name. Such were the men of the Bronze Age, but they would end up "leaving no name in icy Hades." For better or worse, only with the age of heroes are precedents established for all actions. It is a short and frenetic period, to which Zeus decided to put an end as he watched the men who fought one another beneath the walls of Thebes and Troy—and more than once they happened to be his children and descendants.

Hesiod's succession of the ages of the world has Indian, Persian, Mesopotamian, and Hebrew parallels. Each of its elements finds a correspondence in other places. Except one: there is no equivalent to the age of heroes, the fourth age, which precedes the torment of the Iron Age, to which Hesiod himself belongs.

As for the earliest literature, whether it be Homer's poems and hymns or Hesiod's *Catalogue of Women* and *Theogony*, it had to speak about the gods or about an age that had been swallowed up. The only exception is one part of *Works and Days*, where Hesiod describes the tough existence of those who work the land. Humble beings, condemned always to repeat the same gestures.

The heroes were slow to extricate themselves from their animal origins. Chiron the centaur was Achilles's teacher, but was killed by Heracles. And Heracles himself ended up tortured and driven to kill himself by the tunic soaked in the sperm, oil, and blood of another Centaur, Nessus. Heracles had killed Nessus to defend a woman, Deianira, whom Nessus had captured when he pulled her from a river metamorphosized into a bull. Sophocles specifies that one and the same arrow had killed Chiron and Nessus, as if

Heracles had kept that weapon to exterminate a race from which the heroes had learned many secrets. Barely separated from animals, close to the gods, soon extinct—and so the heroes came, and soon went.

The exploits of the heroes were exercises in cunning and force. But cunning and force that would be useless without female intervention. Theseus was the first to understand this. Heracles was still too primitive, he endured women instead of using them. Whereas Theseus, from the very beginning, from the time when he descended on Athens along the isthmus, knew that encounters with women verge upon the ultimate difficulties, those where neither cunning nor force are sufficient. The woman belongs to the enemy, but if the hero succeeds in making her betray her role, her land, the enemy falls, like the body of the Minotaur slashed by the sword.

The phrase "gods and children of gods" appears many times in Plato's *Laws*, from the mouth of the old Athenian. Dances honor "the gods and the children of gods"; certain forms of life can be practiced only by them. Why such insistence? The "children of gods" are the heroes, beings that belong to a vanished age. But a special cult is dedicated to them. Plato never tires of repeating that *all* cults must be kept and celebrated in the city he is planning. This part of the divine that was mixed with mortal women to give birth to the heroes is an enduring part, it belongs to life forever.

As in many other cases, and despite what glottologists suggest, the more correct starting point, with regard to the heroes, was set by Plato in *Cratylus*, where we read that *herōs* derives from *érōs*, because heroes "are born either from a god who fell in love with a mortal woman or from a mortal man who fell in love with a goddess." The hero was therefore distinguishable for being evidence of a period of particularly intense mutual attraction between the divine and the human. A short period that ended in the space of three generations, from the quest of the Argonauts to Odysseus's return to Ithaca.

No return from Troy lasted as long as that of Odysseus. And Odysseus was driven further than all other heroes with the weapons of the mind. He would bring the period to a close. And we might think the killing of Penelope's suitors, the Proci, was the final scene. But the poets of the epic cycle kept a few surprises in reserve.

Telegonus was the son of a daughter of the Sun, and of the last hero. Son of Circe and Odysseus. He had never seen his father. For years, all that he saw around him was a woman—his mother—and the lions, bears, and wolves that wandered around their house. Wherever he looked, there was the sea. But he was impatient to get away. He wanted to find his father. This was also what his mother wanted: "Circe sent Telegonus, the son she had had with Odysseus, to look for his father." When Telegonus said good-bye, Circe handed him a strange weapon with a twisted point. It was a spear tipped with the barb of a stingray. A weapon like none other in the world, said Circe. Hephaestus had forged it. And only Telegonus could use it. The young son left the island. He had no name: he was the One Born Far Away. He traveled long.

There are differing versions about what happened at Ithaca. According to some, Telegonus was tossed by the waves onto an island and began to plunder it. Odysseus turned up to stop him. They fought, and the barb of the stingray stabbed Odysseus in the side, killing him. According to others, Odysseus was warned by the oracle of Dodona that he would be killed by his son. He therefore had Telemachus sent away and imprisoned at Cephalonia. One day he heard shouting outside the palace. A young man wanted to come in—to see his father, he said—and they were refusing him entry. Odysseus thought it was Telemachus. Perhaps he had come back to kill him. He went out armed. But his spear became stuck in the trunk of an apple tree, while the barb of the stingray, on the point of Telegonus's spear, stabbed him in the side and killed him. When Telegonus realized what had happened, he despaired. He told Telemachus they had to give their father a worthy burial. But where? On the island of a divine woman. "On the island of my mother," said Telegonus.

It was a strange voyage that Telegonus made back to his mother, Circe, accompanied by Penelope and Telemachus. On the ship they also carried the body of Odysseus. They had talked long before deciding that the right place to bury him was not Ithaca, where Odysseus was born and where he had returned, but the island of the sorceress who wanted to take him forever. As would now happen. The voyage was long and uncertain, since Circe's island is not to be found on maps. To get there, the help of a god is required. But Athena was there. She accompanied Odysseus, even in death. The three passengers had time to study one another. And they spoke about just one subject: Odysseus. Penelope became increasingly surprised as she gazed intently at the young man who had killed her husband. And it wasn't obvious why Telemachus had at once agreed with Telegonus in arguing that Circe's island would be the most appropriate place for their father's tomb. Perhaps because it was a good excuse, and perhaps the only possible excuse, to meet the daughter of the Sun.

Eventually the three seafarers landed on the island of Aeaea. Circe saw Penelope, of whom she had heard much; and Penelope saw Circe, of whom she had heard much. On the empty island they buried the man who had been their husband, father, and lover. Then they looked at one another. They didn't know what to do with their lives. Athena then intervened. She said that Telegonus ought to marry Penelope and Telemachus ought to go with Circe. "Circe and Telemachus gave birth to Latinus, from whom the Latin language took its name, while Penelope and Telegonus gave birth to Italus, who gave his name to Italy."

Once again, Athena's intelligence had found a path that would have been barred to anyone else. Too bold, too unusual. Athena knew that the last moments of the age of heroes were looming, and she had to end it with an act that had the power of all that had preceded it—and was something unique and unrepeatable, like the heroes themselves.

She wanted Penelope, who had been frightened for years that her suitors would kill Odysseus, to marry the man who had actually killed him. She wanted Penelope's son to go with the woman who had stubbornly prevented Odysseus from returning to his wife. She wanted the divine lover to go with the son that the man she loved had had from another woman. Everything had to stay in the family. These were the last throes of the age of heroes. Athena wanted to enclose Penelope, Telemachus, and Telegonus on Circe's island like insects in amber.

The outside world? Indifferent. Those who came after were above all extraneous. They belonged to another story; indeed, to another era, from which Odysseus's exploits were separated by an imperceptible barrier. At the same time, that new story legitimately followed from the age of heroes—even if it was a legitimacy that was paradoxical and open to doubt, like all legitimacy.

Latinus, Italus: figures that soon faded. They became confused with certain places: Latium, Rome, Italy. Places where more would be *written* about the heroes. And where the *Odyssey* was read, but where there was no mention of Telegonus. Only the learned poets remembered him. During the desolation of his banishment, Ovid called his three erotic books "his Telegonuses" because they had killed their father. If Italy had studied its origins, it would have found Circe and Penelope. But it forgot them. Romulus couldn't be descended from a man who had killed his father and married his stepmother. It needed the piety of Aeneas, the voice of Virgil, and the lineage of Aphrodite. But Athena had already acted and left her mark, moving the center of gravity of the stories from Greece to another peninsula: Italy. There was a shift from the land chosen by the Olympians to the land of jurists and legionaries.

The skin of the Calydonian Boar ended up hanging in the temple of Athena at Tegea. Pausanias could still see it in the second century C.E. It was a worn remnant "that time had shriveled and left without a single bristle." As for its tusks, they had become part of Augustus's plunder after his triumph over Mark Antony, along with the ivory statue of Athena. Pausanias adds that one of the tusks had broken, while "the remaining one is kept in the emperor's gardens in a shrine of Dionysus on the other side of the Tiber, and measures three feet."

Pausanias was neither moved nor surprised when he saw the skin of the Calydonian Boar. Legendary animals could end up even like that. He was impressed, however, by the temple of Athena, "by far the first of all temples of the Peloponnese, for its size and architecture." It had Doric, Ionic, and Corinthian columns, as in a compendium of Greek art. And its architect was a great sculptor: Scopas of Paros. On the pediment were the heroes of the hunt for the Calydonian Boar, including Ancaeus, already injured, brandishing an ax: and first among them, Atalanta and Meleager. The Calydonian Boar was celebrated in the land of she who had been the first to wound it. It was as though history, at its remotest point, and art, at its zenith, had been reunited in the same place. Pausanias also saw in the temple a statue of Mother Dindymene "with a face made of hippopotamus teeth instead of ivory."

When the Palladium was stolen from Troy, various conflicting stories soon circulated. It seems that Odysseus entered Troy through an underground passageway, disguised as a beggar and accompanied by Diomedes. Once inside Priam's palace, he was recognized by Helen as one of her suitors in Sparta. But she didn't betray him. And nor did Hecuba, who also saw him. Indeed, Helen led the two Achaeans to the temple of Athena. It was the feast day to the statue and, during the commotion, Odysseus was able to steal the Palladium. But was it the real Palladium—or the copy? Or one of many copies? The real Palladium was the smallest, a wooden statue you could hold in your hand. The copy is the cause of a fight. Odysseus and Diomedes were already arguing over the Palladium in front of Helen. Helen managed to calm them for a while—her only thought was to get them away without being discovered. In the night, on their way back to the Achaean camp, Odysseus and Diomedes began arguing again. Diomedes took hold of the Palladium and claimed it was a copy. The argument has not yet been resolved, even today.

An abandoned talisman—the Golden Fleece; the rough and tattered remains of a wondrous animal, displayed as a hunting trophy or an ex voto in a temple at Tegea—the Calydonian Boar; a statuette about which no one can say whether it was the original or a copy—the Palladium. This is how the age of heroes ended. In the place where power was concentrated, it melted away. Now it would work its way elsewhere, into other forms, secret and fake.

The Argonauts, the hunt for the Calydonian Boar, the Trojan War, the return of Odysseus: cycles that are interlinked. Everything takes place in less than half a century. Nestor, the old man whom Telemachus meets at Pylos, was "in the flush of youth" at the time of the hunt for the Calydonian Boar. And he had fought at Troy. Achilles's father was one of the Argonauts, who Achilles as a child had seen set sail from Iolcos. Jason leads the Argonauts and takes part in the hunt for the Calydonian Boar. The Argonauts pass Scylla and Charybdis, but so, too, does Odysseus. Wonders abound, especially at the beginning and the end.

In those few decades, in the brief age of heroes, history is reduced to offering material to sing, to narrate, to elaborate. Then Zeus chose to bring it to an end. The wars and novels would be all that was left. Along with the memory of those few years in which everything that could happen did happen, only rather more splendidly than before or after.

V

SAGES AND PREDATORS

My lords, a solemn hunting is in hand

—SHAKESPEARE, *Titus Andronicus*

At one time, there was a murderous visitor who made human corpses disappear deep inside a cave and ripped them to pieces. In that same cave where their predecessors had been devoured, men devoured other, smaller beasts and kindled fire. There was a continuity of killing, in that darkness. But now humans felt they could become another being, distinct from all those they were killing or by whom they were being killed. To kill without touching: no one else could do this. This was the secret. After having fled for thousands of years, they lay in wait, immobile.

The history of no other animal has seen such a swift change in its way of life as that of mankind: from primates gathering fruits and roots, pestered by predators, to an omnivorous—and therefore carnivorous—animal, a biped who goes around in a group hunting quadrupeds often larger than him. Man distances himself from animals, acquiring their powers. There is a double movement, a cross-movement: in order to distance himself—in the process of distancing himself—there has to be an assimilation. Man becomes a predator so that he can distinguish himself from every predator and from every other animal. To distance himself from animal ways, man must become a specific animal. And in particular, that animal by which over a long period he had been killed. This double movement persists, indelibly.

Animals viewed humans for a long time with puzzlement. They realized that something was changing. Humans were no longer just one of many animals that the great predators were attacking and devouring, in the savanna and in the caves. Now humans, too, were attacking and devouring. But they weren't doing so with their bare hands. They were always making use of some strange object. Stones, poles, pikes. And they eventually used something even stranger: they struck from a distance, with obsidian tips that penetrated the skin. They were the only animal that struck from a distance. As humans advanced, in the scrubland or in the forest, a particular scent was detected, something unpleasant and alarming. The scent of hunters.

The hunt is the place where the primordial separation occurs, the divergence from which all others follow. The prey becomes the hunter at the moment when it sets its gaze on a being that is distinct from itself. In that gaze the hunter is born, who until that moment had been just one animal among others. He was *the* animal. Now, having become the eye that observes the animal, he also had to kill it.

Man's detachment from the animal was the great event among all events in history. Every other event follows from it. No story exists about what happened. But countless stories that have been passed down presuppose the existence of that story which hasn't reached us, and which perhaps was never told. Before being a ritual, it was what precedes every ritual, and to what every ritual refers.

Man, for a long time, was a primate among many and, as such, lived for a long time in terror of certain predators, knowing that he was one of their favorite foods. The story of how man became—in the words of William James—"the most formidable of all beasts of prey, and, indeed, the only one that preys systematically on his own species" is one that has no precedent in the history of the earth. The step to predation was an ethogrammatical *spillover*. Immensely risky, disruptive. It altered relations between Homo and every species around him. That step began a process that would never end.

For Homo, there were two mortal sins: *separation* and *imitation*. Separation occurred when he decided to go against the zoological continuum, taking certain animals into his service and regarding others as material that he could potentially use for his own purposes. Imitation occurred when Homo's behavior began to resemble that of predators. Once he had completed the step to predation, Homo didn't know how to deal with that new part of his nature. He chose to circumscribe it in its literal meaning and to expand it indefinitely as a metaphor. He invented hunting as a nonessential, gratuitous activity. It was the first art for art's sake.

In the animal kingdom, creatures carried on living as they had always done. They repeated the same unchanging motions. When Homo transformed himself into a predator, he infringed this order of things. Every killing, from then on, was also a signal that rekindled the memory of that step. And around that memory other gestures grew, and were repeated with regularity. Ritual ensured that Homo didn't stray *too far* from other creatures.

Animals do not imitate humans, though it did happen, in Victorian times, when Beatrix Potter started drawing her characters. The imitation was not only in thought and behavior, but in dress. Indeed, the clothes were almost the first notable feature. Waistcoats, bonnets, tailcoats, shoes. Everything in matching style, even the surroundings. And everything based on one rigid omission: no human was allowed to set foot in that world. Humanity had been erased and replaced by animals, in every tiny detail. Humanity had become superfluous, except as a remote, now extinct, model. A post-human life was being presented.

Beatrix Potter achieved the prodigy of inverting the course of history. Humans had long tried to domesticate certain animals, especially those of small or medium size, nonaggressive, and in certain cases edible. They were much apparent in the farmyard, in the garden, in the countryside. With Beatrix Potter, the relationship was turned upside down: this time it was the animals that used humans as a universal fund of behaviors.

There were two glorious moments in the Victorian age: Darwin linked human beings to primates; Beatrix Potter distributed human behavior among a certain number of small domestic and rural animals.

Man is not a born predator, but he becomes a predator. To do this he had to negate what he was, adding to his body a prosthesis—a sharp flint, a pointed stick, a bow. And then he began to hunt. Without the help of some kind of prosthesis, hunting would have been futile. Negation is therefore inherent to hunting. The hunter is the man of negation. He exists insofar as he negates an initial situation. If man, as Hegel argued, is "the sick animal," his sickness implies both negation and hunting.

All the idyllic pictures of a primitive humanity busily gathering fruits and berries are based on one absence—the absence of predators: as though humanity didn't need to protect itself. Quite different is the picture of a paradise that, in order to be so, needs to protect itself with a "fence," *pairi-daësa*. It is paradise only if it includes a barrier, beyond which stretches pure nature.

There was a time, around 542 million years ago, wrote Oliver Sacks, when "the once-peaceful pre-Cambrian seas were transformed into a jungle of hunters and hunted, newly mobile. And while some animals (such as sponges) lost their nerve cells and regressed to a vegetative life, others, especially predators, evolved increasingly sophisticated sense organs, memories, and minds." This is the dawning moment toward which humans, those recent arrivals, found themselves ready to climb when they transformed themselves from prey to predators. The Cambrian explosion was an unfurling of forms and modes of behavior, each interlinked with the others. And some of the qualities that humans would become so proud of were then tested for the first time, in waters that had become deadly.

To distance himself from the animal kingdom, Homo had to turn to hunting, which was not natural to him, whereas it was natural to other species. To distinguish himself from *all* animals, he had to appropriate certain highly conspicuous characteristics from *certain* other animals. But he did so by extending their application:

Homo became a predator not just because he was constantly killing other animals, but because he was preparing to take over the
whole animal kingdom. Predators have no interest in animals they
don't kill. Not so for Homo, who wanted to exploit all animals.
And the same was true for inanimate nature, which was harnessed
by gradually and cautiously subjecting it to various processes, thus
transforming it. One day people would talk about *technology*.

Herodotus speaks only once about "providence of the divine,"
"*toû theíou prónoia*"—and that is in relation to predators. He
writes that lionesses can give birth only once because their cub,
before being born, tears the uterus with its claws. It cannot avoid
it. It's a predator. But, if this didn't happen, predators would mul-
tiply and would wipe out other animals, which instead reproduce
plentifully. This is the order of things, which was violated when
humans became predators that reproduce plentifully.

Why is it that Homo cannot manage without guilt? The first possible explanation is that taking the life of another living creature
could indicate the cause of that feeling. But the killing of other living
creatures is normal practice for a very large part of the animal world.
Might it be the method of killing? Which has been done, since the
earliest times, in the form of hunting. And yet Homo hadn't particularly excelled in his capacity to kill, whereas he was a favorite prey for certain predators. Then a radical change took place:
Homo became a predator. Or more precisely: a predator who was
different from all others because he used objects specially devised
for killing. This went contrary to all observable behavior in the animal kingdom. Homo made a new and extreme use of imitation.
Certain animals imitate leaves or rocks or other animals, but they
do so to defend themselves or make themselves invisible—or sometimes to prepare ambushes. But they don't imitate the behavior of
other animals that continue to kill them. The unprecedented factor
that distinguished Homo from the animal kingdom was not in the
killing, but in that form of imitation involving the use of prostheses. By likening himself to another category of animals, Homo was

showing that he had no fixed and well-defined nature of his own. He was showing an inclination to metamorphosis. Which was not aimed, though, at escaping from a predator, as often happens with insect camouflage. On the contrary, it was helping him to become a predator. Homo was killing, like many other animals, but he was killing by imitating those animals that were his most deadly enemies. That gesture, which distanced Homo from other animals but also from himself, taking his enemy as his model, was the origin of a state—the state of *guilt*—from which he would not extricate himself.

For many species, killing is a way of passing time. They rest, play, kill. They sometimes copulate. Then the cycle is repeated. Homo kills and butchers meat as well. And yet, in a particular remote and unascertainable moment of time, and in the most far-flung places, he began killing and butchering meat while addressing certain words and gestures to invisible entities. And redoing it, at regular intervals. It was glory and guilt interwoven. If there had been guilt alone, it would have been enough to refrain from killing and to live off plants and their fruit. Yet now guilt was also being celebrated. Why? We need to look back to two facts of devastating importance for the species itself: when Homo became predator, and when he turned to eating meat. Behind these clean definitions, favored by modern scholars, lay a vast and silent wilderness of the past. Those who trod there recognized certain tracks, rekindled in certain gestures, in certain words, in certain carved or drawn figures.

Guilt is inevitable for anyone who is predator and prey. It's impossible to have one single role. There is the guilt of killing and there's the guilt of debt, which places someone in the hands of someone else. According to the Vedic seers, everyone, from birth, is in "debt," *rṇa*, and must therefore expect to be assailed by a creditor or by a predator, who—in the beginning—are the same figure.

Orpheus refuses to go hunting, but dies as prey. And every

predator is hunted by someone else. The lion hunting of the Assyrian kings was evidence of this circle. The ultimate predator is the god, who kills the king when destiny requires it. But the god can also allow himself to be killed, in a lynching. This is what happened to Zagreus "the Great Hunter," who is also the first prey.

Homo learns more slowly than other animals, and with greater difficulty. He never stops being born, and retains physical traces of his prenatal existence. As for his ethogram, it doesn't appear so clearly defined as that of primates closely related to him. This irrepressible initial *delay*, with its consequence of prolonged defenselessness, is the precondition for a learning process that, having once gradually and belatedly begun, can, by way of compensation, develop in countless directions. If Homo had not possessed a radical indeterminacy, he could not have developed his enormous capacities of imitation. The delay in development increases the capacity for development.

Metamorphosis brings about an extension of movement. And movement is a reaction against the inanimate, which dominates the universe. The possibility of metamorphosis is essential for those who want to move on in life. Nothing less was implied in the ancient practices of metamorphosis, which took the form of an incursion into another being: out of curiosity, admiration, erotic desire, envy, self-defense, aggression. The reasons may have been many, but the procedure was the same: assimilation. Something of the other being was made to resonate with something of themselves. Imitation presupposed the ubiquity of the mind. Those who sought to enter another being could find themselves being overrun by the other. The basis of every metamorphosis was possession. Which could be a grave affliction or a marvelous gift. Or both together. The shaman was called upon to cure nervous illnesses because only possession could cure possession.

One day metamorphosis began to become less frequent. Then it was no longer accepted. That which had most sense—transitions of state—now no longer had sense. Indeed, it was better not to men-tion them, to avoid being ill-judged. In only one place did meta-morphosis seem to remain intact: in dreams. Only in dreams did it seem entirely reasonable and normal. Much was lost, much was forgotten. But other forms of virtual behavior were acquired—and continued to be practiced. No comparison could be made between what had been lost and what was gained, each inextricably tangled with the other.

One voice merges into the other, making itself unrecogniz-able. It is an exercise in self-defense. The same is true for visual appearance. It is the camouflage of insects, who try to flee from their predators. But imitating means appropriating something else, extending one's own way of being. Imitation is possible only if the mind lets itself be infiltrated by what surrounds it and is capable of transforming itself into other beings, who weren't yet called *animals*. Homo became a predator through the use of imita-tion, until imitation led to metamorphosis. A certain repertory of imitations was established, a fluid and repetitive process ended up carving itself into a form, becoming an ever-available skill. This skill, of which there are no remaining traces or testimony, except in myths and rituals, has had the greatest consequences for human endeavor, noticeable everywhere, from the earliest times.

If pushed to the extreme, imitation is metamorphic. Not only does it reproduce something that was previously extraneous, but it assimilates it. It brings the imitator inside the imitated—and vice versa. In metamorphosis, the imitator invades an entity from which he allows himself to be invaded. When the imitator goes back to where he started, he will no longer be the same. Something of what he has imitated is now a part of him. And the situation can become desperate when there is no return from metamorpho-sis. Metamorphosis, then, rather than expanding a being, impris-ons it. If, on the other hand, the imitation develops a prosthesis, it takes over a being for a certain time—and can then be cast aside.

But if it goes too far it can become metamorphosis: something that modifies the substance of the being. Sometimes irreversibly. *Substitution* and *connection*—the two perpetual poles of the mind—coexist in imitation and in metamorphosis, they interweave, they stir, they overpower each other. At their extremes: the incessant simulator—the animal, or the plant, or the stone that are the results of metamorphoses with no return, as narrated by Ovid.

When imitation is applied temporarily, it is interrupted at a certain point and canceled out in the imitator, who returns to being what he was before. After the hunt, the hunter's bow is abandoned in a corner. After the performance, the actor removes his costume and goes off for supper with friends. And so there is a separation from the kind of imitation that would transform the imitator irreversibly. A clear dividing line cannot always be drawn between these two ways of imitation. And the whole of human history is a continual attempt to draw that line, if only temporarily.

Concealed in every imitation is some residue from the age of metamorphosis. A powerful and dangerous residue, like all residues. And which cannot be eliminated, since no order can include the totality of ordered material, in the same way that perception cannot avoid excluding a part of what is perceivable.

Imitation: a likeness that can sometimes result in a substitution. The copy is the perfect imitation, which can dispense with the original. When substitution takes place, the act is violent: not just because it eliminates what it replaces, or at least makes it superfluous, but because it shows that the regime of substitution in the end prevails over that of likeness. And it can even use it for its own ends.

In imitation the connective pole, based on likeness, operates to the point of preordaining the substitution. The imitator is by implication a forger, who can substitute and exchange the genuine banknote with the one he has just forged. Hence the latent violence in every imitation.

The prosthesis is defined by the fact that it can always be *detached* from the person who carries it. And it is first of all an imitation. Everything that distinguishes imitation will always be there with it, as a trademark and as a radical doubt. Will the prosthesis be capable of equaling all that it imitates? And if indeed it goes beyond it (this is the most worrying doubt)? The Western way of knowledge was the way of the prosthesis, therefore of imitation. Technology is nothing less than its culminating moment. The Vedic way was quite the opposite: it transformed the totality of the single being at the moment of detachment of the self from the I, of the *ātman* from the *ahamkāra*, which is the "forming of the I."

When imitation entails an appropriation, it also harms what is singular: an inevitable act, since knowledge, above all, means moving ahead in the dark, imitating. The violence of imitation is hidden in every act of knowledge. And first and foremost in this most obscure and critical process is the transition from the realm of metamorphosis to the realm of prosthesis. A transition accompanied by an immense growth of power (which is still occurring) and a gradual elimination of the communality with the rest of nature.

What mankind had lost, in relation to primates, in the fixity and certainty of their repertoire of gestures, it would recover in its capacity for metamorphosis. And the moment came when a certain metamorphosis became irreversible: the metamorphosis into predator, linked to the practice of a meat diet. At that point metamorphosis, which was the guarantee of a perpetual oscillation between forms, turned out to be a mechanism—and a trap—to isolate one form and keep it confined there forever.

The person who lives by imitation is the actor. And the first actor is the priest. There is no theater unless there has first been a relationship with the god. This disturbs and upsets Nietzsche's vision of the *Schauspieler*, the "actor" who discovers he had first been a priest. Simulation—hence imitation—is not an additional, recent quality, but a founding one. Without the mediation of the priest there can be no access to the god. But, for the Greeks, anyone could be a priest. Tertullian, an enemy of the Mysteries, is always blunt and illuminating. On the question of the actor-priest he had already spoken the harshest words: "Why is the priestess of Demeter abused if this is not what happened to Demeter?" If Nietzsche, in the beginning, regarded the actor as the main enemy, for Plato it was the *góēs*, the "magician" or "wizard," the man of the metamorphosis, who had within him, in their latent state, all the possible transformations that would be experienced and which would one day have to be abandoned, like so many garments. Plato saw the actor as man as he was becoming, whereas the *góēs* represented man as he had been in remote times. Two turbulent, mercurial conditions. To be avoided. There was no alternative but to establish an *orthótēs*, a stable, upstanding "justness." Plato hated mutability and irregularity above all things, "since always pursuing the same path, always acting or suffering in the same way is enough to manifest an intelligent life."

Théōsis, "becoming divine": a path followed as much by certain pagans as by certain Christians. *Imitatio dei, imitatio Christi.* Imitation was the only practice that made it possible to begin a process of assimilation to something that was unknown, remote, and overwhelming. At the same time imitation was condemned along with all that is secondary, derived, parasitic, as if it were due to a fundamental insufficiency. And yet the movement was the same: an attempt at incursion, however gradual, into something else, which was then found to be accessible insofar as it already belonged to the one who was imitating: the god, the animal, the character.

To become sanctified, just as to become guilty, one had to imitate. There was no other act that conjoined within it the extremes of good and evil, heaven and hell. One who imitates someone is a potential rival. And the rival is a potential, destructive adversary of the one who is imitated. If the emulator is successful, he can even make the person imitated superfluous. Or at least deprive him of his uniqueness. And this can be no less serious.

The Olympians were never crueler than with those who dared to imitate and emulate them. They feared being overwhelmed by them. To be punished it was not necessary to call oneself an emulator. Mere imitation was enough. Ceyx "addressed his wife by calling her Hera, and she addressed him in return as Zeus, so Zeus transformed them into birds, changing her into a kingfisher and him into a coot."

Simulation differs from imitation only because it doesn't renounce *mental reserve*: however long it lasts, it presupposes a return to the starting point, the necessity (and possibility) of it being divested. Whereas imitation poses no limits. It could continue indefinitely. And imitation could lead to metamorphosis. With possession, the inverse movement occurs: the incursion of an entity that imposes a certain conduct, producing an obligation to imitate something unknown.

The extreme complication—and seriousness—of all that relates to snobbery depends on its intimate and archaic relationship with imitation. *À la recherche du temps perdu* is full of grim and deadly stories that unfold between a *dîner en ville* and a *matinée*. There is something prehistoric about the social vicissitudes that Proust recounts. The snob lives in a delirium, trying to assimilate himself to something unattainable. He is a martyr of imitation. A potential saint or a potential murderer, who is stuck halfway along the path of sanctity or of crime.

Variation is the form most akin to metamorphosis—and a remembrance of that ancient age. It is found in its purest state in music. But Shakespeare's Sonnets can also be interpreted as variations. Or Tiepolo's *Scherzi*. And certain vases from Eleusis, where divine figures change positions and postures each time, might be an early example of this.

The act that has been the most powerful, and still continues to be effective, is a silent act of the mind: the act of substitution, the act with which it was established that *a stood for b*, that *a* took the place of *b*, that *a* represented *b*, that one stone would be called the same as another stone, that a notch on a piece of wood would indicate a star. It is the act of coding.

The bedrock of every mental activity, *standing for* is the secret of *Homo sapiens*, who doesn't even notice it as such, even if consciousness is constantly applying it. *Standing for* is apparent when, at the moment we look at something, it is superimposed and replaced by the mental image of something else. Or: when a stone is replaced by the sound of the word *stone*. And all of this is witnessed by consciousness, an entity that sees the stone and, simultaneously, sees the sound that indicates it. It is the first sign of self-reflectivity, which has always dwelt in consciousness: a silent, often unacknowledged, guest.

In 2014 Noam Chomsky, Richard Lewontin, Ian Tattersall, et al., felt it necessary to publish a manifesto to make it clear that all the current theories about the origins of language are inadequate and sometimes ridiculous. But it is not just language that has escaped the clutches of Darwinism. Another power—more obscure and neglected—hides behind it, like its shadow: the power of *substitution*. Without substitution there can be no words. Indeed, even before being articulated, phonation can already be the vehicle for substitution: the sound can *stand for* the thing. But here, once again, the specificity of language seems to dissolve away. For not only a phoneme, but anything whatsoever can *stand for* a stone— and a certain stone can *stand for* a certain other stone. At this point the substitution becomes the shadow that emerges from the shadow. It is no longer something that depends on language but something upon which language depends. And not just language. Every mental activity is based on internal images that *stand for* something external. The coding occurs in consciousness, indeed it is an unavoidable feature of consciousness. Language is not created alone, but as a branch of mental activity that incorporates all kinds of other nonverbal phenomena, among which one would find everything that was regarded as "specific of man."

A turning point for Alan Turing, in working up *On Computable Numbers*, was the moment when he established that the "states of mind" envisaged for his machine could be counted. "We will also suppose that the number of states of mind which need to be taken into account is finite." And this was not because Turing thought they were so, but because "if we admitted an infinity of states of mind, some of them will be 'arbitrarily close' and will be confused." Once again, it was necessary to sidestep the continuous and therefore treat the "states of mind" as something that they obviously are *not*: individual, well-separated blocks resembling the squares in which the numbers appear on the computer tape.

It was a new application of *putting into focus*, which is a first reduction of elements to make them enter into perception. Thus a discrete and countable unity is created, starting from an undivided totality. And it is the unity of the "states of mind" in Turing's machine. He knew perfectly well that such a formula would cause him difficulty, if only because it introduced a word—*mind*—whose meaning could not go unquestioned. And so he invented a character: *the desultory computer*, a person who cannot stay still at a table and "never does more than one step at a sitting." But this was nothing to worry about. It gave the opportunity to get rid of an inconvenient word. "State of mind" could be substituted by "note of instructions," without causing any detriment. Thus Turing, in one single blow, demonstrated his dexterity in eluding the "mind," where it wasn't strictly necessary, and at the same time he left a boundless field of action for it. Where indeed would the mind have been during the *desultory computer*'s repeated absences from his desk? No one could have said.

How is the *negligible* created? It is created in many ways, but most relevant to Turing was the move from analog to digital systems. The negligible could not be ignored in that transposition, since analog is continuous and digital is discrete. But what power was at work in that move? Substitution. The brain belonged to the continuous, but it needed—vitally needed—the discrete in order to function. If substitution was so essential, the machine could imitate it perfectly, enhancing and expanding that vast area which was dominated by substitution. The brain can act effectively only if it decides to ignore something (for example, the "intermediate positions" in a process: Turing says "we can forget about them"). The *negligible* is the key to all effectiveness. And the negligible is the *residue*. Ignoring the residue is imperative for the brain—and will become imperative for science.

Turing told friends that he wanted "to build a brain," but went on to say he wasn't interested in that organ with the consistency of cold porridge. To imitate the brain, he didn't want to start off from what a brain is made of, but from what a brain does. And not from all of what it does, but only from a certain segment of what it does: that of substitution. Digitality is the most perfect form of substitution that occurs in nature. Thus the *realm of substitution* would become the realm into which the machine would penetrate and would end up being more powerful than the supreme ruler that had preceded it.

But Turing knew very well that the nervous system was not a discrete-state machine like the universal machine he had designed in 1935. Indeed, he explained that "strictly speaking there are no such machines. Everything really moves continuously. But there are many kinds of machine which can profitably be *thought of* as being discrete state machines." These include the brain. To think of it as a discrete-state machine was an enormously fruitful and revelatory idea, even though, strictly speaking, it was *false*. Why? The answer is somewhat disconcerting: the brain is not and never can be a discrete-state machine but, in various circumstances and for various reasons, it *simulates* being so—and succeeds remarkably well in doing so. Even though, in many cases, it is less effective than machines. So that, "as long as the brain worked in *some* definite way, in fact, it could be simulated as closely as one pleased by a discrete machine." Such a machine would therefore simulate an entity (the brain) caught in the act of simulating.

Turing's machine simulates a simulation already being carried out by the brain in order to effectively perform in certain situations. It doesn't therefore imitate the brain, but certain strategies used by the brain. To imitate the brain, it would have to work out why the brain needs these strategies.

The simulation constantly at work in the brain and transmitted to science as its foundation is that of the *closed vessel*. Turing drew on that simulation, and on it he built the universal machine. It is an extremely powerful simulation, which operates in the world of the mind just as much as in the physical world. Simone Weil refers to this point in a page of notes that presuppose a knowledge of the workings of the Bourbaki group (hence of her brother, André, seeing that it refers to the axiom of choice): "Essential contradiction in our conception of science: the fiction of the closed vessel (foundation of every experimental science) is contrary to the scientific conception of the world. Two experiments should never give identical results. We overcome it through the notion of the negligible. But the negligible is the world . . ." This last sentence corresponds with the vision of the Vedic ritualists: *the residue is the world*. Two lines below: "The notion of analogy, of identical relationships, is central for the Greeks. Bridge between the finite and the infinite."

The same word, *simulation*, is used to indicate two processes that are drastically different. We talk of simulation when we imitate in order to deceive. A process in which the will is implied in two ways: the intention to imitate is overlaid with the intention to deceive. But we also talk of simulation for mechanisms (machines) that imitate something: a procedure where there is no will insofar as the programmer acts *before* the simulation procedure comes into effect.

What do the two modes have in common? Incompleteness. But not only this: it is a kind of incompleteness of mind that can be *effective*. Simulation demonstrates that in a vast part of what takes place, incompleteness is *not* a dividing and deterrent argument. One can move forward by successive approximations. And this supremacy of approximation is even more important than the distinction between action that is conscious and that which is unconscious (or not considered conscious). The word *simulation* is therefore appropriate in both cases without any straining of meaning. It is as if the outside world were to give the brain the capacity not only to elaborate constructs that correspond to the world, but to show itself so flexible as to allow constructs that are largely incomplete without rendering them ineffective.

Simulation, imitation, possession, metamorphosis: the wind rose of the mind. And a snake that bites its tail. They are kindred powers: they sometimes amalgamate, sometimes oppose one another, sometimes come close. At the point where they operate, they are easily confused. The art of distinguishing them was called *discretion of the spirits*. To understand possession, it is necessary first of all to remove it from its psychopathological and parapsychological context, where it was confined by those who feared it as *another path* of knowledge (and who did so for centuries, stubbornly and with a persecutory spirit). Nothing is more useful, then, than the impertinence of Paul Valéry:

"I reflect . . .

"Is it very different from that practice that consisted (and still consists) of consulting the 'spirits'?

"Waiting before a table, a pack of cards, an idol or a sleeping and groaning Pythia, or in front of what is called 'we ourselves' . . ."

These few words are enough to lead the question back to its true terms, which are quotidian, ceaseless, and much more insidious than any occultist or ethnographical performance. Possession is something that regularly intervenes in conscious life—and it cannot be otherwise, since every moment of consciousness is divided into at least two parts and contains something more than "what is called 'we ourselves.'"

Simulation presupposes, in the end, a return to the state from which we had begun. But this doesn't guarantee that we can effectively begin all over again. The prosthesis is a way of sidestepping this inconvenience. It always remains available. It can be used or not used—though it still offers the certainty of the object, its fixity.

It would be naïve however to think the most powerful prostheses are extensions of the body (instruments, weapons, etc.). These are prostheses that all depend on other prostheses (formal systems, algorithms), which are sequences of fixed signs on an impalpable *medium*, of which paper is an imitation. The mind has the capacity to project signs outside itself and to let them act as a result. Logic itself is an immense prosthesis—and mathematics can be equated to an experimental prosthesis in continual change. The wonder of the prosthesis is not just that certain mental operations are transferred into an object, such as the computer, but that these operations are applied to the world, which is external to us as well as to our prostheses. No explanation has yet been given for this. For science, the "unreasonable effectiveness of mathematics" is the mystery of mysteries, as E. P. Wigner had the nerve to claim.

Consciousness is recognized in an infinitesimal part of the life of the universe. And it poses the question of how it arose. If consciousness is a diachronic entity, we will have to suppose that logical and mathematical structures have developed over time. Perhaps through evolutionary pressure (there is no other accepted cause according to current prevailing scientific opinion). But pressure in view of what adaptive advantage? The only answer could be that such an advantage was the *correspondence* between certain logical-mathematical configurations and the outside world. In this case evolution would show itself to be an extremely sophisticated mind, capable not only of guaranteeing the applicability of certain mathematical formalisms, but of elaborating them. On the basis of what? What would be the *state of mind* that precedes the elaboration of those formalisms? On the other hand, if there were no correspondence between the mathematical structures of the mind and the outside world, man would be entirely defenseless, incapable of calculating, therefore of developing those prostheses that assure control over certain portions of the outside world. If mathematical constructs were inventions, the outside world would be a perpetual hallucination. If the mathematical constructs were discoveries, the outside world would be a continuance of the mind with other materials.

Western philosophy, starting from Descartes, is seen as a *prosthesis*, an apparatus to be placed over the mind so as to bring order into the world. The apparatus can be innatist, empiricist, idealist, materialist, etc. Each apparatus has its own outline and its own character. Each has vast consequences in the ways in which the subject onto which the apparatus is superimposed will deal with the world. This is not so for Nietzsche. Any page of his writing requires a reaction from those who read it. It can be one of rejection, agreement, or even plain shock. No prosthesis is placed over the mind of the reader.

As for science, once again from the years of Descartes, it can be said that it based its fortune on a vast omission: on ignoring the mind of the scientist who developed it—and ignoring consciousness in general. Each time it has broken this rule (the pineal gland, homunculus, various reappearances of vitalism) science has failed. When it has respected that fundamental approach, science has achieved amazing results. And in the end it has discovered, among its subjects of investigation, those things that it had omitted. In the list of given facts, consciousness, being pervasive and ever-present, cannot be eradicated. Indeed, it could be regarded as *the* prime given. Thus science has realized that it couldn't avoid it—and has found itself before a continent that was not only unfamiliar, but ignored. The omission on which science was founded presupposed

as self-evident what is in fact the fundamental mystery: the correspondence between the world and certain operations of the mind,
its obedience to equations. Once the investigation turns to consciousness, that mystery becomes central, in the same way that—
once upon a time—the opaqueness and unintelligibility of the
external world was central.

To get out of the quagmire of theories of consciousness, Colin
McGinn has put forward the following explanation: "There are
specific features of consciousness and specific features of human
intelligence that make the latter ill-equipped to understand the
former." The incapacity of the human species to explain the phenomenon of consciousness would therefore be phylogenetically
based. H. Allen Orr found nothing wrong with this theory, indeed
he restated it with a certain nonchalance—and almost with a sense
of relief: "The point is that we have no reason to believe that we,
as organisms whose brains are evolved and finite, can fathom the
answer to every question that we can ask. All other species have
cognitive limitations, why not us? So even if matter does give rise
to mind, we might not be able to understand how. For McGinn,
then, the mysteriousness of consciousness may not be so much a
challenge to neo-Darwinism as a result of it."

This rescuing of neo-Darwinism could turn out to be dan-
gerously deceptive. According to McGinn, the human species is
incapable of understanding the phenomenon of consciousness in
the same way that an antelope cannot count. In both cases, it is
said to be a phylogenetical limitation, since we are all organisms
whose brains are "evolved and finite." But no sooner has this argument closed one question than it opens up another, bigger and
more formidable one. We can understand how the human species, with a brain that is a gelatinous substance weighing around
three pounds, is unable to explain a phenomenon such as consciousness. Yet it seems far more incomprehensible that the same
brain can envisage and describe, with an extremely high degree
of accuracy, an enormous quantity of phenomena that take place
outside the human body. Behind the problem of consciousness

looms the no less difficult problem of intelligibility. According to McGinn, evolution has made the human species incapable of discussing what is going on inside its own head while at the same time it has developed an enormous capacity to describe and envisage processes that are going on in nature. A capacity not shared by any other species. It ought to be admitted that this is another of the numerous counterintuitive theories of which science is justly proud. But it's not enough for a theory to be counterintuitive in order to make it convincing. And above all it is not enough to make it true.

The omission of the consciousness-that-watches from the *enumeratio* of elements to be investigated was the crucial step for modern science. If consciousness is omitted, everything fits together—or rather: everything *can* fit together. At least until the moment when we find ourselves up against an invisible wall, which is consciousness itself. Greek science never dared go as far as omitting the mind. We had to wait for the recklessness of Descartes for such a step to be taken. And we had to await the beginning of the twenty-first century for a clear acknowledgment of the unfathomable gap that lies at the center of the fabric of science itself.

On the sixth day of the Creation, Elohim said to man and woman: "Have dominion over the fish of the sea and the birds of the air, over every other living thing that moves on the earth." But that wasn't all. To survive, man and woman had to feed themselves. Then Elohim said: "Behold, I have given you every plant that bears seed, which is on the surface of all the earth, and every tree that gives fruit, that has a seed: they will be your food." For man and woman, the food granted to them would be plants and fruit. Elohim made no mention of dead flesh.

But his words continued—and the most surprising part came with this: "'And to every wild beast, to every bird of the air, to everything that creeps on the ground, to everything that has living breath, I have given every green herb for food.' And it was so."

In the beginning, then, humans and animals alike fed exclusively on "herbs that have a seed" and on fruits. Yes, there were "wild animals," but they fed on plants, like humans. There were predators, but there was no predation. In nature, no living being killed any others. This remarkable peculiarity among primordial creatures was abandoned and overshadowed by the story of the Tree at the center of the Garden of Eden. But the two stories coexist, indeed the story of those foods prescribed for humans and animals alike comes before that of the Tree.

That the two stories are interwoven is revealed most clearly after Adam and Eve's transgression. It was then that "Yahweh Elohim made for man and his woman garments of skin and he clothed them." But those garments of skin must have been flayed from an animal. Dead? Killed? In its wonderfully laconic fashion, Genesis doesn't tell us. But we immediately feel that the gesture of Yahweh Elohim marks a crucial moment. Those "garments of skin" that Yahweh Elohim makes like a skilled tailor are also his first tangible involvement in human life. They could have been conserved as the first relics.

Adam and Eve are clothed not to be protected but because they now feel the shame they hadn't felt before. And their clothing is something entirely new. It implies death, perhaps killing—and implies that it is all right to put the bodies of animals to some useful purpose. Until then, no mention had been made of this.

The next crucial moment will take place after several generations and after the flood. Then Elohim said to Noah and his sons: "All those that creep over the land and all the fish of the sea are delivered into your hands. Everything that moves and is alive shall be your food, like green grass. I have given you all this. But you shall not eat flesh with its life, that is with its blood." Those words established the practice that is still followed—and those rules about eating meat were to be prescribed only for the Jews. Otherwise, everything that moved became material available for man, who could kill it, eat it, use it, transform it as he pleased. Between the sixth day of the Creation and those words to Noah and his sons, there had been an immense transformation, not just for men but for all animals—though a transformation over which Genesis doesn't linger.

What is true for animals is true for the countryside: we begin to think about it when it is already disfigured. And so animals begin to be *thought about* when they are no longer visible, except as pets. From Descartes onward, the great philosophers we encounter in textbooks have made poor attempts at discussing animals. Rather than a way of thinking about them, philosophy was a strategy for not having to think about them. That strategy—applied with greatest consistency by Descartes himself but followed without any fundamental changes in Kant, and eventually by those who claimed to challenge the reasoning of Descartes, up to Heidegger and beyond—leads us to agree with Derrida's observation: "We understand a philosopher only if we properly understand what he seeks to demonstrate, and in truth fails to demonstrate, about the dividing line between man and animal." This doesn't just apply to philosophers. What holds Judaism, Christianity, and Islam firmly together, through thick and thin, even before the obsession about divine oneness tempered by hosts of angels and saints, is a shared silent and continual war, the "war against the animal," a "sacrificial war as old as Genesis."

Christian revelation is responsible not only for the declining reverence toward the cosmos, which from that time is equated to a series of outposts of enemy powers, but also for a certain new, summary, and almost brutal way of dealing with animals: "*Numquid de bobus cura est Deo?*" "Is it about oxen that God is concerned?" As always, we find the harshest words in Paul, and yet it was written in the Psalms: "*Homines et jumenta salvabis, Domine,*" "You shall save men and beasts, O Lord."

So far as animals, Christians followed the Stoics, advocates of a controllable image of what is human. They got rid of everything that didn't fit with it, no longer fearful or cautious, but tenacious. They proclaimed that "we humans have no kinship with irrational beings." And they had no doubts about animals: "'Certainly,' they [the Stoics] say: 'We have no duty of justice toward animals.'" This justice which suddenly stops as soon as it finds itself sur- rounded by *áloga*, by beings devoid of reason, is the final point of Greek impoverishment. Dike, the august goddess of justice that swathed the heavens, is now a domestic power and disappears al- together as soon as she sets foot outside the door and encounters creatures of other species. Plutarch, who had a sharp dislike for the Stoics, once observed: "It might be said we are more sensitive to acts against convention than to acts against nature." It is a muffled reproach: he well knew, even then, that nature was a pale acolyte, whose nature had been forgotten.

Nicolas Malebranche was emaciated, sickly. He was suffering with a "twisted spine and heavily sunken breastbone." He was twenty-six when a bookseller on rue Saint-Jacques handed him Descartes's newly published *Traité de l'homme*. He read it "with such transport that he had palpitations which forced him every now and then to stop reading. The invisible and useless Truth is not accustomed to finding such sensibility among men, and the more common objects of their passions would be well pleased to stir so much of it." From that moment, Malebranche's sole concern was "to be useful to truth." According to Fontenelle, he was unrivaled in forming "the chain of ideas," which in his case was "long and at the same time narrow," and above all contrary to any form of common sense. According to Malebranche, "God is the only one that acts, both on bodies and on minds." For the body, alone, cannot act on the soul, nor the soul, alone, on the body. Every instant therefore is the *occasion* for God to act, in each soul and in each body. A gloriously implausible theory, which had the singular merit of exposing the difficulties of successive scien- tific (and neuroscientific) theories about the relationship between mind and body. All around, a boundless population of automa- tons: animals.

In this regard, Abbé Trublet recorded the following anecdote about Malebranche: "Fontenelle recounted how one day when he had been to see the Fathers of the Oratory of rue Saint-Honoré, a large pregnant dog of the house came into the hall where they were conversing, approached Father Malebranche, and rolled over at his feet. After several useless attempts to drive it away, the Philosopher gave it a great kick, for which the dog let out a cry of pain and M. de Fontenelle a cry of compassion. 'Oh, really,' said Father Malebranche coldly, 'don't you know that it feels nothing?'"

In kicking the pregnant dog, Malebranche was only applying the doctrine of Descartes. But to this, unlike Descartes, he added the reasoning of a theologian: "If [animals] were capable of feeling, it would follow that, under an infinitely just and omnipotent God, an innocent creature would suffer the pain, which is a penalty and punishment for some sin." What Malebranche meant was that, if Descartes was not correct, then it would have to be conceded that billions of living beings, from the beginning of time, would have suffered and would be preparing to suffer, endlessly, yet without having been afflicted by original sin. How could this happen at the hand of a God who was "infinitely just and omnipotent"—and above all *perfect*? Malebranche raised the question in *Recherche de la vérité*, published in 1674. No Christian theologian, since that time, has managed to give an answer.

The question to ask, according to Plutarch, was not why "Pythagoras abstained from eating meat," but why did "man touch blood with his mouth for the first time and put his lips to the flesh of a dead animal." Since Homo was not a carnivore by constitution, his move to a meat diet was a key event in human history. Indeed, the first clearly definable event. All advocates of *verum ipsum factum* ought to regard it as the unavoidable *factum*, yet they seek to ignore it. It wasn't ignored, however, by those who developed certain rituals. The blood sacrifice was first of all a history book.

The desire to eat meat is a sentiment that psychologists tend not to dwell on. Perhaps they regard it as physiological, as inevitable as the fact of breathing. But this is not so. There was an age when humans (and their ancestors with numerous Latin names) were frugivores. At a certain point they discovered they could eat the flesh of dead animals. It was a traumatic and irreversible step. To go against the desire to eat meat involves going against a very long past: a possible and practicable undertaking, as the first Western sect, the Pythagoreans, demonstrated. It was necessary to fix the terms of a *bíos*, of a regimen of life that was contrary to everything around it. That regimen was no less important than geometry. Geometry helped in discovering something that no one had seen before. The *bíos* led to a regimen that no one else had lived. A bold, difficult challenge in both cases, contrary to the general inclination not to know and to eat animal flesh, a dominant inclination since time immemorial.

Theophrastus, Aristotle's favorite pupil, an expert in distinctions, wrote that blood sacrifice could be based on three reasons: "reverence," *timé*, "gratitude," *cháris*, and "utility," *chreía*. Three contrasting reasons, inextricably linked. This already made any single and noncontradictory explanation of sacrifice impracticable. And yet, if sacrifice involved the killing of animals that had committed no injustice, the act itself had to be considered an injustice that the gods wouldn't fail to notice. It followed from this that "in no circumstances must animals be sacrificed to the gods."

Why then did men carry on, from earliest times, performing such rituals? Here Theophrastus pushes the argument much further, into areas that thought had always sought to avoid, then and after. In sacrifice, writes Theophrastus, there is a "pleasure," *apólausis*, that consists of eating flesh—that part of the victim not kept aside for the gods. And "those pleasures lead us to try to obscure the truth of these things." But the gods couldn't fail to notice this either. They watch us while "under the patronage of divinity we slaughter and rip to pieces" oxen, sheep, stags, birds— all animals that are useful and whose flesh we enjoy eating. Harsh, abrupt, right as far as the conclusion: "Thus we testify against ourselves that pleasure is the only reason for continuing to perform these sacrifices." This seems to be the last word—and indeed no enlightenment thinker has managed to argue so effectively against blood sacrifice.

But the question remained unresolved, as was demonstrated by the holocaust carried out by the Jews and by the Greeks themselves: a kind of sacrifice where the victim was entirely burned—and where humans couldn't therefore experience any "pleasures" of eating meat. Theophrastus even recognized that this was the most ancient form of sacrifice. And here we were nearing the final problem.

The most difficult, most crucial, question about sacrifice relates to the *necessity of destruction* that the sacrifice (every sacrifice) implies. Every moral response is insufficient. Yet one hint of an answer is offered by several words in *Timaeus*, where it is said that the world "nourished itself procuring its own destruction, whereas all that it suffered and operated within itself, and from itself, happened by art [*ek téchnēs*]. He who had made it felt indeed that it would have been better if it had been self-sufficient and needed nothing else." The self-sufficiency of the world implies its perpetual self-destruction. Sacrifice would then be just the barely perceptible human contribution to this process. Insignificant as such. But immensely significant as a recognition of the way the world is made, to which the sacrifice is equated as acting "by art."

The world is a broken vase. Sacrifice tries to reassemble it, piece by piece. But certain parts have crumbled. And, even when the vase is mended, many cracks are visible. Some say they make it more beautiful.

The most frequent state in the universe is not life, nor death, but non-life. Death appears in correlation with life. If a living creature fails to take something from outside, it will sooner or later die. This therefore confirms François Bichat's definition that life is a form of opposition to death. The painful fact is that, to keep death away, it is necessary to cause death. When something is taken from the outside world, this means that it must disappear—and very often be killed. Two possibilities that were regarded as equivalent in the Vedic vision of existence. Whereas the secular vision presupposes that man is a self-sufficient being.

To placate an invisible entity is a feeling that can be easily understood. But why the placation has to take place through the killing of an animal is a consequence that has never been fully explained. And yet this has been a feature of very many cultures. Every other question about sacrifice depends on this.

At Delphi, Apollo slit the throat of a young pig, held it over Orestes, and let the blood trickle over his head, his chest, and his hands. This was the purification required by the god for matricide. But why did it have to be an effective act—and a divine act?

Killing precedes the law and cannot be healed by the law alone: this was the premise. Killing contaminates, produces a contagion that has to be stopped. How? By allowing the blood of the animals killed to be poured over the killer. With the butchery of meat there was a continual killing of animals, on which the community relied for sustenance. But that killing was to be carried out in ceremonial form. It was a form of sacrifice. Blood sacrifice was blood poured over a wrong, to heal it—an operation that had always to be repeated, since the wrong was being repeated. The wrong was the killing itself, of men and animals, through malice or the need to be fed. The "unwritten laws" related also to this. No one dared to question them. Orestes can ask for justice, but only after the blood of an animal is poured over him. The blood comes before the word.

In Athens, certain officials, the *peristíarchoi*, had the task of killing young pigs and having their blood scattered in the *agorà*, in the places of assembly and "meetings of the people." Even "in the theatre," according to a gloss on Aeschines. The victims were called *kathársia*, "purifiers." Spectators, purified by the blood of a pig that had wetted the steps on which they were sitting, then watched dramas in which human blood was shed. There were two purifications—one at the beginning, another at the end. Always by way of blood. This was how theater originated.

Propitious: this word, indicating a benevolent disposition of the numinous toward every form of existence, has a mysterious origin, since it presupposes that the deity expects to be made propitious through the shedding of blood. There must be a killing to ensure that the action of the power being addressed, and on whom one depends, becomes favorable. And this is true not only for the gods, but also for the dead: "*Nam olim, quoniam animas defunctorum humano sanguine propitiari creditum erat, captivos vel mali status servos mercati in exequiis immolabant,*" "Once upon a time, in fact, since they were convinced that human blood was propitious for the souls of the dead, during funerals they sacrificed prisoners or slaves bought cheaply at the market." Tertullian commented, with short sharp sarcasm: "Thus they consoled themselves for the death with acts of murder."

The idea that blood could be used as purification from blood had already been deplored by Heraclitus: "They purify themselves with blood when they are contaminated by blood, as if a man covered in mud could wash himself with mud." But that absurdity extended over the whole ancient conception of sacrifice. Sacrifice is an act of guilt, as the only means of placating—temporarily— the guilt that is added to and laid over another act of guilt. And purification with blood derives directly from the sacrificial vision. Abandoning that incongruous gesture meant abandoning a highly developed and widespread conception about everything.

Over the centuries there has been a debate, which still continues, about why, according to Aristotle, at the end of a tragedy, there is a *kátharsis*, "purification." Here it should be remembered that Aristotle preferred not to stray from literal meaning. *Kátharsis* is the result of a *katharmós*, a "purification ritual." And there had to be a *katharmós* when a killing took place. Murder contaminates and produces contagion. To stop that contagion, even before the law intervened, a common animal—a young pig or lamb—had to be killed. Only the shedding of blood stopped a process that had been started by the person who had shed blood. That was the *katharmós*, blood that purifies blood. A process that could seem nonsensical even to the ancients, as the fragment of Heraclitus indicates. And yet they continued practicing *katharmoí* rituals for a long time, trusting in their power. Aristotle suggested that a killing—by murder, sacrifice, or suicide—could be purified by the retelling of the killing itself. It was simply an alternative form of *katharmós*. An alternative with far-reaching repercussions.

"And behold the ornaments of Artemis and the new-born lambs, for you wash away the contagion of killing through killing"; "The law, it is true, requires the murderer to remain silent, but only until the moment when the blood of a young slaughtered animal has flowed over him, at the hand of one who purifies bloodshed"; "The blood on my hand is turning drowsy and fading; the stain of matricide is washed away. It was still fresh when, before the hearth of the god Phoebus, the purifying killing of a young pig drove it away." These words are found in Euripides and Aeschylus. Tragedy shows not only the killing but the *katharmós* that followed the killing, the blood that washed away the blood. The *kátharsis* of tragedy itself was a further purification. "Purification is one way in which the meta-physical can be made palpable," wrote Robert Parker, with superb concision. Tragedy allowed blood, whether flowing or congealed, to return to being impalpable. There was still the same wrong and the need for purification. Which could take place even as anonymous spectators sat on the steps of a theater.

Around the Mediterranean, civilizations performed sacrificial rituals that had their own names and gestures. All of which, in their own way, were based on the killing of animals. If the animal wasn't killed, it had to be sent away forever, into the desert (but this happened only for the Jewish scapegoat and the Greek *phar-makós*). An equally striking similarity among rituals is the coinci-dence in the time when they disappeared. From a certain moment (the fourth century C.E.) sacrifices *were no longer celebrated* in the form that had been normal for centuries. For the Jews, this was because the Temple had been destroyed and the community scattered; for the pagans, because they were now subject to the Christians and ever fewer in number; for the Christians, because the death of Jesus had been the final, nonrepeatable sacrifice that could be commemorated only in the Mass. And yet they all kept the language and mind-set of the sacrifice. This is found in Nonnus as in Augustine, as well as in rabbinical literature. Sacrifice is something that everyone wants to be rid of, but at the same time it is rooted in the language and in certain categories of thought that seem irreducible. And so they remain, even in secular society, which claims to have rid itself not only of sacrifice, but of every form of religious sentiment. Even the language of economics, the language that holds up the world (there is no other language), and which is an arid, euphemistic language, lacking in image (it says "recession" instead of "depression," it talks of "redundancies" when it means "firings"), cannot do without the word *sacrifice*, loaded with history and prehistory.

A head of government declares that he is not asking for "blood and tears." But he cannot avoid asking for "sacrifices." "Blood and tears": the final appearance, in words alone, of the blood sacrifice. In the meantime the ritual sacrifice has become an illegal or meaningless practice. "Illegal" if it involves the killing of a living being, an offense of cruelty to animals. Their killing is allowed only in abattoirs. "Meaningless" if it concerns a simple libation. But the word *sacrifice* still remains. It now means the acceptance of loss, by an individual, of some monetary benefit to assist the well-being of society as a whole. With this operation—and with this deviation of meanings—society takes a step toward becoming the last horizon for society itself. Society is now the invisible entity to which the sacrifice is offered. No other invisible entity is permitted: there is one single god, or many gods, or nature, or even the unknown. But the point is that it is still necessary to talk about "sacrifices." No one is bold enough to declare that the word itself ought to be consigned to the attic. And this is the most eloquent indication that secularization can never be achieved. There is still a superordinate entity that absorbs all the powers in itself. Having passed a certain meridian of history, the choice is between a secular society, but one that continues to perform acts of devotion (though now directed toward itself), and a society devoted to some divine object, but which it can no longer recognize.

Describing ancient Greece, Jean Rudhardt wrote that blood sacrifice "is the central act of worship, the ritual around which are ordered the festivities that gave city life its sacred rhythm." But why should the bloody killing of animals be at the center of a complex religious life? Why the need for blood? Why are animals necessary to establish a relationship with divinity? These same questions arise in relation to the Vedic cult. There is no possible answer unless we look at what lies behind the sacrifice, in a time period where no assistance can be found in writing and only rarely in images. A period in relation to which it is reasonable to suspect that any statement is arbitrary. But this should not deter thought.

When the pathos of blood ceremonies finally began to be examined by historians and philologists through the texts, something unfortunate and unexpected occurred: it was explained away. M. P. Nilsson described how the *pharmakós*, crowned and perfumed, was led around the streets of the city, before being killed and burned. He then blithely commented: "In just the same way that a dirty table is cleaned with a sponge and the sponge is then thrown away." In this way a grim and solemn ceremony was likened to the experience of a housewife. Not that this was groundless: the Laws of Manu had already described the act of someone who does the cleaning as that of a murderer. But it was the movement of thought that now followed the opposite path. The act of cleaning was once considered within the overall category of murder. Now murder was considered within the overall category of cleaning. This was enough to establish a comparative aesthetic of massacre. Pyramids of skulls, disemboweled corpses around the tents, decapitated heads: it was like the scene of a sacrifice that had got out of hand, where the knife had carried on attacking all by itself. But let us go inside the death camps that were scattered across Central Europe: many exterminators operated there—and Himmler could be considered the housewife supreme. They persistently cleaned the table in the Germanic dining room, and each time they threw away the sponge, impregnated with ashes.

The first thing to be said about sacrifice is that it is dirty, contaminating. A sacrifice that has nothing to do with purification is unacceptable. Theologians—according to Porphyry—claimed that the state of ritual purity was a "precautionary protection" or a "sign of recognition," a "*sýmbolon* or divine seal" that ensured that no harm would be done by those with whom one came into contact. Who were these beings, if not the animals who were about to be sacrificed? Porphyry added: "Thus the state in which one finds oneself is contrary to what one does." If that state was purity, it would act "like a bulwark" against something that had to be far more impure and unjust: the killing of the defenseless animal. This is so if, as Porphyry states elsewhere, "the divine is naturally most just, otherwise it would not be divine."

In this respect, Porphyry goes on to talk about "mental sacrifice," "*noerà thysía*," and describes the person who celebrated it as follows: "He appears to the god in a white garment, with a truly pure impassivity of soul and a light body, not oppressed by juices taken from other bodies or from passions of the soul." It was the point of greatest proximity between neo-Platonism and Vedism. In the same way that the internalization of the Vedic sacrifice culminated in the theory of *prāṇāgnihotra*, the "breath sacrifice," so Porphyry's doctrine completed the internalization of the pagan sacrifice. In both cases every tangible object of the sacrifice vanished (its ultimate residue, in Vedic doctrine, was the breath). For Porphyry, on the other hand, not even the mental word was allowed: the offering had to consist only of "pure silence" and "pure thoughts that accompany it." Both ways, however, still shared the fact that no question was raised about the sacrifice itself, indeed it remained like a cornerstone for all thought. And so, according to Porphyry, "we shall continue to imitate the ancient saints, offering as first-fruits the contemplation that the gods have given us and which is essential for our true salvation."

Discovering sacrifices, for the Vedic gods, was like Western mathematicians discovering irrational or transfinite numbers. This meant that sacrifice existed well before the gods—and not at the service of someone, but as a pulsation of life itself. This was the source of the Vedic vision. The sacrifice that escaped in the form of a *mṛga*, "antelope," was like Uṣas transformed into an antelope that escapes through the sky after having had intercourse with her father, Prajāpati. There was always an animal—and an animal that escapes—at the origin of stories about gods and men. Perhaps suggesting that these had been the last figures to emerge in the story of creation. And that the first step, for man, was to distance himself from animals. At the beginning of the beginnings there were only animals.

"The divine guilt is existence," said Utnapishtim when Sindbad went to visit him on the island of Dilmun, beyond the waters of death. "When the Progenitor produced those children born-from-the-mind, there was no guilt and all appeared spectral, insipid. But when he wanted to try sexual creation, desire gushed forth and the arrow was shot. Desire and the wound were produced in that same instant. The wound would never reheal, even if medication was applied. The rituals served this purpose. And those who celebrate them know they are not enough."

Utnapishtim also had this to say to Sindbad: "Men were born in an order that was already an immense disorder, in comparison with the beginning. Slowly, cautiously, they violated it, adding further disorder. But they consoled themselves at the thought that, after all, they were imitating something that had happened even before they were born."

For Christianity the passage to a secular society was much easier, compared with the other two religions of the Book. This because Christians don't have to follow strict rules about butchery. Christians don't have to stick to what is *kosher* or *halal*. They follow rules about abstaining from certain animals, but not about the way they are butchered.

The intractable fact, the killing, is ignored. People act as though it didn't happen. This is implicit in Friday fasting. Orthodox Jews or Muslims, even when they live in a secular society, always ask whether the dead animal they are being offered has been killed in accordance with *kosher* or *halal* rules. And this is enough to make them aware of an unbridgeable difference between them and secular society. The ordinary Christian, however, knows no such kind of objection.

As for secular society: law requires the animal to be stunned before being killed. This is done, it is said, to shorten and ease its suffering. But the animal suffers above all *before* being killed. Tormented, constrained, goaded toward death, so that it doesn't misbehave, doesn't cause delay. Stunning serves to dull the senses of the one who is killing rather than the one being killed. It is a euphemization of death. Its purpose is to persuade the killer that he is killing a creature that is already almost dead. In this way, the Christian is clearly sidestepping the act of killing. An overt compassion for suffering, a silence over killing.

If the critical aspect of sacrifice were the killing alone, a solution would not be hard to find: any kind of plant could be offered as a substitute for the animal killed. But the animal killed was also an animal that, in certain cases, was eaten. And the custom of eating meat is deep-rooted in Homo. It is a legacy passed down from the remotest branches of human history, in a family where changes are not measured over generations, but over hundreds of thousands of years. Certain anatomical features of the masticatory apparatus "point to the beginning of substantial consumption of meat at the end of the Pliocene." It is not enough to say you are vegetarian to cancel out that past.

The Greeks didn't eat raw meat, indeed they were horrified by it. But the "initiates," *mýstai*, of Idean Zeus followed "Zagreus who wandered the night, celebrating the festivities of raw meat." And Zagreus himself, in the *Etymologicon magnum*, is described as "the Great Hunter," "*ho megálōs agreúōn*." The savagery of the Bacchantes, who rip animals to pieces, repeats the savagery of the Titans, who had ripped Dionysus to pieces (the same verb, *sparássō*, is used), and then threw his limbs into a cauldron and offered them to his brother Apollo at Delphi. "Into the fire they threw Bacchus, over the bowl," says a surviving line of Euphorion. The Bacchantes were not gripped by a recurring, mad euphoria. What they were doing was primarily repeating and recalling the "ancient grief" suffered by their god. In the same way that Dionysus is a bull and a killer of the bull, so too does he rip to pieces and is he himself ripped to pieces.

Who is the Great Hunter? Apart from Zagreus, there are other Great Hunters among the gods. Zeus is the Great Hunter. And Hades is the Great Hunter. An invisible plumb line drops from high in the sky, through the whole earth, and down to the lowest point of the underworld: it is the Great Hunter. In none of its parts does the divine agree to separate itself from the act of chasing prey. At no altitude, in the transparent air of Olympus, in the turbulent air of the earth, in the perpetually dark air of Hades, does the sharp outline of the Great Hunter disappear.

"There are good reasons to suspect that much, if not most, of the bone behaviorally related to stone tools from the early Pleistocene is the result of scavenging, not hunting." This sentence from the leading twentieth-century authority on bones, Lewis R.

Binford, has marked the end of that bold and rudimentary theory of man as "mighty hunter" (a hominid Nimrod), which had
reached its peak with Washburn and Lancaster's article "The Evolution of Hunting," in 1968. Persistent research by the paleoarchae-
ologist Binford, coinciding over the years with the startling results
achieved by C. K. Brain on the relationship between hominids and
predators, dispelled a vision of the past that is still to be found in
schoolbooks and natural history museums.

Before becoming the hunter feared by all animals (and fabled
exterminator of the elephants of Torralba), the human ancestor
had spent several hundred thousand years scavenging, less effectively but with as much purpose as hyenas. If phylogeny is not
an empty word—and it certainly isn't, unlike every conception
of man as a *tabula rasa*—that intractable past, which dates back
to the point between the Pliocene and Pleistocene, therefore to
around two and a half million years ago, has to be taken into account by every Thucydides of prehistory.

Hunting, then, will no longer appear as the precondition and
basis for every sequence of human development, but as a crucial
and belated discovery and acquisition, almost to the point of being considered the true threshold of all *modernity*. But this implies that it was preceded by a much longer, rougher, and more
tormented history. If sacrificial rituals were also a way of sinking
into the well of the past, it is plausible that in them might be found
the traces—and the only surviving annals—of that prehistory of
prehistory.

If "substantial consumption of meat" has been established
toward the end of the Pliocene, and the activity of group hunting
is established at around five hundred thousand years ago (though
Binford moves the date much closer to today), there remains a long
interval in which man would have fed on animals that he himself had not killed. They were what paleoanthropologists today call
"residual carcasses," where men appropriated the remains left by
the "primary predators."

There was therefore a terrible twofold relationship between the forefathers of *Homo sapiens* and predators. These were first of all the killers lying in ambush, against whom defense was futile. But Homo fed on their residual carcasses. Therefore, in order to survive, he depended on his traditional killers. Eating a corpse that had been killed by his own enemy was as if—vicariously, through the carcass—he were eating himself. Remote origin of self-reflectivity.

Frugivorous primate, then granivorous hominid, then predator: these are the stages recognized by paleoanthropologists. The divisions between them were etched deeply. And, in fact, there was only one disrupting break: that between the granivorous hominid, who still fed on seeds and roots, and the predator, who had a set of teeth where bicuspids and molars no longer predominated, but in which the role of incisors and canines was accentuated. The whole long intermediate phase, however, presupposed that hominids had found a new position—what the paleoanthropologists call an "ecological niche"—in the food chain. It would be the position of *saprophagous carnivores*. This marked the long period in which Homo modeled himself not on tigers but on hyenas.

Bipedalism, which ancient tradition associates with the nobility of man who looks up toward the sky, may also be connected to the activity of stripping the flesh from animal carcasses, if the increased speed and running capacity of *Homo ergaster* (who lived much earlier than the Paleolithic hunters) is regarded as a "determining factor for sighting carcasses and swiftly approaching them, and then swiftly escaping in the event of the primary predator returning."

The first animals that the forefathers of *Homo sapiens* sought and were able to imitate were hyenas, the only animals capable of something not even the great predators knew how to do: with their mighty jaws they smashed the bones of their prey and sucked the marrow, which was rich in protein. Homo had to imitate this with the help of sharpened flints and stones used as hammers. Paleoanthropologists place the scene in the African bush, close to running water. Hyenas, inasmuch as they were the first animals that Homo imitated, were also his first rivals. Blumenschine and Cavallo have gone as far as supposing that the disappearance of various species of hyenas can be traced back to rivalry with the ancestors of *H. sapiens*, who "may have started to supplant hyenas by getting to the kill first."

Two macroevents stand out in prehistory: the transition to a meat diet, and the transformation of Homo into a predator. They extend over an indeterminable number of years and are linked by another major and uncircumscribable macroevent: the transformation of Homo into a scavenger. They are points of a triangle that imprisons a vast part of prehistory and remains lodged inside datable history—and, earlier still, in the physiology of *Homo sapiens*. They are phylogenetic events. The slowest, most laborious, agonizing achievement in the history of the human species has been the acquisition of its dominant position in the food chain. Every other achievement follows from it. And, if they are compared in time, every other achievement has been like a sudden inroad.

There are many signs to show that man is not a primary predator, but a predator only *through imitation*. Perhaps the most eloquent of these signs is the human inability to get about in the dark. For the primary predator, however, the night is the time for hunting. In watering places, a magnetic center for animal life in the savannah, hyenas are the first predators to appear, toward sunset. They look about, they drink before hunting. In man's long apprenticeship to become a predator, the hyenas were probably the first model, the easiest to imitate, where the behavior of the scavenger, as man had long been (though, as Binford observed, man always remained "the most marginal of scavengers"), became more closely combined with that of the predator that man would soon become.

At first, his technique involved using implements that stripped the flesh from carcasses already flayed by predators. Dating from long before the sophisticated Acheulean instruments, these tools were sharpened flints or stones used to hammer the carcasses to be stripped, as the Hadza and the San tribes of sub-Saharan Africa still do today, or as chimpanzees do when they crack nuts.

Hyenas were the first philologists. The only bodies they dealt with were those whose life belonged to the past. They went straight to the bone and broke it apart. They had stronger jaws than those of any other mammal. They were looking for something that others ignored: the marrow. They were experts in crushing bones, even into fine pieces. Humans to them were like provincial up-starts wanting to make their way in the savannah. The hyenas did their reconnoitering at sunset, went about counting the carcasses. This was the *ordo rerum*. No one was able, no one was allowed, to disturb it.

As a model, Homo first chose hyenas, then *Dinofelis* and saber-toothed tigers. The first uncontainable impulse toward imitation became apparent when Homo realized his body would never be adequate. He needed a prosthesis, something extraneous, some-thing to hold. And it could even be a sharp piece of flint. Fire was also a prosthesis, though it couldn't be held. It was one further step, something that assisted in the invention or development of other prostheses. The first prostheses were used for stripping the flesh that remained on carcasses and above all for cutting into them, breaking open the bones and sucking the precious mar-row, like a protein-rich drug. Flints, at that time, were used as hammers. It was a very long period of time, where imitation was already occurring but still had to be developed. It reached its cli-max when men—after several million years of being preyed upon themselves—attempted to become predators.

A hut (called "base camp"), stocks of gathered food, distribu-tion of food, women who wait for the men to return from the hunt, even monogamy. For a long time this was the story that people told, claiming it to be fact. After decades of studying the bones of hominids and what surrounded them, Lewis Binford expressed doubt: "Even if our currently used inferential strategies turn out to be faulty, I strongly doubt that methodological advances will ever return us to the view that hominid life at the Plio-Pleistocene boundary was a watered-down version of modern man. One conclusion arising from the current research is that early hominids were very different from us." *Very different*: if research has difficulty understanding beings of twenty thousand years ago, it might be supposed to be all the more doubtful and inadequate when it investigates beings that lived more than two million years ago. Only a few points are fixed and certain: the discovery that people can live (indeed, perhaps live better, with the help of proteins) by eating the flesh of dead animals and crushing their bones to suck the marrow; the imitation of other animals that are highly skilled at doing this.

Scavenger: a strong, clear word. It indicates the animal or human that eats the remains of an animal already partially eaten by the predator that has killed it. In some languages, such as Italian or French, the word used is a euphemism: the scavenger becomes a *spazzino* or *éboueur*, as if it were an urban garbage collector. This eliminates the fact that the scavenger clears up the remains by eating them. With such lexical distortions a vast part of human history is sidestepped and forgotten. The only traces of them that remain are a few incisions made by the tools of hominids on bones already marked by the fangs of large cats or gnawed by hyenas.

If the hyena, this "interesting animal," was the first step (or at least one of the first steps) on the mimetic ladder that would transform man into the king of the food chain (in which he had previously been just one of the intermediate steps), then we have to reconsider how hyenas, though viewed with contempt and repugnance, still occupy a very high position. There is no doubt that their downward-sloping back and rear legs, which are much shorter than those in front, instill a universal feeling of horror.

But something else is also operating: an untold, unacknowledged, unpalatable history that also helps us to understand why imitation has always had derogatory associations, from the time of Plato. Not because humans remember the long period during which they imitated hyenas, but because the very process of imitation—and above all of imitation as an essential expedient for survival— required humans to recognize the unstable basis of their existence, which had to be consolidated, first of all, by adapting themselves to the way in which the most effective scavengers existed, and then by rising up, taking a staggering risk, to assimilate the behavior of their persecutors: the predators.

It was not only due to their physical appearance that hyenas stirred repugnance and fear among humans. There is something more serious. Hyenas are seen as symbolizing those who thrive on the killing done by others. But this applies in just the same way to people today. People cannot survive without killing, but no one wants to be involved in the killing. Humans have become predators—and are proud of it—but most of them in their daily lives follow the model of the hyena: they eat what has been killed by other people. And these other people are obscure beings, no less remote than hyenas. No one knows who they are. They spend a large part of their lives in abattoirs.

Eaters of remains: this is how human ancestors appear at the Olduvai Gorge, the site with the most plentiful evidence so far. The assemblages of bones "were commonly dominated by anatomical segments from the heads and lower limbs of animals." To explain this, Binford "reasoned that if hominids had had initial access to carcasses by virtue of having killed them, the parts introduced into sites identified as home bases would not be parts of marginal utility but instead would be anatomical parts yielding far greater amounts of edible tissue." Consequently: those bones had to be what remained of the carcasses that hyenas had stripped, though not entirely, of their flesh. The hominids had merely finished off their work. This is the situation from which they would one day move on to become hunters—and so, at last, to have prey all to themselves. During a very long interval they had lived as the parasites of predators, preparing for the irreversible step that would allow them to be fully acknowledged as predators. One factor—eating the flesh of animals killed—would be common to both phases. The proteins and fatty acids ingested when the remaining flesh was torn from the carcasses acted as a slow and certain drug.

The incubation period prior to that fateful step, the transformation of Homo into a predator, was extremely long and cannot be determined with any certainty. The stages of human history: first fruit eaters, then imitators of hyenas and discoverers of the drug that provided proteins, and finally imitators of their killers, with such skill that they could rival them, gaining the upper hand. And after that, managers of traveling circuses.

About one and a half million years ago, Homo emerges as a sick animal in the case known as KNM-ER 1808: an African woman who died through an excess of vitamin A, "a very rare symptom in human pathology since it only appears after ingestion of large quantities of raw carnivore's liver." What the paleoanthropologist finds most striking, however, is that the hypervitaminosis, incapacitating in itself, would have gone on for several months. This leads to the assumption that the woman, immobilized by the illness, had been nursed. Someone must have protected and fed her; someone must have given her water. It is the first sign of the existence of a community. Fire had not yet been harnessed; hunting in groups did not yet exist. But for several months various representatives of Homo ergaster helped a woman suffering from an illness to survive. She had eaten too much raw liver, having taken it from the abandoned carcass of an animal killed by those predators who were potentially her killers.

The fact that humans, for a long stretch of their history, had eaten remains left by other animals is helpful in understanding the strict and meticulous Vedic rules about leftover food, as well as the deep revulsion felt today when it comes to eating food touched by others. A part of the past has to be disregarded—and rejected. But only the Vedic ritualists managed to integrate the rules governing leftover food into a metaphysics of residue, of all residue. A metaphysics that is implicit in their theory and practice of sacrifice.

Hyenas appear in a Vedic myth that is so brief and obscure that Indologists have generally ignored it, or (in the rare instances where they have written about it) they have distorted it, until Stephanie Jamison, with stubborn insight, began to tease its tight knot apart. She arrived at a convincing reconstruction of the sequence of facts, starting from the eight texts of the Black Yajur Veda which provide an outline in intermittent flashes of texts two or five lines long, leaving vast areas of darkness. All might have happened like this:

The Yatis, priests of Indra, are celebrating a *soma* sacrifice, which also involves an animal sacrifice. A group of young hyenas surrounds and attacks them. At this point "Indra gave the Yatis as food to the hyenas," a phrase repeated—to the letter or with minimal variations—at the beginning of all eight texts. Stephanie Jamison persuasively demonstrates how, in this instance, the verb *prāyacchat* doesn't have the generic meaning of "to deliver" but means "to offer something as food." This is the nub of the story: Indra, king of the gods, offers some of his priests to a group of hyenas for them to tear apart. Nothing is said about the reason for this act.

Besieged by the hyenas in the area of the sacrifice and gripped by panic, the Yatis commit several ritual errors: they tip the precious *soma* onto the ground, jump on the altar to defend themselves, vomit the *soma*, one of them laughs (a "nervous laugh," observes Stephanie Jamison) having once jumped on the altar. Perhaps he thinks he is safe. But at that very moment the hyenas, which hadn't dared to launch their final assault, now attack the Yatis and eat them: "Ripping them apart one by one, the hyenas ate them to the south of the high altar," in the words of the *Kāthaka Saṃhitā*. Since that time, "there must no longer be foolish laughter" (unintentional but all the more fearsome Vedic sarcasm).

"Each account is short, almost telegraphic, but on reading all the accounts together one gets a picture of terror and confusion, of an act in the course of happening, that seems to me rare in early Vedic literature," is Stephanie Jamison's dry comment. But who were the Yatis? They are mentioned three times in the *Rgveda*: in two cases alongside the Bhṛgus, a mighty dynasty of *ṛṣis*, as faithful worshippers of Indra. In the third case it is said that the Yatis, like the gods, "made the living worlds expand" and "brought here the sun, which was hidden in the sea": one of the most enigmatic and magnificent formulations, set in a hymn that is one of the metaphysical high points of the *Rgveda*.

Why then should Indra have to exterminate the Yatis? Was it perhaps one more of his famously reprehensible deeds, like the decapitation of Viśvarūpa or the attack on the bright chariot of Uṣas? Caution is necessary. The Yatis, for one thing, commit serious ritual errors. And this would be enough to condemn them. Whether those mistakes were voluntary or involuntary is entirely irrelevant for the Vedic ritualists. They were errors just the same, which made them "impure," *amedhyá*, and therefore unfit for the sacrifice.

What caused the Yatis' errors? Panic. Surrounded by the hyenas, they tried to escape. The mistakes they make, which justify their killing by the hyenas, take place *after* the hyenas have appeared. It's an obvious case of cause and effect being inverted. How can this be explained? We are led to think that the Yatis had started a rite of atonement even before committing the errors that would have required them to carry it out.

The summoning of hyenas by Indra to massacre his priests harked back to a time—a time long past—when men had not worshipped the gods through the celebration of blood sacrifices but had imitated hyenas. That memory would not disappear and a compromise was required. Which had to be found *inside* the sacrifice, since the sacrifice is never a guaranteed solution, but a continual trial. The hyenas were now returning to practice pure killing on those who professed to have escaped from the anguish of killing since they were practicing it ritually, in the sacrifice. And, in the sacrifice as well, there was a moment of hesitation and paralysis. As the *Śatapatha Brāhmaṇa* explains, "in the beginning man dared not act against the victim." To enable humans to return to their privileged position of being the only animals that perform sacrifices, it was necessary to go back to how things were at the very beginning: the Yatis had no longer to be officiants but victims, as had happened with Prajāpati, the Progenitor. During that sacrifice in which they were about to sacrifice an animal, they themselves would be sacrificed through the action of other animals. Perhaps this is also why they jumped on the altar, not just to defend themselves. Perhaps it is for this reason, and not just out of scorn, that one of the Yatis had let out a "foolish laugh." Perhaps it was the conscious laugh of one who knows he is about to be killed and also knows why. That laugh was an invitation to the hyenas that were about to claw him. Whereas previously they had been hesitating, in front of the altar "they did not dare," just like man in front of the first animal he was about to sacrifice. But now the officiants would be sacrificed in exactly the same place where animals were usually sacrificed: "It is in the vicinity of the Uttaravedi [the high altar] that animal sacrifices are performed, and the animal-sacrificing Yatis, by a sort of ritual symmetry, become sacrifices to animals."

Let us now try to go back in time, to reconstruct the course of events: Indra had given the Yatis as food for the hyenas in the same way that the hyenas had once left carcasses of animals killed by big cats or by the hyenas themselves as food for humans. And this was not allowed: it would have meant the return to pure killing, whereas the thinking of the Vedic ritualists centered around the transformation of pure killing into something else: into sacrifice. How could this conundrum be resolved? By transforming the sacrifice of an animal into a sacrifice in which the officiants are the victims and are eaten by animals. And this is what Indra had arranged for the Yatis.

It all had to take place at the same moment in which a pack of hyenas was besieging a group of priests intent on celebrating a *soma* sacrifice. Compressed into one single unit of time there had to be the besieging of the hyenas, the ritual errors committed by the frantic priests, and the final form of the sacrifice, which became a sacrifice of atonement for the errors just committed, and where the priests themselves were killed and abandoned like leftover carcasses. A scene of mayhem. If there was ever a theater of cruelty, it was here.

Unlike the Egyptian priests, the Vedic ritualists knew nothing about history and scripture. But they had an astonishing memory, which went back a long way and was contained in the underlying ritual gestures and stories. The story of Indra and the Yatis, though marginal, incomprehensible, and repugnant, opens up an unfathomable prospect if examined closely. And yet that wasn't the final scenario. As often happens in Vedic myths, behind the curtains there are other, even more remote scenes. Which allow us to glimpse the reason Indra turned to the hyenas to exterminate the Yatis. We have to go back to the beginnings, when the gods, the Devas, lived on earth with the anti-gods, the Asuras, their older brothers. They were all children of Prajāpati. "In the beginning this earth belonged to the Asuras. The gods owned only what they could see when sitting down. The gods said of the hyena: 'All that it shall go round three times will be ours.' The hyena went around the whole earth three times. In this way the gods conquered the earth." The gods are therefore indebted to the hyenas, indeed they owe what they possess to them. Transposed into human history, this means that, if humans hadn't imitated hyenas, they would never have arrived at their position of dominance. The scene is then interwoven with a valuable ethological detail. As Hans Kruuk has observed, hyenas tend to interrupt their feeding by wandering in circles within a radius of about twenty-five yards. It is an eloquent example of *Übersprungbewegung*, the "diversionary movement" that many animals adopt, as if to amuse themselves or distract themselves from something—possibly very important—that they are doing. It is as though certain animals have grown bored of doing nothing more than what they are doing at a certain moment. And it is like a first attempt, on the part of the animal, to emerge ritually from the constraints of its compulsory gestures. This singular custom enabled the Devas to conquer the earth. But the gods couldn't allow themselves to appear so dependent on hyenas, exactly as would happen, later, with humans, who did all they could to set themselves apart from hyenas and denigrate them. Indra, the king of the gods, had to intervene. And so it happened that "Indra, having transformed himself into a female hyena, went around the earth three times." And so the gods acquired the world, attributing the enterprise to Indra and not to a hyena. Celestial etiquette.

One morning in summer 1981, Lewis Binford was walking along a dry riverbed in South Africa. And he noted this: "Around each turn in the valley there came into view groups of ungulates clustered near water holes. Lying in the shade of great trees near one water source might be groups of blue wildebeests: ten, twenty-five, even forty individuals would not be uncommon. As we approached, a great bull would rise to its feet, shake itself and, engulfed in dust, lower its head slightly to gaze in our direction. Ostriches ran across our path. The ubiquitous springboks would stare at us but go on feeding, slowly wandering along the valley towards shade or an area of tawny grass. The valley, with its water sources, was truly the domain of the ungulates.

"The only clue to violence in the landscape was the occasional vulture perched in the tree tops or soaring above us, eventually to land and add its number to a feathered group taking a meal around a dead animal. When one looks around the environment in a little more detail, carcasses or parts of them are easily spotted: silent indications of violent death are constant features of the land surfaces around the water holes.

"If one remains in the area for some time, however, the ostensibly placid rhythm of the land is seen to be anything but subtle. The ungulates certainly rule the water sources at high noon: but as the sun begins to kiss the western horizon they begin gradually but deliberately to move back towards the valley margins and climb the dunes out of the valley. The abandonment of the daytime domain of these animals is striking, as they disperse out into the vast rolling landscape away from the water and disappear. In the slanting light of sunset, the predators, lords of the night, move into the valley to occupy the water holes and exercise dominion over the land used by ungulates during the day.

"Generally, the hyenas are the first to arrive, approaching the water hole slowly and passing old carcasses of ungulates killed previously by predators, and of other animals which died less violently near water. The hyenas may gnaw on these relatively dry bones, but eventually go in to drink, for they almost always take water before hunting. The actual search for food may not begin in earnest until much later in the night, so it is not uncommon for the hyenas to remain in the immediate area of the water source, gnawing bones, moving body parts around, and engaging in various social activities. After dark, some calling (the characteristic 'whooping') may occur; later on, the hyenas leave rather deliberately to make a kill and secure fresh meat. Lions and leopards, too, often visit the water sources during the night, since they also need water during the active hours of hunting and pursuit of game. The roars of the lion are commonly heard late in the evening between ten o'clock and two o'clock, when they may travel great distances visiting water holes along the way before stalking and attacking prey.

"Between about two o'clock and four-thirty in the morning, activity seems to subside: at least, the sounds of predators dwindle away and the night becomes still. Just before sunrise, lions' roars increase: predators tend to be moving along well-travelled routes which frequently take them through or past water. As the full rays of the sun flood the landscape, the vultures are already soaring, searching for the previous night's carnage. Gradually, as the warmth of the sun returns to the valleys, the ungulates reappear, moving back to the water sources. The cycle begins again." Water and carcasses—the first coveted landscape.

After being the sole representatives of Homo in Europe for more than a hundred thousand years, the Neanderthals saw groups of outsiders—*Homo sapiens*—infiltrating their territory from the east. For a long time they coexisted. What happened then, in those ten thousand years (45,000–35,000 B.C.E.) that are euphemistically called "the Transition," anticipating Flaubert's *Dictionnaire des idées reçues*, is not known for certain and is perhaps unascertainable, though never as in recent decades have paleoanthropologists allowed themselves such free rein in attempting to reconstruct it. Genocide? Lewis-Williams talks of a "probably intermittent rather than sustained genocide." But, according to Ezra Zubrow, even a "small demographic advantage" in the order of "a difference of two per cent mortality" would have been enough to cause a "rapid extinction of the Neanderthals." Other explanations have been offered, pointing to hunting strategies or to the choices of environments or climatic factors. Hypotheses that all have one element in common: a vast amount of personal judgment—and lack of evidence-based arguments. But this doesn't alter the fact that, on looking at those ten thousand years of transition in a scenario that stretches between France and Spain, described by some paleoanthropologists as a *cul de sac*, one finally plumbs the depths of all possible conflicts: a primordial confrontation, source of every story line in which there is a clash of opposites. Whatever he does, *Homo sapiens* will always be a *foreigner*, a new arrival in lands already occupied by others.

On the relations between *Homo sapiens* and Neanderthals, paleoanthropologists should always bear in mind the words of Simone Weil: "At the time of the succession of the races at the dawn of humanity (e.g., when the *Homo sapiens* of the paleontologists substituted earlier specimens) the losers may have appeared to the victors like an animal species rather than human . . . But one of those losers could have been God incarnate. This is perhaps one of the origins of the image of God dressed as an animal."

Homo sapiens needed an incubation period of more than fifty thousand years before reaching agriculture, domestication, a sedentary existence. A phylogenetically close relative, *Homo neanderthalensis*, continued living alongside him for around thirty thousand years—the most recent find so far, in Gibraltar, dates from 28,000 years ago. *Homo sapiens* saw him disappear. Or made him disappear. In both cases, the history of his relationship with the Neanderthals is the immense, unwritten gothic novel behind all novels.

The Neanderthal of Marillac was a superpredator who fed in particular on herbivore quadrupeds. The food regimen of wolves living in the same area at that time was not much different. Nor that of *Homo sapiens*, who overlapped with the Neanderthals. But the Neanderthals died out a few thousand years later, whereas *Homo sapiens* continued on till today. Marylène Patou-Mathis, after twenty years of research on the Neanderthals, during which she had "followed, dissected, interpreted" their every trail, concluded that all the theories about their disappearance were inadequate. But she added, without batting an eyelid, that "today, among the most convincing theories, one opts for that of a 'stress' engendered by the arrival of different men (but who resemble them)." The power of stress.

A child at the beginning of the twenty-first century is not much different, anatomically, from one born around sixty thousand years ago. But the first signs of fixed dwellings, in communities that discover and practice agriculture and domesticate animals, are said to date back to around 10,000 B.C.E. Why only then? According to paleoanthropologists this is the "sapient paradox," for which no explanation has yet been found. And yet the paradox might have another purpose, becoming extremely useful material for paleoanthropologists to carry out a self-examination that has yet to start.

Indeed the paradox is only a paradox if we suppose that *Homo sapiens*, having once reached what the experts tend to call his "modern" anatomical makeup, has nothing better to do than discover and develop agriculture, choose a sedentary life, and domesticate various animals. And thereby finally abandoning his existence as hunter-gatherer, which, it is presumed, consisted of no more than a tireless search for the food necessary for survival. That interval of fifty thousand years, prior to a sedentary existence, then comes to look like a tedious delay. Why had *Homo sapiens* waited so long before *sorting himself out*? Fifty thousand whole years? Maybe this reconstruction has much to do with the mental outlook of paleoanthropologists in the late twentieth century and very little with what was going on in the final stages of the Pleistocene.

In the midst of all this, the amazing discovery is made in 1995 at Göbekli Tepe: a site that radically contradicts all the unspoken assumptions of paleoanthropologists. Starting with the basic facts: around 10,000 B.C.E., at the center of the Fertile Crescent, namely the region containing the sites of all the most significant finds for understanding the beginnings of agriculture (Çatalhöyük), there was a population of hunter-gatherers that spent its time erecting slabs of stone weighing several tons, often covered by reliefs with figures of wild animals and geometrical forms. No evidence—not even rudimentary evidence—of any agricultural activity; no evidence of domestication of animals; no evidence of a sedentary existence. Göbekli Tepe was not a place where people lived. It had another purpose—and no one can be sure what. And yet we can be sure that hundreds of people must have worked on creating this site. And it has to be acknowledged that this unknown population of hunter-gatherers had other concerns, apart from hunting, and digging up roots.

Most of the animals in the Göbekli Tepe reliefs are hostile to humans and to be feared: if birds, they are birds of prey; if insects, they are scorpions, spiders, and centipedes; if quadrupeds, they are foxes, wolves, big cats, or other, composite beings that don't look harmless. But there is also a charming line of ducklings. The stones cut in the shape of a T, the perfect circle in which they are arranged, already show a high degree of abstraction. The animals merge into each other on the surface of the stones. Indeed, it seems they *have to* merge into each other. Bare stone is avoided. As if the slabs of stone, which sometimes weigh tons, could not exist without these animals appearing on their surfaces, almost as though they were tattoos—though sometimes they are not engraved but appear in high relief.

"In the great family of composite beings in Mesopotamian art, 'demons' and 'monsters' are distinguished as follows: the beings that wander about on four legs as animals are called monsters, those that walk with the erect posture of man are called demons." This is how Klaus Schmidt, who discovered Göbekli Tepe, set out the criteria of his work—and recognized how, as a result, "the true identity of each composite being . . . has not yet been identified." Whereas the first human beings that took shape, whole, in the stone, always had a spectral appearance. Eyes blank, limbs rough-hewn. If a unique quality is inevitably attributed to Greek statuary, this is largely due to it having been released unscathed from the restraints of that past in just a few years, which, in comparison, were the blink of an eye.

Leopards, vultures: animals that man doesn't eat, and which eat man. They dominated the pictures of Çatalhöyük. They kept watch on the walls of the houses. They were the heirs of other fearsome animals carved onto the T-shaped pillars of Göbekli Tepe. Even if humans had already formed themselves into a society, they still felt a great need to contemplate those animals, or perhaps to gaze at them when they awoke: those animals from whose grips they couldn't be sure they had escaped.

"All there are at Çatalhöyük are houses and middens and pens," observed Ian Hodder, after many years spent excavating the site: a very large village of buildings crammed together for no apparent reason, certainly not for defense. With no distinct divisions, with no specialized, functional areas. Each house consisted of hearth, dormitory, cemetery, sanctuary, workshop, storehouse. All that can be noted is that in many of those modest-size multi-purpose dwellings the occupants felt a special need to depict animals that were generally dangerous—first of all, in frequency, the leopard—or to stick animal horns and skulls into the walls, painting them and carving reliefs. James Mellaart, the site's first archaeologist, described these spaces as "sanctuaries." But then he realized that these were *areas* of the houses. And that there was no trace of any separate sanctuaries that were just sanctuaries.

One day, after 650,000 animal bone fragments had already been excavated, Nerissa Russell identified the first leopard bone. It was a claw, used as a pendant, with a circular hole in it. It had been found next to a human skull coated with plaster. And both of them close to the skeleton of a woman, who was clutching the skull in her right arm. After half a century of excavations, that claw pendant was the only leopard fragment unearthed. But leopards were visible everywhere in the site: painted, in relief, sculpted, in sandstone figurines. Ridden by women or placed close to women. And other women and men in the paintings were wrapped in leopard skins.

Erwin Rohde, the most like-minded of Nietzsche's friends, made a point without which the terrible novelty of the Homeric world can only be lost: the *lightening* of life, its total abandon to splendor, even in the midst of every atrocity, if it is true—as Giambattista Vico wrote—that "the atrocity of the Homeric battles and deaths . . . gives the *Iliad* all its wonder." Nothing is more heartrending than the sight of Hades that opens up for Odysseus. Exhausted, delirious, the souls continue to live—and this is part of their torment. But they know they can no longer have any involvement on earth, where light reigns. And this is the origin of Homer's radiance. "The living being is left in peace by the dead. In the world only gods reign, not pallid specters, but figures well fixed in a body, who operate wherever, and live on calm peaks 'and over it is spread a glorious splendor.'" The Homeric scene is not a beginning, but something close to an end. Behind stretches a boundless, dark region, infested with specters, roaming shadows, bodiless voices. This, if it ever existed, is the only line dividing Greece from the whole of prehistory.

Indeed, the greatest obstacle, if we want to understand something about prehistory, came from the fact that in the meantime human life has become immensely *lighter*. To such an extent that the world can no longer exert pressure on those who observe it— at least in certain experimental situations, like the one permanently reached in the nineteenth century, especially among those who belonged to the upper class and lived on income, during the years of Queen Victoria. This was the favorite human material for Henry James. Instead of sharp flints, he collected phrases dropped in conversation, anecdotes, gossip, social visits, lunches, dinners, afternoon strolls. On the basis of all this, James reconstructed a web of intrigues that, by then, had nothing to do with the world outside. Nature was an occasional backdrop. Everything happened inside, or sometimes in the street or in comfortable surroundings. But what could happen if the *lightening*, the choice to discard the world like an irksome ballast, became a rule of life consciously practiced?

Some of Henry James's most important stories are ones he didn't write. They are "little *sujets de nouvelles*," buds that never blossomed except in the contracted form of his *Notebooks*. And yet one sometimes suspects that this very form was the *final form*, the most appropriate form for a story that, countless times, grew out of a few words spoken by someone in conversation, during one of the countless social gatherings at which James had been present—and which were the very soil, tilled and re-tilled, of his literary output. This is what happened over a phrase uttered by Mrs. Procter, in which James recognized "the tiny little germ of a tiny little tale," of which only the outline remains.

At Torquay, on October 28, 1895, James noted these words in his notebook: "I remember how Mrs. Procter once said to me that, having had a long life of many troubles, sufferings, encumbrances and devastations, it was, in the evening of that life, a singular pleasure, a deeply-*felt* luxury, to her, to be able to *sit and read a book*: the mere sense of the security of it, the sense that, with all she had outlived, *nothing could now happen*, was so great within her. She had, as it were, never had that pleasure in the way or degree; and she enjoyed it afresh from day to day. I exaggerate perhaps a little her statement of her individual ecstasy—but she made the remark and it struck me very much at the time. It comes back to me now as the suggestion of the tiny little germ of a tiny little tale."

Straight after, James noted the outline of that story so lucidly that one can hardly regret it never having been narrated in full: "There would be an old, or an elderly, person whom one would have known, would have met—in some contact given an opportunity for observation. This old person—in the quiet waters of some final haven of rest—would manifest such joy—such touching bliss—in the very commonest immunities and securities of life—in a quiet walk, a quiet read, the civil visit of a friend or the luxury of some quite ordinary *relation*, that one would be moved to wonder what could have been the troubles of the past that give such a price to the most usual privileges of the present. What could the old party (man or woman) have been through, have suffered? This remains a little suggestive mystery. The old party (the time of life a thing to determine properly) is reserved, obscure, un-communicative about certain things—but ever so weary and ever so rested. One wonders, but one doesn't really want to know—what one is really interested in is guarding and protecting these simple joys. One watches and sympathizes, one is amused and touched, one likes to think the old party is safe for the rest of time."

One can try to transpose James's "tiny little tale" into the boundless story of *Homo sapiens*, who tried, for several tens of thousands of years, through trial and error, and proceeding in numerous directions, to lighten himself of the world. Distancing himself first from animals. And protecting himself from nature in general. With gradual relief and concomitant anxiety, since every innovation was at odds with deep-rooted behavior. Humanity was increasingly resembling Mrs. Procter, who, "having had a long life of many troubles, sufferings, encumbrances and devastations" had come to appreciate "a deeply-*felt* luxury," which was this: "to *sit and read a book*." It might seem a small thing, but not if we connect it to what it implicated: "the sense that . . . *nothing could now happen*." Mrs. Procter, after her troubled life, and *Homo sapiens*, after thousands of years of history, aspired most of all to one and the same condition: to be protected, separated from the world thanks to an insuperable barrier that averts every intrusion from outside—every last attack from predators. Mrs. Procter and *Homo sapiens* also had the same idea in the *luxury* they were looking for: *to read*, sitting in an armchair. Reading, in fact, whatever one is reading, always involves reexperiencing past events, which might now appear fascinating. And even amusing, like a nonstop entertainment. But—above all, *distant*. There was nothing small-minded in that feeling, if one took account of the torments and protracted heartache that it followed. Mrs. Procter could be displayed as an exhibit in a natural history museum or at Madame Tussaud's as an epitome of Western humanity living in the largest empire at the end of the nineteenth century. The fact that *Homo sapiens* continued during those years to launch himself into exploits of greed and conquest, in various continents, was certainly not incompatible. It was a vortex that hid, at its center, a scene of perfect peace: Mrs. Procter sitting in her armchair reading, barricaded against whatever intrusion, and above all comforted by the thought that "*nothing could now happen*."

Mrs. Procter's feeling was obviously illusory, if for no other reason than the three evils that the young Buddha witnessed before leaving his father's palace: sickness, old age, death. And everyone knows that the world always finds a way of making itself felt, and that every attempt to avoid its intrusions cannot last long. And yet a vast historical movement had stirred, nourished, and developed that illusion, of which Mrs. Procter was a representative example.

Henry James had a very clear awareness of all this. But it wasn't the story he wanted to tell. His narrative genius always drove him to search out what remained unsaid in the interstices of other stories that were written around him, even in those he most admired, in Stevenson or in Turgenev. Mrs. Procter couldn't help him to tell the story of how a late solitary calm could be shattered as a result of some outside occurrence. James was aiming higher. He wanted something far more subtle and insidious: how that peace would self-destruct, through the action of some corrosive agent, *from within*.

Starting from what Mrs. Procter had already told him, James went on: "One watches and sympathizes, one is amused and touched, one likes to think the old party is safe for the rest of time." This might seem to be a conclusion—and yet it is here that James's demon is let loose, beginning the transformation of "the tiny little germ" into a story. It was a ritual moment, recurrent in the *Notebooks*. The step to elaboration was indicated using a formula that in its complete version appeared like this: "*Voyons un peu les détails*." At that precise moment James's storytelling antennae began to quiver—and the notebook became the shorthand recording of what those antennae were receiving. This is what occurred as a result of what James had heard Mrs. Procter say. Here the tone suddenly changes. It is no longer Mrs. Procter who is talking, but James who is following his whim: "Then comes the little denouement. Isn't the little denouement, must it *not* only be, that some horrid danger becomes real again, some old menace or interruption comes back out of the past? The little safeties and pleasures are at an end. What I seem to see is that somebody, a fatal somebody, turns up. *Voyons*:—I seem to see something like an old fellow whose *wife* turns up." *Voyons*: it's as though we are witnessing a golden moment of narrative invention. Something is taking shape in the shadow: "What I seem to see is that somebody, a fatal somebody, turns up." A phrase that could be the cartouche of the novel in general.

Mrs. Procter's words become the bastion to be destroyed. How? The "horrid danger" has to emerge, which is always lying in wait—and is enough to frustrate any expectation of *being safe*. And this is where the details appear: meanwhile Mrs. Procter is transformed into an old gentleman whose wife reappears. A situation that might seem very commonplace, especially if the wife was "the source of the complications, the burdens that preceded." But not so—and here James's demon finally has a free hand. The wife who reappears is not bitter, vindictive. On the contrary, she is "repentant, reconciled, compunctious, reunited." But this is precisely what the old fellow dreads: *disturbance*. The reappearance of his wife "invades him still more with her compunction than with her—whatever it was of old." The solitary gentleman is forced to realize, to his horror, that he may have a double: the wife who has reappeared. And this is enough to destroy the architecture of solitude. In his show of meekness, his wife is not only a double. She is a rival: "She has come (genuinely, but selfishly) for peace and quiet—*she* wants to read a book, etc., but hers, somehow, puts an end to his." Savage words: how one can destroy someone by simply sitting there in an armchair reading a book, not too far from him. James realizes just how savage they are and stops himself short, like a torturer struck by a fit of benevolence: "I note this, I see it all, I feel for him." Writing is *seeing everything* and taking note.

With a few strokes, James has created an unbearable situation, no less than certain scenes in Dostoyevsky. How to get out of it? "At last, abruptly, he disappears—he vanishes away, leaving the wife in possession." Where will he go? Perhaps, like Wakefield in Hawthorne's story, into the house on the other side of the square. He will try once more to be invisible.

And the wife, the terrible wife, the "fatal somebody"? James explains, intensifying his vision. "Then I see *her*—having exterminated him—given up to the happy stillness as *he* was. She is in his chair, by his lamp, at his table: she expresses just the same quiet little joy that he did. 'It's such a luxury to just sit and read a book.' It's the same book—one I have seen *him* read." Here is the violent origin of imitation, that primordial venture that led humans in a distant past to imitate their persecutors. There is a silent sinking into prehistory. But from the peak of "perfected civilization." James wants to explain immediately that his old fellow and the wife belong to the "specifically refined and distinguished order" (indeed, he insists, they are "*raffinés*"). He, in particular, is "a man of the world, absolutely, in type, a man of quality, as it were." And this is what makes "this contentment with small joys, this happiness in the mere negative, sufficiently striking." From Paleolithic to *décadence*, the mental background to what is going on remains just the same.

The story prompted by Mrs. Procter remained in the planning stage, but already it had a title: *Les Vieux*. Though it still lacked "the *faire*, the little hard, fine, repeated process": this was James's way of describing writing. But perhaps *Les Vieux* had already been written, in those two pages of his *Notebooks*. Nothing more was needed.

VI

ZEUS'S LAST NIGHT
ON EARTH

For sixteen generations Zeus had intercourse with women from earth. The first was Niobe, the last was Alcmene. Niobe was the daughter of Phoroneus, "he who is called the first man," said Solon to the Egyptian priests when he wanted to talk about "the most ancient things we have." The priests smiled and said: "Solon, Solon, you Greeks are still children." For the Egyptians these were all recent stories. But for Zeus, Niobe was the first woman on earth. There was never a time when a woman could not be seduced by the god. Once chaos had dissolved, the world became flooded with the loves of the gods ("*Aque Chao densos divom numerabat amores*," we read in the *Georgics*). *Dense* loves, like the points on a straight line, arrows massed on the same target. The same adjective, *densus*, indicates a relentless succession of blows and the formless embrace of mist. But once he had reached the time of Alcmene, Zeus was forced to do something he had never done before: disguise himself as a man. Having abandoned the realm of metamorphosis, he entered that of fakery. *Incipit comoedia.*

Heroes were often hunters before anything else. Or at least they began their exploits through the practice of hunting. Unlike them, Heracles had to deny the hunter in himself in order to become a hero. It was his poisoned arrows that decimated and scattered the Centaurs, masters of every hunter. It was also his arrow that shot Chiron's knee by mistake and made that immortal being, the master of every Centaur, feel he wanted to die. Heracles transformed the emptiness, the gratuity of hunting into a purposeful enterprise. It made him become more clumsy, made his body heavier. Each single muscle in him became discernible, each at the service of another and all together having some purpose. Previously, the body of the hunter had been a neat, flowing line, similar to the arrow with its undulating shaft, similar to the back of the animal that the arrow would reach.

Heracles knew he could not improvise. Everything had already been prepared for him. He was deprived of the feeling of adventure. He was the first son who had no choice but to follow his father's plans—and those of his stepmother. But what a daring, derisive, and impudent game Zeus had played to engineer the birth of Heracles . . . Perhaps because this was Zeus's last opportunity to play around with women from earth.

Zeus knocked at Alcmene's door disguised as Amphitryon, as though he had made a surprise return from his expedition against the Teleboans, weighed down with weapons. Alcmene greeted him with amazement: in the middle of the night Amphitryon seemed to be enveloped "in a golden snowstorm." Silhouetted in the doorway was the mighty figure of Alcmene. Her strength was apparent even before her beauty, though she was very beautiful; and, as soon as she raised her eyes, there was a certain gravity in her gaze, of one who knows how things stand and will keep her silence, forever. Only in Hera's gaze had Zeus found anything similar.

That last night began at the moment when Alcmene opened the door to Zeus and recognized Amphitryon, the husband with whom she had never even once "joined in love," while Zeus recognized in Alcmene the expression of Hera, his wife-sister whom he was once again on the point of betraying. And it continued, protracting into three nights, spent in intercourse between Zeus and Alcmene, while the Hours had unharnessed the horses and were relaxing in their celestial apartments, paying no heed to that inadmissible delay, and the men were struck down by a drowsiness that always overcomes them when they become involuntary witnesses to divine events they are not supposed to understand. But if Zeus, as Diodorus Siculus declared, had no wish to act that night "through erotic desire, as with other women, but to beget the child," then why did that night last longer than every other night, almost as if to allow him endless pleasure? It was one of those enigmas that Zeus scattered across his adventures. During that inexhaustible intercourse Zeus turned his thoughts back to another sharp, intense pleasure he had experienced with Alcmene's great-grandmother Danaë, when he had descended upon her in a golden rain inside an underground chamber of bronze that was sealed from outside. He always remembered its coldness and its glimmering green darkness, that rigid box at the center of which was a soft pile of cushions and white clothes with embroidered animals, and on it a pearly warm body that the coldness of the surrounding metal could not subdue. That bronze cell was empty, apart from the sumptuous bed sparsely lit by a thin aperture in the ceiling—and, beside the bed, suspended by an invisible thread, a round mirror, where repeatedly, that night, Zeus saw a diffused glittering light lose itself on the breast of the prisoner.

With Danaë, Zeus came close, closer than ever before, to forgetting himself. His body was scattered into droplets that were also coins—light, tinkling coins, moist on contact with Danaë's skin, clung to her and hid themselves everywhere, beneath her armpits or in her groin or behind her knee. The rain came in waves, constant in the sepulchral silence. This princess of Argus, reclining on two enormous cushions, watched with curiosity, in the half-light, as the coins slid over the fabrics of the bed and piled between her thighs. From her head, from her hair, like a rock clad with moss, fat drops poured down her back and formed a lake around her buttocks. Other thin coins worked their way between her toes, and then coiled themselves into an eddy around Danaë's famous long, thin ankles.

But Zeus was not thinking now only of Danaë. Far more distant than she, and of the same lineage, at the sixteenth generation before Alcmene, Zeus remembered Niobe, daughter of Phoroneus, the first woman on earth with whom he had had intercourse. He had always been attracted to the women of that house of Argus: his earthly love affairs had begun in that family, and in that family they would end. Alcmene was the last mortal he would touch. He knew that the children born from those love affairs would no longer be as noble as they had once been—"and he was unwilling to have the better followed by the worse." The god also yielded to the course of time.

This night with Alcmene would mark the end of a whole chapter of Zeus's life, when every woman lived knowing that she ran the risk of being terrorized or intoxicated by his visits. A long complicity had been created between him and those beings who had served, among other things, to set history on its course. But history was now hurtling down alone, like a boulder freed from the mountainside. There was one last exploit to be performed: to give birth to that hero Heracles, who would be the exploit itself, its looming, blind, inexorable grief. Zeus was about to abandon himself to a new, useful paradox. For the most human of heroes to be born, Zeus—the one for whom everything, including love and glory, was toil—had chosen to transform himself into a man like all other men, adopting the role of a husband in an ordinary mortal couple.

Having removed his weapons, and then as he washed and oiled himself, Zeus felt himself obliged to tell Alcmene, with the voice of an exhausted and happy warrior, about imaginary episodes in a war he knew nothing about. And, as he spoke, he shook inside with a feeling of hilarity he had never felt before, and hence no one else had ever felt, whereas now it emerged clearly as a form that would be fixed once and for all. This was the birth of comedy, Zeus's final gift, the gift of misunderstanding and laughter that he would leave as a legacy to those beloved beings he had to abandon. Alcmene carried on listening to him, concealing her doubt in her piercing gaze. Her majestic body was now splayed out on the bed, her head resting on her snow-white arm. Zeus didn't know what new stories to think up about his nonexistent war with the Teleboans. He felt like one of those tavern drunkards who stubbornly return to anecdotes they've only just finished telling.

The moment approached when their bodies would touch. Zeus was solemnly immersed in thought. He readied himself for intercourse with Alcmene as if it were an onerous task. And meanwhile he thought: what a strange experience to be human, without a glimmer of divinity. And even more to be an actor, to perform the part of a strolling player who invents a different scene every night. How much easier, more natural, to be a swan, a white bull, an eagle, or even a woman, as he had been when he seduced Callisto. Alcmene continued watching him. Trained in *sōphrosýnē*, in that capacity to steer clear of extremes, which the Greeks much revered since they knew it was alien to their own inclinations, she hoped the night would bring her a modicum of pleasure and some refreshing sleep. But that night was three nights—and filled with pleasure alone. Alcmene became gradually more and more surprised, in the bed, before her husband, who was turning into an unfamiliar and overwhelming lover. She found out everything that women, for many generations, had discovered when they had sex with Zeus. At that point they no longer spoke, they no longer whispered a single syllable. They watched and reflected. Zeus, embarrassed at first by his own form as an ordinary man, now felt, to his surprise, that he was returning to his normal self. And not just as when he roamed the earth in his many forms in search of adventure. But as he used to feel on Mount Olympus, in his marriage bed, or wherever he found himself with Hera—for everything around her became a bed. On that last night with a woman from earth, he thought things would once more be just. That final night should be accompanied by a double gift: to his bedfellows and to his wife, who had kept count of his betrayals. His gift to Alcmene, and through her to all women, would be the wondrous capacity to take one man for another as well as to take a god for a man or a man for a god. To Hera he would be giving a secret lover: Heracles, the "glory of Hera." Now, with supreme care, he had to father him. Zeus worked at the form of intercourse with Alcmene, in its slowness and in its frenzy, since he knew that such form would correspond with Heracles's strength. "The immensity of time taken to procreate prefigured the exceptional strength of the being that was begotten," noted Diodorus Siculus.

For Zeus, this was his most exotic adventure. Never had he

ventured so far from himself—as in an improvident gesture of homage. And yet, at the same time, he felt he was back in Hera's bed, which he had so often deserted. The more the night went on, the more clearly Zeus recognized Hera in Alcmene, in the same way that Alcmene recognized Zeus in Amphitryon. He was betraying Hera on behalf of Hera. Never did Zeus feel such marital devotion as on that night of infidelity with Alcmene. Hera could not tolerate lovers, but Zeus wanted to give her this lover he could never admit to. And he prolonged that night like someone who is searching for a gift—and who knows that the longer the search, the more special the gift will be.

The encounter between Zeus and Alcmene introduced a new genre into literature and into the ways of the world. It was no longer tragedy—and couldn't really be described as pure comedy since, as Hermes observed, "gods and kings" appeared onstage. Slyly he added, "*Sit tragicomoedia.*" The forms, from then on, became composite. The extremes of comedy and disaster would coexist, like old companions, alternating and suddenly combining onstage.

Alcmene was now exhausted and had fallen asleep. Zeus vanished. In her sleep, Alcmene traveled back through the generations of women in her family, encountered Niobe for the first time, like a sister with whom she spoke at length about something known only to them; and then she reached Danaë and spoke of metallic boxes and children, water, snow, and gold. Looking at Danaë, Alcmene felt a sense of pleasure and anguish, a soft embrace and burning sensation she could not explain. She woke with a start. Someone was knocking loudly. She opened the door and saw Amphitryon weighed down with weapons, tired, with a glint in his eyes. But he was not swathed in a golden snowstorm. Alcmene had learned long ago not to react to her first impulse. She greeted Amphitryon with cautious affection. The warrior began to undress and to talk. He told stories of war, in bursts of sudden frenzy, all stories that Alcmene now already knew. Meanwhile the night passed, a nor-

mal night. Amphitryon washed, oiled himself, and continued his
stories, unperturbed. Alcmene no longer knew what to think. She
was in a state of exhaustion after that night of lovemaking that
had lasted three nights. It was impossible to keep a clear head. She
found herself at last stretched out on the bed just as the sky was
turning light. She recognized Amphitryon's perfumed body beside her and felt his hand searching for her. "But we haven't slept a
wink," she barely managed to say—and fell asleep again. Amphitryon kept watching her, dismayed. Then he approached and took
her, asleep, without any feeling of pleasure. He had faced every
kind of adversity for that woman, had been banished from his city,
had fought a bitter war to avenge her brothers. And Alcmene had
always been with him, but he hadn't been able to touch her because
there had always been some promise or magic spell that forbade it.
Now all his promises had been kept. He had come back home and
found a sleepy, unresponsive woman who had clearly been lavish-
ing her body on someone else.

While Alcmene continued sleeping, lost in oblivion, Amphitryon began to ponder what he would do with her. He would
solemnly burn her alive forthwith. He saw no other solution. Alcmene woke—and outside they were already erecting a sturdy pyre,
built carefully with uniform rows of large logs. On top they had
prepared a comfortable bed which, for Alcmene, would be her
last—though she wasn't yet aware of it, even when they dragged
her from her bed, still drowsy with sleep, and laid her on the pyre.

Zeus watched from above. Alcmene raised her arms toward
him as the flames began to crackle. Zeus gave a sign to two of the
celestial nymphs, the Hyades. From the vault of the cosmos each
produced an amphora, from which they poured a continual flow of
water. It fell onto a rainbow that could be seen in the dawn light,
and from there it showered onto Alcmene's pyre, gently extin-
guishing it before the flames could touch her body. Alcmene kept
looking up to the sky with her mouth open in silent entreaty, as
streams of water trickled between her lips. She realized the rain
was her salvation—as well as being a salutation, an allusion. She

thought of Danaë, of the gold that had rained down on her from the ceiling, she thought of the golden snowstorm that had enveloped Zeus when he had come to find her in the night. That gold might never perhaps reappear on earth. And yet the droplets that streaked her face, mingling with her tears, still bore some trace of its flavor. The rain, her humble savior, was heralding something vast and specific, though as yet indistinct: the new chapter in Zeus's reign would be founded on metaphor. A firm yet elusive foundation: since metaphor is a memory.

Even if the heroes were sons or descendants of Zeus and of mortal women, and this brought them close in life to the gods, nonetheless like humans they faced death. To become immortal, one had to suck the milk of Hera, the archenemy of the mothers of the heroes. Hera, Zeus's third consort, had given birth to Ares, Hebe, and Eileithyia—all inhabitants of Olympus. But her milk was ever-flowing. It could also be sucked by those who would otherwise die. Hera found herself, at every moment, in the condition of women who had just given birth. And, in that state, she pursued women who were giving birth or about to give birth from Zeus's seed. It was hardly a minor secret of divine physiology.

Zeus was pondering this while Hera slept. She drew little Heracles to her breast: he was already condemned to his labors. But Zeus didn't want him to vanish one day into Hades. Heracles clung to one of Hera's nipples and began sucking with passion, like a lover. Hera gave a sudden start and pushed him away. But the milk flowed and an immense arc spurted into the sky. The drops congealed on the dark vault, in a long, frayed ribbon. Other drops finished up on earth, strewn among the fields and deserts. And so the Milky Way was formed. And white lilies sprouted on earth, the same lilies that the Archangel Gabriel would offer to Mary, at the moment of the Annunciation.

Zeus's subterfuge was based on an earlier story. For the gods, too, every story comes from another. One day, as Dionysus was leading his rowdy army of Bassarids and Silens toward India, he was struck down by madness. It was not a divine delirium, but a fierce *lýssa*, pure madness, that made him froth at the mouth. Hera's revenge didn't just afflict Semele, but also her son. Zeus had to be prevented from realizing what was going on, since he would immediately have gone to Dionysus's aid. And the revenge would not have been fulfilled.

So Hera decided to seduce Zeus, with the same tactics she had used with him since she was a child. Once again, Zeus succumbed. Under her spell, he rejected Taygete, Niobe, and Io, the lovers Hera most hated. She let a golden cloud envelop them, as in a marriage chamber, as they lay on the grass in a soft hollow, surrounded by mountains. Then Zeus fell asleep. And this is exactly what Hera wanted, so that "the deep suffering of Dionysus who knows no suffering" would last as long as possible.

But Zeus eventually awoke, on the peaks of the Caucasus, and reconstructed Hera's deception. He threatened to suspend her once again from the sky. He would tie her hands once more with the same gold chain. He held that threat in reserve for his greatest fits of fury. Then he thought how he could punish Hera and save Dionysus at the same time. He ordered her to offer her breast to Dionysus and "let him suck with his adult lips" her "sacred drops." She would then have to "rub her milk over Dionysus's body and clean away the ugly patches of the disease that destroys the mind." Hera obeyed. If this is what had happened then, to save Dionysus, the same had to be done once again, to save Heracles.

Even to the naked eye, the Milky Way seemed to the ancients to be the vastest, most boundless entity to be seen. Looking up at night, they could gaze at a pearly swath that resembled nothing so much as a still river with a mass of tributaries. The Olympians did not let themselves be awed by that indomitable immensity. As eminent rhetoricians, they sought to deal with it through antiphrasis. They devised the most unlikely story, as often happened in the tales about Heracles, to explain the origin of something that belonged to every life. It had nothing to do with the immensity of space and the immeasurability of numbers, but with

the *continuum*, which would one day become Georg Cantor's torment and his paradise. It was marked out in the sky by the Milky
Way, continuing then onto the earth and beneath the earth. For, as
the *Jaiminīya Brāhmaṇa* states, "in truth the bright world is so to
speak continuous [*saṃtata*]." It was the current that flowed ceaselessly from the "celestial pail"—the Vedic seers called it *kośa*. And,
just as it acted in the sky, so too did it act in the mind, meeting and
colliding with the singularities of the discrete. That which in India
was evoked by enigmatic hymns was for the Greeks a sash of stars:
each star a droplet spurted vexatiously from Hera's breast. An un-
equaled example of cosmic *sprezzatura*.

On Mount Olympus, time had long been punctuated by detailed reports of Heracles's exploits. And whole periods had been
marked by events that related to him. It was said: "This happened
when Heracles was Omphale's slave," or: "When Heracles captured
Diomedes's mares." Heracles would now become a dweller in the
sky, even if not always present, even if he had no seat. Zeus had
invited him to be one of the Twelve. But Heracles knew too much
theology not to be aware of the trap. "If I become one of the Twelve,
one god will have to be expelled," he said. "And how can I accept
an honor that means dishonoring a god?" Zeus gave a wry smile.
Who could know more about the Twelve than Heracles? He had
suffered it to his own cost—and for a very long time. He had always been the Thirteenth, the sacrificial discharge of the totality,
the residue that in the end is burned. Heracles had been struck
down by madness *after* having completed his twelve labors. Something in him, by destiny, was too much, in comparison with a
measure calculated with irksome precision. It would remain like
this even on Olympus, even if everything now became lighter—
and Heracles could have moved about as a guest, a family member,
a hero, a man, a god, without anyone ever being rash enough to ask
for explanations about his nature. Heracles's story—so the Olympians, and Zeus in particular, thought—would remain first and
foremost a story about Hera. The goddess, as well as being a tireless

persecutor, had also, at one time or another, been Heracles's wet nurse, stepmother, and mother-in-law. In those changing roles, and in that perpetual role of guardian of cosmic laws, she had surrounded him so much that, wherever Heracles looked, all he could see were Hera's round eyes. But in the circle there remained a vast spectral gap: the role as yet unrecognized, from which all others depended: that of mother. Zeus came up to Hera with a solemn expression, as happened on the rare occasions when they could talk alone. And he said: "Now is the moment. Now you have to perform the act you have always been delaying." She opened the door and let Heracles in. His face was scorched as usual by the sun, the tips of his hair graying. But in his gaze, for the first time, was an appearance of unease that no monster had ever made him feel. Hera meanwhile had stretched out on the bed, not even greeting him. She arched her great body, lifted her peplos as though it were a curtain. In Zeus's presence, with a cautious and timid gesture, Heracles approached Hera's bed and hid his head beneath her robes. Then also his mighty body disappeared, while the peplos of Hera's supine body swelled. And eventually Heracles's feet were covered by the folds of cloth. There was silence. And the shapeless white mountain, on the bed from which Hera's noble breast and divine head were all that could be seen, settled back to immobility. A long, faraway groan could be heard, the voice of a woman, an animal, and a child, and something dark rolled onto the floor, like a sack. It was the huddled body of Heracles, to which Hera had just given birth. "He whom the goddess, white-armed Hera, had once hated among all the blessed gods and mortal men, she now loves and honors more than all other immortals, except the mighty son of Cronos." The other gods, whom Zeus had allowed into the room, watched the scene in silence, as if they had always known it had to end like this.

VII

SPUMA FUI

Ovid, at the age of twenty, was a provincial boy from a respectable family seeking his fortune in Rome. He balked at the idea of entering a serious career of the kind that parents generally favor. Rhetoric inclined him not to the law, but to verse, which gushed from his lips like the prose of Monsieur Jourdain. The first god he encountered was Cupid. The god had scurrilously removed a foot from his hexameters and had softened them into elegiac couplets. It was theft—and Ovid would spend his life demonstrating how theft was first and foremost an erotic act. From now on, epic gravity was no longer de rigueur. Ovid was now moved by the lighter meter to sing of some "girl with long and well-groomed hair." Thus *Amores* was born, faithful only to the irreverence of the god that had filled the poet's "vacant breast" with a single, generic, and imperious word: *amor*.

Ovid's impudence extended even to the king of the gods, from the very beginning of the *Metamorphoses*. In the first of his amorous adventures, Zeus addresses Io by calling her a "virgin worthy of Jupiter"—and up to this point he is being playful, though immediately after he shows no restraint and portrays himself as a god "who does not come from the common people," "*nec de plebe deo*." So were there common people among the gods? A puzzling idea, but the poem had hinted at this a few lines earlier. On Mount Olympus, to the left and right of Zeus's palace were the open doors of the dwellings of the other gods. Then, scattered here and there, the houses of the common people ("*plebs habitat diversa locis*"). No wonder that, soon after, Ovid ventures to talk about a "Palatine of heaven." Olympus, according to his description, is a celestial duplication of Imperial Rome. The man who was about to dedicate thousands of lines to an uninterrupted sequence of wonders felt no need to make any distinction between the dwellings of the gods and those of his fellow citizens. Never had the life of the gods been superimposed to such an extent, in the smallest and most intimate details, on that of the inhabitants of a metropolis, of that city that claimed to be *the* city. But this in no way diminished the numinosity of the wonders that were about to be told. And this is the particularly scandalous aspect of the *Metamorphoses*: the account of a world filled with wonders and inhabited by characters—above all gods—who reason as though the wonders were now only to be found in poems. Young Ovid had expressed this crudely in a couplet in *Amores*: "I speak of the wondrous untruths of the ancient poets, / that no day has ever seen nor ever will see."

Elegy was breathing in a dense forest, with waters and a dripping grotto at the center. A suitable place for the deity. She was light, with an amiable limp, her dress puckered, flimsy. Strolling among the trees was the thin, nervous poet whom many were talking about in Rome, though not so much for literary motives. He was thinking about what to write. He was drawn to everything apart from loud tragedy, with its stereotypical mask, its painted buskins, its uniformity of language. There again, by that time, tragedies could no longer be written. They—like sacrifices—were a matter for imperial officials. Ovid gazed at Elegy, who gave him a wry smile. She still had the fragrance of the new. He pretended to want her because she was young, concise, and suitable for messages of love. But these were excuses. If he wanted her it was because he felt she symbolized poetry itself: cursive, casual, and very private. When he was among the Getae, at the icy mouth of the Danube, he continued talking in couplets, and it was a submersed delirium, still marked by that tremor. There was no longer any occasion for love messages—and even the letters to Rome were a soliloquy.

Beneath a heaven of *exempla*, euphoric because Cupid had made the hexameter become lame, Ovid was describing for the first time the room in semi-darkness, assailed by the heat (*"aestus erat"*) a moment before she glimpsed her lover's foot in the doorway. At that moment Ovid is already the fully fledged modern writer. For him, everything is material for literature: the whole of mythology, the ritual gestures are presented like a wheel of variants, an ever-ready repertory of prescribed gestures, combinations, images. A religious resonance is sensed in Ovid only in his literature. It is the only *numen* to which he always bows. Otherwise, how hard it is to endure a night of chastity just because next day the *puella* has to celebrate the rites of Ceres . . . Then, in the midst of brazen love talk, Ovid notes a terrible discovery: that it is death that destroys what is sacred. "*Scilicet omne sacrum mors inportuna profanat,*" "Importunate death profanes all that is sacred." As if the imminent labor of secularization, which has always been going on, were not due to an impiety of mind, but to the natural impiety of death, which breaks down every barrier, like an intruder. The meagerness, the paucity of funeral rites, up to the squalor to which they are reduced, would then be the signal of this painful process: death, a perennially hostile witness, has not only shunned the ceremonies that sanctify it but circumvents all that is sacred in anticipation of defiling it.

Ovid was one of the first, if not the first, to use all the precautionary ploys that are considered peculiar to the moderns. "*Expedit esse deos,*" "It is fitting that gods should exist": this is what he says in *Ars amatoria*. But if something is "fitting," does it necessarily have to be true? The gods belong to the good manners of existence. But does this perhaps diminish their power? Or invalidate their necessity? Ovid's urbanity places him at a watershed between magic and parody. For him, *carmen* means "incantation, magical evocation," as in the original meaning of the word, but also "poem" as Ronsard or Mallarmé meant it. And "*carmen perpetuum,*" the formula with which he sought to define his *Metamorphoses*, means both "endless incantation" as well as "continuous poetry," which opens with the beginnings of the cosmos and ends at the very moment in which it is written.

Ovid therefore goes as far as suggesting that, if writers need gods, which are their raw material, gods also need writers: "*Dei quoque carminibus, si fas est dicere, fiunt,*" "Even the gods, if one may say so, come into being through poetry." Such words express a new and extreme risk—absolute literature—and Ovid is well aware of it, with a certain trepidation. Which is why he inserts "*si fas est dicere.*" And he wrote these words *ex Ponto,* on the Black Sea, where he had been banished for having committed or for having seen a *nefas,* something "nefarious."

The *Metamorphoses* is the last appearance of the gods in their full panoply. The next occasion, four centuries later, was the *Dionysiaca* by Nonnus, but everything there was already an immense, prolonged hallucination. Around Ovid, on the other hand, in the recently established Empire, the gods were still officially present. Meanwhile, in Galilee, a young Jewish child, Jesus, was growing up. In Rome, the only preoccupation, if any, might have been the ease, the familiarity, with which Ovid talked about the gods. "The marvelous thing is made plausible, the gods are humanized, the annals are written as if copied from a parish register; the heroes might have been acquaintances of the author's father" (a note by the young Ezra Pound).

Among Latin writers, Ovid was the most brazen toward the gods, but also the most flexible when it came to naming the divine. Aphrodite appears and offers him "a leaf and a few berries" of myrtle, which she had taken from her hair. This was enough to sense the *numen*: "*Sensimus acceptis numen quoque,*" "As soon as I took them I felt the divine." And suddenly everything changes: "*Purior aether / fulsit et e toto pectore cessit onus,*" "The purest air / irradiated and all weight vanished from my heart."

Where in Rome could frivolous women buy wigs? "Under the eyes of Heracles and before the chorus of virgins." Thus meaning: at the Circus Flaminius, in front of the statues of Heracles Musagetes and before the group of Muses that follow him. Wigs and statues: Ovid was the best guide for finding and placing them side by side. The various cults were also an excuse to catch sight of the most attractive *puellae,* the girls who seemed to congregate in those places. "Rome has all that has ever existed in the world," said Ovid, using a similar expression that had been used in India for the *Mahābhārata*. "They go to the theater to see and be seen." But the same could be said about ceremonies. There was plenty of choice, between "the rites of the seventh day celebrated by the Jews of Syria" or "the Egyptian temples of the heifer dressed in linen," dedicated to the cult of Isis, or other ceremonies that Ovid doesn't specify. And he compares them, for the purposes of amorous pursuits, with the "bustle of the Forum," where the lawyers argued beside the fountain of the Appian Nymphs. Sign of a total openness and amenability toward every form of the sacred and profane. This was Ovid's own view—and the condition that he preferred, which could only be found in the age of Augustus.

Ovid at first sought to follow the example of Tibullus, Propertius, Cornelius Gallus, using the elegy to chart the changes of heart of those pierced by Eros, between euphoria and despair. But then he conceived a rash and unprecedented plan that distanced him from everyone: a short treatise whose subject was *concubitus*, "coitus" and its pleasure. The usual material for an elegy became the pretext for arriving at that single purpose. No one in Rome— nor in Greece—had dared to undertake anything similar.

But how to do it? First of all by transferring the material of the elegy into another form and register: that of the didactic genre. In the same way that Virgil, in the *Georgics*, had shown in some way how to cultivate the land and make it flourish, Ovid had written about how to achieve *concubitus* and enjoy it. In both cases, it was an education and at the same time a celebration.

The *Ars amatoria* declares it in no uncertain way: it will be a shrewd and patient pursuit in which *concubitus* is the target. Flaming passions, steadfast love: they are occasional consequences, but not the actual object of the short treatise. And like every pursuit of love, mixed in it is a certain savagery: "*barbaria noster abundat amor,*" "our love abounds with barbarity" (anticipating what Baudelaire would one day write about "the natural ferocity of love"). Likewise, as in every hunt, the movement is perpetual, since "*errat et in nulla sede moratur Amor,*" "Love is a wanderer and lingers in no place."

Around him people were celebrating the "*Pudor priscus,*" the "chasteness of past times," but Ovid had the effrontery to treat it as a "survival" of the "*rusticitas*"—or the peasant crudity—of "ancient ancestors." And he added, defiantly: "*ego me nunc denique natum / gratulor: haec aetas moribus apta meis,*" "I am pleased to have been born now: / this is the age that suits my nature." Ovid stood out, lone admirer of the present, in the midst of a throng that praised times past and the "*simplicitas rudis,*" "rude simplicity" that he was very happy to escape.

Aphrodite had warned Ovid: "*Praecipue nostrum est quod pudet,*" "Our specialty is what is shameful." But the poet did not give in, and so he went on to discuss positions in *concubitus*. And here too, in terms of acrobatics, he is aided by a mythological *exemplum*: "*Milanion umeris Atalantes crura ferebat,*" "Melanion lifted Atalanta's legs onto his shoulders," since that position allowed him more than any other to admire the long legs of the great huntress. And Briseis let herself be touched by Achilles's hands, "still stained with Phrygian blood," indeed—Ovid suggests—"it was this that gave you pleasure, lascivious girl." If myth was a repertory of exemplary deeds, they must also be extended to "*quod pudet,*" to what people are ashamed to say.

Concubitus—not the cosmos, as in Lucretius, nor the earth, as in Virgil—can be chosen as the subject of a didactic poem only if it is written tongue in cheek. The subtle poison of parody now penetrated the veins of an august genre that dated back to the time of Hesiod. But the amorous torments of Propertius or Tibullus, from whom Ovid had drawn inspiration, also became specific examples in a repertory of possibilities that anybody could try out. And thus it lost that characteristic of uniqueness and unrepeatability to which the voice of the elegiac poet aspired. Propertius could no longer say to Cynthia: "*Tu mihi sola places*," "You're the only one I like," nor expect Cynthia to respond to him as her only lover.

The word *concubitus* occurs seven times in the three books of *Ars amatoria*, whereas there are only two occurrences in *Amores*. It appears another seven times in the fifteen books of the *Metamorphoses*. And there's a subtle link between the two works. The *Ars* is a didactic tract that self-destructs. It teaches detailed rules about something that, according to the author himself, defies every rule, because it requires "a thousand different methods to win a thousand different minds." It is pointless listing precepts if the only certain argument is that of training oneself in the art of metamorphosis, so that the chaser of girls "*utque leves Proteus modo se tenuabit in undas, / nunc leo, nunc arbor, nunc erit hirtus aper*," "will, like Proteus, melt into smooth waves, / will now be a lion, now a tree, now a bristling boar."

The commonplace about man as an amorous hunter must have been obvious in the Rome of Augustus no less than in every successive age. Ovid discussed it as only true writers know how: he took it literally, and from the start of *Ars amatoria* he spoke of the hunter who "knows well where to spread his nets for stags," returning constantly to images of the hunt. But he wasn't just exploiting a supposed piece of proverbial wisdom. Like Léon Bloy, Ovid sought the mirror image of divine truths in commonplaces, and he wasn't frightened to pursue them, even where they led him into forbidden territories. And the more dangerous they were, the more lightly he trod.

The word *puella*, "girl," appears eighty-three times in *Ars amatoria*. We know this from the *Concordance of Ovid*, which Roy J. Deferrari and Martin R. P. McGuire compiled with Sister M. Inviolata Barry, of the College of Our Lady of the Lake. A noble concordance of both pagan and Christian civilization.

Having spent years studying the Augustan age, Ronald Syme wrote of *Ars amatoria*: "The tract was not meant to be taken seriously—it was a kind of parody. Augustus did not see the joke." Alternatively, it could be said that he saw it too well. As an eminent politician, he knew that parody was something not serious but grave. So grave, one day, as to justify banishment.

Though by nature he was the person least suited to undertakings of this kind, it was Ovid who wrote the work that sought to penetrate deep into the ritual geology of Rome and to bring it to light in the form of an account that followed the periods of the calendar: *Fasti*. The most irreverent poet was called upon to write about the most sacred of things. Ovid himself was the first to doubt his suitability for the task. Once again, he sought the help of Elegy, his "indulgent maidservant in love." But the poet now continued: "*sacra cano signataque tempora fasti*," "I will sing of the sacred rites, marked by the Fasti." And immediately the question arose: "*ecquis ad haec illinc crederet esse viam?*", "who would think a path could ever be found from down there to these things?" From the erotic games of *Amores*, how could he tackle the arcane practices of Rome when by now "the Greek tide had submerged everything, destroying the taste for and knowledge about traditional explanations"? With these words, Ovid had unintentionally described, in the form of a question, the farthest bounds of his territory and at the same time the irreducible peculiarity of his poetry: the capacity to move just as effectively from the imperious presence of the *numen* to a fearless nonchalance in discussing the facts of life. Both elements would grow together, one over the other, like tropical vegetation, in the *Metamorphoses*. Or, in certain cases, one element might be used to hide and circumvent the other, as happened in the *Fasti* with regard to the Lupercalia.

Omphale, the Oriental queen, thus appeared to Faunus, the Latin name for Pan, god of rugged Arcadia: "*Ibat odoratis umeros perfusa capillis / Maeonis, aurato conspicienda sinu*," "Maeonia passed by with fragrant hair loose on her shoulders, / with her wondrous golden breast." Beside her, a sturdy slave held a parasol to protect her moon complexion from the sun. Omphale entered a richly decorated cave. While the servants prepared food and drink, the queen began to dress Heracles with her most precious ornaments. She wanted to make him into a woman as much like her as possible. It wasn't easy: one belt was too tight and snapped; her bracelets wouldn't slide onto his wrists; and his big feet wouldn't fit into her sandals. Meanwhile Omphale had taken Heracles's club and the skin of the Nemean lion. Dressed up like this, they dined and stretched out beside each other on two beds. They lay there immobile, like two twins. They couldn't touch each other because a feast was to be celebrated the next day and demanded ritual purity.

Faunus had watched the whole scene, moment by moment. He wanted nothing more than to touch the body of Omphale. He waited until the middle of the night, then approached, groping his way in the darkness. He stretched out his hand, felt the hairy skin of the Nemean lion, and drew back. Moving across, he touched the soft garments and lay down alongside them. He tried to lift them up. At that point, *"tumidum cornu durius inguen erat,"* "his swollen penis was harder than a horn." He slid his hand beneath the light dress and found a muscular thigh, covered with a thick layer of hair. Heracles woke and threw the intruder off the bed. As soon as the servants brought light, Omphale laughed. From then on, since Faunus had been deceived by the clothes, he required celebrants to take part "naked at his ceremonies."

Ovid had made a scurrilous attempt at an explanation that explained nothing about the origins of the Lupercalia, a wild, archaic festival. Some nineteen hundred years later, in the tranquility of Cambridge, J. G. Frazer tried to find a reason for that puzzling ritual. According to his reconstruction, young men, naked apart from a leather thong tied to their hips, ran around the perimeter of ancient Rome. The Luperci used their thongs, made by flaying goats they had sacrificed, to whip whoever they came across, but above all women, "who held out both hands to receive the blows, persuaded that this was a safe mode of securing offspring and an easy delivery." Frazer's account is euphemistic and says nothing about the details that up to now, as Dumézil observed, "remain unexplained": having sacrificed the goats, the foreheads of the Luperci have to be smeared with blood from a knife, then other young men dry the blood with a piece of wool soaked with milk—and "the young men have to laugh once the blood has been dried." This is what Plutarch wrote. No one has managed to explain the need for the blood and for the laughter. As for the women having their hands whipped, the ritual didn't always have to stop there. A mosaic found in Tunisia shows a woman held by her armpits and legs by two young men while a Luperco is whipping the lower part of her naked body.

Frazer described the Lupercalia with just the same impassiveness with which he had described the bloody rituals of many obscure tribes. And those descriptions were easily juxtaposed. But in the case of the Lupercalia it was essential also to look at events that had taken place in Rome, and especially those of February 15, 44 B.C.E., one month before the assassination of Julius Caesar and a year before Ovid was born. And remembering also that February 15 was a special day in Rome: "Once a year, for one day, the equilibrium between the regulated, explored, divided world and the savage world was broken: Faunus occupied everything."

On that February day of 44 B.C.E., Caesar, sitting on a golden throne, at the height of his glory, was watching the furious race of the Luperci. Among them was Marcus Antonius, naked and glistening with oil. The crowd opened before him as he approached Caesar and offered him a diadem set in a laurel crown. Caesar made a gesture of refusal and the crowd applauded. Antony repeated the gesture and Caesar refused again. The tumult of applause grew. Caesar then got up from the throne, pulled the tunic away from his neck, and offered his throat to whoever wished to cut it. "According to Cicero, who may have witnessed the scene, Antony was drunk as well as naked when he attempted to crown Caesar king of Rome."

Ovid wrote *Fasti* after years of fierce civil war, and that episode, which was seen as "a first outline of the imperial cult," must still have been in many people's minds. According to Plutarch, the Lupercalia recalled the rites of Mount Lyceum in Arcadia and was therefore linked to stories of cannibalism and metamorphosis. Frazer was content however to use his all-purpose word: *fertility*. But the rite remained unfathomable and forbidding. Ovid, a shrewd ethnographer and cold man of letters, chose to steer well clear, perhaps because it meant *too much*. And the best way for him to distract attention from it could have been to go back to his role of poet of amorous games that were sometimes lewd and often comic. Nothing could be more diverting than the outrageous story of Faunus, where Heracles appeared as a woman's slave, dressed as a woman, and was mistaken, if only temporarily, for a woman. A story presented as a "myth full of ancient playfulness." So ancient that only Ovid recalled it.

With equal scruple, Ovid wrote a tract on cosmetics, dedicated to women's faces, and the *Fasti*, a poem "dug from the annals of the earliest times." Both in elegiac couplets. "*Culta placent*," "refined things are pleasing": this could have been his motto, though he offered it only as opening advice for beautiful women.

In Rome, each year was punctuated with moments that were *fastus* and *nefastus*. Days and hours. The days of *fastus* were those in which the praetor could pronounce three words: "*Do, dico, addico*," "I give, I say, I adjudge," and thus apply the law. *Nefastus* were the days in which those three words "may not be spoken." Immense, intractable, largely uncomprehended: this was how the bulk of ritual traditions appeared in the Rome of Augustus. Remote, arid material. But the *princeps*, like all men of power, observed the cult of tradition. And Ovid displayed scrupulous accuracy in his arduous task—only occasionally allowing a certain impatience to emerge.

The year opened with a fig, a date, honey in a white bowl, and a coin with a ship on one side and a two-faced Janus on the other. From that moment on, there was a disparate string of festivities and celebrations. On April 15, the day of the Fordicidia, the Capitoline Hill was awash with the blood of pregnant cows, and the oldest of the Vestal Virgins burned the calf fetuses. Their precious ashes would be used on April 21 for the festival of the goddess Pales.

Ovid recounts how he had held the ashes of those calves in his hands. During another festival, the Robigalia, he had witnessed the sacrifice of a female dog ("we saw the foul guts of a vile bitch"). He asked for an explanation from the *flamen,* who said it was to do with Maera, Erigone's dog, which then became Sirius: "this dog is set on the altar in place of the astral dog, and is put to death only because it has the same name." Cold, technical, frightening priestly nominalism. For another rite, Ovid tells how he jumped among various fires. He didn't spend the whole of his time at the doors of *puellae.*

Many goddesses had particular roles: Fornax for ovens; Robigus for rust, Carna for door hinges. But a temple to Mens, the mind, was also introduced after a defeat by the Carthaginians. Ovid moved easily amid the vast jumble of gestures, relics, etymologies, events. And at times he admitted to feeling confused by a "swarm of doubts." The interpretations were too numerous and incompatible. Once, almost in defiance, he listed nine interpretations—and had no wish to choose which one he thought was right. Around him the Romans continued unbendingly, celebrating rituals whose meaning they understood less and less. They knew, with their perfunctory clarity, that the city was founded on its rituals.

The *Fasti* could be described using the comments once applied to an obscure custom by which foxes had torches fastened to their tails: "*factum abiit, monimenta manent*," "the fact is forgotten, the memories of it remain." It was Ovid's fate to record how much of the remote past had stubbornly survived in the Rome of Augustus and, at the same time, such features of its ephemeral present as the makeup on a woman's face.

The *Metamorphoses* is above all the record of that remote period in the world during which everything was transformed into everything else. This made life impossible for anyone who wanted to have a name and a form, without further change. The gods put an end to this situation, in that they further transformed it. And they were the first to have a name and a form. If humans can claim so much, it is only because the gods had already achieved it. But the gods created nothing—indeed the very idea of creation seemed strange and incongruous to them. The gods were simply masters of transformation. And when the world became settled, they continued to apply the primordial power of metamorphosis to individual cases, to individual situations, so that life wouldn't lose its adventurous character. And so the indelible outlines paraded by the gods mingled ceaselessly with the whirl of apparitions from which they had broken away.

The *Metamorphoses* is a collection of self-sufficient stories inside other stories. In their immediacy, each of them could stand alone without the others. But each is illuminated by its context, and from that context alone it acquires a further significance. Aphrodite forgets her sanctuaries, even ignores the heavens in her pursuit of the young hunter Adonis. While her son Eros was giving her a kiss, the cane rod of one of his arrows had grazed Aphrodite's breast. This was enough for his mother to fall into a new passion, which would soon draw Aphrodite toward the goddess with whom she had least in common: Artemis, who appears and vanishes into the thicket, on the mountains. Aphrodite, though eager, soon exhausts herself in that "*labor insolitus*," an exertion to which she was not accustomed. She had no interest in hunting, it was just an excuse to be close to Adonis.

It was then that she put him on his guard and told him the story of Atalanta, the blond woman with whom she was least compatible, who brought death to anyone who hoped to marry her. That salutary story served no purpose. Adonis was killed by a wild boar, Atalanta was transformed into a lioness. Two predatory beasts. But what was the secret link between Atalanta and Aphrodite? Irresistible physical love. Once beaten by Hippomenes in the chase, Atalanta had become a lover subject no less than Aphrodite to "*concubitus intempestiva cupido,*" to inappropriate and intemperate sexual desire. One day she was roaming the forest with Hippomenes, who was now her husband, when they came across a sanctuary to Cybele. Solitary, empty. Close to the temple, a small cave, full of very old wooden effigies of gods. Hippomenes made Atalanta lie down there. The images averted their eyes before the pleasure of the lovers. For that insult they were transformed into a pair of lions that couldn't have intercourse.

Ovid wanted to give full emphasis to the sexual desire in two female figures: Aphrodite, who propagates and protects desire, and Artemis, who shuns and punishes it. Atalanta, the counterpart of Artemis, is the woman Aphrodite evokes just before her lover Adonis is killed. She was the most powerful link, which eluded words.

Since Ovid's *Metamorphoses* recounts some two hundred and fifty instances of metamorphosis in fifteen books, and every metamorphosis is a *miraculum*, a "wonder," the first formal question posed in the work will be this: how to move from one wonder to another, considering also that the stories take place in every corner of the earth as it was then known, and over a time period that goes from immediately after the flood up to the reign of Augustus? In the language of rhetoric—and musical composition—it is the *question of transitions*, the most difficult formal problem that Ovid had to resolve. And, for a writer, nothing has as much importance as the challenges of form.

More than in book one, which is still partly occupied with the description of cosmic events (the portrayal of chaos, the four ages of the world, the Gigantomachy, the Flood), it is in book two that the narration is caught up in a crisscross of stories—and therefore of transitions from one to another. This is the sequence: at the beginning, the race of Phaeton, who cannot guide the horses of the Sun along the tracks of heaven and comes very close to setting ablaze not just the earth but the universe, before plunging into the river Eridanos. Much more than in the lines on chaos and the flood, here Ovid proves himself to be a remarkable cosmic poet. But this time the narrative subject, despite its immensity, is the uninterrupted story of an adolescent wracked by an obsession: as an illegitimate son, he asks Helios for some sign of unconditional love that will convince him once and for all that he is his son. And Helios grants it by allowing him to do something that not even Zeus would allow: to drive his chariot for a day. And from that moment we follow events as if we were captives inside Phaeton's head—and with him we are swallowed up. Just twenty lines later, however, Helios has to shake off his paralysis and take back the reins of his horses, still "maddened and trembling with terror." In this phase of the world, no pauses are allowed, moments of grief cut deep and are very short. And immediately we ask: what will follow the catastrophe?

The answer: another story of amorous intrigue. As in book one, where the story of the flood and the killing of Python, the last survivor of an age of monsters, is followed by the story of Apollo and Daphne, likewise, after the disaster of Phaeton, comes the story of Zeus and Callisto. The world suddenly empties and what happens is concentrated on a woman's body and an eye that peers at it. It is the epiphany of Artemisian beauty, the origin of stories of the cruelest kind. The pattern is repeated over and over (indeed, it will be the bloodstained golden thread that emerges so often in the *Metamorphoses*), but from the first appearance of Daphne all its distinctive features are already present. There is a huntress of extraordinary beauty, whose only thought is about hunting and roaming the forests. Her hair flows loose, her dress is short, her hands are holding a bow or a javelin. This is the primordial vision of desire: a figure that is seen fleetingly and vanishes like a hallucination (the origin of Baudelaire's passerby).

But why does Daphne have to be the first to appear—and not for example Syrinx or Callisto, whose story Ovid tells a little later? Because she was Apollo's "first love"? Or perhaps simply because Apollo met her on the same mountain where he had just shot Python? There's a third, more plausible reason. The story of Daphne will form the basis for all tales of erotic love and meta-morphosis because it is the only one where a god dared—for just a few moments—to doubt the sovereignty of Eros. The question was: who possesses the most powerful arrow? Still puffed up with arrogant pride at having shot Python, Apollo mocks Eros, "a lech-erous boy," who is playing with his bow. The god is going too far. Young Eros answers with a highly theological proposition: "Phoe-bus, your bow will shoot everything, / mine will shoot you," "*Figat tuus omnia, Phoebe, / te meus arcus.*" And he goes on to add: "in-asmuch as all living creatures are less / than gods, so too is your glory less than mine." This is cosmic arithmetic. Immediately con-firmed, since one of Eros's arrows wounds Apollo, piercing him "to the marrow," while Apollo fails to hit Eros. In fact, he has other things on his mind. He's already in love with Daphne, who runs away from him. Eros has shot her as well, with a lead-tipped arrow that drives away love.

Since the story of Daphne is only the first of many love stories involving the gods, we might imagine that Eros appears frequently in them. But Ovid's theology is as rigorous as it is well disguised. He prefers not to linger on the stories, and even less on their ce-lestial purposes. For him theology must make its pronouncements only in rare and treacherous passages. Otherwise it has to be re-constructed in the weave of the plot. The theology is ever-present, but implicit in the form. The same is true for Eros. Despite being so powerful and pervasive, he appears on only three occasions. In book five, Aphrodite asks his help to shoot Hades, the king of the dead. Once again it is a question of power. Aphrodite realizes that, in the tripartition of the world among Zeus, Poseidon, and Hades, the part of Hades still escapes the arrows of Eros: "You conquer and control the gods of the heavens and Jupiter himself, you conquer and control the lords of the sea and he who reigns over the lords of the sea. Why then not Tartarus? Why not expand your empire and that of your mother? That is one third of the world." When Eros is involved, everyone talks like theologians, even Aphrodite.

Eros then disappears, to reappear in book ten. It's as though the *Metamorphoses* demands his presence every five books. Indeed, there was a gap. His mother, Aphrodite, spoke hastily, as if her powers were the same as those of her son. But that was how it was. The goddess discovered this when her breast was grazed by one of Eros's arrows. It seemed a trifle, but "the wound was deeper than it seemed." Ovid gives no respite: in the very next line Aphrodite is lost in an amorous swoon and neglects her duties as goddess: "she prefers Adonis to heaven," "*caelo praefertur Adonis.*" And so, for Eros, the circle is complete: his supremacy is declared not only over Apollo and all the Olympians (book one), not only over Hades and the kingdom of the dead (book five), but even over his mother, Aphrodite (book ten), and it remains unshaken. The *Metamorphoses* can now proceed toward the estuary of book fifteen, mixing its waters more and more with the murky and poisonous waters of history.

Ovid's humiliation (the humiliation of the whole of literature) is being compelled to end the *Metamorphoses* with the catasterism of Julius Caesar, and the announcement that Augustus would follow likewise. Since then, literature lives under the threat of being *press-ganged into service*. The finale of the *Metamorphoses* cannot but taint everything else: it debases it in its obsequiousness. If the work culminates in Julius Caesar and his adopted son (who here becomes his natural son—the last, tacit metamorphosis) being assumed into heaven, then the gatherings on Mount Olympus can only be compared to meetings of the Senate, where the senators pretend to make decisions and meanwhile submit to the will of the sovereign. If Augustus is going to rise up toward Zeus, then Zeus will be brought down much more to the level of Augustus. The immeasurable distance between gods and men, though born from "one same race," as Pindar wrote, was reduced—and potentially canceled out. The glittering saga of the metamorphic world, in two hundred and fifty episodes, ended in a scene that implicated its final decline.

Using Mount Olympus as a *mirador*, Hera was incessantly scanning every corner of the earth. She suspected that Zeus, her bedfellow, brother, and consort, might be carrying out one of his devious erotic forays in some place. One day her view was hampered by a thick mist. Hera was also a skilled meteorologist. She investigated the reasons for this phenomenon, "surprised that rapid clouds, on a splendid day / had made it seem like night; she noticed they were not the effect / of the river, and nor had they come from the damp earth." She realized then that the mist was a trick by Zeus to hide himself. Hera, an expert in "*furta mariti*," "the larcenies of her husband," acted immediately, she too using her cosmic powers. She scattered the mist, but meanwhile—as in a Feydeau farce with doors and windows that open and close—Zeus had already transformed Io, priestess at Hera's sanctuary in Argus, into a "splendid heifer": and this made his seduction, carried out on his divine consort's most sacred domain, all the more odious.

It marked the beginning of a scene of transcendental, high comedy between two consummate actors. Hera paced around the heifer. She feigned interest, admiration. "It's really beautiful. But who owns it?" Zeus attempted, as on many previous occasions, to adopt the expression that least befitted him: that of the innocent. "I don't know. It must have been born from the earth." "Then let me have it as a gift," replied Hera, allowing her consort no reprieve. He felt a pang: "*crudele suos addicere amores*," "it is cruel to surrender one's own love." But it would be equally suspicious "to refuse a small gift to a member of his family and his bedfellow." So Zeus yielded, on the strength of a cogent logic: "*si . . . vacca negaretur, poterat non vacca videri*," "if . . . the heifer had been refused, it might appear to be no heifer." With the solemnity of a Roman lawyer, Zeus had reached the conclusion that it was better to hand over his lover as a gift to his wife. But that was not enough to allay Hera's suspicions. The splendid heifer would be kept under surveillance, like a high-risk prisoner, inside an enclosure where Io had once officiated for Hera.

Up to this point a remarkable comic humor had prevailed.

Never had such a powerful lens been trained on the tiniest gestures in the marital comedy between Zeus and Hera. Now, with a sudden leap, the action moved to pathos. Io, the beautiful priestess whom Zeus had described as bringing good fortune to whoever welcomed her into his bed, was a lonely heifer, forced to graze in the lands of her childhood without anyone recognizing her. Her father was Inachus, the river that flows through those pastures. Io approached him. She drank from the water that was her father. She saw her reflection in it and was horrified. Then, with a hoof in the dust, she traced the letters that told her story. Her father deciphered them and understood. In tears, he embraced his daughter the heifer, but soon Argus, the servant hired by Hera to guard her, hauled her out of his arms. He led her then to lone pastures. He squatted down on a hill, surveying the horizon with his hundred eyes.

Io is transformed by Zeus into a heifer; and by Zeus she is transformed back into a woman. Her son is Epaphus, whose name means Contact. Zeus's touch has worked on her twice: metamorphosis was not yet constrained by irreversibility. All other metamorphoses recounted by Ovid are irreversible. Irreversibility is humanity, wounded by the arrow of time.

The most subtle gesture for showing gods the meaning of irreversibility, the scourge of all humans, is libation: spilling a noble liquid onto the ground, losing it forever. It was a gesture of homage: recognition of the presence and the privilege of an invisible entity. But it could also be meant as a gesture of conversation. A way of telling the gods: Whatever we do, we are this spilt liquid. The gods also appear sometimes with libation cups in their hands. That gesture of the gods overflowed with countless meanings. But it was certainly a way of resuming conversation: a nod of approval toward that same gesture performed so frequently by humans under the eyes of the gods.

Gods, like witches, cannot cry ("the faces of the gods cannot be streaked with tears"), but they give out deep groans of unknown provenance. This happened to Apollo, who had shot his unfaithful lover Coronis and was now trying unsuccessfully to use his healing powers upon her. "Now we will both die," murmured Coronis, dying and revealing that she was pregnant with Asclepius. Apollo's groan then followed—a groan more animal than human or divine. Ovid says that the god differed little from the "heifer who sees a hammer / raised over the right ear of a suckling calf / before it strikes the hollow of its forehead with a dry thud," "*haud aliter quam cum, spectante iuvenca, / lactentis vituli dextra libratus ab aure / tempora discussit claro cava malleus ictu.*"

This analogy may help in understanding the ultimate difference between Ovid and the Latin poets before him. Not even Lucretius, who pointedly expressed much harshness toward the gods, had ever gone as far as describing such a gesture, such silence, such a sound. It was the one instance—the only instance—where what happens in slaughterhouses and during sacrifices coincided. And nothing resembled Apollo's pang of suffering more than the mute pain caused to an animal that watched such a scene. Wouldn't Winckelmann and others one day say that Apollo positioned himself outside passion, in a "noble simplicity and calm greatness"?

That instant marked the origin—untiringly concealed—of all worship. If there hadn't been that instant, there would have been no need for the doctrine—exoteric and esoteric—of sacrifice. And a writer now named it, using it as an ordinary similarity set in one of the numerous adventures of gods with women of the earth. Just as no one before had dared to describe a catasterism as "the price of rape" (and above all allowing a goddess to utter such words), likewise Ovid a few lines later described the suffering of a god as being much the same as that of a heifer who witnesses the killing of its calf during a sacrifice. But wasn't sacrifice supposed to be an act that sought to please the gods? And why did Apollo perceive it through the eyes of the victim?

We won't find an answer to this in Ovid, who carries on in the whirlwind of his narration without looking back. Ovid is someone who just wants to describe what is going on. And, if possible, everything that is going on. Not only the *miracula*, the "wonders" interspersed throughout the *Metamorphoses*, but countless intermediary passages that writers generally tend to pass over—and which were now articulated in a few vivid, unquestionable words.

In the pagan world, two of the heaviest indictments against the eating of meat were the section on Pythagoras in book fifteen of Ovid's *Metamorphoses* and Porphyry's *On Abstinence*. In both cases the killing of animals for food appeared like something more akin to an original sin. "*Primusque animalia mensis / arguit imponi*," "He was first to protest / about animals being served at table": for Ovid, this was the first point in Pythagorean doctrine, not the discovery of irrational numbers or metempsychosis. And when Pythagoras begins to speak, a breath of noble eloquence pervades the verse. The speculative implications are various. The first guilty person, "*non utilis auctor*," was identified in the one who "envied lions for their prey." A crucial passage: here the *imitation of the predator* is described as the origin of every evil. That unknown person who began it "*fecit iter sceleri*," "paved the way to crime." But not only this: the whole sacrificial system was implicated in the crime, made worse by attributing its institution to the gods: "*Nec satis est quod tale nefas committitur; ipsos / inscripsere deos sceleri numenque supernum / caede laboriferi credunt gaudere iuvenci*," "And it is not enough that such wickedness [the sacrifice] is committed; but / the crime is attributed to the gods themselves and it is believed that the celestial divinities / take pleasure in the killing of working oxen." With these words, Ovid, the master of unambiguous concision, questions the justification of the sacrificial act, which in all the other stories of the *Metamorphoses* was the fulcrum in relationships between gods and men. In the poem, there were few events in which sacrifice didn't play a central role or at least have a strategic position. And none of the characters, except Pythagoras, who only appears at the end of the poem, had dared to refute sacrifice *in itself*.

Through Pythagoras, Ovid offers not only a number of dry and peremptory formulations that taint the theology of sacrifice at its root, but he introduces doubts and identifies subtle psychological perceptions. What distance is there between one who offers "indifferent ears" to the groans of animals slain by the sacrificial knife and one who is ready to kill in general? "*Quantum est, quod desit in istis / ad plenum facinus? quo transitus inde paratur?*" From sacrificial killing, the way—*transitus*—is opened to any other killing whatsoever, to "the fullness of the crime." And those ears that are indifferent to victims with their throats slit on the altars can also remain indifferent before anything else touched by the knife.

The exposition of Pythagoras's doctrine at the end of the *Metamorphoses* is the only metaphysical digression in the work. It casts a retrospective light on the tangled stories that have preceded it over the course of fifteen books. And it is not clear how a world based entirely on sacrifice can coexist with that devastating argumentation about sacrifice itself. The conflict is made immediately clear: as soon as Pythagoras has ended his divinely inspired discussion—"*quoniam deus ora movet*"—Ovid moves on to Numa, presented as a faithful disciple of Pythagoras himself. But what is the first act of Numa, king of Rome? "*Sacrificos docuit ritus*," "He taught the sacrificial rites," a first civilizing gesture. And indeed these rites were the strategy through which Numa "introduced the arts of peace to a population accustomed to the savagery of war." With this it might be said that Pythagoras's entire doctrine was canceled out by his disciple. There again, Ovid had already suggested this: the master's words had been wise, "*sed non et credita*," "but not believed."

If Lucretius objects to sacrifice, this is an inevitable consequence of his opposition to the Olympian system. But Ovid and Porphyry, each in their own way (Ovid in *Metamorphoses*, Porphyry in *On the Cave of the Nymphs*), celebrated the order of Zeus in its various forms. How could this be reconciled with the attempt to undermine it from within, declaring the impiety of sacrifice?

And Ovid, with his intrepid eye for detail, goes further, focusing on the culminating moment in the sacrificial act itself, seen from the victim's side: "*Victima labe carens et praestantissima forma / (nam placuisse nocet) vittis insignis et auro / sistitur ante aras auditque ignara precantem / imponique suae videt inter cornua fronti, / quas coluit, fruges percussaque sanguine cultros / inficit in liquida praevisos forsitan unda,*" "The victim, immaculate and of great beauty / (to be admired, indeed, has been its downfall), decorated with gold and with headbands / is led up to the altar, it listens to the prayer without understanding it, / it sees fruits placed between its horns from the soil / that it has cultivated and, once it is struck, with its blood / it stains the knives that it may once have seen plunged into clear water." In the *Iliad* one could read the description of the havoc caused to Achaean and Trojan warriors hacked to death, but never, prior to Ovid, had there been a description of what the sacrificial victim felt the moment before being slain.

Immolation is different from *killing.* Is it simply because someone (a priest, a person in power, an ordinary man) has declared it to be a sacrifice? The Romans, who were strict ritualists, didn't think like this. Immolation takes place when something has been sprinkled with *mola salsa,* a mixture of spelt flour and salt prepared exclusively by the college of Vestals. The *mola salsa* is sprinkled on the forehead of the victim, on the altar, and on the sacrificial knife. But why, without that mixture, was *immolation* not permitted? The custom and the prohibition were introduced by Numa, the only king of Rome who "spent most of his time celebrating rites and instructing priests." He was also on overly familiar terms with the divine, it was said, if it is true that Egeria, a nymph, wasn't just his advisor but his "spouse." Numa was an expert on sacrifices and secrets. He taught the Romans to worship a Muse "who was called Tacita, the silent or the mute."

Numa is claimed to have clarified directly with Zeus how expiatory sacrifices were to be celebrated. It was a story that dated back to the annalist Valerius Antias. Plutarch considered it to be "mythical and laughable." He nevertheless reported it, impeccable anthropologist that he was, because "it revealed the attitude of men of that time toward the divine." The same happened with Ovid in *Fasti*.

According to Ovid, Numa sought above all to "soften the Quirites [citizens of ancient Rome], too ready for war." To get them to abandon their "wildness," *feritas*, he persuaded them to pour libations sprinkled with *mola salsa*. Which was therefore an essential element of the sacrifice from the very beginning.

But Jupiter appeared one day with a terrifying sequence of thunderbolts. The people were in panic. The normal sacrifices were not enough. Jupiter himself had to be invoked. Numa then performed the first act of theurgy, even if the word didn't yet exist. A suitable place was needed to receive the deity: a clearing in a shady wood on the Aventine Hill. It required the assistance of two woodland gods, Faunus and Picus. Help that could not be obtained "without violence," *"sine vi"*—a lesson for all future theurgists. And finally Jupiter agreed to be *drawn down* from the sky. For this they called upon Elicius. When he trod the Aventine, the treetops shook and the ground began to quake. The dialogue that followed was a concentration of brutality and guile, a Roman version of the dialogue between Zeus and Prometheus at Sicyon, when Zeus allowed himself to be deceived. It needs to be followed as Ovid has related it. Numa asks for *"certa piamina fulminis,"* a safe way for warding off the lightning. Jupiter says: *"Caede caput,"* "Cut off a head." Numa plays dumb, mistaking *caput* with *cepa*, "onion." He promises that he'll cut the head of an onion. "Of a man," Jupiter explains, like a regular at a saloon bar. Numa pretends that Jupiter has asked him for a man's hair and not his head. Jupiter explains again and "at this point he demands the life." This is the crux: for the gods it is important to obtain *that which is living*. So sacrifice has to take away human life. It couldn't be clearer. But Numa is obstinate. He now pretends that Jupiter has been talking about fish. At this point the tension is broken. Jupiter *laughs*. He has appreciated the comedy of that "man not ill-equipped at conversing with a god." And also capable of averting a human sacrifice.

In history, it wasn't so easy, nor so rapid. Human sacrifices had been abolished by senate decree only ninety-seven years before the birth of Christ. Had Roman senators been thinking about something mythical or legendary? No. They were sober, hard and pragmatic. They didn't use senate decrees to recount fairy tales. They remembered that little over a century before, "in obedience to oracular commands of the Sibylline books, two Greeks, a man and a woman, and two Gauls were buried alive in the Forum Boarium." That day, Jupiter had not laughed.

One day metamorphosis, which had been the everyday wonder, became an intermediate punishment between exile and death. It was Aphrodite who announced it: "*Siquid medium est mortisque fugaeque / idque quid esse potest, nisi versae poena figurae?*" "If there is something between death and exile / what else could it be if not the punishment of changing aspect?" At the end of his life, Ovid became one of his own characters.

For Pausanias, a century after Christ, it still seemed perfectly obvious that there had been an *age of metamorphosis*. And never did he speak so clearly about it as in his book on Arcadia: "People at that time were guests and table companions of the gods by reason of their justness and devotion. The good were openly honored by the gods and the unjust suffered their wrath with equal force. It then also happened that certain humans became gods, those who still retain this gift today, such as Aristaeus or Britomartis the Cretan girl, or Heracles son of Alcmene, or Amphiaraus son of Oecles, and also Castor and Pollux. So it was also credible that Lycaon was transformed into a wild beast and that Niobe, daughter of Tantalus, became a stone. Today, however, when wickedness has reached such a peak and has spread over the whole land and all the cities, a man no longer becomes a god, except in words of flattery toward the man of power, and the wrath of the gods is held in abeyance until the unjust have left the world."

During the reign of metamorphosis people became what they were. And the change could be seen as plausible. Whereas later an opaque veil spread gradually across the world. There was a collapse in every visible relationship between what people were and how they appeared. Punishments were postponed to another world. And there was no longer any hope of being "guests" of the gods. All of the stories about wonders could only sound dubious. And all that remained was a trace—a ludicrous trace—of that other age, when men in power were flattered by those who treated them as divine beings. A sad farce, which no one believed. Neither those in power, nor their flatterers.

Poros, whose name means Passage, was the son of Metis, Wisdom, first lover of Zeus and swallowed up by him. Dionysus didn't yet exist, wine was unknown. The gods got drunk on nectar. Penia, Poverty, appeared dressed in rags. She was continually roaming about at the celebration. Poros moved away from the group. Like a sleepwalker, he went into Zeus's garden and stretched out on the soft grass. Penia followed him and stretched out beside him. Poros felt Penia's hand and the outline of her body. He turned onto her and penetrated her, in silence. This was how Eros was conceived. Poros continued dreaming, delirious. When he woke he was alone and had no clear recollection of the night, except for the sensation of something liquid, damp, that he had permeated.

"*Michtheîs' en philótēti*," "mixing in love": these are the words most frequently used in *Catalogue of Women* to describe sexual intercourse. Used above all for Zeus. Two substances that mix together—and can be divine or human, but at the moment they come together they are no longer separate: Eros is this tendency to become lost, dissolved into a composite that did not previously exist.

In sexual love the body secretes those humors that are its sacrificial surplus. Saliva is the single element in which the two fundamental forms of sacrifice—expulsion and communion—converge.

Expelled, in sputum; assimilated to another kindred substance, in the kiss. "*Spuma fui*," says Aphrodite to Poseidon. To remind him that, if Poseidon is the sea wave, she is his foam. She could appeal to other relationships, but Aphrodite preferred to recall the moment when she had been joined to Poseidon in the same matter. The wave becomes foam in the same way that liquidity becomes sexual love. Matter suited to the physical metamorphosis of Ovid, more than the atomistic metamorphosis of Lucretius. There is an affinity in things, which supports their changes. Which are not just a gathering and dispersal of particles.

Strolling among blackberries, sunflowers, mulberries is already a strolling among stories. And, when night falls, the stories continue, among bats and overhanging rocks. Nature is not silent, but has been silenced. The precarious magic of the word is enough to revive those blackberries, those sunflowers, those mulberries, those bats. The poetic word, according to Ovid, "*exit in inmensum*," "expands into the immensity" and does not allow its way to be blocked by any "historical fidelity," "*historica fide*." It is hard to express it better—or more succinctly.

An old man was watching some seabirds in flight. He was resting on a beach. He saw a kingfisher and a coot flying and remembered who they had once been: Ceyx and Alcyone, faithful and desperate spouses, now reunited in their existence as birds. But another old man approached and pointed to another bird skimming across the waves. It was a merganser—and had once been Aesacus, Priam's wild son. Ceyx and Alcyone had lived in Thessaly, Aesacus in Phrygia. Distant lands, separated by a vast sea. And they had lived in different periods. One day they came across each other as birds, watched by an old man, on an unknown beach. They were the last witnesses of the age of metamorphosis.

VIII

NOCTURNAL COUNCIL

Having already reached seventy, the age at which—according to the rules he himself had set—he could no longer be one of the "guardians of the laws," Plato writes his *Laws*, the most ponderous, exhausting, and prolix of his dialogues, in one last, anxious attempt to lay down *in writing* how a just society should be, after he had made three failed attempts, in Syracuse, to put this into practice. And he abandons the picture of the just society he had outlined in the *Republic*. Now, oppressed by what he sees around him, he will have to make do with another model, "second in value," watered down and reduced. But he is still determined to outline it.

The opening is abrupt. The speaker is an old nameless Athenian, whereas in the *Republic* it was Socrates who held the reins. The setting is Crete, considered by Greece to be where everything began. His interlocutors: two other old men, a Cretan (Clinias) and a Spartan (Megillos), on the road from Knossos to the cave where Zeus was born. The first word is *theós*, "god." It is the start of a question that, for Plato, is *the* question: "O strangers, is it a god or someone among men who was at the origin of the institution of laws?" Words from which we can grasp the main purpose of the *Laws*: to answer an urgent and pressing question: can it still be claimed that *tò theîon*, "the divine," permeates and infuses the laws to which men submit? Or do such laws merely reflect the changeable whim of men, who think the gods themselves are the product of their volatile arbitrary will? A question that is much like another: does the divine exist in itself? We can already deduce from this that the *Laws*, unlike the *Republic*, is not a bold proposition for a new social system, but a last defense, in the face of a world willing and prepared to carry on without the divine. Plato is making a final plea, and a desperate one, since—as Clinias observes—"the part that persuasion can play in such matters is fairly small." And the Athenian, the counterpart of Plato himself, reiterates: "If the theories of which we speak [of those who claim to be wholly born "not through any god or art, but . . . from nature and from chance," a definition that would be perfectly suited to Darwinists] had not been, so to speak, widely disseminated among all men, there would have been no need to resort to theories that claim the gods exist; but now they are necessary [*nûn dè anánkē*]." With this reliance on a *necessity* Plato reveals his condition of self-defense. Having reached the moment to conclude the immense arc of his thought, he is compelled to go back to where he started: to state "that first of all the gods do exist," even if it is hard for this to occur without "resentment and rancour" toward those who make such a task necessary. And then there are—as will appear clear—the "*hoi polloí*," "the many," who attacked and overwhelmed Plato and his doctrine in a city that suffered "what many of the cities of today suffer." Now, for one last time, Plato would attempt to illustrate his doctrine, though in the most elementary and even more meticulous terms, along the interminable and unconcluded walk toward Zeus's cave.

The *Laws* is presented as a conversation among three old wise men who have abandoned all youthful intemperance. It proceeds cautiously, judiciously, and by slow progression. But, hidden among the folds of the text, like poisoned barbs, we find some of the most caustic and provocative statements that Plato ever wrote.

The Athenian has just stated that "human affairs are not worth being taken with much seriousness." And this itself is outrageous, seeing that the three friends are doing all they can to find the best form for what is eminently a *human affair*: society. How do we interpret these words, which erupt—quite unexpectedly—in the middle of detailed and instructive discussions in book seven of the *Laws*? It's as though the elderly Plato were being forced into something against his own nature—and from time to time could no longer keep up the pretense. He still had five books to write of what would be his final work, and which would turn out to be among the least loved and least read. More details, precepts, distinctions. A sense of futility, a dogged pursuit of his purpose. The just city, the just life, the just constitution, but knowing that nothing he evokes can be achieved. An immense sadness of exposition—together with the inability to accept defeat.

The Athenian will not give in: "What I mean is: there has to be a serious treatment of what is serious and not of what is not serious: now, by nature, the god is worthy of all the seriousness for which a blessed being is worthy, whereas man, as we have already said, was invented as a plaything for the god, and in truth this is the best that has happened to him." If man is a plaything, his highest aspiration can only be that of *taking part in a game*. And here Plato doesn't hold back: "This is the way of being that every man and every woman must pursue: playing the noblest of games, devised in a way contrary to those that are practiced today."

Men are not only "puppets," *thaúmata*—continues the Athenian—but the truth is accessible to him only in "minuscule fragments." This is too much. His old friend from Crete, Clinias, cannot stop himself: "Stranger, you are putting down the whole human race." But the Athenian apologizes and explains: "I have said what I have said because I saw and heard the god." The Athenian is worried and concerned not about man and his society but about "the god." This is the premise of the *Laws*: to build a bastion so that the god can be *seen and heard*. With Aristotle, one of Plato's last pupils, all of this was over. In his *Politics*, the god and the gods are spoken about because religion is a part of society, not because society must help in a perception of god. Since then, everything has remained in Aristotle's terms. The *Laws* is a *final* work for this reason as well.

A disruptive innovation introduced by the sophists in Athens was the idea of *nómos* as *convention*. And therefore as something extraneous to *phýsis* and independent of it. "Nature" was in danger for the first time of being subordinate to "*nómos týrannos*," the "tyrannical law" that Hippias referred to in *Protagoras*. At the same time, convention was declared indispensible for human life.

It was a shock that left nothing untouched, and Plato's work could be read as a prolonged response to that shock. But once convention—an active agent of *substitution*—was in circulation, it could no longer be banished from it. It had to be absorbed and controlled. A difficult task, since convention itself is the prime weapon for anyone wanting to take control, insofar as it presupposes arbitrary will. From the *Republic* and the *Laws* there was a long, grueling struggle that failed to reach a conclusive outcome. Interrupted, often resumed, the conflict between *nómos*-convention and *phýsis* (anything that is understood as "nature") would become persistent, in expectation of reaching further extremes, which still await us.

In the *Laws* Plato has the "penetrating gaze" of the old man, but also professes to play like an "old child," trying to say something ineluctable with the tone of a tractarian, abandoning the subtleties and whims of thought that usually abound in his work. It is a gesture of sad submission to common paths, whose purpose is to safeguard a few points that cannot be abandoned. And those points emerge every so often. Indeed, they converge on *one* point: *ho theós*, "the god." That which has to be safeguarded—and on which everything else depends—is the presence of the god. When this becomes explicit, there is a sudden jolt and the prose condenses into a sharp formulation: "The god for us is the measure of all things, supreme in rank and much greater than man, contrary to what some say." This "contrary to what some say" isn't referring just to Protagoras, who had proclaimed that man was the measure of everything, but to the whole world that surrounded Plato—and had already sometime earlier begun that long process that would make the active presence of a *theós* entirely superfluous. The *Laws* is a last attempt to hold back a rising and inundating tide.

It is no longer the time, says the Athenian, "of those ancient lawgivers who used to legislate, according to what we are told today, for those sons of the gods who were the heroes, and being themselves born from the gods they established laws for others

who were like them, whereas today we are no more than men leg-
islating for others born from the seed of men." Harsh words. The
city he is describing is not much different from those that would
emerge thousands of years later. A secular city. But one that wants
to distinguish itself from every other city for one single feature: its
capacity to preserve, in unadulterated form, "the divine," *tò theîon*.
This, the Athenian suggests, is what we are reduced to. And this
was what he was stubbornly aiming for as the only salvation for
men born from the seed of men.

What Giorgio Pasquali wrote about the *Seventh Letter* is also
true of the *Laws*: "Difficulties also arise from the prolixity of style,
which can properly be attributed to his age without any irreverence to Plato. No one denies that this prose is austere and solemn,
nor that it abounds with audacities sometimes greater than in his
young writings. But certain thoughts and certain expressions return too often; and things are rarely said in the simplest and most
concrete way." We detect a disconsolate relinquishment of the
delicacy, the inventiveness, the imperative of form—and a steady
inclination toward a few points, which have to be safeguarded.
Safeguarded from what? From the whole of subsequent history.
Not just Syracuse but the whole world was getting out of control.

Having reached the moment to decide what governs events,
two paths open up: either to admit that "that which is mortal [*tò
thnētón*] acknowledges no law" and "all human affairs are chance
events [*týchas*]" or otherwise, the Athenian declares, to recognize
"that it is a god and, along with the god, fortune [*týchē*] and occasion [*kairós*], that govern all human affairs." With the addition, he
continues, of another element: "art," *téchnē*. This neat and memorable formulation would become famous. Stobaeus quotes it
three times. And, at first sight, this would seem to be the watershed. But there is a snag: the same word, *týchē*, is found on both
paths, once in the plural and once in the singular. If the god
excludes fortune, how can he coexist with it, how can he keep it

on his side, together with another elusive element: "occasion," *kairós*? And to what extent can human design, *téchnē*, intervene to correct the course of affairs? If Zeus feels subject only to *anánkē*, "necessity," which is an order superior even to divine order, *týchē* becomes more ambiguous: if it indicates a necessity, it doesn't guarantee an *ordered* necessity. *Týchē* could also merely produce an indefinite series of *týchai*, unpredictable "chance events"—and then one would end up on the first path, which ignores the law. In Plato, right to the end, there is a vagueness, a superimposition of hostile powers.

The role played by *téchnē* in the governing of affairs is explained immediately after—and once again with an unexpected twist. The example given is the art of a ship's pilot, who "provides help in the event of a tempest." The storm is the *kairós*, the "occasion" that manifests the *týchē*—and precedes every human intervention. But the pilot, if he knows his art, can respond to the tempest, can steer through it, can react to its force. The Athenian pauses at this point and asks: "Isn't this better than its opposite? Am I right?" A very swift passage, that almost prevents us from noticing the tremendous novelty of the theory: the only human intervention possible in the ordering of affairs—*téchnē*—would just be a way of conspiring with the "tempest" of the world, barely deflecting it.

Plato is worried about equality. On the one hand, many voting procedures presuppose it and enforce it; on the other, "for unequal beings equality would become inequality." A phrase that instantly presupposes the existence of beings who can be described as "unequal." It is followed by another consideration, where Plato seems to confirm his own doubts: "There is an old and true saying that equality generates friendship, a correct and harmonious formula; but what equality there is that can do such a thing is not absolutely clear and therefore absolutely torments us." That word *sphódra*, "absolutely," immediately repeated, is the indication of a profound difficulty. Plato wants the just constitution to be "a cross between the monarchic and the democratic constitution." And democracy cannot exist without the application of equality. But Plato also knows that equality doesn't exist naturally and can be imposed only by introducing a distortion. The *equality that generates friendship*, according to the Pythagorean saying, is only that which exists among initiates, insofar as they are participants in something that is essential, identical, and intangible. But initiates are also *ánisoi*, "unequal beings" par excellence, in comparison with the social body of the uninitiated. Democracy has an esoteric foundation, but degenerates as soon as it is transformed into an automatic procedure. Yet without automatic procedures there *is* no democracy. This conundrum still remains. Plato was just the first to point it out, almost unwillingly.

Who are the "unequal" ones? Certain people encountered while traveling: "There are always, among the masses, certain divinely inspired men—not many—with whom to establish relations at any cost; they are born in well-governed cities no more than in those that are not; their tracks should be followed by anyone who lives in well-governed cities, journeying by sea and by land, and, if he is not corrupt, you should investigate to strengthen that which is good in your own customs—or to correct that which is lacking in them. Without these observations and investigations no city will remain perfect, and not even if such observations are conducted badly."

Discussion about communism is futile unless we go back to Plato—and, once we have gone back to Plato, we need to follow his reasoning step by step. After a long and rambling "prelude," the Athenian had reached the point where he had to propose a *nómos*, a word that means "law" as well as a musical "mode"—and Plato played on this double meaning. The prelude had to be followed by a song. Starting from where? From the finest constitution, even if, to the "surprise" of the listener, it is immediately declared that, "apparently, on the basis of analogy and experience, a city can be established in a form that is second to best." A fragment of a phrase that passes unobserved, a perfect example of Plato's stylistic ploys, especially in the *Laws*, where he pretends to follow the line of a gradual discourse, but only to set off deadly salvos here and there. In just a few words, and somewhat to the surprise of his listeners, he states here that the best constitution can never be implemented. Why? The text does not explain, overcoming the obstacle in silence. What the lawmaker can propose is only that which is "second," less than the best. But how will the best be established? Here again, Platonic cunning intervenes. No declaration of principle or metaphysical elaboration. Only the reference to "an old saying," of Pythagorean mold: "It is said that things are truly shared among friends." To build the best city, the only thing necessary would be to implement those few words. With what outcome? The answer couldn't be more direct: "women shared, children shared, property shared." All this would be handed down to the humanitarian, popular communism of the nineteenth century. But Plato has something essential to add: it would be necessary for "everything that is the so-called private [*ídion*] to be totally expelled from life." Words in which the venom lurks in two points: above all in that "so-called" attributed to "private," as if the category itself were illusory; and in that ejection "from life," "*ek toû bíou*," which contains something cruel and irremediable. Indeed, every vision of society as *koinōnía*, as a "community" of different beings, leads straight to results so radical as to be unacceptable. What can be the importance of shared women, children, and property, apart from the perception, the judgment? Is it necessary to share even "the eyes and ears and hands," therefore the mind? But how can the justness of every detail of life (even the smallest) be established—in what the eyes see, moment for moment, or in what the ears hear? On this Plato has given no answer. He has not explained how it can happen, in fact he has excluded this possibility. But at the same time he has stated that it would be a good thing if it happened. Indeed, nothing would be "more just [*orthóteron*] and better." It's a noose from which it would be hard to escape. Plato doesn't want to give any further indications, but here he certainly clarifies why the *man of metamorphosis* is his prime enemy, since he is the one who not only doesn't banish any character but is able to pass from one character to another, like playing on different keyboards and finally returning to himself. According to Plato, the first of these men had been Homer.

The claim of shared interests, if it is to be rigorous, requires that society is a single mind, a superorganism—as ethologists would one day say—outstanding examples of which are to be found in societies of insects. And this for Plato would be the ideal model for whatever constitution. But can Plato possibly be so naïve or so fanatical? Certainly not—and he immediately confirms this. Such a society, he states immediately and concisely, is conceivable only for "gods or children of gods." Plato's guile becomes apparent here: that hideous image of society, even if unworkable, is to be thought of as the best, to be approximated as much as possible.

This passage of the *Laws* should be read alongside another passage that Plato had written in the *Republic*. The transformation of society into a single sensorial and desiring apparatus, into a single mind that moves first in one direction and then in another, is not the improbable, unattainable result of a certain constitution. It is indeed what naturally happens in a society when the *hoi polloí*, "the many," gather together and become a single body producing opinions. *Dóxai*, "opinions," is the key word. Once this process is complete and society has become a single "big animal," another character will immediately appear, as in a circus: the tamer, capable of making the "big animal" do whatever he wishes it to do. This tamer, according to Plato, is the sophist, described as someone "who doesn't really know what is beautiful or ugly, good or bad, just or unjust among these opinions and these desires, but applies these terms according to the opinions of the big animal."

There is an obvious resemblance between the two situations, one that is perfect and unattainable, where society becomes a single mind and a single sensory apparatus, and the other that sees the spontaneous emergence of the "big animal," which the sophists-tamers carefully train and steer at every movement. The two pictures can be easily superimposed. Just one difference remains: in the first case—the perfect society—people don't seem able to adapt to the model, which applies instead to "gods and children of gods" (and the children of gods have all disappeared with the end of the age of heroes); in the other case—the "big animal"—there is an automatic process that begins whenever "the many" gather together: a process that is therefore inevitable in *any* society that has a minimum of cohesion. From which it follows that while the greatest evil inevitably happens in a society, the greatest good is something that a society cannot manage to achieve. But the deep malevolence of that-which-is ensures that those two images—of the worst and the best—are terrifyingly close.

The prime enemy, according to Plato the teacher, is "private and domestic" life. People do things inside their homes which escape the attention of the lawmaker: "many and trivial and invisible to all." These vary, according to "the suffering or the pleasure" of the individuals. "So trivial and so frequent" that it would not be "decent" to punish them by law. What should be done, then? "To remain silent about them is impossible" in the view of the legislator. And we feel the pain of recognizing that a vast, formless part of life escapes the law. To such an extent that heavy words toll out: those continual and minor infringements that take place "in the dark" contribute toward "damaging the written laws."

From Plato to the French Revolution, the original defect of all legislation that claims to be perfect is that of seeking to make citizens "as happy as possible" (as is stated in the *Laws*). Collective happiness corrupts thought. It will be enough then for the man from underground to object, through Dostoyevsky, that he *doesn't* want happiness for the whole social edifice to collapse. Indeed, for it to reveal itself as a powerful machine for producing, among other things, unhappiness.

Even media theory and ideas about entertainment as a dominant social category had already found a name and curt judgment
in Plato: "A musical aristocracy was replaced by an unfortunate
theatrocracy." As Plato has coined the word *theatrokratía* immediately after having stated that there were "two mothers of
constitutions"—monarchy and democracy, one exemplified ideally
by Persia and the other by Athens—this implies that *theatrocracy*
can be given a place between them as a third fundamental type of
regime. This doesn't in fact relate to a simple shift in the way the
audience behaved at musical entertainments, suddenly "eloquently
silent as it was, and convinced it knew the difference between the
good and bad in music." If this change were confined to music,
Plato observes, "it would not have been such a big thing." But this
was just the first stage of a complete upheaval: "What began at that
time among us in music was the opinion that everyone knew about
everything." And the consequences were those of "corrupt impudence," enemy of all "justness," not only in music.

The novelty here lies not so much in the warning against excesses of liberty—present throughout Plato—as in having identified the *theatergoing public* as the driving force behind an upheaval
so drastic as to constitute in itself a new form of regime. It is the
realm of opinion whose genesis is stated here for the first time. For
Plato, it is the regime suited to those who are unsuited to philosophy, beings "painted with opinions, like those whose bodies are
tanned by the sun." It is the realm of *dóxa*, already then perfectly
defined. At that point Plato places it alongside the two fundamental forms of constitution. Present-day sociologists, as well as fierce
"critics of culture" of the Frankfurt mold or impenitent enemies of
the "system," cannot claim to be moving on unexplored ground.
Old Plato, in his *Laws*, had already described the main features of
what they are talking about.

A word that obsesses Plato is *orthótēs*, "justness," applicable to
sounds, to words, to thoughts, to desires, to whatever aspect of life.
A word that is always under threat, avoided, scorned. But in the

Laws, Plato obstinately returns to it, trying to find it—and to impose it—in every aspect of ordinary life. Sometimes a sober exasperation becomes apparent: "To deprecate an irremediable state of affairs, where error has been pushed so far, is not a pleasant task at all, though necessary."

But *orthótēs* mustn't be interpreted as probity and rectitude, almost as if behind it we might glimpse the cane of a metaphysical schoolmaster. To understand it, we have to start off from the opposite extreme, from *manía*, that multiform "madness" presented in *Phaedrus* as the very basis of knowledge. And here we encounter Plato's style at its boldest and most arrogant. Here we read these shrill words: "People of today, who have no sense of beauty." Plato's art of concealing the most cutting phrases in the flow of conversation reaches its peak in *Phaedrus*. The dialogue form serves for this too. But what is the context? Fairly abrasive. Socrates is broaching a delicate point: "The men of old who invented names regarded madness as neither evil nor disgraceful. Otherwise they wouldn't have attached this word to the noblest art, divination." So "madness" and "divination" were originally close and akin to each other in *manía*. At this point the moderns turn up, lacking any sense of beauty, and they wrongly insert a *tau*. So that a new word, *mantikḗ*, is formed, which must be kept well apart from "madness." When it comes to etymologies, whether true or false, we know from *Cratylus* that Plato's irony runs wild. The same happens here, at the beginning of the most paradoxical passage, in which Socrates talks about "raving correctly," "*orthôs maínesthai*." And this is the original form of *orthótēs*.

Once the Athenian had dwelt firmly on *orthótēs*, on "justness," which has to be found and applied in every circumstance of life, the time had come to ask: "What therefore is justness?" The answer is clear—and comes as no little surprise: "We should spend our lives playing such games as sacrifices, singing, dancing, that allow us to gain the favor of the gods, fend off our enemies, and win in battle." Playing is the height of seriousness and everything else is dependent on it, even the protection of the city against its enemies. This is already far removed from every moralizing stricture. The Athenian wants men to be playthings who are conscious of being so. If this were the case, their playing would become something extraneous to the game: it would become practical, indeed highly useful, because it would incline the gods to protect society from its enemies. A very bold theory that was never applied, and maybe it was impossible to apply it. But the Athenian wedges it at the center of his pragmatic reasoning. And it is a wedge that threatens the stability of the whole edifice—and eventually allows it to collapse. There's a strong suspicion that this is precisely what the Athenian wanted.

Anyone who has visited Delphi or Olympia, or the Heraion of Argus or the temple at Bassae, or Epidaurus or Dion, or Troezen or Messene, or the sanctuary of Perachora or Dodona, or countless other Greek sites furrowed by ruins, knows that there is an inextricable nexus between a place and its buildings. At first it is the place—intact—and it seems to contain within it all that would be added: human intervention, construction. We might ask how this was formulated in the mind of the Greeks. The Athenian speaker in the *Laws*, having listed in minute detail the correct divisions of the territory into equivalent parts, ends with an observation that thwarts his previous arguments: "With regard to places, we mustn't fall into the error of thinking that there are not those which are more suited to making men better or less good." Why? Obviously for reasons of climate, for plenty or lack of water, for exposure to the winds. But not only this. There's another reason, which he adds at the end. Certain places, says the Athenian, have a "divine breath," "*theía epípnoia*"—and this distinguishes them from all others. And it is the point to which the legislator must devote his whole attention. The rest follows from it. As proof of this, over the centuries buildings have been ravaged by fire, demolished, laid to waste. But the "divine breath" of places has remained.

Not only can places have—or not have—"a certain divine

breath." But they can also be the "haunts of demons," "*daimónōn léxeis*," in the sense that *daímones*—numberless powers and presences—can live there. And as a result they "receive with favor or disfavor the colonies that succeed them." The world is never uninhabited, it is never a *tabula rasa* on which to arrange inhabitants with sovereign whim. First and foremost, we are all the guests of someone. To ignore this can only bring disaster. The Athenian wanted to recall this, at the end of a long peroration on the perfect city, which he was the first to consider unachievable.

What, asked the Athenian, are the "biggest" questions. "To think rightly [*orthôs*] on the gods and to live well [*zên kalôs*]." Once again, *kalós* is the key word. If life is not swathed in beauty, which is after all the first meaning of *kalós*, it has no hope of being the "biggest" question. Here it is not just Plato who is speaking. The whole of Greece is included in that formula, which had not been applied elsewhere, and would not be repeated after.

What is the purpose of listing in meticulous detail the *purifications* connected to every sort of crime and transgression, if "broadly spread teachings" declare that people can manage without the gods, since they don't exist? And, if the gods don't exist, to whom will the purifications be dedicated? The Athenian becomes impatient: how can we, "without a certain irritation, prove that the gods exist?" But ready to undertake every thankless task, he prepares himself even for this. Above all because he wants to go back to the "spring" from which all those "researchers of nature" who "have not reasoned well but have erred" have drunk. And what is the object of their error? The soul, the belief that the soul comes "after" the elements, as their epiphenomenon. A doctrine in line with the opinion that prevails, more than two thousand years later, in the scientific community. Even though, instead of soul, people today talk about *mind*. It's enough, however, to replace "soul" with "mind"—and the doctrine remains unchanged. Plato had done something similar, but in the opposite direction.

For the Athenian, the essential point is to recognize that the invisible—the soul—envelops the visible and goes before it. For "the soul is older than the body" and consequently all its assertions come before "heaviness, lightness, hardness, softness." All would seem to be resolved by putting the soul in first place. But the situation becomes more complex: "One single soul or several? Several, I will answer for you. Anyhow, let us assume no less than two, the soul that acts well and the soul that does the opposite." This splitting of the soul is surprising, but Clinias the Cretan agrees, as though it were obvious. And there is another surprise: the Athenian explains that the soul "combines with the mind [noûs] . . . educates [paidagōgeî] all things guiding them toward what is right and happy."

The two companions follow without seeking explanations. But, from the moment when "mind" appeared, the whole argument changes direction. A wonderful correspondence between world and mind is now described: "If the whole course and translation of the sky and all that it contains are of a similar nature to the movement and the circulation and reasoning of the mind and proceed in congenial harmony, then it must be said that the best soul regulates the whole universe and guides it along that same path." This leads to the amazing parallel being made between reasoning (including mathematical calculation) and the outside world. An amazement that will be repeated among various scientists over subsequent millennia. But it is discovered, to further amazement, that this movement of noûs can also be "mad and irregular": evidently the work of what the Athenian has just termed ánoia, an anti-mind that produces "the opposite of good."

But will the movement be guided by the noûs itself or by the psyché? Here, as elsewhere in Plato, the question remains unanswered. The Athenian has not offered a demonstration but a revelation. At the end of which he abruptly sets out something akin to a credo. But expressed in question form: "Since a soul or several souls are the manifest cause of all this, and are good inasmuch as they have every virtue, shall we say that they are gods, that finding them in bodies, like living beings, they give order to all the heavens, and that they act in whatever other way? And shall there be someone, once this is recognized, who will continue to claim that all things are not full of gods?"

The Athenian knew that those who are pure and rigorous deniers of the gods are not so numerous. Indeed he had to admit, grudgingly, that some of them are "of naturally just character." It was far easier to find those who claimed to have some acquaintance with the gods but were convinced the gods had no interest in human matters. Otherwise—they said—there could be no explanation for why wickedness is so often rewarded and virtue punished. The Athenian vented his annoyance on these people as well. To imagine that the gods neglect small things is, for him, no less impious than denying the gods themselves. Attributing negligence to the gods is like denying their nature, which is to watch over everything. Aren't the gods "the greatest of all guardians"? The answer, on this point, was inflexible: "It would not be difficult to prove to anyone who thinks this that the gods care about small things not less, but more, than about great things." Nothing is too small for a god.

But there was one last category of impious people, of the most despicable kind: those who believe they can gain favors from the gods, as though the gods were corruptible officials. And here once again the Athenian showed his intolerance of all that is private: small domestic sanctuaries, solitary sacrifices, secret invocations. The hidden life of Athens that was now brought into the open. And roundly condemned, not so much as a laughable pretension to corrupt the gods, but because it was hidden, the work of men and women ready to fall into the snare of "concocters of private initiation rites." And here, against a scene teeming with soothsayers and witches, emerges yet another figure, the memory of whom is even more potent: Alcibiades, who himself had been accused of celebrating initiation rituals *in private houses.*

The "guardian," as propounded and portrayed by Plato, is the closest the West has come to the concept of the Vedic ṛṣi. And just as the Saptarṣis watch over the earth from the stars of the Bear, so the guardians of the city, "equipped with a keenness in every part of their souls, will go around observing every part of the city, transmitting to memory all they have seen and telling the elders about all that happens in the city." But if this is what "young guardians" do with such inquisitorial scruple, what will happen with the elders? Plato's *Laws* is the point of contact between the Vedic ṛṣis and Bentham's Panopticon. The guardians mustn't miss a thing: "In each person's last moments a guardian of the laws should take charge." Ordinary inhabitants of the *pólis* should resign themselves to not being able to die *alone.*

The Nocturnal Council is the supreme institution evoked in the *Laws.* How does it operate? This is already explained in its description: "Council of those who superintend [*epopteuóntōn*] the laws." To superintend, to oversee: this is how *epopteúein*, the verb used by Plato, is normally translated. Enough to liken the Nocturnal Council to the *Aufsichtsrat* in German company law. But Plato's word also implies another: the verb corresponding to *epopteía*, "vision," which is the highest grade of initiation in Eleusis. The members of the Nocturnal Council had to contemplate just as much as oversee. That was the supreme grade of political vigilance.

The Athenian's secret aim is perfect wakefulness. Only continual wakefulness guarantees control. And it is at nighttime that differences become apparent. Just beings remain awake. This is also why there is nothing higher than the Nocturnal Council. Only by staying awake at night can "a large part of political and domestic affairs be done." And so "the time spent awake must be maximum," with a minimum of sleep "for bodies and for souls." These seem to be instructions for everyday life, but here the Athenian's ultimate purpose is revealed. The ideal city doesn't sleep and lets nothing escape its round of surveillance, which is protective as well as enlightened: "The leaders who keep watch at night are a terror to evildoers, whether enemies or citizens, and are respectful and admired by the just and the temperate, useful for them and for the whole city." Their precedent is to be found among the great predators, which operate only at night and surprise their sleeping prey. But the Guardians remain immobile. They sharpen their vision and awareness, while for the others it becomes clouded. And yet the affinity with predators remains. The Nocturnal Council will never be simply benevolent.

But it would be naïve to think of the Nocturnal Council as a sort of special police corps. Looming behind the variegated forms of life in society there had to be another form of ulterior thought, removed from appearance and yet which governed appearance. The guardians that make up the Nocturnal Council are those philosophers who are also empowered to act: to act from a point of invisibility, and to act invisibly. Plato tried in vain to convey all of this at Syracuse.

How many festivities will there be, each year? The Athenian answers: three hundred and sixty-five, "without exception, in such a way that there is always some authority who sacrifices to one of the gods or demon gods on behalf of the city and its inhabitants and its property." The celebration is perennial—and there is no celebration without a sacrifice. The law contents itself with establishing one for each month, dedicated to each of the Twelve. Otherwise, it will be for "the exegetes and priests with the priestesses and soothsayers to assemble with the guardians of the laws to establish the order of what the legislator has necessarily not specified." Therefore hundreds of festivals and sacrifices to various gods and demons. The guardians decide this too.

Social control, much idolized by the powerful figures of the twentieth century and injected into the physiognomy of the twenty-first century, was already a practice that Plato considered desirable and had organized in every detail.

For society to be superimposed on nature and acquire a sort of second naturalness—an overweening stratagem—it had to function with a regularity comparable to that of nature itself. And this can be achieved only by introducing a new and fateful factor: control. Here, too, Plato displayed no reticence—and his formulation would serve as a model for the social engineers of Soviet Russia or the China of Mao Zedong and his successors. "Now that the whole city and the whole territory have been divided into twelve parts, shouldn't perhaps the roads of the city itself, the houses, the public buildings, the ports, the market, the fountains, and above all the sacred precincts, the sanctuaries and other places of the same kind, have their own specially appointed superintendents?"

The Athenian sought above all to give practical instructions. Unambiguous, if possible, and easily applicable. And so, if imitation was—as it seemed—the source of all evil (and of all good), then it was important to ensure no one was tempted to use it wrongly. Men tend to imitate "the gods and the children of gods," but if it is said, in the stories handed down about them, that they had employed "fraud and violence," then anyone would have felt justified in repeating such deeds. Yet who had put such stories into circulation? "Poets" and "certain mythologists." Here, poets and mythologists are coupled together for the first time without any clear distinction, as "deceivers." But the Athenian breaks off the discourse: "The lawgiver knows more, as is right, than all poets put together." In one fell swoop, these few brutal and hurried words summarize and clinch the ancient dispute between poetry and philosophy that had been developed with an abundance of arguments and distinctions in the *Republic*. It is as though, having reached a point where action now mattered more than reasoning, the Athenian was assuming the task of putting into action, with a few summary words of justification, what had been concluded in the *Republic*. But this happened to be occurring at the very moment when any prospect of practical action was proving vain. The figure of Philip of Macedonia was about to appear. And, behind him, Alexander. It was only a matter of a few years.

It is not only music—and changes in music—whose consequences reverberate on the whole of society. Ancient China took much the same view. But Plato also adds "games" (primarily those for children), as "material of supreme importance for those who lay down the laws." It is crucial that the games are always the same and that "there is enjoyment in the same entertainments." Indeed, if some change is made to the games, or even just to the "shapes and colors" that children like, then everything else will be affected. In fact, "there will be no greater ruin for the city." A further effect—and here he reaches a delicate point: "It will despise what is old, it will value what is new." The starting point must be games, those games that for children are partly "innate," *autophyeîs*, and are partly "discovered when they play together." Only in this way will proper order be established. One doesn't start off from work to arrive at play as its epiphenomenon, but the other way around. Likewise one doesn't start off from war to understand athletics. Because "athletic activities are useful both for peace and war, both for public and private life, whereas all other physical labors, whether done for fun or seriously, are unworthy of a free man."

According to Plato, the great ascendancy the Egyptians had over the whole of Greece depended primarily on one major principle: to eradicate the new at all cost. In what way? By attaching "every dance and every song" to the sacred. By "consecrating" music, "preordaining feasts," the sequence of hymns and dances. "Anyone who presents other hymns and other dances for celebrating certain gods would be banished by the law-guardians along with the priests and priestesses." This is the closest approximation in history to a perfect world.

The Athenian declares all this in a confident tone. But then he stops, becomes suddenly cautious ("since we have reached this point of the discussion, let us yield to what is convenient for ourselves"). What is the doubt? Certainly, there might be a temptation to transport the Egyptian principle to Athens: "But how could one legislate on such things without becoming totally ridiculous?" It is the fear of ridicule that blocks the discussion. Athens has now rushed ahead. Egyptian fixity is useless. The Athenian knew it. He sometimes allowed his secret thoughts to slip out, then took a few steps back to look for some adjustment, some compromise. He was thinking about his own city, so fierce in deriding people.

The dances the Athenian allows in his city are those of a warlike and a peaceable kind (or simply "unwarlike," *apólemoi*, since peace is evidently more difficult to define, compared with war). But there is also a third kind, which spoils the order: they are dances connected to nymphs, pans, satyrs, and silenoi to celebrate "certain purifications and initiations." "This kind of dancing is not suitable for citizens." "*Ouk ésti politikón*," "it is not political," and so it is "better to leave it alone."

As always in the *Laws*, it is in the nooks and crannies of the more detailed prescriptions that we find the underlying ideas: here we realize that something is slipping away from social order and tends to disturb it. These are certain "purifications and initiations"—and the dances that accompany them. Better to leave them where they are, in the forests, with the nymphs and the silenoi. Let the city be content to celebrate its wars and its peace. But it has to be assured above all that "all is set in order, and thereafter no further change is made either in dancing or in singing." Change is banned: "Thus, by dedicating itself to the same pleasures, the city itself and its citizens will remain, so far as possible, just the same and will live well and happily."

The demand for immutability is found in all the Athenian's arguments. But here another element no less significant emerges:

the dances connected to "purifications and initiations" are to be banned, even if they are part of the worship of "gods and children of gods." The rules of society and the rules of initiation clearly do not overlap and do not coincide. Initiation *is not political*, the Athenian would say. Society can only therefore claim to be immutable if it distances itself from what pertains to initiation. It is a crucial point, on which much of the construction set out above depends.

Tragedy is also banned from the city, in the same way as initiations. The scene is described by the Athenian: one day the authors of tragedies arrive at the new city, and ask to be allowed in. What answer should be given to these "divine men"? The Athenian suggests these firm and courteous words: "Excellent strangers, we ourselves are authors, to the best of our ability, of the most beautiful, the best tragedies; our whole constitution indeed is an imitation of the most beautiful and best life, and we believe this to be the truest tragedy." A supremely arrogant reply with a hint of humor. The authors of tragedies, whether they be Aeschylus or Sophocles or the ill-reputed Euripides, are refused entry because their art is already applied by the constitution of the city. Which turns out to be an "imitation of the most beautiful and best life." Wasn't this perhaps the intention of tragedy? Certainly not, if we look at its history. But the Athenian utterly ignores this. And above all he doesn't want to allow a traveling company to "set up its stage in the central square" and bring in its "fine-voiced actors." The constitution of the city is already a work of art in itself. It is, indeed, *the* work of art, which makes all other art superfluous. How, in fact, can that "imitation of what is the most beautiful and best" be equaled? And what other purpose could art have, even when practiced by those "divine men" who write tragedies? Unperturbed, the Athenian rejects the evidence.

Euripides, "son of the woman who sold vegetables," hadn't been forgiven for introducing "everyday things" into tragedy.

So he had become "the scourge of families." The voice here is that of Aristophanes. Behind the sexual farce, handled with impassive confidence, loomed the old metaphysical torment: *mímēsis*. Aristophanes invokes it immediately through the mouth of the tragedian Agathon, who appears smooth and perfumed as a courtesan: "When writing dramas about women, / one must partake of those manners in one's own body."

Words to which Aristophanes, the wise literary critic, provides an immediate reply: "So, when you are composing a *Phaedra*, you go about wiggling your ass." This ribaldry sums up the literary theory contained in *Women at the Thesmophoria*. Aristophanes suggests that Euripides is not to be condemned for speaking ill of women. In fact, the mischief committed by women every day is far worse than that presented in his tragedies. Euripides is to be condemned for speaking too much about women, something inevitable for one whose aim is to describe everyday life. And those who talk constantly of women end up resembling them, as is shown by the case of Agathon, but also by those more distant and insidious instances of poets such as Anacreon, Ibycus, Alcaeus, who were inclined toward Ionic voluptuousness. Imitation is implicit in storytelling. And imitation is the harbinger of metamorphosis. And therefore of the ill that has to be avoided. Aristophanes's attack would be continued with Plato.

"The tribe of poets cannot adequately recognize things that are good and those that are not." Once again the Athenian is saying something most revealing, though hidden among a list of what to do and not to do. What is stated here, in just a few words, is something that Plato hadn't dared say so clearly even in the *Republic*: the "tribe of poets" is simply not capable of distinguishing good from evil. And is to be treated therefore with suspicion and caution. The notion that art generally lies *beyond* good and evil is now presented as a simple affirmation from which the appropriate consequences are to be drawn. The "age-old quarrel between poetry and philosophy" is founded in ethics: poetry can only pursue its own ends, following a feckless impulse. It cannot therefore be confined within that *orthótēs*, "justness," to which Plato directed his every thought. Nevertheless it continued to operate: Athenians imprisoned in the quarries of Syracuse eased their suffering by reciting passages of Euripides that they knew by heart, in the same way that Andrei Sinyavsky repeated lines of Pushkin, or Józef Czapski reconstructed the plots of Proust for his companions in Gryazovets prison camp.

In the *Sophist*, the sophist is the one who can give an answer to everything. In the *Republic*, the poet is the one who can transform himself into everything. "Wondrous" beings, who yet have nothing "healthy" about them. Resembling the *góēs*, the "magician," more than the wise man. The shamanic legacy, the echo of the age of metamorphosis, can be gleaned in the poet. The sophist opens up the prospect of the future where someone—the politician—will have to give an answer to everything. And the politician can then only listen to the suggestions whispered by the sophist.

Why does the magistrate who oversees *paideía*, "education," need to know that "this is by far the most important among the highest appointments of the city"? Because "the first growth, if well started," gives a strong advantage to anyone wanting to achieve *télos*, "perfection," which, for the Greek and for Plato, is the essential requirement. In this there is no humanistic implication (in the modern sense of the word). The principle is applied to the whole of nature, to "all plants and domestic and wild animals and to humans." And here Plato proceeds with a marvelous *aside*: "Man, we affirm, is a domesticated animal, but if he has a just education and a happy nature he is wont to become the most divine and sweetest animal, whereas if not trained in an appropriate and fine way he becomes the most barbarous of those that dwell on earth." Events in life are decided for the most part by *paideía*. This is a useful sort of mechanism because, in the oscillation between the wild and the divine, which is generally inherent in man, the impulse toward the divine prevails. Nothing is said here about society and about the services that have to be rendered to it. When it comes to the ultimate choices, there are only two possibilities: man as the fiercest animal, and man as the most divine animal. Plato is, as always, inclined toward the prospects of *tò theîon*, "the divine." This was the purpose of education.

In a few lines, with extreme sobriety, the Athenian lists the paradoxes of sacrifice: on the one hand, he says, the custom of "sacrificing men" is something that still exists even in his time "in many cases"; on the other, he states that in the past "people didn't even dare to taste the flesh of oxen." And "no living creatures were sacrificed to the gods," but only sweets or fruits drenched with honey, to avoid "contaminating the altars of the gods with blood." On the one hand, human blood was the precondition for sacrifice; on the other, blood was generally regarded as a contaminant. And yet the same terms—*thýein*, *thýmata*—were applied to both practices. Sacrifice therefore managed to contain within itself the most radical contrasts. But this didn't worry the Athenian—and his interlocutor Clinias echoes him: "The matters you have related are much reported and to be believed."

Distinctions: the usual name for laws is *nómima*, "customs," "traditions." Plato states that they must not be described "either as laws [*nómous*], or as unutterable [*árrēta*]" (and *árrēta* is a term specific to the Mysteries). Why? Traditions are not unambiguously formulated laws, but a sort of pervading and protective membrane that allows laws to exist. Or rather, to use an alternative image, they are "buttresses" to the edifice of laws. If those buttresses were not there, the whole building would collapse. The *politeía* (what would one day be called "society") is made up of bonds, nexuses, links. Laws are one of these nexuses. But they in turn need to be supported by other "bonds." This is how ordinary life operates. The laws the Athenian attempts to formulate might be the visible and definable part, but certainly not the whole.

For him, there are two main difficulties. First of all, what matters is not the composition of a certain human type, but of "one who wants to become divine," *tò theîon* being a category that cannot be translated into any other, and is irreducible. There is then the reference to "unwritten laws," which means that the provisions of the written laws cannot be exhaustive, especially when it is added that unwritten laws are the "bonds of every constitution" and therefore the only forces that hold together the written laws. Which is the same as saying that the written laws are not self-sufficient nor self-supporting. Here the insuperable gap appears between the Platonic legislator and the moderns—even if, at the same time, Plato had prepared almost all of the contrivances that would later be used by the moderns.

Pindar sat on an iron chair, in his cell at the temple of Delphi, and there he sang his hymns to Apollo. Beside him, statues of the Moirai. "But in place of the third Moira are Zeus *Moiragétēs* and Apollo *Moiragétēs*." The cantor had before his eyes the image of the god and of destiny, together. The Moirai had once even fought beside Zeus against the serpent-footed Giants. But it wasn't always like this. Sometimes Zeus had to bow before them, like the time when his son Sarpedon had died.

Pindar had sung of the "*nómos basileús*," "the law that reigns over all, / over mortals and immortals, / and guides them with a supreme hand, justifying that which is most violent." But was that law the god or necessity—or both? According to Philemon, "men are slaves of kings; a king is a slave of the gods; a god is a slave of necessity." Zeus could guide the Moirai, like a caring father (Ate, akin to the Moirai, was his "eldest daughter"), but the Pythia would reply, as Herodotus records: "It is impossible even for the god to escape from the Moirai"—or "from *moira*," therefore from that "portion"which is destiny.

The divine system of the Greeks follows the rule by which, in the words of Simonides, "the gods do not fight against necessity." Zeus's arbitrary will recognizes and accepts only this limit. And on this tension everything is interwoven. A dramatic tension, for which Plato gives the driest and most memorable formulation by stating "how much difference there is in reality between the nature of necessity and that of good." In translating this fragment of a sentence, Simone Weil wrote in the margin: "Revelation," underlining the word three times. If one wishes to touch the true bedrock of Greece, this is it.

In the *Laws* this theme could hardly fail to emerge, like every other great Platonic theme. Once again, the style is colloquial, but the direction of thought is all the more clear. Necessity, says the Athenian, "cannot be repelled." Not even the gods fight against it (and here reference is made to the words of Simonides). But then, straightaway, comes the axis around which the *Laws* rotates: *tò theîon*, "the divine." It must indeed be understood "which of the necessities are divine": this power that eludes the gods and occasionally opposes them is itself *divine*. This is what most interests the Athenian: the necessity implied in world order must be well distinguished from "human necessities, as they are considered by many." Otherwise an unfortunate misunderstanding would arise. But there is also a double movement—by gods and by men—toward necessity. The "divine necessities" are defined by the fact that the god "cannot but apply them and generally learn from them, if he wants to be able to take serious care of mankind." From which it is inferred that the god wants to learn from necessity and must also "take serious care" of mankind: two principles that aren't at all obvious—and yet which the Athenian here presents as such. Men, however, have to *learn* from necessity if man wants "to become divine." There is a chiasmus, at the center of which necessity resides: something about it has to be learned if (in the case of men) one is to become divine or if (in the case of the gods) one is to act as such. Here again, what is presented in the *Republic* as an unresolved and perhaps irresolvable tension is absorbed into a word that pervades and includes everything: *the divine*. At the same time, it is stressed that "no god fights nor will ever fight" against necessity.

In ancient India, it was said that the world is made of fish that eat one another. "Fishes and beasts and winged beings / eat one another, because Justice [*Díkē*] is not with them; / but to men [Zeus] has given Justice, which is much the best." Everything changed when "the son of Cronos established this law [*nómos*] for men." This is what Hesiod said to Perses. Until such time as *nómos*—or *dharma*, in the Indian tradition—intervenes, mutual oppression is the rule, which reigns unopposed among animals. But is the *nómos* that intervenes between men something occasional, revocable, and superimposed upon nature—or does it also form part of necessity, in the same way that the animals that devour one another are obeying necessity?

Around the fifth century B.C.E., in Athens, the word *nómos* defined both the law that Pindar describes as "king of mortals and immortals" and the convention that dictates, through arbitrary will, the power of substitution. Two powerful and consequential conceptions, which until then had no prospect of coexisting in any other part of the world. And they were able to coexist only in the acutest conflict, which became the very stuff of Athenian history, between the Persian war and the battle of Chaeronea. It was *nómos* in the form of convention that won. As it would then win everywhere. And already when it had appeared, proclaimed by the sophists, it can be said to have won. But Pindar's "*nómos basileús*," like Heraclitus's "*theîos nómos*," "divine law," was not destined to die. Plato also represented the attempt to remain faithful to that vision, which was now cornered and wounded, close to its end, and almost desperate, and found its last variant in the *Laws*. And yet that vision would be found again, unscathed, in Plotinus.

"No pity is due to someone who suffers from hunger or anything else of that kind": no phrase by the Athenian more clearly illustrates the difference from what would be the Christian precept. Not so much for the crudeness of what is said, but for the explanation that immediately follows: pity is to be reserved for someone who, "by practicing temperance [*sōphronôn*] or some virtue or a share of some virtue, is nevertheless a victim of misfortune." The astounding novelty of Jesus is nonselective pity. Food or drink is given to anyone who is hungry or thirsty. Whereas the Athenian reveals here, with tough clarity, the punitive character of *areté*: no pity is to be given unless there is "some virtue or a share of some virtue" (the revealing feature is in the word *share*, as though the champion of *areté* is content with little, provided he can regard someone as his ally). But the emotional force is then lost—and pity becomes a sort of prize for those deserving it. Whereas Jesus will leave the door open to the unknown, without asking for any certificates of good conduct.

It is always useful to study the modulations of the Athenian, his often unexpected shifts from one theme to another. He has just finished talking about science, and the teaching of science, when the discussion turns to hunting. Why? For similarity. "Hunting and all that is connected to it must now be dealt with in a similar way." But the reason for the similarity is not explained. Certainly, like science, hunting is "a most complex matter." But what are its elements? A list follows, where the Athenian hides far more than he reveals. There is therefore the hunting of water animals, the hunting of birds, the hunting of mammals—or rather "of animals that walk," and these include bipeds: humans. "The hunting of men needs to be included, both in war and in the frequent search for friendship, which can be commendable or reproachable." The discourse is flat, didactic, apparently unremarkable. But here the Athenian has already introduced, as though by sleight of hand, a disturbing strand of thought: war is regarded as a variation on hunting; above all the manifold "search for friendship" appears as a further variant, the only one that can be described as "commendable or reproachable." In just a few lines, and unobtrusively, the Athenian has juxtaposed hunting with science, as if the hunting of hares were much closer to the doctrines on the "gods of the heavens"; he has included war in the much vaster category of hunting, as if there were no essential difference between killing enemies in battle and on a hunting expedition; lastly he has compared war with the "search for friendship," which in its various forms includes amorous courtship. From the sexual desire directed toward "loved ones," *erómenoi*, to war, to the hunting of hares, to the study of celestial bodies: one single strand links these activities. That of hunting. But the Athenian doesn't stop at such ventures, which might all be considered noble: hunting, he adds, also includes "theft, banditry, and group attacks." The category of hunting appears in the end as a true multiheaded monster. And, in resolute tone, it is stated that the legislator, in the face of such a tangle of forms, cannot impose "rules and punishments for all of these kinds," but "reproach or commend that which relates to hunting" according to whether or not it is appropriate to the labors and the occupations of the young. Far more fundamental than the individual legislative prescriptions, however, would be grouping together the hunting of animals, war, and erotic pursuits under one single word.

Plato never loses any opportunity to connect hunting to knowledge. Even those who are described as "land stewards or *kryptes*," a body of overseers who "must explore every territory, summer and winter, armed, to protect and investigate all places," will prepare themselves for these functions through hunting, practiced "not for the pleasure that is found in it but for the benefit to be gained from it."

The close connection between hunting and knowledge doesn't imply just a celebration of exploration and its adventures. At the end of the hunt there is always dead prey. It is not just the practice that matters, but the identification of something to hit. The final nexus is this: between knowledge and the act of hitting. This therefore prevents knowledge from leaving its object intact, as happens with contemplation. Or with mystical knowledge, described as *epopteía*, "vision," which can therefore be equated with the simple act of looking. There are two fundamental possibilities here: when *knowledge* is discussed, it has to be specified whether it is a knowledge that transfixes its object or simply looks at it.

"To define the sophist is certainly not the easiest thing," the Stranger (in the *Sophist*) says straightaway. It will be a "difficult and painful hunt" to search him out. But in what direction? Among hunters. And, of the many kinds of hunters, who will be closest to the sophist? Barb fishers. And not even those fishing with a trident, which strikes the prey in whatever parts of the body, but fishing with a hook, which wounds the prey "in some point of the head or mouth." The Athenian says about hunting what people would one day say about technology: that, depending on how it is used, "it improves the souls of the young" or else it can produce the contrary effect. The tight nexus between *hunting* and the *soul* is implicit. Those who choose a certain form of hunting are also shaping their soul in a certain direction.

The exceptions immediately follow: it is recommended to avoid—in this order—fishing in open sea or with a hook, "man-hunting by sea" (therefore piracy), as well as theft "in the country or the city." What remains? The hunting of quadrupeds, where the prey is eventually caught by men "with their own hands" if they are among "those who practice divine courage." These hunters are even described as "sacred." And are totally opposite to the "nocturnal" hunter, who operates only with nets and snares. For him the Athenian orders that "no one shall ever allow him to hunt anywhere." But why so many warnings and distinctions, when everything in the end focused on the hunting of quadrupeds that were not even so fearsome (big cats had abandoned Greece long before)? The Athenian must clearly have been thinking of other kinds of hunting.

The sophist is the hunter being hunted, forced into a corner by another hunter, who is Plato: "If the sophist . . . finds some hiding place in which to take cover, he has to be pursued step by step, relentlessly dividing into two every place that shelters him, until he is caught. In no way can he or anyone else boast of having escaped a search conducted so methodically and concertedly." It is the description of a cruel and persistent search, where *diairesis*, the incessant "division into two," is the most effective way of identifying and capturing the prey. *Diairesis* is that "method," *méthodos*, which is the search itself. And its result is not so different from that barb fishing with which sophistry had been equated from the beginning. Here again it was a matter of transfixing a prey "in some point of the head or mouth."

Having reached book eight, the three friends, on their walk toward the cave of Zeus, have to negotiate a particularly tedious and exhausting stretch. Through the Athenian, Plato wants to show that he is a practical man: he advises them not to move the stones marking the boundaries between properties and generally to keep out of extremely tiresome disputes between neighbors; he talks about wholesale and retail business; about importation and exportation (to keep both to the essential minimum); about the administration of water; about the arrangement of districts and individual houses. His comments each time are well argued and sensible. Unusual for one who, for a lifetime, had had extreme and disconcerting things to say. His patience remains unruffled. How can this insistence on even the most obvious detail be explained? There was in Plato an uncontainable desire for dominion and control, which constantly impinged on his thought. The notion that the sophist, the philosopher, and the politician were three faces of a single being was perhaps not a doctrine to be applied to the world, but certainly to Plato himself. The *Laws* is the demonstration and final admission of this, amounting almost to the subdued frenzy of an unappeased will.

The Athenian abhors retail trading. Not a matter for free men. A law should establish that "only a resident alien or a foreigner can engage in retail trade." The reasons for this revulsion are not explained. The only example offered is that of the innkeeper (equated once again with the retail trader) who extorts excessive sums from his guests. But fraud and deceit are also found in other activities.

Why then rage against retail trade as an "unseemly" activity? If trade has to be allowed, it will only be "out of strict necessity" and in any event only "the minimum number of traders" will be allowed. Even if, reluctantly, the "power of money" is recognized as being capable of creating an equilibrium in the distribution of goods. The real enemy that emerges behind the trader is trade itself, as if the Athenian were predicting that this unseemly and marginal activity, limited to those who are not completely free, might seep into the veins of the city, distorting its nature. And this is exactly what happened—and was already happening, though to a rudimentary degree compared with later developments. But unlike Aristotle, who wanted to deal with the subject, Plato stopped there at the threshold, with a gesture of refusal that pretends to have moral grounds, but is above all metaphysical.

Obsessed by completeness—and the need to pass judgment and apply justness to every aspect of life—the Athenian finds himself dealing with three knotty questions, which he joins together: the man who commits suicide, the animal that kills, and the object that kills.

In the case of suicide, he fails to indicate what "purifications," *katharmoí*, are required. "The god knows," he says, but he doesn't explain what he knows. And he advises relatives to go to the "exegetes" for instructions. It is the only case in which he avoids setting out his own rules. Though not where burial is concerned: "The tombs shall be isolated, with no neighbors, on the borders of the twelve districts, in places that are barren and have no name. They shall be buried without ceremony, without a stone and with no names to indicate what tombs they are." All the Athenian's roughness and severity is concentrated in these words.

He follows it by considering the case in which "an animal, of burden or other kind, kills a man." Here, too, "the relatives of the dead man shall prosecute the killer for murder." And the Athenian prescribes that the relatives appoint a jury of land stewards: "once convicted, the animal shall be killed and cast beyond the borders of the territory." But the frenzy of judgment doesn't stop here. There is still the case in which "something inanimate robs a man of his soul." With the exception of lightning or of "any other body sent from the god." But in other cases? Once again, the relative of the dead man "shall choose as a judge his first neighbor and so will purify himself and his whole family. As for the guilty object, it will be cast out beyond the borders, as is done with the animals." What then shall be cast out: trees broken by the wind, collapsed walls, fallen boulders? Beyond the borders, one wanders among silent tombs of suicides, carcasses of animals, and "guilty objects."

At this point the Athenian utters not a word about the oddity of the situation in which he has found himself. But he pauses for a moment, as if to banish some doubt. Indeed, the greatest of all doubts: why are laws necessary? To which he provides an immediate answer: "As a prelude to all these matters it must be said that men need to establish laws and live according to such laws, otherwise they would be in no way distinguishable from the most savage animals." Having seemingly forgotten that he had accepted at the beginning of his discourses that laws had been established "by the god," the Athenian now proposed a minimal theory that allowed him to support "order and law," "*táxin te kaì nómon*" (which would become *law and order*), as the ultimate defense in differentiating from the "most savage animals": such, in the end, was his lack of confidence in the ability of men to live together.

"Since we have agreed that heaven is full of many good things, but also of things of an opposite kind, though no louder, there is— we say—an immortal battle, which requires a wondrous vigilance, and we do battle having the gods and demons as allies, we who are property of the gods and demons."

It is the Athenian's practice from time to time to introduce the fragment of some esoteric meteorite into the middle of an otherwise smooth and gradual discourse, which is resumed immediately after those dazzling words without any explanation being given. They can indeed be presented as something implicit (here: "Since we have agreed that . . . ," even though there is no place where what follows has been agreed).

The *Laws* has an underlying bitter, desolate tone. It presupposes that the radical and rigorous action that Plato had long yearned for, which he had tried to put into effect three times at Syracuse and had proposed in the *Republic*, had turned out to be impracticable. Another, less exalting task remained: to attempt to limit, circumscribe, hold back—if at all possible—a new order of things that was being imposed, without having to declare it. A few years later, once the whirlwind of Alexander had gone, that new order would be established in Alexandrian form: unprincipled, multifaceted, parodic, pluralistic, easily understandable to someone born more than two thousand years later. With one single but notable difference: at that time the cults—the numerous cults—were still alive, even if they were becoming an increasingly private matter.

Plato didn't manage to give a definitive form to the *Laws*, but he appended a short and imposing epilogue: the *Epinomis*. While the last books of the *Laws* emit a sense of persistent gloom, the *Epinomis* resumes a superbly peremptory manner that is far more congenial to Plato. Such is the difference between the *Epinomis* and the *Laws* that many scholars argue that the text is apocryphal. Presumptuous philology. The same argument could be used to demonstrate the opposite, as if Plato had had a sudden burst of pride, which compelled him to return to the terms of his most hidden and unrenounceable doctrine, as in a farewell. The relationship between the *Epinomis* and the *Laws* is strongly reminiscent of that between the Upaniṣads with the Brāhmaṇas: a shift from expansive detail to aphoristic concision.

In Diogenes Laërtius, the *Epinomis* bears the subtitle "Nocturnal Council." It would be appropriate to follow this. The whole dialogue, indeed, is to be read as if Plato had finally decided to reveal some fragment of the founding doctrine of that enigmatic council. It begins abruptly: Clinias the Cretan tells the Athenian that the three friends had certainly managed so far to deal with "all that related to the institution of the laws." But in doing so they had overlooked "that which is most important to discover and say": what it means "for a mortal to be a wise man [sophós]." It is as though speaking about the ideal order of a society hampers, rather than helps, the discovery of what is wisdom. What was in danger of collapsing was the whole impressive edifice of the *Laws*. And here a crucial point was made: thinking is *not* a social virtue.

The Athenian replies, first of all, that the soul doesn't have a clear idea where to find wisdom, even if it has a vague notion that "it is part of its nature to possess wisdom." The *téchnai* will certainly be of no assistance: agriculture, hunting, the arts—none of these activities bring wisdom. And above all, "imitation does not bring wisdom in any way."

What remains, then? Number. "If we removed number from human nature, we could not achieve any thought." The outcome is immediate: "And so by necessity we must place number at the base of everything." The procedure is apodictic—and the Athenian warns that, if that necessity had to be justified step by step, "it would require a discourse even longer than all previous ones."

They are coming near, says Clinias, to "great discourses on great things." Yes, replies the Athenian—and "the most difficult thing is that they must be totally true." This is the sign that speech is crossing a threshold through which there is no return. Then Clinias, a perfect antiphon, invites the Athenian to pronounce "the fine words that come to mind about the gods and goddesses." For now it must be "the god himself [who] guides us." It is followed by a silent prayer by the three friends. After which the text has no more to do with the meticulous discourse of before, as though the Athenian now wanted to devote himself to what could only be overlooked by every theory of society. For it related not just to mankind but to the cosmos and that "single bond that naturally binds everything." A bond that could be recognized only through number. The most noble and hazardous task for thought was to establish what it comprised and how it was formed. Simone Weil described it succinctly in a letter to her brother, André: it was a matter of "establishing an identity of structure between the human mind and the universe." With a vibrant eloquence that had rarely emerged during his reasonings on society, the Athenian then launches into a phantasmagoria about the order revealed in the movement of the "divine race of the stars," which had first appeared in the enameled sky of Egypt. This passage, "a splendid page on the dance of the stars," according to Simone Weil, was also the variegated cladding of a number: $\sqrt{2}$, the ratio between the diagonal of the square and its side. A ratio that cannot be defined using a rational number. $\sqrt{2}$ was the number that marked the discovery of incommensurables. And Plato chose to devote several extremely complex lines to it at the end of the *Epinomis* (990c–991a), as though, before sealing up the vast structure of the *Laws*, he had wanted to inset a jagged diamond. For the incommensurable was none other than the *diabolus* or the *deus in Mathematica*. Or both. According to Iamblicus, the discovery of incommensurables "enraged the divinity." Its author "perished in the sea, like a criminal," because—as some used to say—"he had divulged the secret of the irrational and of the incommensurable." That discovery certainly appeared as an affront to reason, a scandal that has not since then abated, up until young Törless. According to Paolo Zellini, incommensurability "generates a confusion in science, toppling the idea of being able to control nature by resorting to whole numbers alone." According to André Weil, incommensurability was a "drama" and had consequently "marked the ruin of Pythagorism." His sister, Simone, replied that certainly there had been "a drama of incommensurables, and of immense significance." But she immediately added: "I think that this emotion was joy and not anguish . . . I think they were not astonished because there were relations that numbers could not define, but intensely happy to see that even that which is not

defined through numbers is yet always a relation." Perhaps that
was the wisdom the three friends had gone to look for. Or at least
this can be supposed from the final words of the *Epinomis*: "It will
be a thing most just [*orthótata*] if we make those who are part of
the Nocturnal Council refer to this wisdom, once we have duly
selected and evaluated them." Words that Plato set down in the
final sentence of what would be his final work.

IX

THE NIGHT OF THE HERMOCOPIDS

There is something infinite in this city: wherever we enter, we come across some traces of history

—CICERO, *On the Ends of Good and Evil*

Hermes, with pointed beard and erect penis, was present everywhere in the city. He was present at sacrifices and received trays of offerings. The vases show figures that talk to him, caress him, show him something, question him. A girl clasps his shoulder as she gazes into his eyes. A boy brushes the tip of his beard and has hung a light garland from his penis, as from a flagpole. There is familiarity, affection, playfulness toward such blocks of stone, no less than to certain animals—or to certain gods. Disfiguring herms, cutting off penises: gestures that struck at the most secret and yet the most conspicuous part of city life. One spring morning in 415 B.C.E., when Athenians woke and saw the havoc, they immediately realized the seriousness of what had taken place. It started a period of panic. Many didn't dare to go out for fear of being arrested. Many were condemned to death. Some fled. The lists of properties confiscated can still be read, carved on stelae.

Three and a half years after the night of the hermocopids, Aristophanes's *Lysistrata* was performed for the first time. At a certain point the leader of the chorus finds himself among a group of men with erect penises and says: "Be reasonable, cover yourselves with your cloaks, lest one of the *hermokopidai* see you." Scholars have reasonably inferred from these words that it was not just the faces of the herms that were disfigured that night. Their erect penises would also have been mutilated. With academic precision, Debra Hamel points out that the erections in the performance of *Lysistrata* were "not real, of course, but prosthetic."

According to Aristophanes's Lysistrata (and no one is more reliable about what was going on in Athenian minds), tragedy is, above all, women's stuff: "It's no surprise that tragedy is ours; / we are nothing other than Poseidon and the boat." This is sharp humor, once the reference is understood. Sophocles had written two tragedies—now lost—about the story of Tyro. We can imagine what would have happened if these tragedies had been saved instead of *Oedipus Rex* and *Oedipus at Colonus*. Tyro, in love with the river Enipeus, was sighing on her bank when Poseidon, god of the sea disguised as the river, seduced her. The god then plunged back into the waves. Tyro gave birth in secret to twins and exposed them in a cradle shaped like a boat. And so, says Lysistrata, we women "are nothing else than Poseidon and the boat." In few words—and with a brazen reference to a story twice told by a great tragedian—Aristophanes had summed up the female propensity to let herself be ruled by a fixed idea. And he had defined it as the main stuff of every tragedy. Lysistrata was hinting that men would not have been capable of offering such rich literary material. Tragedy, instead of being traced back to its Dionysian origins, was being linked to obsessiveness: in the desire for revenge, in the memory of a horror, in the immensity of a passion. Electra, Hecuba, Medea: the distinctive feature of tragedy was seen in these figures. Aristophanes wanted to show disrespect toward what most stirred reverence and terror. So he couldn't miss the opportunity of referring to the hermocopids.

The *hetaîroi* were members of informal "clubs" of young men who belonged mainly to the upper classes. Their numbers varied between fifteen and thirty. When the Athenians found that the herms had been mutilated, they immediately thought of them. But there must have been more than one of these clubs, since the destruction was throughout the city. Several days later, a certain Dioclides recounted how, deep in the night, close to the theater of Dionysus, he had come across a gathering of some three hundred men, split into groups of fifteen or twenty. They were lit by the full moon. He immediately thought it was a meeting of *hetaîroi* who were plotting something. Dioclides named forty-two men he had recognized. His story was later shown to be false. That night, there had been no full moon but a new moon. Yet his story, at the time, seemed plausible. And it was immediately linked, according to Thucydides, to an attempt to overthrow the democratic regime. This was Athens: herms

stood not only in front of temples and sanctuaries but at crossroads
or before private houses. They were something that no one would
fail to notice every day. Nothing more usual. But they were the image of a god. To attack them meant striking at the central nerve of
a city that was preparing to embark upon a reckless war: the expedition to Sicily. Several modern scholars have tried to argue that
the night of the hermocopids was an act of bravado by spoiled and
insolent youths. But it was an act of bravado for which twenty-two
men were condemned to death and various others had to escape
into exile. Once his story was found to be an invention, Dioclides,
too, was executed. The night of the hermocopids remains an un-
solved case. The first to say so was Thucydides, who was in a position to know more about it than anyone who lived after: "No one,
either then or later, has been able to say anything with certainty
about those who committed the crime." Yet one point is certain,
and curious: the night of the hermocopids was closely linked to the
scandal of the Mysteries, in which Alcibiades was embroiled. Teu-
kros, the accuser of the hermocopids who was finally believed and
whose testimony led to the conviction of fifteen men, had admitted
that he had been involved in a private celebration of the Mysteries.

When the night of the hermocopids took place, it was the eve
of the departure of the expeditionary fleet for Sicily, which was to
be commanded by Alcibiades. And during those days Alcibiades
himself had been placed under investigation, suspected of having
celebrated the Mysteries in private houses, including his own. At
the very moment when Athens was about to launch a cold-blooded
military campaign, the city was shaken by two scandals involving
impiety, which shook its religious foundations.

Alcibiades asked to be judged before his departure for Sicily.
This was refused. So he left, but when he was recalled to Athens for
his trial, he went and joined the Spartans instead: whom he advised
to attack Athens. Meanwhile he seduced the wife of one of the two
kings of Sparta. Then he betrayed the Spartans, too, and joined the
Persians. In the end he betrayed the Persians by returning to Athens. But in 407 B.C.E. Alcibiades was leading the procession from

Athens to Eleusis, protecting it with an armed escort. For several years the procession had been discontinued because the Spartans had occupied the neighboring areas. During that time, Eleusis had been reached by sea. But the procession was part of the initiation. The perfect fulfillment that Eleusis granted was not achieved without first the procession. That September, when the Athenians once again trod the Sacred Way, it was, according to Plutarch, a "solemn spectacle and worthy of the gods." They were thankful to Alcibiades and called him "high priest," in the same way that eight years earlier they had accused him of having acted as a "high priest" celebrating the Mysteries in private houses and had commanded the priests and priestesses of Eleusis to curse him. One of the priestesses, Theano, had refused to comply. It was her task, she said, to pray and not to curse.

Three centuries before the night of the hermocopids, at the end of the war between Eleusis and Athens, it was agreed that "the Eleusinians would be subject in all other respects to the Athenians, but would carry out the Mysteries in their own way [idíā teleîn tèn teletḗn]." Ídios here means that, for the Mysteries, the Eleusinians would act outside the jurisdiction of Athens. But ídios also means "private"—and Alcibiades would be accused of having celebrated the Mysteries in private. It was already an enormous concession that thirteen miles from Athens there was something totally outside the power of the pólis. But it would have been unacceptable for that extraterritorial prerogative to be hidden within the walls of private houses, in the city.

Politics, in Athens, was fierce and pervasive. Those who kept out of it did so also to avoid the risk of being killed. Socrates stated this clearly to his judges: he would never have reached that age if he had involved himself in politics pursuing what was right. And now politics was about to kill him all the same. It was a deadly game that didn't even spare those who kept out of it. Or it spared them only for a certain time. None of the traps and subterfuges practiced up to the times of the cardinal of Retz, and from then up to the Chinese Communist Party in power today, had not already been tried out in those brief years in which Athens imagined itself to be imperial. A careful reading of Thucydides is enough to establish this. The *agorà*, by reducing the spaces and people involved to a minimum, was the ultimate workshop in which all kinds of political action were tested out, whether perfidious or noble, but above all convoluted and contorted. The fundamental playing positions were established in just a few years and would remain the framework for every future game. Politics was one of those things capable of evolution only in their secondary branches.

But in the political game in Athens, compared with those that would follow it, there was an additional element: "impiety," *asébeia*, a capital crime that makes it necessary to delve into the secrets of Athens. Brazen and unscrupulous, the Athenians were also capable of using impiety as a deadly weapon—and therefore to look to a sacred sphere that had to be protected and preserved. Anaxagoras, Phidias, Aspasia: all three were accused of impiety. All three very close to Pericles. But it was Pericles himself—according to Pseudo-Lysias—who asked the Athenians to "strive to judge the impious not just by the written laws that regard them, but also by the unwritten laws according to which the Eumolpids make their exegeses." Pericles was drawing attention to a twofold justice and a twofold law. The first: written and administered by the people obeying formal rules known to everyone; the second: unwritten and administered by just one family in Eleusis, the Eumolpids. No one else—not even the other priestly family in Eleusis, the Kerykes—was authorized to perform *exégēsis*, namely the interpretation and application of that law. Pericles's friends were tried and convicted by normal tribunals: Anaxagoras was forced into exile, Phidias ended his life in prison. And Pericles himself wept before the tribunal as he defended Aspasia. Here, between written and unwritten law, there is a conflict and an overlap of the highest intensity. And such tension defines the distinctive feature of Athenian law, during its period of dazzling glory, at least until the archonship of Euclides, in 403–402 B.C.E., when it is decreed that "the authorities cannot apply unwritten law in any circumstances." Indeed, unwritten law, or references to other ancient unwritten laws, could be the pretext for arbitrary measures of whatever kind. But that decision also brought an end to the age in which the interpretation of an unwritten code, carried out by a single family of Eleusinian priests, could be applied as law. A law that affected first of all those who did not show *sébas*, "reverence," before that-which-is: the feeling first "for all, for the immortal gods and for mortal men," which had stirred the vision of Kore as she was gathering "roses, crocus, and beautiful violets." Where the essential detail is "for all": even the gods feel *sébas*, reverence before that which appears. It is this that establishes what men and gods share in common. And this is the ultimate sense of all *asébeia*: impiety is the failure to give recognition to that reverence. Three years after the archonship of Euclides, Socrates was sentenced to death.

There was a general terror about accusing anyone of impiety; so people were convicted for some other reason. Aspasia for procuring sexual favors; Socrates for corrupting young men; Phidias for embezzlement. But the weight of the sentence was due to the impiety that swathed it like a cloud and gave an importance to the crime that was not apparent from the written law. Impiety indicated a behavior that shook the foundations of ordinary life. And as those foundations grew flimsier and more insubstantial, impiety was used as a subterfuge to justify arbitrary power. As Aeschylus had said: "The reverence [*sébas*] of one time, invincible, intractable, unassailable, / which penetrated the mind and the ears of the people, / is gone. What is left is fear. Success, / this for mortals is a god and more than a god."

The Athenian *pólis*, according to Burckhardt, "like the monarchy in Spain, was something sanctified, a religion that resorts to extreme measures against any heresy." They had discovered freedom—together with the ways of persecuting it. They had discovered the excellence of the individual—and had immediately set up procedures for banishing him. Anyone who stood out from the others lived in a perpetual state of siege. He knew he was at the mercy of informers, who were a recognized profession. People lived in an atmosphere of "public terrorism." If Sparta had invented such ruthless institutions as the *krypteía*, which was the equivalent of a license to kill helots, Athens had done no less to instill fear, though in other ways. Common to both cities was the intention of giving paramount importance to "public utility" (otherwise called "*utilitas populi*," when Odysseus claimed to have defended it and advised Agamemnon to sacrifice Iphigenia). Now even religion became ornamental. And "public utility" would be the first political legacy left by Greece to Europe, long before the ignorant and ruthless utilitarians laid claim to it for the school of Bentham.

As to the hermocopids, historians from Thucydides until today have relentlessly examined successive reports and counterreports over some sixteen years that sent many to their deaths or into exile. Thucydides, in just a few words, had the final say: "It is not clear whether those who suffered all this had been punished unjustly, but it is certain that the rest of the city at that moment felt an evident relief." Much more apparent is the fact that contemporary sources as well as subsequent historiography have glossed over the meaning of the actions themselves. What was the point of mutilating the large number of herms that stood before temples and private houses? And why did both Thucydides and Plutarch state that "for the most part they mutilated the faces"? Whereas they say nothing about the penises, which Aristophanes couldn't resist mentioning. As to the celebration of the Mysteries "*en oikíais*," "in the houses," there is no explanation about what happened and why. A revealing detail is then given: Thucydides writes that certain "resident aliens and servants," as well as reporting the private celebration of the Mysteries, had indicated that "other statues" (*agálmata* this time, not *Hermeía*) had been mutilated by groups of youths. Immediately "the affair escalated" and the train of events was interpreted as a bad omen for the imminent expedition to Sicily and as evidence of a conspiracy. Time has done nothing to clarify what happened. But the fact remains that to throw the Athenians into panic required, before anything else, an attack on the statues and on the Mysteries.

Embólima are "lyrical digressions" in a stage tragedy that suddenly interrupt the course of events to celebrate other events, other stories, which might even have no plausible connection with the story being told. And *embólima* usually appear when events in the tragedy have reached a critical and delicate point, when it seems as if there's no way out. Euripides was particularly fond of this device, more so than anyone else. And, in *Iphigenia in Tauris*, a paean to Apollo is begun at the very moment when the protagonist's plans need to be kept secret; in *Electra* there are two digressions, on the golden lamb and on the Nereids. But the most eloquent example is in *Helen*, this "new Helen," as Aristophanes says, a play that seems strange and disconcerting from the start.

Menelaus and Helen, in Egypt, have just worked out a highly risky escape plan. And they have managed to dupe the Egyptian Theoclymenus, who thinks he is going to be Helen's husband. But the plan could be exposed at any moment. At this point the chorus appears and speaks about Demeter and her search for Kore. It isn't clear what connects the vicissitudes of Demeter, origin of the Eleusinian Mysteries, with the story of Helen. But the link is discovered in the end: it is the Mysteries themselves.

Helen, over the course of time, had been accused of almost every evil act. But never, until this chorus, of having celebrated the Mysteries "in her bedroom," "*en thalámois.*" An accusation similar to that made in those same years against the most handsome of Athenians: Alcibiades. It was claimed that he had dared to celebrate the Mysteries in the houses of others, and also in his own. And the verb used was *poieîn*, to "do," "perform." Not to imitate or parody, as the moderns have often understood. The wrong was in this: in transferring the Mysteries into a private, intimate place.

No differently to what certain Neoplatonic Florentines were to do in the Orti Oricellari, some eighteen hundred years later. With the difference that, once out of those Orti, or gardens, no one had any idea about the Mysteries.

As soon as we touch on the story of the hermocopids and the Mysteries celebrated in certain Athenian houses by Alcibiades, we realize we are close to the secret of the Athenians. Among the "strange things" about their story, nothing is as strange and as unexplainable as these two episodes. In Euripides's play, Helen speaks *also* of this, superimposing the two figures of Helen and Alcibiades. But in doing so the drama doesn't clarify their double mystery, indeed it heightens it. Thucydides makes no comment about the celebration of the Mysteries in the houses. He says only that it happened "*eph' hýbrei*," "out of arrogance." But *hýbris* can be interpreted in many ways. It can be mere impiety. Or it can be a belief in the capacity to deal *alone*, in the privacy of a house, with the power that acted only in one place—Eleusis—and in one temple. This, according to Euripides, was indeed the only wrong that Helen had committed: celebrating the Mysteries "in her bedroom" and confiding "in her beauty alone." Another form of *hýbris*.

The *embólima* were a device that annoyed Aristotle. The chorus, we read in his *Poetics*, "should be part of the whole and share in the action, as in Sophocles and not as in Euripides." And immediately after, he condemns the *embólima*, which he regards as an arbitrary digression: "What difference can there be between singing these digressions and transferring a speech or a scene from one play to another?" As so often in the *Poetics*, Aristotle identifies with clinical precision the watershed that divides forms. The enemy here is the apparent disconnection between one lyrical intermezzo and the rest of the play. But the real object of the criticism is mythical stereoscopy: so long as mythographical narration exists (and in Euripides it still does), every event is boxed up in another—and there is no way of escaping from this hallucination where one story is the enlargement of the detail of another, and container and content are continually being exchanged.

The mythical tree is a network and is never reduced to a linear sequence. Aristotle spoke the voice of what literature would become, once it had freed itself from myth: a plausible concatenation. But Euripides had already anticipated his reply (and his own defense) in the very last lines of *Helen*: "Many are the forms of things divine, / many unexpected things are plotted by the gods. / And what seemed likely has not happened, / the god found a path for the unlikely."

In the twenty-first century, massacres have replaced sacrifices. They mark out the course of time, of a formless, convulsive time, in the same way that sacred ceremonies marked out the circular course of the calendar. The officiant can sacrifice himself along with his victims; or otherwise he can keep a distance, as far away as a remote control allows him. The massacre can be a final, conclusive act; or it can be one element in a series. The basis remains the same. Compared with any other act—whether political, military, diplomatic, or subversive—the massacre offers a certainty: the guarantee of effectiveness. It is the only act of undoubted efficacy, among countless other acts about which one might have doubt. It is the safe anchorage of meaning. The motive can be wholly private and secret; or wholly public and declared. But the difference between the two acts is much less than what they share in common: the certainty that killing is the only unshakable foundation, the only gesture whose meaning is certain.

This, too, had its origin in Greece: at Sparta, where, according to Isocrates, "the ephors are entitled to choose as many as they wish to put to death without trial." Athens, as always, was more articulate—and certainly less effective: the concept of massacre was introduced not through the destruction of human life but of simulacra, on the night of the hermocopids. But what happened to simulacra presaged what would happen to the living. And so one mysterious night, whose secret has never been revealed, heralded the end of Athens itself.

X

THE CONTEMPLATOR

Greek by name, Egyptian by birth, Plotinus was born at Lyko-polis, the city of wolves. It got this name because, "when the Ethio-pians were invading Egypt, many packs of wolves gathered and attacked them, chasing them beyond Elephantine." His sole biographer—Porphyry—has nothing to say about Plotinus's child-hood, except that when he was seven, and already going to school, he would visit his wet nurse and bare her breast "out of the urge to suck it."

At the age of thirty-nine, after eleven years at the school of Am-monius in Alexandria, Plotinus applied to join Emperor Gordian's expedition to Persia. "He ardently wished to acquire a direct knowl-edge about the philosophy practiced by the Persians as well as that which thrived in India," writes Porphyry. It was as though Plo-tinus had foreseen that in the Upaniṣads he would have found the form of thought that most resembled the *Enneads*. But Gordian met military disaster in Mesopotamia and "Plotinus only just managed to escape and took refuge at Antioch."

Henri-Charles Puech, a most congenial commentator, was in-clined to imagine for some time that among the ranks of Shapur's army, against which Gordian was moving, there was Mani, "founder of one of those new religions that was preparing to invade the Em-pire." It was a magnificent scenario, this encounter, on opposing sides, of Plotinus and Mani, one attracted by the East, the other by the West. But it seems not to have been like this. According to Hans Heinrich Schaeder, the Shapur campaign in which Mani took part was that of 260 C.E. against Valerian, sixteen years after Gordian's expedition.

Seven centuries after Plato, Plotinus wasn't claiming to be the bearer of any new speculative ideas. What Plato had said was true—in the same way that what Parmenides had said before him was also true, even if Plato claimed to have confuted Parmenides. The tripartition of everything, the three natures, the descent of one from the other: "So Plato knew that from the good comes the mind, and from the mind comes the soul." All that could be left was "the teaching of these doctrines whose antiquity is proven to us by the writings of Plato." But that truth hadn't yet had the opportunity for "deployment," it still had to be further clarified. Above all, there was still much to be said about all that regarded the ineffable—the good and the one. This was the origin of the *Enneads*.

Nothing gives so clear an impression of a changing age as what happened in the sky around the birth of Jesus. The stars had been gods, a particular species of gods: "the visible gods," as Plato's Athenian could still say. Their figures and their movements, drawn on a dark canvas, were the model of every dance and of every order. Everything on earth was irregular, sporadic, sudden. Everything in the sky moved with order, slow nobility, continuity. And there were even those on earth who sought to imitate the sky.

But at a certain moment—difficult to pin down, except with a vast approximation in time and space, several decades before Jesus, and in a vast region that stretches from Iran to Palestine— this notion became strained, empty, and vacated its place for something else, entirely different. The structure of the heavens, their sequences, their evolutions, remained just the same. But now those rotating spheres emitted no music. They now weighed heavily on the people, like barriers, like tight metal circles around their necks. The spheres were still the places where powers lurked. But these were nefarious powers. The greatest urge was to escape from that ambush, crossing the skies as though passing a series of customs posts. Fearful of remaining trapped inside one of them, like in a "dungeon"—the Mandaeans called it *mattaratā*.

Plotinus knew that this view was widely held, even among his pupils. Yet for him, if he gazed at the heavens, everything continued to appear just as it had appeared to Plato. Once again, the cosmos had to be spoken about as divine. But around Plotinus, *world* had become a disparaging word. Smooth-talking Christians described it as what had to be renounced in order to follow them; and Gnostics, in their various tribes, spoke of it as a prison from which to escape. Plotinus, in his firm mildness, disapproved of all this. But he had no inclination to discuss it. He preferred to speak of that *other* world, the world up there, the model for everything.

If *that* world were not supreme beauty, "what would be more beautiful than the visible world?" He then added, as if with a sigh: "A world that is wrongly condemned by some, except insofar as it is not that other world."

"A continuous and evident and manifold and ubiquitous life": this is how the life of the stars appeared to Plotinus. "Whether they be in the lower spheres or high up in the heavens, why could they not be gods, inasmuch as they move regularly and rotate around the whole universe?" It is this that the Gnostics steadfastly refused to understand, according to Plotinus. Out of arrogance, above all, because they were confusing their individual souls with the soul of the world. A fatal error. It is true—admitted Plotinus—that "the union of our soul with the body is of no gain for the soul." But how can something that applies only to the soul of the individual be transferred to the soul of the world? It would be like "criticizing a whole well-governed city by considering only the class of potters and blacksmiths."

The soul of the individual is enveloped by the body. Whereas the soul of the world envelops and unites everything else. If the soul of the world is not perceived as something *bigger* than the whole visible world, thought is lost. This was a crucial mistake of the Gnostics. And it meant disregarding a vast part of the divine. Through what aberration ought we to consider human wisdom as being greater than the wisdom of the stars? Above all, adds Plotinus, the stars always live "at leisure." And why then shouldn't they be better than us at understanding "the god and all other intelligible gods"?

Recognition of the *beauty of the world*, which Simone Weil, alone, would one day talk about once again, was assumed not only generally in Greece, but in its science. It was the bond that connected numbers and metaphysics. With the Gnostics it was a bond that eventually frayed—and snapped. Plotinus accused them of seeking and predicating that severance: "How can the world survive if it is severed from that [from the intelligible world]?" What follows is a passionate plea: "It is indeed a meaningless question to ask. Anyone who is incapable of looking at this world must be truly blind, devoid of any perception or intelligence, and thus be so far from viewing the intelligible world."

But the sectarians—Christian and non-Christian—would win. From then, the "bond," *desmós*, with which the soul of the world held everything together, was not immediately perceivable. Whereas Plotinus had alluded to something else: to a feeling that is part of everyone's life, so long as it lasts and so long as there is someone ready to celebrate it.

Against the world's critics and detractors, both pagan and Christian, Plotinus used an argument to which there was no answer: the god "will be present in everything and will be in this world, in whatever manner, so that the world participates with him. If he is absent from the world, he will also be absent from you." Here Plotinus doesn't try to go into much detail. The formulation is abrupt, imperious. The world had to be saved, most of all from religious denigration. Otherwise how could people think of following the tortuous route of the soul as far as the farthest borders of the mind—and from there once again into the multitude of bodies? All would harden into a head-on conflict, which did not relate to the experience of someone like Plotinus, who was practiced at moving within himself.

No one can say where Gnosis started. It is like a wind that blows from the Persian plateau to Syria, Egypt, and as far as Rome. Ever more turbulent after the revelation of the Gospels. Always an admixture, as though its constitution prevented it from claiming

a single ancestry. Among Gnostics there is always a family atmosphere, even if they thwart or ignore one another. The true Gnostic, just like the initiate, doesn't like to be recognized as such. He
produces no documents. Cultivates anonymity. Seen from outside,
he displays passions, feelings, sympathies, just like anyone else,
and more so. But he always retains an unswayable detachment
from what surrounds him. A detachment that is difficult to identify. Only another initiate can recognize him.

Gnosis, whether Christian or pagan, is above all knowledge:
knowledge that is being sought, that is self-sufficient, extraneous
to the world, indifferent to merits and virtues, basically amoral,
cosmopolitan. The Gnostic crosses the world as though he is barely
touching it; or, alternatively, as though he is swallowing it whole,
in the same way that the sea can hold everything within it, since
it is too vast to be contaminated, and yet it transforms, disperses,
disintegrates whatever plunges into its immensity. Already widespread across the eastern Mediterranean, Gnosis flourished after a
Jewish sect sought to spread the teaching of its master, Jesus. The
element that sparked it off was personal salvation. In whatever
way it was reached, whether along the farthest and least compatible routes, it remained the crucial point. Why think, if the person
thinking cannot be saved? And what is the world, other than a trap
from which to escape?

Plotinus pondered all this from his observatory, in Rome,
toward the middle of the third century of the new era. In Egypt,
where he had grown up, he had witnessed the proliferation of doctrines and sects, which now darkened the sky and its Platonic light.
It was time to oppose them.

Plotinus wrote reluctantly about the Gnostics, trying to re-
strain himself ("That's all: it's enough for us to have said this
about them"). But one sensed that inside him was an even greater
pent-up fury, a physiological incompatibility, as well as alarm and
disappointment, since he felt under siege from the Gnostics. They
had infiltrated his pupils. Perhaps even the most brilliant among

them. Plotinus despaired about being able to deter them: "For my part, I feel a certain sense of shame in front of several friends who had encountered these theories before becoming our friends and still cling to them, I don't know why." This "I don't know why" reveals Plotinus's sorrowful conviction that the world was moving farther and farther away from him. But there was still the obligation to say it. Refuting such theories was not the most important point—and Plotinus entrusted this to Porphyry and Amelius. They would know how to pull the abstruse arguments of the Gnostics to pieces.

Apart from making a few metaphysical gibes, Plotinus concentrated on reflections that were above all psychological. What he couldn't tolerate was the arrogance of the Gnostics, their conviction that they were *the only ones*: "Man must strive to become better, but why do they believe they are the only ones who can do so?" What Plotinus detested above all was a certain Grand Guignol. For reasons of taste: "They must stop that tragic tone when they talk about the dangers that are encountered, they say, in the spheres of the cosmos, which have nothing other than benevolence toward them." Plotinus cultivated quite different ways: "One must not insult those who are inferior to the first, but gently accept the nature of all, while moving swiftly toward first things."

Plotinus's dialogue with the Gnostics is a scathing, closely knit argument: "They will say: It is the soul that generated when it lost its wings. But the soul of all does not suffer this. They will then say: It generated when it fell. But then they must tell us what is the cause of the fall. In what moment did it fall? If it has been so forever, it will remain fallen, as they themselves claim. If it had a beginning, why not before then?" Plotinus found the language of the Gnostics, above all, irritating. How they spoke about a *new land*, and claimed to introduce "newness in words." There was a proliferation of conjectures, a mass of new terms. They spoke of "exiles and imprints and conversions." Words, "empty of meaning," according to Plotinus. Useful only to persuade people they have "a doctrine of their own." But here a more serious suspicion arose: perhaps these new theologies "have nothing more to do with ancient Greekness," which knew how to speak "with clarity," *saphôs*. It wasn't just a question of speculative argument. Plotinus was aware that Greece itself, the Greek style of presenting things with that fearful clarity which culminated in Plato, was on the wane. And yet the Gnostics were plundering much from Plato, but at the same moment in which they were laying claim to "a philosophy of their own" they ended up "outside the truth."

In the realm of the mind, inhabited by "intelligibles," *tà noētá*, Plotinus was demanding that Occam's razor be applied. "Down there the least possible number of entities needs to be admitted." And this already separated him forever from the Gnostics, who were tireless multipliers of entities. It was not only a speculative but an aesthetic demand. The geometric transparency of Plato's intelligible realm was invaded by "generations and corruptions of every sort," as though a powerful migration from below risked forever obscuring the sky of ideas.

The most difficult question remained open: evil. The pace of thought was now becoming faster, more pressing, as in a cross-examination in which the prosecutor hastens to present the final irrefutable evidence, with the tone of one who has unmasked a conspiracy. A conspiracy that sought to make evil rise, to lift it from the visible to the invisible world, to attribute the cause of evil to the soul itself, and, beyond it, to dare to place it even higher. In this way the entire architecture of the mind and of the world appeared disfigured. From one end to the other it was crossed by an "inclination," *neûsis*, toward evil: "If they say that the soul, by inclining itself, has created matter, then previously there had been no place toward which to incline itself and the cause of the inclination was not the darkness but the very nature of the soul." Thus the ultimate purpose of the Gnostics was revealed: to place evil inside the soul. And this was only the first step. If evil was a necessity, it had to extend as far as the cusp of that which is, as far as the "first things." A deadly wave was gathering from below, and ended up crashing down and submerging the vertical structure that, according to Plotinus—and Plato—held up the world.

In Plotinus, too—though far different from the clamorous vicissitudes enacted by Gnosis—there was a cosmic dramaturgy of which various episodes were recounted here and there, in sudden flashes. "We—but what we?" This is the abrupt beginning of one such episode. Where were we before being born? We were in the soul, which is "one and infinite"; we were a "mind joined to the whole being." And "some were gods" (nothing more is said to explain this). We were not "separated and cut away from the mind." And it is true that we are still not wholly separated from the mind.

But something happened: an "other man" came toward us. He was looking for us and eventually found us. Indeed we were not "outside everything" (only our head protruded from the heavens). Man was shadowed by another man: we are not told who he was, nor where he came from. And eventually the pursuer managed to join up "to the man whom each of us then was." It is a process that is repeated for all souls that are born. Something dramatic, silent, inevitable. What follows from it? A new being is formed, which Plotinus calls *tò synámphō*, "the dual one." Something monstrous, it might be said. But it is normality itself. One point is certain: "We are no longer what we were" and sometimes "we are he who was added to us," while the first being disappears into the background, as though he had never existed.

Plotinus's style doesn't allow any recourse to arcane names, nor to fierce confrontations. He recounts a silent pursuit, on a barren stage, adding no color. Reminiscent of certain coded story outlines in Kafka's *Diaries*.

Worshipper of the *one*, Plotinus ended up describing a lost and disparate world. And the more lost and disparate, the more it responded to the *lógos* that governed it. From here, with a transitional passage, he moved on to the psyche of lovers: "The greater the presence of opposites, the more each person has a desire to live and the more he is attracted toward the one. Often lovers [but Plotinus uses the neuter, *tà erônta*] destroy those they love, when they are transitory, by seeking their own good, whereas the desire of the part toward the whole attracts to itself all that it can."

Immediately after, it was theater that offered the all-encompassing image: if "the good person and the bad person each have their own role, and the bad person has more roles," this is because an invisible dramatist has arranged each of them in the appropriate place. "In the same way that actors are given their masks, costumes, sumptuous robes or rags, the soul is given its destiny, certainly not at random." After which the soul "performs its actions and the other things that it will do in its own way, as though it were a melody." And the sounds produced will also be shrill, because "the perfect sound is that produced by all sounds." It is an all-encompassing vision, which even includes the figure of the executioner, anticipating Joseph de Maistre: "In the beauty of everything even the ugly sound has its place, and that which is against nature is in accordance with nature in everything. Such a sound is certainly worse, but it doesn't make the totality worse at the moment in which it sounds, in the same way that the cruel executioner doesn't make the well-governed city worse. He, too, is needed in the city, and it is good that he is there."

There was no doubt about the closeness and affinity between the *gnôsis* that Plotinus was writing about and what the Gnostics were saying. In both cases it was the pivot around which everything else revolved. And it was always a knowledge that *saved*, the ultimate aim of thought. With the Gnostics the differences were above all in approach: there was nothing more incompatible with Plotinus than that patched-up plethora of stentorian mythologies with those arrays of iniquitous archons and female hypostases who invariably ended up in dens of ill-repute. The style congenial to Plotinus was the opposite: it consisted of playing subtly with pronouns, referring as little as possible to the few entities about which it made sense to speak: the soul, nature, the mind (or intellect), the intelligible, simulacra, first things, the good, the principle. But there were inexhaustible combinations and movements among those few entities. Sometimes the words of Plotinus are most suited for illuminating certain maxims in the manuscripts of Nag Hammadi. While Irenaeus and Hippolytus fought against the Gnostics as political adversaries to be defeated, Plotinus disagreed, knowing that they were looking for something very similar to what he was searching out in his own thought. But the Gnostics did so with a display of gestures and claims that deep down Plotinus found repulsive.

The scandal of the Gnostics also consisted—and perhaps above all—in the fact that they had a total disregard for virtue. Plotinus could hardly avoid pointing this out: "This, too, is testimony about them, that they have developed no theory of virtue. They have totally failed to write about it, or to say what virtue is, how many forms of it there are, or how many fine and varied definitions have been given of it in the works of the ancients. Nor even how virtue is achieved and possessed and how it takes care of the soul and purifies it."

It was a remarkable omission, which was enough to demolish—and implicitly to deride—the whole edifice of Greek thought. Everyone—not just Platonists and Aristotelians, but Stoics, Cynics, Epicureans—felt the need to argue about virtue, with conflicting theories that nevertheless converged in the conviction that virtue needed to be talked about. And now these sects arrived on the scene and ignored even the word. They spoke only of *knowledge* and, as though it were a consequence of it, of *salvation*.

Where had something of this kind already happened? In the Mysteries. Plotinus knew this but did not want to say so. It might have sounded like praise. Whereas discernible in that refusal was the wish to demolish from within the entire framework that had held the social structure together, not just in Greece but in Rome.

The virtue of the free citizens of Sparta was very different from that of the Athenians, or the virtue of Plato from that of Chrysippus, or the virtue of Cato from that of Lucretius. But the word itself remained—and it implied a rule of conduct, whatever that might be. Whereas the Gnostics, by abandoning it, allowed *any* *conduct*. The abjection of the Carpocratics was only the most obvious symptom of an inclination that was inherent in every kind of Gnosis: total anomie. And so Plotinus, the man far removed from any official social zeal, was clearly sounding the alarm about the *licentiousness* that would then become a constant feature of a Western world which was increasingly frightened of the progressive corrosion of laws—and restraints. Sexual licentiousness would be the first and preferred signal of it.

Plotinus deplored how the Gnostics had abandoned not one but all of the virtues. At the same time, it cannot be said that Plotinus followed the notion that had long been dominant, according to which *aretè* was something sovereign and final. On the contrary, virtue served in his view as a support only if man had already lapsed. From what? From "contemplation," *théa*. The true weakness of humans lies in their incapacity to remain in a constant state of contemplation. And it is then that virtue offers its services. Once stirred, it will allow people to regain a certain inner order, will make them "lighter," will guide them "toward the mind" and, "through wisdom," toward "that"—the pronoun form perpetually used by Plotinus to suggest what lies beyond being. It is a humble and valuable function that is entrusted to *aretè*: a sort of training and persistent exercise to restore the condition of the contemplator. Having reached that point, virtue disappears. It begins the "flight of who-is-alone toward what-is-alone." And with these words Porphyry chose to end Plotinus's *Enneads*. No other expression could provide such clear evidence of the distinctive nature of his master's teaching.

The procession of virtues, as they are practiced in society, is the very image of the exoteric. The wise man passes unobserved in that procession, as though he wishes only to behave as a decent man.

He will be moderate, just, courageous, prudent, depending on the circumstances. But is this perhaps his purpose? Certainly not, according to Plotinus. Anyone who has understood what are "the models in the mind, prior to virtue," will no longer live "the life of the decent man in the way that social virtue considers it," even if "occasionally he will happen to behave in accordance with those virtues." But his purpose is another: "He will choose another life, that of the gods, since he wants to become similar to the gods and not to men of respect." There could be no clearer declaration of the wish to be disentangled from moral considerations. The *toû spoudaíou bíos*, the "life of the serious man" (*spoudaîos*, in Plotinus, indicates someone who practices in the right direction), can only separate itself forever, at this point, from the life of "men of respect." Seen from outside, they might even be confused. But a vast gulf separates them.

In spite of what he himself claimed, Plotinus's thought was devastatingly new in comparison not only with Plato but with all those who had gone before him. And this could already be felt in the way he interpreted the word *theōría*, which for him meant not "theory" but "contemplation." At least once, Plotinus admitted that his thinking could only stir bewilderment, being an unsolvable "paradox." And this is what happens in the opening lines of *Ennead* III, 8: "If, before speaking seriously, we were to say playfully that all things desire contemplation and aim toward this end, not only rational creatures but irrational ones and the nature in plants and the earth that generates them, and that all things achieve contemplation in a different manner, some truly reaching it, others through imitation and image, would the paradoxical nature of what we are saying be tolerated?" In a sentence of eight lines, filled with embellishments and refrains, but abrupt insofar as nothing precedes it, Plotinus had indicated his irreducible novelty. And he expressed it "playfully," as though he wanted to tone it down. Whereas immediately after we realize that in that way he was compounding it. This is how the discourse continues:

"But, since we are among friends, there is no danger if we speak playfully of our own affairs." Words that are revealing, almost shameless in admitting the esoteric nature of what at that moment was being said.

The more Plotinus insisted on *play*, the more serious the discourse was becoming: "Might it be that we, at this moment, while we play, are contemplating? Not just we, but all those who are playing like this, are doing and playing because they wish for contemplation. In conclusion, any child or adult, whether he is playing or serious, ventures to play or to be serious with a view to contemplation, playing or being serious, and every action tends toward contemplation." A vortex is produced, where "play," *paízein*, which seems to be a lesser activity requiring justification, ends up absorbing in it every form of "being serious," *spoudázein* (a verb that often indicates *thinking* in general). The course of the argument is irresistible and ends with a distinction between voluntary and involuntary ("obligatory," *anankaía*) actions, which Plotinus defers to another lesson ("But we will speak about this later").

Something else was urging: "Let us speak now of the earth and of the trees and of all vegetation, about what contemplation there is in these, and in what way the things produced and generated by the earth can be traced back to the act of contemplation, and in what way nature, which is said to be devoid of imagination and reason, possesses contemplation within it and does what it does through contemplation, which it ought not to possess." Now the game is revealed: contemplation is no longer a human characteristic, mixed up with many others, but the fundamental characteristic of the whole of nature. Indeed, it can be said that nature operates only if it contemplates and because it contemplates. Compared with the tone of playful paradox at the beginning, we have reached the opposite extreme, a cosmic vision, where the role of man is no different, in essence, from that of the trees and vegetation. And at this point the listener and the reader might stop and allow themselves to pause, to contemplate to what extent this vision departs from everything that has been argued, both before and after.

There is a mild and destructive irony in Plotinus. Aristotle had written, in the *Nicomachean Ethics*, that, according to Eudoxus, pleasure was the supreme good, "because we see that all beings desire it, rational beings just as much as animals." A sentence behind which we perceive the litany of good sense. Plotinus begins his *Perì theorías* with a sentence exactly the same as that of Aristotle, but where *pleasure* is replaced by *contemplation*, and along with animals there is now vegetation and earth.

That the world, from beginning to end, is crossed vertically by contemplation; that it is not just the object but the subject of contemplation; that the changeability of that-which-is is due to the continual transition from one to the other way of contemplation: these are theories that might be enough to form a firewall between those who, by inner nature, are driven to follow them and those who can only regard them as a baseless eccentricity, far removed from all reality. To clarify these theories, Plotinus wanted to make nature itself speak, even though it is not accustomed to do so. This was a further irony. Nature spoke as follows: "It was proper not to question me, but to understand and remain silent, in the same way that I am silent and it is not my custom to speak. But to understand what? That whatever is generated is an object of contemplation for me, in my silence, and it is naturally so: I myself am indeed born from contemplation and I enjoy contemplation; and that which contemplates in me creates a thing to be contemplated, just like geometers draw while they contemplate; but I do not draw, yet I contemplate, and the lines of bodies emerge as if coming from me. And I have the same passion as my mother and those who have generated me; and indeed they, too, are born from contemplation and my birth does not follow from their action, but since they are reasons superior to me and they contemplate themselves, I have been generated." The style was that of a whimsical, drawing-room Sphinx: but it conceded nothing, faithful to its vocation of accu-

mulating, rather than solving, enigmas. And now Plotinus came to
help out, like an old friend, to explain what nature *wanted to say*.
For one thing: nature is a soul, and a soul that descends from an
earlier and superior soul. Its strength is a "silent contemplation,"
which looks neither up nor down, is not searching for anything,
but "carries to fulfillment the object of its contemplation, which
has splendor and grace." But what kind of contemplation does nature have on that which it produces? "Silent and indistinct." And
yet life is carried on between beings that have clear outlines—and
who speak. How can the transition happen?

"Creation has been revealed to us as being contemplation. Indeed it is the fulfillment of contemplation, which remains such
and does nothing else, but creates inasmuch as it is contemplation." Never as in these words is Plotinus's intention so fully
declared, which consists in eliminating "creation," *poíēsis*, as a primary power, reducing it to an epiphenomenon of contemplation.
It's a reversal of perspectives. Contemplation, which presupposed
a prior creative process, becomes its origin. All that appears comes
from the immobile contemplator, who—insists Plotinus—"does
nothing else." Even for the most *oriental* Greeks, these notions
must have seemed bewildering. Whereas they would have seemed
very close to the truth for the Vedic Saptarṣis, who would merely
have added something on *tapas*, the ardor that the seer cultivates
inside and which nurtures contemplation itself.

If *theōría* is "contemplation," *theórēma* is "object of contemplation" and not "theorem." This object is splendid in itself, and full of
charm. Plotinus immediately adds, however, that if nature is
equipped with sensation and intelligence, these exist in it like in
a person asleep compared with someone who is awake. The
object of contemplation, in its splendor, is therefore like a sequence of figures that appear in a dream. The same dream in
which nature appears to itself. It is a "silent and indistinct" vision.
Which presupposes another that is "clearer." Nature, therefore, defers
to a higher vision, of which it can offer only an "image," *eídōlon*.

Similar in this respect to men, since "a contemplation with no power creates an object of contemplation with no power." Here, once again, *poieîn*, "creation," is introduced. But with unexpected consequences, in regard to people. Plotinus now goes on to explain why people *act*: "Men, when they are weak in contemplation, create action [*tèn prâxin poioûntai*] as a shadow of contemplation and of *lógos*." The action depends on a "weakness of the soul," which makes it impossible to achieve an "adequate vision, that will manage to fill them." Men therefore move to action, because "they wish to see that which they haven't managed to see with the mind." It seems almost as if Plotinus has sensed the faraway roars of Cieszkowski and Marx and all the many other turbulent champions of *prâxis*, to immediately counter them with a theory that is their antitype. And, as if addressing them, he reiterates the point: "We will always observe that creation and action are a weakening or a secondary consequence of contemplation."

Plotinus stated and repeated that the *one* does not think. And so it was not "thought of thought," as Aristotle argued, but something akin to a fragrance, from which the mind emanated. And the mind continually thinks. From matter to the soul, from this to the mind, from the mind to the one: there was always something that was transmitted and transposed from one power—Plotinus called it "hypostasis"—to the other. Not so when it reached the one, which remained isolated, intangible, enveloped in itself. A great remote, immobile, solitary, living entity that does not think, because this would diminish it, like every other act.

The whole chain of progressions, emanations, imitations on which the cosmos was based depended on that initial break. The universal concatenation presupposed a hiatus at the beginning. "Another thing is to exist in something other and to exist in itself." All of a sudden the "mind," *noûs*, and *noētón* appeared as something successive, detached from something that "has no need to think."

Anyone who had followed Plotinus's arguments into the tortuous links he had established so as to pass from matter to the soul and from this to the mind, culminating in the vision of the mind that contemplates itself, would have good reason to suppose that knowledge—and, in its supreme state, self-knowledge—would be the final point of arrival. But, having got there, one discovered that this was not the end. Indeed, a chasm opened up, beyond which loomed something that had no concern about knowing anything, including itself. ("It is not absurd that it doesn't know itself: it has nothing to know in itself, being one.") And yet, from the opposite edge of the chasm came a *gift*: "This gives something that is better and bigger than knowing, and it is the good of other things, or rather of the things that are in it, to the extent to which they manage to touch it." Beyond the chasm there was therefore the possibility—not the certainty—of establishing a *contact*, for all that went on in the mind, in knowledge and in self-knowledge. But at this point the being would have to stop considering itself in terms of knowledge. There existed an unknowing, above, indeed at an immense distance above knowledge. In the same way, knowledge could observe, from a vast distance, the ignorance of *homme naturel*, from whom it had one day been unbound.

Viewing the world's affairs, Plotinus observed that everything, without exception, depended on something else, which dwelt in them and to which they were fastened. He called this something *soul*. Then he saw that the soul was also necessarily attached to something else, which gave it articulation and form. This he called *noûs*, "mind." But had he, with the mind, arrived at something self-sufficient, something initial? No, before the mind there was the one. "That," *ekeîno,* is what he very often called it. It was immobile, it needed nothing, it was dependent on nothing. And it wasn't the mind, but something else, without which however the mind could not exist. But what was the origin of the mind? Had it originated from that total immobility? Thanks to something that resembled a movement, without it being a movement: an *epistrophé,* a "turning" of the gaze of the one toward itself, as if the pupil of the eye, instead of looking outward, turns within. In that moment the mind was born. It was the gaze of the one turned toward itself. And so self-reflectivity emerged.

For Plotinus, the "mind"—if this is how we translate his *noûs* (and though inadequate, no other word seems more appropriate)— was not just that mode of being that is felt by everybody who is conscious. *Noûs* is also an order, an articulation of elements. Indeed, it is the only order to which one must refer in relation to the essential, therefore the *tò kalón*, "the beautiful," and the *tò díkaion*, "the just." Every other order, reached through the use of "reasoning," *logismós*, is dismissed by Plotinus. That is not the true order, but an arduous attempt at discovering something that *was already present*: so, too, "anyone who is capable of using reasoning in the best way will be amazed as to why reasoning could not find anything different to create (whatever the object of knowledge, even in individual natures, might be) which in a reality in a perpetual becoming would be more intelligible than a rational order." Certainly, there is a difference between the order of the mind and the order of the world around it: "Up there everything is all things, down here each thing is not all things. And the single man, insofar as he is a part, is not everything." What is ineluctably absent is the perception of the *symplokḗ*, of the "mesh" of everything with everything. This is why each individual being cannot be "perfect." But that mesh stands behind everything that appears.

Supreme knowledge—that which "is in that which is" (a formula used by Plato in *Phaedrus* and implied by Plotinus)—does not consist of words set out in propositions, but only of "fine images," or rather "simulacra," "*kalà agálmata*." This is the dividing line that allows Plotinus to state that language is subordinate to images. And from this comes the whole theory of hieroglyphs, up to Kircher and the seventeenth-century pansophists. Of course, by *images* he means not "those drawn, but those that are." But what are images "that are"? Those that are found "in the soul of a wise man." Mental images. This is—*down here*—that which most resembles what is *up there*—the dwelling place of gods and "exceedingly happy," *hypereudaímonas*, beings—it is the knowledge that it is not "other in other," but "is in that which is." What is more: "fine images," Plotinus adds, are no different from "ideas, of which the ancients said that they were 'beings and substances [*ónta kaì ousías*].'" At this point the vast and unbridgeable gap that Plato had established between "fine images" (always suspected of leading to some sort of delusion) and "ideas" is canceled out and the *kalà agálmata* become the element itself of supreme knowledge. Even though Plotinus had just declared that he wanted to show himself worthy of being called Platonic ("if we wish to be deserving of being called so"), here the doctrine of Plato was subjected to an entirely new twist. Never as at that moment had "fine images" been glorified. Plotinus was anticipating Baudelaire.

No one has managed to state with such eloquence and precision as Meister Eckhart what the image is in Plotinus and what process in his view replaces the crude craftsmanship of the demiurge: "*Imago proprie est emanatio simplex, formalis transfusiva totius essentiae purae nudae . . . Est emanatio ab intimis in silentio et exclusione omnis forinseci, vita quaedam, ac si imagineris rem ex se ipsa et in se ipsa intumescere et bullire in se ipsa,*" "The image is properly a simple, formal emanation, infusing all the pure naked essence . . . It is an emanation from the depth of silence, excluding whatever externality, it is a certain life, as if you imagine a thing that swells up from itself and in itself and boils in itself." The fundamental terms remain (emanation, infusion, silent depth, abolition of that which is external, and finally above all, "a certain life"), with a further heightening of style, in that "*intumescere et bullire in se ipsa.*" The doctrine was still there.

Plotinus was not—and did not seek to be—a philosopher like Aristotle. His writings: a long, uncontainable gloss on Plato. But what did they add? If ever there was an example of what Thomas

Aquinas would call *"cognitio dei experimentalis,"* "experiential knowledge of God," it was Plotinus. Every word, for him, was an attempt to explore that boundless place that had never before been written about so extensively and persistently in Greek, except in some passages of Plato. But Plotinus was concerned only about this, since *"pánta eísō,"* "all is within." Whereas Plato had always thought about other matters as well. Including how to deal with men of power. Plotinus's approach was very different. "Anyone who is serious [*spoudaîos*, here he doesn't even use *sophós*, "wise"] doesn't think that those with many possessions or men of power are worth more than private individuals, but he lets others take these things seriously."

It is not Plato but Plotinus who is the true inventor of interiority. Christian mysticism, from *The Cloud of Unknowing* to Jean-Pierre de Caussade, applies, varies, and elaborates what Plotinus had described and circumscribed: the territory in which an individual ventures into the divine. When Christian mysticism dried up, it was followed by the *Innigkeit* of the German romantics, branching out as far as Proust. Close to Plotinus we encounter Schubert well before Kant. In the century of the moderns, interiority loses its thread and the psyche is invaded by the flow of associations. This is where Freud began.

Zōé, "life": a word that Plotinus introduces into all the crucial intersections of thought, and which ends up absorbing thought itself, and going beyond. *Zōé* is given no definition, but defines everything else. Woven into a delicate demonstration, this sentence suddenly rings out: "We don't try to find out whatever life is." Is this a reproach? We cannot tell, since the text moves straight on to something else.

Zōé is not a key word in the speculative lexicon like *ousía* or *eîdos* or *enérgeia*. It is all the more surprising when it appears. It appears only once in Aristotle's *Metaphysics*, but in the passage that perhaps, in all his works, most resembles Plotinus. And the statement that introduces the passage already seems pure Plotinus:

"Contemplation is the sweetest and the best thing." It is followed by a passage that seeks to define what is "the god," *ho theós*: "If the god is always in that happy state in which we sometimes are, it is a marvelous thing: and it is even more marvelous if it is even greater. So indeed it is. And life [*zōḗ*] belongs to him. Life is the act of the mind and he [the god] is the act. The act is his life that itself is dependent on him, the best and eternal one. We therefore say that the god is a living being, the best, eternal one, inasmuch as life and continual and eternal duration belong to the god. This indeed is the god." They are riveting words, of great concision and density—and might have served as an introduction not only to *Ennead* III, 8, on contemplation, but to the very many passages in which Plotinus speaks about "life." Their strategies are radically different. Aristotle comes out with the word *zōḗ* only once, in a culminating moment; Plotinus introduces it everywhere, discreetly and resolutely—and almost in passing he recalls that "we don't try to search for what life actually is."

Contemplation is not a state devoid of progressions, indeed the essential steps occur within it: "from nature to the soul and from this to the mind." If it is true, as Parmenides argues, that "being and thought are the same," then this is a state that has to be reached—and only contemplation allows it. And "thought," *noeîn*, in Plotinus will instead be *the life of the mind*. This already points to the peculiarity of Plotinus, who immediately declares: "And every life is one of thinking, which however is sometimes more, sometimes less obscure, like life itself." But, if contemplation has achieved its effect, both thought and life will now be "more evident." Plotinus then defines them as "first thought and first life." This implies that life has various levels—and indeed immediately after he talks about a "second life" and a "second thought," and likewise about a "last life" and a "last thought." There is therefore a sequence of steps, in life and in thought. And these culminate in the "truest life," which "is the life for thought."

The unshakable justness of thought was enough for Plato. Not so for Plotinus, who measures thought by its correspondence with the "truest life." And everything is traced back to contemplation, which is at last defined: "And contemplation and the object contemplated are this living being and this life and the two are equally one." No one had ever devoted so much attention to the word *life*.

But what does he call "first life"? In no circumstances does Plotinus abandon an image. Gradually, through a succession of embellishments, he returns there. But now onto more difficult ground, that which opens up "beyond" the mind, where an irreducible duality of *noûs* and *noētón* no longer exists, but something is discovered that "will not know itself." A very dangerous area. Plotinus, as though afraid, asks: "What will it have, then, that is venerable?" It is something difficult to reach. In comparison, the mind is a familiar reality. And yet "something of it is in us." But how do we perceive it? It is "like a sound that fills an empty space and the people who are listening in that space are aware of all or not all of it." The mind must now perform its supreme feat. It must "withdraw" and, "if it wants to see it, it must be not entirely mind." To reach that being that lies *beyond*, the mind—which Plotinus had just said was "all"—has to renounce (to what extent?) itself. And it has to recognize that "this is the first life, an act that runs through all things." It is the life that possesses "all with precision and not in general terms." For the mind, there is nothing left but to turn toward its "beginning," which is described as "preceding all things, if all things must be after him."

What will it be? "The power of all." Without that power there isn't even the *first life*. Here we are approaching something that is "above life and a cause of life." Life itself descends from it like from a "spring." And here we encounter the greatest problem: it is "a spring that has no origin" and never runs dry. This is the first image, which perfectly matches the "stanza of plenitude" in the *Bṛhadāraṇyaka Upaniṣad*: quiet and always at the same level, the spring flows into all rivers. And it is immediately replaced by another image: an "immense tree," whose sap permeates every branch but does not disperse and "remains in the root."

"Why be surprised?" adds Plotinus. If this were not so, there would be nothing. Once we arrive at this which is "simply the one" then we must ask no more, even if we can say nothing about the one, since "it is not being, it is not substance, it is not life." Now the *first life* has really reached beyond itself. The spring, the immense tree, simply the one: names of something that is also called "the good," *tò agathón*. The mind searches for it, but it mustn't make the mistake of thinking it: "In expressing the good, do not add a thought to it; to add something to it, whatever it might be, means diminishing it." The task of the mind, which has gone through everything, is now simply to be silent. Even thought is inappropriate, since "the mind needs the good, but the good has no need of the mind." In the end, the mind has to do without itself.

And here Plotinus recalls what the mind *has been*, as if during the course of his journey he had abandoned it: "Yes, the mind is beautiful, it is the most beautiful being, in the pure light and in the pure splendor it envelops the nature of beings." To look at it causes "dismay" in "anyone who sees it and penetrates it." And yet there is something that lies *beyond*, "which has no need of anything and not even to think." And it is there that thought has to reach: to eliminate itself.

In everyday life, *ágalma* meant first of all "statue." But *up there*, in that heaven where the gods live? Plotinus explains: "It mustn't be thought that up there the gods and the blessed ones see propositions, but all the things they are told are fine simulacra [*agálmata*], which we can imagine to be in the soul of the wise man, simulacra not drawn, but which are." In heaven, simulacra are things that are "said," *legoménōn*, but not in words—and nor through a "written" trace. In a language that is used "up there"—and an echo of which arrives on earth. So immediately after, Plotinus adds: "I think this is what the wise men of Egypt have sensed, whether through an exact science or through an innate understanding: to draw things wisely they don't use written letters, which are articulated into speeches and sentences, nor do they use that which imitates the sounds and expressions of propositions, but they carve simulacra [*agálmata*] in the sanctuaries, and each of them is a simulacrum of a single thing, in every detail, so that each simulacrum is both science and wisdom, which exist all together, and not a reasoning or a deliberation."

"Often, having awoken myself to myself from the body and being outside other things, but within myself, and seeing a most wonderful beauty and trusting especially then to be sharing in the best destiny, since I live the supreme life and have become a single thing with the divine and being founded in it I have come to found myself on that activity that lies beyond every other mental entity, after this residence in the divine I descend from the mind to reasoning and I ask myself why then, and also now, can I descend, and why then was the soul able to enter into the body, being what it seemed to me, though still in the body."

A sinuous sentence, split into three in Hadot's translation and into four in that of Bréhier, it thrusts the reader into a continuity of movement: the experience, prior even to the reasoning, from which the *Enneads* emerge.

The starting point in Plato: it is not the world that contains the soul, but the soul that contains the world. In *Phaedrus* he talks of the "ridge of the sky," from which can be seen that which does not appear in the world, because it lies beyond its shell, envelops the world, and shows itself as consciousness. Every conscious thing inside the world is derived, without knowing it, from this entity.

If this were not so, consciousness would be none other than an appendage of the physical-chemical compound with which all that is conscious is made, and could at most communicate with other beings within the scope of empathy. Whereas consciousness shows itself in its entirety when it passes beyond the shell of the world and sinks into the element with which every other form of conscious-ness itself is made. Within the world, on the contrary, conscious-ness is entirely subordinate to the physical-chemical compound. It is the bond of necessity that grips it. This is enough to banish any suspicion of panpsychism, an easy error that eludes Ananke.

Man is immersed in the cosmos, but his head remains out-side it. This is the physiological factor that is the cause of every friction with the world and every detachment from the world, which is a return to the head. *Timaeus* explains it in terms of a metaphysical naturalism. The head is the "root" of man, it is to be regarded as a "celestial" and not a "terrestrial" plant. Man is therefore "suspended," *anakremannýn*, from high in the sky, like a marionette.

This vision is repeated precisely by Plotinus: "Their head [of the souls of men] is fixed above the sky." The idea that the head is the root helps us to understand the picture of the *arbor inversa*, "the upturned tree" that is found at a crucial moment in the *Bhagavad Gītā*. But the reference here was found in Homer. Speaking about men whose heads soar above the sky, Plotinus was reproducing—with modifications—three magnificent lines of the *Iliad* that de-scribe Eris, Strife, "sister and companion of man-killer Ares, / who at first is a little thing and then fixes her brow / in the sky, while she treads on the earth." In Homer, Eris, a terrifying and fickle power, sometimes minuscule and sometimes gigantic, manages to "fix" her brow high up in the heavens, imposing her woeful pres-ence on the entire cosmos; in Plotinus the souls of men have their heads "fixed above the sky."

The situation of Eris and the soul is divergent: Eris occupies the entire cosmos, as far as its ultimate limit—and flaps against it with her wings. Nothing in the world can avoid sensing her deadly wheeling. But the soul is the opposite: if her head protrudes be-yond the cosmos, this implies that the powers of the cosmos can-not reach a particular part of her. And that invulnerable part is indeed her "root." As we read in *Timaeus*: "He placed the soul at the center and stretched it across everything and even outside, enveloping the body with it."

But why had Plotinus wanted to reconnect the image of the soul that shuns the world to that of Eris, who rages over the world? All his subtlety is revealed in this allusion to Homer: the soul has good reason to feel itself released from the world, but at the same time the world, up to the highest heavens, is invaded by Eris, an unconquerable and murderous conflict that accompanies every event.

If the divine exists, it can only be that which "envelops the whole of nature," as we read in Aristotle's *Metaphysics*, in line here with Platonic doctrine. The divine can therefore be found in the world only as something that filters into it from outside. It is essential for this *outside* to be recognized.

We can look at art—for example, at a painting—in two ways: either as a representation of something else, which belongs to the world and can be perceived in the same way as the painting; or as a representation of something of an invisible nature, however that might be defined. And in both cases the work of art has to be treated as a *mímēma*, an "imitation," a fateful word.

Plotinus made a clear distinction between the two paths: if in a painting we recognize "in the perceptible the imitation of something that exists in thought [*en noēsei keiménou*]," only then does art provoke a mixture of unease and wonderment. This is the source of *páthos*, the "emotion" that occurs in a process inside the person who is looking. And at this point Plotinus sounds out a formula that reconnects metaphysics to myth: "*kinoûntai hoi érōtes*," "the Eroses are stirred." Of course, he adds straightaway, some beings are so lethargic that they cannot even recognize "all the beauties in that which is perceptible" and will never be capable of feeling a "reverence" toward the world around them. If this is the case, then "nothing else will stir them," and they will even encounter art without noticing it. Dry, peremptory words.

"Up there, power possesses only being, and being only beauty. How indeed could beauty be without being? And how could being be devoid of beauty? If beauty is lost, being is lost. This is why being is desirable, because it is the same as beauty, and beauty is adorable for the fact of being. Why investigate which of the two is the cause, if their nature is one?" Before Plotinus could formulate these questions, several centuries had had to go by for a civilization that placed the adjective *kalós* at the head of every list of qualities and wanted beauty to be applied not just to appearance but to any human act. Plotinus's voice was one of the last and clearest to state it. What happened after looks no longer like a history but a tangle of stories, where the roles that beauty had to play were to some extent suspect, and being no longer seemed to need such dubious company in order to exist.

The difficulty for Plotinus did not arise from the relationship between beauty and being, but between beauty and the good. These, for him, were so interwoven that he felt the need to distinguish them. Which of the two had precedence? The good. Why? Because it didn't need to be perceived in order to exist. Whereas beauty, in order to exist, needed to be seen. And immediately "it generates suffering." To see beauty, one has to be awake. Whereas good exists even for those asleep. "The good has no need of beauty, whereas beauty needs good": this is the ultimate difference. And their way of acting is different: the good is "sweet and mild and delicate," whereas beauty is always accompanied by "dismay and wonderment and a pleasure mixed with suffering." Plotinus adds: beauty "draws those who do not know away from the good, like the beloved is drawn away from the father. Indeed it is younger." Each time he comes close to *realia*, Plotinus suddenly becomes laconic. Bréhier, a magnificent translator who often failed to resist the pitfalls of paraphrasing and explanation, rendered the passage as follows: beauty "draws us unknowingly away from the Good, like the beloved draws his fiancée away from the house of her father; since he is younger than the Good." This conjures up fairy-tale scenes of kidnapped princesses or village girls. But Plotinus had made no mention of them.

Ekeî, "up there" or "down there," in the sky or in Hades, is an essential word for Plotinus. It is the word that indicates that *other place*, without which every place down here cannot exist. If that *other place* did not exist, thinking would have no meaning. Sometimes in the *Enneads*, as in book V, 8, 10, 19–23, in a sentence of four lines *ekeî* occurs four times. There are hints of a drama: Zeus appears "from some invisible place" and dazzles "those who are below." Only a few manage to keep their gaze fixed upon him— and they follow him, as do "other gods and demons and souls that are capable of seeing these things." Up there beauty is a light that shines on whoever, as though he were climbing on high ground and enveloped by the "fair color of the earth" that he is treading. It is "beauty from deep down." Then "anyone who has penetrating sight sees in himself that which is seen." This is the moment that makes it possible to understand exactly what possession is: "So he who is possessed by a god, by Apollo or by one of the Muses, contemplates the god within himself, as soon as he has the strength to look at the god within himself." No convulsions or frenzies are needed. Psychiatric case notes are of no help. It's enough that someone has "the strength to look at the god within himself." A singular procession. The one who looks is not caught and absorbed into something external that overwhelms him, but he welcomes within him and recognizes as his own something that is the god itself.

But is possession likely to last and, above all, is it desirable? Is it not a way of making another, potentially valuable, movement impossible? Plotinus suggests so. It is not enough to be joined to the god in silence: an opposite movement is also needed, toward separation. But what benefit will we gain from it? "We will begin to be aware of ourselves, to the extent to which we are another," in comparison with before. An oscillatory movement is created. On the one hand there is the fear of losing contact with the god; on the other "the desire to see him as other than self, outside ourselves." Man is constitutionally unable to be one. By nature he is always deficient or excessive. And this is how he must be. On the one hand men are "those who see, on the other [they are] the sight that another sees." Without self-reflectivity there is no thought—and there is no contact with the divine.

Life up there is easy, everything is transparent, light on light. There is no resistance. The splendor is infinite. The sun is all the stars—and each star is the sun. Each thing shines over everything, yet each thing is everything. Movement is also pure, indistinguishable from what is moving it. Everything that appears has an outline that distinguishes it from every other thing, but by studying it at length each thing is everything. There is no void to fill. Nothing wears out. Insatiability prompts no urge to scorn that which satiates. He who watches can only watch more, for he sees the infinite. On the other hand, life is no toil for anyone, when it is pure life. This life is a wisdom that reasoning does not reach, because it is always whole, and nothing is lacking from it that then needs to be sought. All things up there are statues that look at themselves. A happy vision. We do not see the statues, because we are weighed down by a mass of propositions. And beyond, what is there? A large remote, immobile, solitary animal, which does not think, because thinking would diminish it, like any other single act, because the animal is already the whole act.

In order to approach the god, a sequence of preliminary acts is essential: one must be purified. "It must then be stated to what extent purification [kátharsis] can be achieved; in this way it will appear clear who it makes us resemble and to what god it makes us identical." For Plotinus, purification is an act that can have extreme consequences: assimilation to a god, to the extent of becoming identical. That is enough to take away from purification any assumption of morality. Plotinus explains, "The effort is not aimed at becoming faultless, but at being a god." But what god? Here, too, Plotinus replies: "One of those that have come from up there"; and once having arrived "here, they have settled in the mind." Certain gods have taken up residence in the mind, at the end of one of their journeys. Started where? They are gods that "follow that which is first" and that "first" is not a god, but something previous. These mobile beings could therefore go back to what precedes them and enter what was first; or alternatively sink down into a *here*, which is the mind of whoever. This is perhaps why, in myths, the gods are often traveling.

Purification, for Plotinus, involves "the elimination of all that is extraneous." What remains, then? Perhaps the good? It would be a mistake to think so. Nature (and the soul is nature), even if traced back to its unspoiled state, is never the good: "It will unite [with the good] turning itself [toward it]." Three words were enough to express this sentence: "*Synéstai dè epistrapheîsa.*" Once the purification is complete, the soul must merely steer itself toward something alike ("The good, for it, is to unite with that which is alike").

But how is the good to be recognized? For the fact that the soul contains the "imprints," *týpous*, of the good. And this requires contemplation: "To match the imprints with the real things of which they are the imprint." If there is no contemplation, the imprints remain like inert traces. It is the contemplating eye that reawakens them. But it is assumed that the soul is already predisposed to that contemplative act which for Plotinus is the only effective act. Nothing else is required.

There is a crucial point on which Plotinus differs from Plato, or at least from *Timaeus*: the creation. Plotinus doesn't feel the need for the demiurge. On the contrary, he presents him as a slightly grotesque figure who struggles to compose, piece by piece, the thing created ("but from where would he get things he had never seen before?"). Plotinus's picture is the opposite: "The creation takes place effortlessly." It is not a gradual process, but instantaneous, total and "free of obstacles." The very idea of a creator as gradual composer is negated here. Plotinus turns it upside down: "It's as if in the causal syllogism the conclusion came before the premise." This sentence would be enough to deny whatever is founded on Aristotle—but also on Plato. What remains then, that can account for creation? "There remains the fact that all things exist in something that is other." Of course, "all that is here comes from up there, and up there was more beautiful." If the demiurge is eliminated, each element of everything can only be seen as a copy of something else, which exists elsewhere and is more beautiful there. It is no longer man that produces copies of copies: the world itself, in its entirety, is a copy.

With Plotinus, the theory of imitation, always split between wild approval and condemnation, reaches a turning point. For him, imitation is not a peculiarity that is developed within life, assuming certain characteristics, that can be good or bad. Imitation is life itself, in its totality. "The true life is there," in *another* place: where it is good, indeed the cause of good. That which men live, "the life of the moment and without the god," is "a trace of life, which imitates that other life."

Plotinus follows, step by step, a path trodden by Plato—and it is Plato's boldest path, which leads "beyond essence," as is stated in the *Republic*. But in a world made of copies, and copies of copies, as was described by Plato, Plotinus introduces the "primal image," *archétypon*, which he encounters at the "end of the journey." And throughout the journey he does nothing but repeat the progression of the Mysteries: a passage from "simulacra," *agálmata*, that stand in the vestibule, to the *ádyton*, the secret niche where "the spring of life, the spring of the mind, the beginning of being, the cause of the good, the root of the soul" are to be found—and it is discovered that they are one single thing. A passage from the "image," *eikón*, to the archetype, which is the origin of the image.

"That which is the cause of all things is none of them. It should not even be called *good*, because it produces it, but at the same time it is the good above all goods." Yet that nameless origin, which belongs to no place and to no time, and resembles nothing as much as the Vedic *brahman*, is something that can be *touched*. Exactly as in the Mysteries, this is the point of divergence: a knowledge that is a contact—and for this very reason is distinguished from every other knowledge: "It is not situated in a certain place, as if to deprive other things of itself, but is present for he who is able to touch it, absent for he who is unable to do so."

If what exists at the beginning cannot even be defined as *the good*, in what other way can it be described? Plotinus speaks then about "first nature," which carves forms onto the soul. The soul must therefore be "without qualities," like matter, which couldn't otherwise receive the "imprints" of all things. This, more than anything else, was why Musil called Ulrich "the man without qualities."

Hēsychía, a key word in Plotinus, means both "silence" and "calm." Silence because it precedes and is greater than language; calm because it contemplates what is happening from an immobile center. Indeed, it makes it happen. It is the *mind*, *noûs*, which— "without wavering and in calm"—offers something to matter: *lógos*, "which streams from the mind." This flow is the constant act that governs the world. A silent act that cannot be seen. There is no need here for a demiurge that acts, that shapes once and for all. The flow is uninterrupted, it is the *continuous* itself. If all thought is a search for the continuous, Plotinus suggested how to find it, at any moment.

Plotinus mistrusted theurgy, he preferred not to rely on the Egyptian practices that Iamblicus had celebrated. But he recognized one point: the soul needs to be charmed (*epōdé* is the technical term he used) in order to soothe its pains, similar to the pains of childbirth. But his solution was quite different from theurgy. For him, relief could come from the repetition "of the things al-

ready said, if the charm operates repeatedly." Here Plotinus talks
about himself and what would one day be considered his work:
those courses of lessons that retraced, relentlessly, the same
words—*noûs*, *psyché*, *agathón*, and few others—discerning and
illustrating their relationships, changing the angle of observation
each time. The *work* itself, the *Enneads*, was the invention of Porphyry. Whereas for Plotinus it was a rapture persistently repeated,
modulated, varied, to soothe "the labor" of the soul.

Six hundred years had passed, but the questions raised by Plato
were still there, unanswered. For Plotinus, it was a matter of unraveling certain strands and reconnecting others. And finally to
trace them back to different points in Plato's writings. Reiterations,
variations. Laborious elucidations. Every so often, a ray of light.
The tone became suddenly intimate, imperious: "*Áphele pánta*,"
"Do away with everything." They were the last two words of his
tractate *On the Knowing Hypostases*. But what was that "everything"? In the first place *society*. Plato would not have been so bold.
Even his most daring speculations were woven into a *politeía*. Indeed, several of them are to be found in the *Republic*. With Plotinus, however, links with society were severed. Something of this
kind had happened only in India with the *saṃnyāsins*, "renounc-
ers," those first individuals living outside the world, destined to
become the model of what acts upon the world.

In describing the sage, Plotinus alternates the word *sophós*,
which dominates the whole Greek tradition, with the term *spoudaîos*, which is commonly used to mean someone who is "serious,"
who strives, who exerts himself. From here also the meaning of
"weighty," when referring to words or things that have mass. Con-
verging with the Sanskrit *guru*, which means first of all "heavy."
And corresponds with a certain *way of living*. At this point it is
Plotinus himself who raises a question that might seem provocative: "What sweetness will there be in such a life?"

The answer was instant. What pleasures will there be for the
spoudaîos? Not intemperance, nor bodily pleasures, nor even

"excessive joys" (Plotinus comments in brackets: "for what ben-efit?"). The only pleasures, for the *spoudaîos*, relate to the presence of the good. But the good is always present. And the *spoudaîos* is always present too. It follows that for him "sweetness is con-stant." But how is this state recognized? "*Tò híleōn toûto*": "*c'est la sérénité*," Bréhier translates—and Harder follows the same line ("*Heiter ist der Edle immerdar*"). But "serenity" has a psychologi-cal timbre. *Tò híleōn*, on the other hand, has another past: it is a technical term used in sacrifice. It comes from *hiláskomai*, a verb used by someone who wants to appease, to propitiate the god. For Chantraine its primary meaning is "'to seek to win favor, to be reconciled' (in Homer the object is always a god)." Thanks to the propitiatory act, which can be a blood offering, the offended god (it is always assumed, from the start, that the god is offended) be-comes benevolent—and, by contagion, the officiant is rendered benevolent. From here the meaning, for *híleōs*, of "allowed by the gods." From here the sense of relief—and in the end serenity—for the man. *Híleōs* eventually becomes *hilarós*, "cheerful," "good-humored," which still has this meaning in modern Greek. And the composite *hilarotragoedia* implies that *hilaritas* has an underlying *tragoedia*. This was also the meaning behind the title of Giorgio Manganelli's book with this title.

If Plotinus's *spoudaîos* is "serene," he reaches this after a long and silent period of attempts to win the favor of the divinity. This "disposition," *diáthesis*, once achieved, is an immovable state, which presupposes a troubled past. But this is enough for the happiness of the wise man: "If we search for another image of pleasure for the life of the *spoudaîos*, it means we are not searching for that life."

It is no surprise, then, if many people find the happiness of the sage hard to believe: "Such a being does not live, some people say. And yet he lives, but his happiness, as well as his life, escapes them." What is irritating about the sage is that he makes him-self hardly noticeable. His serenity is also irritating: "[The sage] would certainly wish all men to be well and that no ill should befall them; but, if this doesn't happen, he is equally happy."

A deeply Plotinian irony. Which is followed soon after—and almost inadvertently—by the only clarification on the relationship between the sage and power. "He will lessen and ignore, through neglect, the excesses of the body; he will remove the powers." As though this were nothing.

"Life in everything, which is superabundant, creates all things and streaks them with life and never ceases to create living, beautiful, and attractive toys": the many toys include humans. Plotinus's vision was already to be found in Plato. But, once again, Plotinus pushes to the extreme. What are wars? "Pyrrhic dances." Consequently: "Like a theater play, this is how the killings and all the death and destruction and conquests of the city must be contemplated: they are changes of scenery and costumes and the groans and laments of actors." It is hard to find anything as shameless in its mockery and vanification of suffering and death. But not only this: ordinary men "take toys seriously because they don't know what is serious and because they themselves are toys." Here is a declaration, more than ever before, of the split between the *spoudaîos* and everybody else. The rest of humanity is stuck away among toys and treated like a group of puppets, assembled for a show that may even be amusing, but remains irrelevant. No less than the Gnostics, though in another manner, Plotinus turns the human comedy into a game. But immediately after, he raises objections against himself that will always remain effective and unanswered, even if Plotinus tries to refute them: "How can we say that something is according to nature or against nature, if we say that everything that happens is according to nature? And how will it be possible for someone to be impious toward the divine, if such a person is what is created, as if in the theater a playwright has put an actor on stage who insults the author himself?" A superb example of a thought that has the capacity to speak against itself.

Plotinus knows very well that, by talking about toys and puppets, he hasn't answered the question on evil. And he formulates it in the most immediate way: "Why are there unhappy people, if they commit no injustices nor have any blame?" This time, however, Plotinus comes up with a new answer: "We will say more clearly what is the reason for this and why it is appropriate." But the greater clarity, in order to be obtained, implicates a larger difficulty. And Plotinus proceeds with a sudden *aside*: "This is therefore the reasoning—let us attempt it; and perhaps we will succeed." In this apparently superfluous inlay we notice Plotinus's last distinctive characteristic, his capacity to let those who follow him sense the cadences, the pace, of his thought. Then, immediately after, we enter an entirely new line of reasoning, like in a vortex. First of all: "Every life is activity, even life of little importance. An activity that isn't like that of fire, but a movement not casual, even if it is not always perceived." Plotinus had promised something clearer—and he immediately offers something of darker, denser thought. The point is to understand the specific nature of the activity, which is life itself. That activity contains within it a *lógos* that "moves life, giving it form." But what will such an activity resemble? "The activity of life is an art, like that of someone who moves about dancing: the dancer resembles this life according to art, and art moves him in the same way that life itself does." To find a similar sentence we have to race forward as far as Nietzsche: "The world as a self-producing work of art," "*Die Welt als ein sich selbst gebärendes Kunstwerk*." Or else sideways, to Śiva the cosmic dancer. But Plotinus doesn't pause to consider this prospect. He is eager to explain that the *lógos* that operates in the activity of life "does not devote itself fully to each thing," in that it doesn't have the integrity "of the one mind and of the one life." Consequently, "by placing the parties against each other and producing conflict and war" *lógos* becomes torn apart. And yet it remains as one, "in the same way that a theater play, which is one, contains within it many battles." The theater, which in the passage on toys and puppets might seem to play down every conflict, reveals itself here as being intrinsic to the constitution of the world. Which now appears like a "single living being," which is in accord with itself even if composed of conflicting roles. And this because "everything follows *lógos*." But *lógos*, in order to exist, needs difference—"and the maximum difference is opposition." It will therefore be *lógos* itself that "will push alterity to the extreme and out of necessity it will create opposites and it will be perfect not merely through difference, but if it creates opposites as well."

Evil is useful because it awakens. "It makes the mind and intelligence alert so that they oppose the paths of iniquity." This is already stimulating. But there is also another way of using evil: "This pertains to the greatest power: to place evil at the service of good and be capable of utilizing that which has become formless to make other forms from it." A doctrine no different, in its foundation, from what flashed through the mind of Baudelaire in his dream about the brothel-museum: the perception of the "mysterious utility" of an evil which, "thanks to a spiritual mechanism," can also "turn into good." It is essential that good knows how to deal with the substance of evil. Not simply because the punishment of evil is a cautionary example. This is enough for weaker minds. Whereas evil can also be valuable material from which to draw new forms.

At the "end of the journey," the unnamed traveler finds himself alone, in front of something that also exists in solitude and has no form at all, not even "mental form." But who is the traveler? Anyone following the Platonic tradition would have answered: the wise man, or the soul that has followed the line of thought to the final stage. Not Plotinus. When it reaches the state of being *sola ad solum*, the soul "no longer says it is another thing, it doesn't say it is man or animal or an entity or everything." Neither Plato nor anyone else in his tradition would have dared write that the soul, having reached the maximum proximity with that which lies "beyond the essence," casts off all possibility of calling itself "man or animal or an entity or everything." Where the possibility of being an *animal* is just as surprising as the possibility of being *everything*. And Plotinus is careful not to underline the newness of what he is saying. It was enough for him to relate what happens at the "end of the journey."

XI

STATUES

Hugo von Hofmannsthal climbed up to the Acropolis, bewildered by an excess of "names, figures" that "merged one into another with no beauty," as though they were dissolving "into a greenish smoke." A question was nagging him: "These Greeks, I was wondering, where are they?" And "the gods, eternal?" Instead they disappeared. They were "uncertain ghosts, fleeing." And their stories? They were "Milesian tales, a decoration painted on the wall, in the house of a courtesan."

Hofmannsthal then invokes the shadow of Plato and reopens *Philoctetes*. That was not enough. "These gods, their judgments, these men, their deeds, they all seemed to me excessively alien, deceptive, insubstantial." The traveler carries on walking. He goes into the Acropolis museum. In the third room, in a semicircle, five *kórai*. "Statues were here, women, in long dresses . . . In that instant something happened to me: an unnamed fear . . . The room, as it was, square . . . filled in an instant with a light much stronger than real light: the eyes of the statues had suddenly turned toward me, and in those faces was a wholly inscrutable smile." It didn't last long, that light—indeed, it cannot be said whether it lasted at all. But even when Hofmannsthal pulled himself together, that material was still before him. There was now "something liquid" about it. It came from one place and revealed the will to reach another. He thought: "Has a universe not opened up to me, in the twinkling of an eye?"

What happened to Hofmannsthal, on that day in 1908, in the Acropolis museum, illustrates the changes in attitude toward ancient Greece, from Hölderlin up to today. Those images now had the air of "Milesian tales": attractive, illusory, and above all, one had to be beckoned in by a courtesan in order to see them. Difficult to find more beautiful figures and associations. But one was then overcome by a sense of extraneousness. Or otherwise those tales became mixed with "a fragrance of strawberries and acacia, or ripe wheat, the dust of roads and open sea." Something intoxicating and tremendously fleeting. This Greece offered no guarantee of stability. It promised nothing—and it had vanished, leaving behind it a trail of mutilated statues. And yet from statues could come the sudden eye-opening flash of inspiration: more from statues than from words. "Something liquid," *tò theîon*, the divine once again.

Hermann Usener experienced a "philological immersion into the material," bold as never before, unflinching before even the tiniest detail, combined with a sudden totality of vision, freed from any tangible element. In his *Götternamen* there are impressions and glimpses of general assertions with vast implications, about which there is no attempt at justification or discussion. They resemble, instead, certain ancient statues freshly unearthed: "Only finished, limited phenomena and relationships are those in which and through which the feeling of the infinite enters consciousness. In the beginning, it is never the infinite in itself toward which feeling and thought are elevated. Not *the* infinite, but *something* infinite, divine is presented to man and is conceived in the spirit, minted in the language. In this way an unlimited series of divine concepts is created, which at first have an independent value. Each of these concepts, to the extent to which it denotes a divine force, is imbued with infinitude. But this quality is extended only in depth, not in breadth; it relates only to the point, the line covered by the concept. For our thought, accustomed to a unitary divinity, these figures of gods can be grasped only as single forms of phenomena or irradiations of divinity . . .

"The originary spiritual conception could only be to grasp and name the single being or the single phenomenon. Prior to particular concepts, momentary or single concepts had to be revealed. If the momentary emotion confers the value and the power of a divinity upon the thing that stands before us, which makes us conscious of the immediate proximity of a divinity . . . then the *momentary god* is perceived and created. The single phenomenon is made divine in its full immediacy . . . that single thing, which you see before you, that thing itself and nothing more is the god." These last words seem to be addressed to Hofmannsthal at the moment when, a few years later, he would enter the semicircle of the *kórai*.

Usener's *momentary gods* were acquired from his studies of classical antiquity insofar as they were protected by the shield of the rigorous philologist, but they came from a book on which a sentence of *scientific death* had been decreed: the *Symbolik und Mythologie der alten Völker* by Friedrich Creuzer. Just the same as would one day happen with Nietzsche, for his *Birth of Tragedy*. The concept had originated from the blazing center of German Romanticism and would then be transmitted to Usener—and from him to his pupil Aby Warburg. For Creuzer, the symbol itself was enough to bring proximity to the gods, if it incorporated "the *momentary*, the *total*, the *unfathomability of its origin*, *necessity*." Because then, and only then, the symbol "denotes the appearance of the divine and the transfiguration of the earthly image."

The clash between Nietzsche and Wilamowitz, between two incompatible visions of Greece, with all its acrimonious consequences, had been anticipated, sixty years before, by Creuzer and Lobeck. And just as the subject of dispute between Nietzsche and Wilamowitz was Dionysus, for Creuzer and Lobeck it was Zagreus. In what was then almost Biedermeier Germany, a potentially scandalous description appeared in print on the same page as a note referring to Lobeck and his "erudite arrogance, which is never so ridiculous as when it is applied to this unconquerable terrain" (meaning: the land of Dionysus): "In substance, this is the story: As soon as Persephone had grown up, all the gods wooed her. Demeter was afraid of a bloody conflict between her suitors, so she hid her daughter in a cave and left her under the guard of the serpents that drive her chariot. But Zeus transforms himself into a serpent and makes love with Persephone. From this intercourse Zagreus is born with the head of a bull. He became his father's favorite, was made to sit beside his throne and even granted the power to hurl the thunderbolt." This was followed by several lines on the ambush by the Titans and the slaughter of Zagreus, until Pallas succeeded in taking his beating heart and delivering it to Zeus.

Jacob Burckhardt never set foot in Greece. In a letter to Eduard Schauenburg in 1847 he wrote: "In the Vatican I could show you the spot where my eyes seemed to open up to antiquity. I was in front of the statue of Nile recumbent." Nile is naked, mighty, bearded, with the hem of a *himátion* on his right thigh and his left arm resting on a sphinx. Sixteen tiny beings are climbing and playing on his body, together with a crocodile and a mongoose. They are the Pecheis, the children that represent the cubits reached by the Nile in full flow. From that day Burckhardt ceaselessly observed how "in the ancient writers there are very many strange things, that few people notice."

Between 650 and the Persian invasion of 480 B.C.E., in Athens as well as in the islands, in the Peloponnese, and on the coast of Asia Minor or in Magna Grecia, many craftsmen, mostly anonymous, but whose names are occasionally recorded, modeled statues of young women covered by layers of drapery and pleated fabrics. Standing upright, with feet together, they gradually became more fluid. One foot, generally the left, a little in front of the other, slightly bent, one hand that holds an offering, three fingers that clutch a hem of drapery. The expressions were very different, but they seemed to belong to one and the same family. The craftsmen often worked on commissions from distant places. They knew exactly what they were required to do. The *kórai* were a new zoological species that appeared in well-circumscribed surroundings and died out in a little under two hundred years.

Sometimes we know the name of the craftsman or the dedicant or the goddess to whom the *kórē* was dedicated. Not the name of the *kórē* herself, or with very rare exceptions, such as in the Geneleos group, where the *kórē* is a young girl of the dedicant family. This anonymity of the image signals the crossing of a threshold, into a place where the simulacrum is self-sufficient in its muteness.

"Nikandre dedicated me to the archeress who hits the target."
Thus speaks what is thought to be the first surviving Greek statue
in marble. Nikandre was a woman of Naxos: the statue was found
at Delos. The figure is a woman of natural proportions. There is a
hole in her left hand. Perhaps she held a bow, to represent the goddess. Perhaps to represent the donor. But the real peculiarity, for
Greece, is the first words of the inscription: "Nikandre dedicated
me . . ." Here it is the statue that speaks.

They had bronze eyelashes, fixed into the eye sockets of the
statues. Some that have survived can be seen at the National Archaeological Museum in Athens. Only during the period of almost
two hundred years of the *kórai* did anyone feel the need to forge
bronze eyelashes. Then the world managed without.

The peplos was held in place by long pins that could become
deadly weapons. The sole survivor of the disastrous expedition
against Aegina (the reason: to recover two wooden statues, of the
goddesses Damia and Auxesia) was surrounded by the wives of his
dead comrades, who stabbed him to death with the pins of their
pepluses, "each demanding where their husband was," according to
Herodotus. It was a lynching not unlike that suffered by Orpheus,
though simpler. To the Athenians "the women's action seemed a
thing more terrible than the disaster." And they decided then to
change the fashion, which marked the beginning of a period of
supreme elegance, as testified by the *kórai*. They substituted the
Doric peplos with the Ionic chiton. Made of linen instead of wool:
lighter, softer, more Asiatic. It came from lands where the women
were judged by their ability to keep their dress above their ankles.
And above all, the chiton needed no pins, but had delicate buttons,
on which the terrifying face of the Gorgon could sometimes be
seen in relief.

The *kórē* is a momentary being, fixed in stone. It is this, before
its name and its function. These can be added—a partridge or a
fruit in her hand, an inscription on a fold of her peplos—without

changing anything of essential importance. Many *kórai* at the Acropolis were dedicated by men. They are not the goddess, they are not the dedicant. Many puzzled historians describe them as maidservants in the perpetual service of the goddess. But why this certainty? We know only one thing: they are as they appear, they remain in a form that appeared only once.

"Did they represent the divinity to whom the statue was dedicated, or the dedicant, or neither? Curiously enough, in most cases we do not know": after many years studying the *kórai*, Gisela Richter came to this conclusion. This uncertainty, this inconsistency, this irreducible affinity between dedicant and dedicatee are the surest and most discernible basis for that possibility of assimilation to the divine about which Plotinus was writing. Ten centuries before him, certain figures of young women had already demonstrated what his words were suggesting.

When the Athenians climbed back up the Acropolis after its devastation by the Persians, they decided to extend its area. To fill the sloping ground, they mixed the earth with statues that were lying around. And not just marble statues, but bronze and terracotta statuettes, vases, coins, and stone slabs with inscriptions, as though every record of the past had to be wiped out. There was no further mention of them until one day in February 1886, when a team superintended by Panagiotis Kavvadias was excavating the ground to the northeast of the Erechtheion and found a ditch with a heap of fourteen *kórai*. The last to see them intact had been the Persians. Herodotus recounts how, "when the Athenians saw they had now climbed up to the Acropolis, some threw themselves down from the walls and died, others took refuge inside the temple. Those Persians who had climbed up first, hurled themselves against the doors and, having opened them, killed the supplicants, sacked the temple, and set the whole Acropolis alight."

The war between Persia and Greece was also a war of religion. The Persians abhorred statues; the Greeks worshipped them. The Persians considered it "foolishness" for anyone to think that gods could have a "human shape." The Greeks were more flexible. They thought the gods could *occasionally* have a human shape. But above all they thought the statues could also be divine. The real difference was concentrated on the *agálmata*, on the "simulacra." A subtle and metaphysical difference, not easy to recognize. The Persians did not in fact reject the gods of foreigners. Indeed: "The Persians accept foreign customs more than any other people," writes Herodotus. So throughout Assyria and Arabia they had accepted Aphrodite. But *not* the statues. This had to do with the condemnation of untruth, from which everything else followed: "The vilest thing for them is lying." *Druj*, "falseness," was the power that loomed over everything, in perpetual conflict with its twin power: *aša*, "order" and "truth," just like the Vedic *ṛta*. The Greeks were much more accommodating when it came to untruth, and reluctant to give it a cosmic role. They preferred to think in terms of *apátē*, "deception," and admitted that such deception was not alien to the life of the gods.

There was also another point of divergence between Persians and Greeks: the Magi. This name originally indicated a Median tribe. Then it became the name for powerful Persian priests. Nothing of the kind was to be found in Greece, where there had never been a priestly class. But the Magi also differed "from other men as well as from the priests of Egypt," whom Herodotus (and the Greeks) regarded as priests par excellence. What marked them out? The act of killing. "The Magi kill any living thing with their hands, except for dogs and man, and they consider this a great thing, killing ants and snakes alike, and other animals that crawl and fly." The Magus who kills ants and considers it "a great thing" is associated with someone who rejects statues and regards lying to be a capital sin. In the Persian legacy there is a persecutory absoluteness that remained alien to the Greeks. But the Greeks and Persians shared other traits. The sacrificial rites could be very different, as Herodotus recounts, but it remained implicit that the sacrificial act involved everything. When the victim was torn apart and cooked, Herodotus recounts, "a Magus approaches and sings of the birth of the gods, how they say that it came about."

The *kórai* remained invisible for 2,366 years. The eye could not catch sight of the eye, which was that of the *kórai* themselves, their pupils, the only point on the opaque human body where a minuscule circle catches a reflection. And the reflection indicates that this is where the mind operates. Once the *kórai* that we know today had been buried, the Athenians seem to have forgotten them. There was no further attempt to model such statues with their thoughtful expressions, with their robes that hung in many folds, vertical or undulating, always parallel, like stage wings.

"The Egyptians describe all those who do not have their language as barbarians," writes Herodotus. And the first barbarians to arrive in Egypt speaking Greek were "certain Ionians and Carians who were voyaging for plunder." The Greeks landed in Egypt as barbarians and pirates. But they had weapons of bronze—and an oracle had foretold the persecuted Psammeticus that "revenge would arrive from the sea, on the appearance of men of bronze." At first, Psammeticus had not believed the oracle. Then someone brought news that "men of bronze had come from the sea and were plundering the plain." Psammeticus realized that these would be his allies. And with their help he reconquered Egypt. "They were the first men speaking a different language to settle in Egypt." Barbarians, pirates, finally mercenaries.

If Egypt is the *primum*, the Greeks had the privilege of being the first barbarians. And from this came the fragrance of all that originated from Egypt, whether it was the Mysteries or the *kórai*. They transposed everything into another language, yet retaining something—the aura or the shadow—of the original. A number of statuettes have survived in which the Egyptian precursors of the *kórai* can be recognized. Naked, with rounded headgear (the *pólos*). One in bronze, with angular forms, found at Delphi. Others in ivory, found in a tomb at the Dipylon Gate. One of them gazes at us from a display cabinet at the National Archaeological Museum in Athens: large fixed eyes, the clear outline of breasts, waist, and buttocks, arms hanging straight, feet together. "But, though evidently connected with Eastern prototypes, one feels that there is something distinctly Greek in these figures," observed Gisela Richter. They were the first words of the barbarians.

Ágalma, "statue," also means "simulacrum" in general, and "mental image." "Do not stop carving your statue [*ágalma*]": words of Plotinus. But what statue is he talking about? An invisible statue. A mental image that has to accompany us at any time. Those who ignore the existence of such invisible statues are unlikely to understand Greek statuary and what separates it from everything else.

After seven centuries Plotinus took the words of Plato, in this case from *Phaedrus*, subtly varying them (as he continually did). He reused not only the word *ágalma*, but the verb that went with it (*tektaínein*, "to model"). In Plato, however, the context is erotic. It is the *ágalma* of the "beautiful ones," of the lovers, that is to be modeled and decorated. And one turns to those simulacra "in order to venerate them and celebrate Mysteries" (*orgiásōn*, a word that can refer only to what happens during the Mysteries). And this is none other than the *way of life* pursued by those who follow the procession of Zeus. There is no better way. If another god also had to be followed, nothing would change since "in relation to each god to whom each has been a choral dancer, he spends his life honoring and imitating him so far as possible."

The first statues were the dead. This was the assumption. The Egyptians, supreme literalists, were among the first to understand and apply it. The dead can be dressed, oiled, painted, eviscerated. But they remain immobile. So "words like *corpse* (mummy, body, remains) and *image* (statue, form, etc.) in Egyptian have the same determinative." Modeling statues implies something to do with the dead. In Egypt it was clear from the very beginning and pervaded the whole of their art. For the ancient Greeks it was an assumption and a challenge. They wanted a life force other than that of normal life to pulse through those motionless beings.

Opposition to the gods means opposition to statues. The noble status of the simulacrum upsets the new Christian piety, which sees the whole pagan perversion concentrated on its relationship with statues. And statue is linked with theater, since the simulacrum is the actor on the stage of the mind. Clement of Alexandria rages: "You have made heaven into a stage and the divine for you has become a drama and you have made a comedy with demon masks out of what is sacred."

The assumption is that statues were alive—and revealed the sovereignty of appearance. A deeply held conviction, among the most difficult to eradicate. Not even the droppings of swallows smeared over the statues of Olympian Zeus or of Asclepius at Epidaurus or of Athena Polias could convince people of "the insensibility of the statues." This was what Clement exclaimed, irritated by that stubborn resistance.

When Perseus saw Andromeda chained to a rock he thought she was a statue because of her supreme beauty. This sounded obvious to the Greeks—and to them alone. But the Judeo-Christian rage against images, which culminates in regarding idolatry as "*summa offensa*," the "worst outrage," does not arise so much out of a conviction that the Lord could not be represented, as from the rash move that had induced him to create man *in his image*. The first idolater, strictly speaking, is the Lord himself. And this was a particular worry for certain Fathers of the Church. Tertullian, with his usual perspicuity, wrote: "*Ipse homo, omnium flagitiorum auctor, non tantum opus dei, verum etiam imago est*," "Man himself, author of all depravities, is not only a work of God, but also his image."

A crucial question, posed by Simone Weil: "Why was it good to make a bronze serpent, and a crime to make a golden calf?"

The sky is also an *ágalma*, according to Plotinus: "A great simulacrum, beautiful and lively and produced by the art of Hephaestus." The sky was therefore a subtly decorated work of art: "The stars twinkle over its face, others on its breast, others where there were convenient places." And so, even in its relentless extension, *ágalma* is still a statue. And this also makes it possible to look at a statue as though it includes the sky in it.

Plato writes that certain gods "we worship seeing them clearly": they are the stars, the sun, the moon, the sky. It is enough to go into the open air to encounter one of these gods in our own field of view. For other gods, the invisible ones, statues have to be built to resemble them. But this means that even the invisible gods allow themselves to be seen, and that humans can recognize their appearance. *Ágalma* is the essential word, as an intermediary for the invisible. A word that implies reverence and worship.

A traveling miracle worker, "Apollonius of Tyana, having spent the winter visiting all the temples of Greece, set off for Egypt as spring approached." He was looking for a boat on which to sail. So one day he reached Piraeus, where "a ship was moored ready to set sail for Ionia." But on the ship was a merchant who was trying to prevent others from boarding. Apollonius began an exchange with this merchant, which Philostratus has reported in its entirety: "Upon Apollonius asking him: 'What is the cargo?' he replied, 'I'm transporting statues of gods to Ionia, some of gold and stone, others of ivory and gold.' 'To dedicate them, or for some other reason?' 'To sell them to those who want to dedicate them.' 'You therefore fear, good man, that we will steal them on the ship?' 'This is not my fear,' replied the other, 'but I am sorry they travel along with so many people, and that they are exposed to the company and customs of worthless people, such as those to be found on ships.' 'And yet, my dear friend,' replied Apollonius, 'on ships where you come up against barbarians—since you seem to be from Athens—though they are full of the usual disorder of the crew, the gods were carried on board with you, and they did not think of being contaminated by you. Yet you foolishly turn away from your ship philosophers, who are the men most agreeable to the gods, and this you do earning money from the gods? Sculptors of old did not behave in this way, nor did they go around the cities selling gods: they carried with them only their hands and tools for working the stone and the ivory, and from material still formless they produced their works in the temples themselves. But you are carrying the gods around ports and markets just as if you were selling wares from Hyrcania and Scythia—I won't say what—and you don't think you are doing something impious? In truth there are men who, in the way of charlatans, stick images of Demeter or Dionysus on their bodies and say they have been brought up by the gods they wear upon them. But to make a living out of the gods themselves and not even to feel satisfied by this food is, I would say, a detestable trade, indeed pure madness, if you do not fear the consequences.' And with these words of reproach he boarded another ship."

The only thing new, in comparison with "sculptors of old," is that the craftsmen then moved about with their tools and carved the statues in the temples. In the end, though, they, too, would be sold. We know that Theodorus of Samos worked for Sparta, Smilis of Aegina for Samos, and Endoeus of Athens for Tegea. Their commissions came from far away. And it seems people were confident the craftsman knew exactly what he had to do. Yet in statues created not in temples but in craftsmen's workshops, something of the divine presence still persisted. Otherwise the merchant of Piraeus wouldn't have worried about those statues being contaminated by the company of ignorant passengers. There was a blend of wiliness and devotion in him that only the Greeks knew how to practice. The merchant knew very well that his job involved selling simulacra, but he recognized their divine aura, indeed he wanted to protect it. He insisted that the statues sail alone, undisturbed by human presence.

The throne of Amyclae was a long wooden bench, with no armrests. It was made of planks with gaps between. At the center, over a wider plank, was the simulacrum of the god: "No one has measured it, but at a guess it would be around thirty cubits," observed Pausanias. It was "an old and crude image." It had a face, feet, and hands, but otherwise it resembled a "bronze pillar."

A helmet, a bow, a spear: nothing else. Its body was a trunk, over which a new robe was placed each year, woven in a special room, which the women weavers called Chiton. The fifty-foot-high statue loomed over visitors, pointing its spear at them. They turned their gaze to look at those places on the bench that were expecting someone. But no visible being would ever occupy them. Protruding from beneath the bench, under the feet of the god, to support the immense statue, was the outline of a tomb. It contained the body of Apollo's lover, pink-cheeked Hyacinthus, whom the god's discus had injured. Along the backrest of the bench, thirty bronze panels recounted stories: Taygete and her sister Alcyon kidnapped by Zeus and Poseidon; Heracles fighting with Cycnus; Theseus, who slays the Minotaur; Cephalus kidnapped by Eos; Hera watching over Io; Admetus yoking his chariot to a boar and a lion. And still more, alternated by sphinxes and panthers. The god looked down, as a unique being, but beneath him was the vast expanse, generally empty, of the divine. If the other gods had visited Amyclae, they would have sat on that bench. Otherwise some story about them would have remained as a record, embossed on the backrest. And everything, just like every foundation, rested on a dead being, watched over forever by his killer and lover.

Pausanias recounts how at Sparta he saw the only two-story temple, dedicated to Aphrodite Morpho—"the Beautiful." J. G. Frazer, in his commentary, compares it with the basilica at Assisi frescoed by Giotto. In the lower part, says Pausanias, was an armed wooden statue of Aphrodite. On the upper floor, another image of Aphrodite, "on a throne, veiled, with chains to her feet." Even back in the time of Pausanias, the stories told about those chains were not believed ("I won't follow them even for a moment"). The chains must have been a punishment: the goddess was said to have forced the daughters of Tyndareus into adultery. Pausanias comments: "It would have been entirely foolish to make a cedarwood figure, calling it Aphrodite, in the hope of punishing the goddess."

Nietzsche recalled "the veiled and chained figure of Aphrodite Morpho" as an example of "how oriental Greece still seemed in the times of Pausanias." Everything went back to the fact that the Greeks "spent a long time looking about, happily learning as amateurs; even Aphrodite, for example, is Phoenician." In describing the simulacrum of Aphrodite Morpho, Pausanias uses the word *zōdion*, "small image" (diminutive of *zôon*, "'animal,' as opposed to that which is not animate"), a word that also indicated signs of the zodiac. Pausanias would probably have used the same word if he had seen an African fetish.

The nudity of the Greeks is different from any other in antiquity, in the same way that every statue of Aphrodite is different from any other Mediterranean goddess. And only in Greece was there a prohibition, also told in myths, on seeing a goddess naked. Actaeon is the eponymous hero of Greek statuary. Even if the body of the goddess later appeared naked, its potential was discernible from the beginning. The assumption was that the pure beauty of a body might have a dazzling effect. This can be deduced from Aristotle, who at the beginning of *Politics* posed a central question: is it true, as some argue, that "certain men are slaves everywhere and others nowhere?" Aristotle clearly understood what problems it would cause if he supported such an idea. And yet he himself thought that slaves were such *phýsei*, "by nature." The difficulties arose as soon as one went any further. The question would certainly be resolved if free men were distinguished by the fact of possessing "a body like the pictures [*eikónes*] of the gods." Then "everyone would say that the remainder ought to be slaves of those others." But perhaps this might not be the case. There were also slaves whose bodies looked like the "pictures of the gods." So that, almost to increase the confusion, sometimes "slaves have the body of free men and free men have only the souls that make them such." At the same time, Aristotle let it be seen how every conflict between servants and masters, between slaves and free men, might have vanished if masters "by nature" had *all* been born with bodies resembling those statues and paintings of the gods (these were their *eikónes*) encountered while walking around Athens.

The classical is separated from the archaic (from *any* form of archaic) through a reduction in the number of elements: fewer animals, fewer attributes, fewer colors, fewer causes, fewer gods, fewer words. Less fixity. Few details are chosen to describe everything—and those details have to carry the power of what has been excluded and is initially attached to such profiles like an invisible halo. It is this that makes the sculpture of Phidias or the Master of Olympia irreducibly different to everything that went before and came after.

Disciples of Winckelmann and absorbed in their studies, the Olympians began to hear the deafening sound of the Dionysiac procession when Creuzer published his *Dionysus* in 1808, a time of full romantic fervor. Kuretes and Korybantes, Mimallones and Telchines, Bacchae and Bassarids: they were so many ranks of like beings, contrary to the singularity of each of the Twelve. Bells and tambourines came closer and closer. When young Nietzsche published *The Birth of Tragedy*, Olympus was already under siege, on every side. But another forty years had to pass before a Greek scholar at Cambridge, a shrewd and daring woman, ventured to write that the Olympic gods, after years in which she had venerated them in their neoclassical integrity, now seemed "like a bouquet of cut-flowers whose blooms are brief, because they have been severed from their roots." And this led her to a surprising conclusion: "My sense of the superficiality of Homer's gods had deepened to a conviction that these Olympians were not only non-primitive, but positively in a sense non-religious . . . On the other hand, the cultus of Dionysus and Orpheus seemed to me, whatever its errors and licenses, essentially religious." Jane Harrison had the gift of frankness. She was able to express what her various colleagues (Gilbert Murray, F. M. Cornford, A. B. Cook) had sensed but hadn't had the courage to declare.

What stands out in her words is the assertion that the Olympians were something "non-religious." How could such a reversal have taken place? Several millennia had passed and a Cambridge scholar now discovered that Zeus, Apollo, Aphrodite, Athena were something extraneous to religious sentiment, because they were *superficial*. And her feeling was certainly shared, not just by a few colleagues but by a certain European climate in 1911.

But as well as being superficial, and therefore to be deplored, the Olympians are unfathomable. Nietzsche had said much the same: "The Greeks were superficial—*through their depth*!" The more one investigates the stories of the Olympians, the more one detects a resistance to any attempt at explanation. It is the gods who give an explanation of anyone who tries to explain them—more than the other way around. What might have led Jane Harrison into doubt is that such unfathomability of character was accompanied by an irresistible fragrance. Those figures were light, and perhaps they suggested a prospect of impermanence, like a bunch of fresh flowers. They didn't impose that punitive gravity that Europe was accustomed to associating with everything to do with religion. But it was Europe that had lost something along the way, it was Europe that had gradually lessened every sense of the religious. The Olympians remained intact. And their indomitable strangeness consisted in this: they were gods, but they were not to be weighed down by feelings of compunction. That sense of superficiality that emanated from some Mediterranean gods was something that others had not managed to acquire. This is why the Olympians were so flexible and well disposed to being statues. And as such, after many centuries, they continue to exist. They have the privilege of not demanding homage. They return to being what they perhaps were from the beginning: images of self-sufficient, unconnected, sovereign life.

Cassiodorus recounts how, when Rome was devastated by Alaric's Visigoths, more statues were left to guard the city than inhabitants.

XII

O EGYPT, EGYPT . . .

Don't you know, Asclepius, that Egypt is the image of heaven; or more accurately, the colony of all things that are ordered and done in heaven? The truth is that our country is the temple of the world . . . O Egypt, Egypt, only the fables of your religions will remain, yet they will be unbelievable to future generations, for whom nothing else will be able to tell the stories of your pious deeds except the letters carved in stone that will tell their story not to the gods and men (for the men will be dead, and the gods will have transmigrated into heaven) but to Scythians and Indians, or such others of savage nature.

—GIORDANO BRUNO, *The Expulsion of the Triumphant Beast*

The youthfulness of the Greeks, their recklessness, and even their impudence became clear to Herodotus in Egypt. Hecataeus the logographer had gone before him. Hecataeus, like everyone else, had boasted about his family, tracing it back to distant times: sixteen generations indeed. After which he was related to a god. The Egyptian priests listened patiently and silently, and made no comment. But they took him into a vast temple. Tall wooden statues, in a line. Three hundred and forty-five. All *piromi*, they said, a word "equivalent in Greek to *excellent men.*" Those *piromi* had succeeded one another for that number of generations. The priests felt it their duty to tell Hecataeus about them, "not accepting from him that a man could be born from a god." Gods certainly existed. But they were not so accessible. The Greeks, these upstarts, were creating confusion, whereas the Egyptians knew that "for 11,340 years there had been no god in human form." Moreover, during that same period "none of the affairs of Egypt had undergone any change, either in what comes to them from the earth, or in what comes from the river, or in relation to sickness and death."

Who were the Greeks for the Egyptians? First of all they were those they encountered in the marketplace and to whom they sold the heads of sacrificed animals. Heads they would otherwise have thrown into the river. And they made sure to pronounce certain words over those heads: "If any evil is about to threaten those who sacrifice or the whole of Egypt, may it fall on that head." Unfamiliar with the "innumerable" rituals that studded Egyptian life, the Greeks were seen as blasphemous traders, on which to discharge the *accursed part* of the sacrifice.

For the Greeks, the Grand Tour was Egypt. Instead of sex, lemons, and Roman ruins, they discovered shaven-headed priests who treated them as curious and fundamentally ignorant foreigners. According to Diodorus Siculus, those who traveled to Egypt included Orpheus, Musaeus, Melampus, Dedalus, Homer, Lycurgus, Solon, Plato, Pythagoras, Eudoxus, Democritus, and Oenopides. This was apparent from books kept by Egyptian priests that listed visitors. Plutarch, a century later, added Thales to the names, and stated that Eudoxus had also translated from Egyptian. Each had pursued a particular branch of knowledge. And Diodorus Siculus concluded: "All things for which the Greeks are admired came from Egypt." Thus the Greeks had acquired Egyptian wisdom like an imported commodity. The Egyptians were entirely responsible for its origins. And this favored the smooth and open-minded way in which the Greeks passed it on as a gift for modernity.

According to Herodotus, the wisest Egyptians were the priests of Heliopolis. And Herodotus had spoken with them. But he made an immediate proviso: "About their stories, those regarding the gods, I intend to make no mention whatsoever, except to give the names, for I believe that all men know the same about them." These last words have been understood in conflicting ways. The more presumptuous commentators are convinced that Herodotus was referring to the fact that all men know very little about divine things. And this is so, they say, because those same things, in themselves, are inexistent. This is remarkably naïve if we think of the numerous passages in which Herodotus stops himself talking about certain divine matters. Because they exist *too much*—and are capable of affecting those who don't know how to deal with them. This is the underlying assumption.

So the words of Herodotus can only have a very different meaning. *All* men know one and the same thing in relation to the gods. They may not know their names, as happened to the Pelasgians. But they are aware of their existence like that of water or fire. The words of Herodotus, in their disarming simplicity, are disconcerting. Even before being named, the gods are present and active. They are obvious, to all. Later, they might even be canceled out, forgotten. But at first they are an irrepressible presence. Many will make a solemn attempt to establish "divine things," *tà theîa*. No one will manage to assume such things as naturally as Herodotus does, as if they were obvious.

The pride of the Egyptians, according to Plato, lay in not accepting that there could be anything new. "If you look carefully, you will see that painting and sculpture in that country go back thousands of years—and when I say thousands it is no figure of speech but reality—and they are neither more beautiful nor more ugly than those made today, using the same technique." This is what the Athenian said to his two companions as they made their way slowly toward the cave of Zeus. Crete, Sparta: these were already examples of rigor, fixity, and antiquity in their regulations. But no comparison with Egypt, which remained the model of that which accepts no change, having found *orthótēs*, "justness," in every aspect of life. But how could this be understood by the other inhabitants of Athens, a city that is *philólogos* and *polýlogos*, which "loves and multiplies words," when every word is open to the suspicion of inculcating and instigating something new? The same is true for sounds, due to the unfortunate "tendency of our pleasures and of our sorrows always to express themselves with a new music." Whereas in Egypt, "the melodies conserved until today are the work of Isis." The goddess serves in this way as a protection against any innovation.

In Egypt, time was measured in thousands of years; in Greece, in centuries and decades. Herodotus and Plato are continually recalling this. Whatever happened in the short term could be reversed. This was what lay behind the perennial turmoil that unfolds in the *pólis*. In Egypt, the same doctrine was refracted from one sanctuary to another. But there were intrigues and disputes among priests. In Greece there was no priestly class to speak. At most, there were the three prophetesses of Dodona, or the Pythia at Delphi. And it was said the prophetesses of Dodona were doves that had flown from Thebes in Egypt. One is said to have begun talking with a human voice. Herodotus did not believe this fantastical story. He thought it was not a dove but a woman kidnapped in Egypt and sold as a slave. "By then saying that the dove was black they are indicating that the woman was Egyptian," he added.

Egypt was the source of imitation. Darius, king of Persia, wanted "to imitate their life"; Orpheus wanted to "imitate their funeral customs." But what is imitated has to be rigid: it is a mold, from which countless copies are made. Plato distrusted copies. He wanted to go back to the mold. At Heliopolis, even three centuries later, visitors were shown the houses where Plato and Eudoxus had stayed. There, according to Strabo, Plato had "spent thirteen years with the priests." Whereas according to *De doctrina Platonis* by Alcinous it was three years. And Diogenes Laërtius speaks of sixteen months.

When Strabo visited Heliopolis, the "great houses" of the priests "who studied philosophy and astronomy" could still be seen. But the priests had gone. Except that "those who celebrated the sacrifices explained the holy things to foreigners." Plato and Eudoxus had once pestered the priests to tell them about certain doctrines that "they held secret and were reluctant to divulge." Indeed, Strabo observed, "the barbarians concealed the major part of things."

The characteristics of the statues were established by the assembly of the gods. So humans, and in particular kings, simply had to comply: the poison of imitation, loathed by Plato, was eliminated. Attempting to imitate what the gods have prescribed may be unsuccessful, but nothing more. The gods can forgive that. Whereas the inexorable chain of *mímesis*, when it is applied to the affairs of the world, and passes from man to man, is a conundrum from which there is no escape. As for the Olympians, they were not concerned with establishing measurements and proportions for the statues. They were too curious and eager about worldly matters, as was shown before each occasion they intervened. And so Plato remained obsessed with *copies*.

According to Plato, Egypt and Mesopotamia succeeded much earlier than Greece in recognizing certain truths about the "gods of the cosmos"—the stars—thanks to the "beauty of their summer," which makes the sky clear and bright. But this should be no discouragement, indeed: "Let us state as a principle that the Greeks turn what they have taken from the barbarians into something more beautiful and they develop it to perfection [*télos*]." Here, in a few words, is a statement of the incomparable difference between the Greeks and anyone else: the cult and the practice of perfection. The Greeks do not claim to have invented anything. They know they are a young race, surrounded by wise civilizations "for countless millennia." Their claim is to "take care of all these gods in a more noble and just way compared with what happens in the traditions and worship practiced by barbarians, thanks to education, to the oracles of Delphi, and to the public worship recognized by law." An enormous claim, which at the same time shows most clearly the relationship between the Greeks and all barbarians. Certainly, it was recognized that barbarians conserved true doctrines of remote origin. Yet they needed to be perfected in a way that only the Greeks believed they could offer. A declaration of extreme humility, and at the same time of wild arrogance. But it was on this, according to Plato, that Greece was founded—and there is no more reliable a witness.

The barbarians were therefore the opposite of what the word has come to mean in modern times. They were not new, rough, inarticulate, strong people. They were civilizations much older than Greece—particularly Egypt, Mesopotamia, Persia—that had achieved a noble and immovable wisdom. But something had produced a rigidity and had blocked them. Now it was for the Greeks to fulfill the immense work undertaken before them, making it more flexible, supple. And indeed simplifying it. This, too, was the genius and wonder of the Greeks. Nietzsche once put it like this: "The superior *moral* nature of the Greeks is revealed in their sense of totality and simplification, by showing us *simplified* man they cheer us, in the same way that the sight of animals cheers us."

Herodotus observed the Egyptians: guardians of purity, they require their victims to be uncontaminated, their heads are shiny and shaven, they wash too much, they sell the heads of sacrificed bulls to Greek traders to be rid of them. They would never kiss a Greek on the mouth. And the Greeks, impure people who disembarked at Naucratis, regarded them in much the same way as people today read the classics. There was no familiarity. They would then set off again with those smelly bulls' heads, cargoes of grain, and scarabs.

For the Greeks, *Egyptian stories* seemed much more abstruse than those that went around about the Olympians. The Egyptians also spoke about the kingdom of the dead with a nonchalance unknown to the Greeks. It was said that one of their pharaohs, Rhampsinit, had gone down alive into Hades and played dice there with the queen, sometimes winning, sometimes losing—and had returned to earth with a gift from her: a golden napkin. At this point Herodotus feels compelled to declare: "It is my gift in all of this discourse to write what someone has said, as I have heard it." And immediately after he adds a crucial observation: "The Egyptians were the first to teach that the soul of man is immortal."

"The women urinate standing up, the men crouching down." This is one of Herodotus's first observations to illustrate how the Egyptians and Greeks were diametrically opposite. Someone might one day have said: the Greeks had Herodotus, who wanted to travel as far as Elephantine *to see* what the Egyptians were and how they acted, noting it down. Whereas the Egyptians were never interested in any detailed knowledge of the Greeks. As in Vedic India, Egypt is self-sufficient, inured, impermeable. Egypt, like India, is a place from which people do not travel. Whereas what came after is always a starting point for a long journey. Which presupposes, however, an untiring attraction for a fabled *place of invariance*.

The ancient Egyptians knew very well how to enter the invisible: through the *false door*. They had many of them, often in pink limestone, in their monuments and their tombs, built over the previous five thousand years. The notable element of false doors is their jambs. Not just two, but many. Always more numerous, ever narrower. They leave less and less space for the door itself. Which may be cramped, minuscule. And always made of stone, like their jambs. There is, in the end, no certain prospect of being able to pass through it. But it is the only access to the invisible.

The outer jamb of false doors was heavily decorated with images of everyday life. They corresponded to the variety of that which is apparent. Broad and manifold. The next jambs did not display images and the sphere of the visible became increasingly narrower. The same happened in life, on moving closer to the doorway that stood at the end. And one might pass through it at any moment—or even just at the last moment.

Scheintür, the "apparent door": this is what German Egyptologists call the architectural feature that other languages call "false door." But the German word is more appropriate. In the word *false* there is always a reference to *truth* and to *deception*. Whereas the "apparent door" is just a point of transit that appears in certain places. And which might even not be recognized.

The wonder of the Pyramids, according to Diodorus Siculus, lay above all in their appearance as "a sudden creation," with no relationship to what was around them, "as if they had been dropped down from above by some god in the midst of the surrounding sand." The same can be said about Egypt in general. There is an irreducible extraneousness between Egyptian antiquities and everything that surrounds them. This is what led to Egyptomania, as though reaching Egypt already meant passing through an "apparent door."

The first difficulty for the world of the dead lay in this: that no one could portray it in such a way as to make it more attractive than life on earth. Even in the representations of eternal bliss, there was something tedious and repetitive. Whereas even the most ordinary image of the world of the living could stir an astonishing desire. In Egypt, during the New Kingdom—the same centuries (the sixteenth to the twelfth centuries B.C.E.) during which the Vedic civilization flourished—the Ba of the dead—if this is what the soul can be called—desired nothing more than to stroll in its garden, perch among the branches of a sycamore (for it had become a swallow), enjoy its shade, drink water at its own pond, "without ever stopping." These were the highest pleasures to which it aspired, if no power had shut it in a cage, if the assembly of the gods had redeemed the dead person to which the Ba belonged.

The tomb was far from being a solitary and generally abandoned place, as happens in the secular age. If anything, it was a point of transit, a sorting office. There was a continual coming and going, helped or hindered, from one world to another, in a perpetual movement. "Enter and leave my tomb" was the wish of the dead. His most fervent desire was that his soul, transformed into a swallow, would enjoy the shade of the sycamore that he had once planted, while the statues in the funerary monument gathered the fresh food presented as sacrificial offerings and the body of the dead rested in the tomb. It was a new stage of life. The deceased expected no resurrection. It was enough for him to live as a swallow. But he expected to carry on living.

Close to the funerary temple of Ramses III, at Medinet Habu, was an enclosed garden—eighty-five feet along each side, with twenty trees inside, and a pond in the middle with fish. Around the temple and the garden, a high wall. It would be difficult to find a better approximation of the primordial garden or the *hortus conclusus*, or even of paradise in the Persian sense. The garden grew beside the sepulcher. One passed through it to get there. And, on leaving the sepulcher, one entered the garden. The vision of Sir Thomas Browne, who juxtaposed ashes and garden in two symmetrical texts, *Urn Burial* and *The Garden of Cyrus*, had been anticipated three thousand years before, in Egypt. As indeed Sir Thomas Browne had sought to demonstrate with his hieroglyphics in prose.

In the Egyptian *Book of the Dead*, chapters 76–88 list a series of metamorphoses that the dead can achieve: to become a golden falcon or divine falcon or lotus flower or Ptah or a god that brings light to darkness or phoenix or heron or swallow or Sa-ta serpent or crocodile. Whether as a plant or animal or god, every part of existence can be reached. But if the dead person wished to return to life on earth, it was essential to eat the sacrificial offerings, taking them from those basketfuls of food left in front of the pink granite of the false doors.

Some two thousand years before Plato, in the Pyramid Texts, it could be read how the primordial god, the Solitary, the One, had given birth to the gods: "Atum is shown in the form of a masturbator at Heliopolis. He took hold of his phallus to excite desire: twins were procreated, Shu and Tefnut." According to another version, with one spit Atum had created Shu and with another spit Tefnut. Other texts say that the world was born from his tears. Sperm, saliva, tears. It required a bodily fluid, shed externally, for something to exist.

The Ogdoad of Hermopolis was the origin of the Gnostic archons, the Sefirot, the Neo-Platonic emanations, the archangels of Ahura Mazda. The whole Mediterranean is populated with these composite beings, transformed—though still recognizable—as they voyage from shore to shore.

Even more than its antiquity, its hieratic nature, its secrecy, it was animals that made Egypt different from all that surrounded it—and made it a world in reverse, proud of being so ("in many matters they have customs and laws contrary to those of other men"). Egypt's many gods were something about which Herodotus preferred not to speak, unless "compelled by the story." But the same "obligation" to remain silent was true in regard to sacred animals. No gods, no animals: the picture described by Herodotus, the most valuable that we have, is based on a vast omission. It was a meticulously crafted setting in which it was easy to become lost. But what stood at the center had to remain unnamed.

On November 26, 1922, a date to remember, Howard Carter found himself in front of the treasure of Tutankhamun. The tomb was protected by a guardian: a jackal made of black resin, dressed in linen. Its body was wrapped in a thin muslin shawl, tied at the throat, decorated with blue lotuses and sunflowers. It was finished with a golden bow, behind the neck. Its eyes were set with gold, calcite, and obsidian. Silver claws. This is how the god Anubis, "Master of Secrets," appeared. And, for the Egyptians, the animals themselves were the first of the secrets.

Herodotus had noted: "Egypt, though bordering on Libya, does not have many animals. Those that they have are all considered sacred. Some live with the people, others don't. But, if I had to say why they regard them as sacred, I would end up talking about divine matters, which I shrink more than anything from describing. Moreover what I have stated about these things, barely touching upon them, I have stated because I am compelled."

The insuperable divide between Greece and Egypt certainly wasn't due to the difference between the gods. That Ptah was Hephaestus, that Osiris was Dionysus, that Isis was Demeter, that Mut was Hera, that Hathor was Aphrodite (or Artemis), that Amun-Ra was Zeus seemed obvious, just as in a tourist guidebook. It was simply a question of finding new ways in which the gods and new names appeared, related to those already known. The Egyptian animal cult, on the other hand, was regarded as "astonishing and beyond belief." For the Greeks, the gods could occasionally transform themselves into animals, but it seemed inconceivable to worship the animals themselves. This was the only form of *humanism* attributable to the Greeks.

Nothing about Egypt seemed as strange as their devotion to animals—"excessive," according to Diodorus. No one was embarrassed to be seen practicing the "liturgies" that they required. They considered them equal to the "most solemn ceremonies of the gods." They prostrated themselves on the ground to worship them—with that gesture, *proskýnēsis*, that would one day be normal in the Orthodox churches. They didn't forget that the first five gods had been "revealed to men in the form of sacred animals."

It wasn't just the ancients that were astonished by the Egyptians' relationship with their animals. According to Henri Frankfort it was "the most baffling, most persistent, and to us most alien feature" of their religion. Animals, for the Egyptians, are not qualities, they are not metaphors. What is adored is "*the animal as such.*" The archaeologist's particular embarrassment consisted in the first place in bringing to light hundreds of mummies of cats, gazelles, dogs, falcons, jackals, crocodiles, bulls, goats, sometimes dating back to five thousand years before. They might have seemed a mockery to his very profession, which was so rigidly fixed on what is human.

What feature made the scarab and the crocodile, the ibis and the baboon objects of such reverence? Frankfort asked this, and his answer, in its simplicity, is illuminating. In animals—in *all* animals—the Egyptians, he thought, worshipped "their inarticulate wisdom, their certainty, their unhesitating achievement, and above all their static reality." A reality finally immutable: it was perhaps this that the Egyptians were yearning for. It was their way of reacting to a very acute sense of impermanence.

Typhon raged. With his enormous body, which towered over the mountains, by shaking his shoulders from which sprang a hundred serpent heads, he attacked heaven. He wanted to avenge his ample-breasted mother, Gaia, for having been supplanted by that group of loquacious and luminous beings that had taken over on Mount Olympus.

The gods then fled, ignominiously, without even putting up a fight. But where to go? Typhon's many monstrous arms sprang up from every point of the horizon. There was just one place—Egypt— where there was some hope of hiding among other animal-headed gods, who were far more numerous and generally impassive. For the gods of Greece, going to Egypt was like seeking protection from their parents. When compared with Egypt, they felt like children. The same feeling would one day be transmitted to the men of Greece, who imitated them.

Afraid and exhausted, the gods reached Egypt and were transformed: "Apollo became a kite, Hermes an ibis, Ares a barbel, Artemis a cat, Dionysus took the form of a goat, Heracles a fawn, Hephaestus an ox, and Leto a shrew." Only Zeus and Athena, closed inside the walls of the mind, retained their own forms. The other Olympians were like a pack of beasts on the loose, driven by fear.

When it was all over, when Typhon plunged into the sea and, to suffocate the consuming fire, Zeus threw a mountain down upon him (one day they would call it Etna), the gods set foot once again in the vast halls of Olympus. A thin layer of dust had settled there, its air like a museum on days of closure. They resumed their normal life, but had a new thought concealed within them; the memory of that brief period when they had been animals, in Egypt. To be transformed and to transform: this was the first of their powers. It was the first of their secrets. When they looked at humans, so rigid in their forms and yet so mobile in their expressions, they couldn't stop seeing them as unknown and persistent seekers of that same power that for the gods was like breathing. Seekers doomed to fail—or only to partial and fleeting successes. Metamorphosis was a secret for humans too. They yearned to achieve it—and they knew that to achieve it they had to encounter a god and become a part of him, for only this is metamorphosis—but at the same time they prayed that the god should remain invisible. They knew, in fact, as Burckhardt would one day note, that "metamorphosis manifests itself in the majority of cases as punishment, indeed as revenge; but on other occasions it is a supreme favor or a sign of pity from the gods or even the only possible salvation." But rarely did the gods show signs of pity. As for salvation, nothing was less certain.

About Ptah, god of the earth and demiurge—whom the Greeks called Hephaestus—it was said: "He created the local gods, built the cities, founded the districts; he put the gods in their places of worship, he fixed the offerings for them, he founded their shrines. He ensured that their simulacra would please their hearts. And so the gods entered their simulacra made of every kind of wood, of every kind of stone, of every kind of clay, or every kind of thing which grows upon him [Ptah], where they have taken form."

Egyptian rigidity, essential for understanding every aspect of their life, was what the gods wanted. They wanted there to be images of them. Everything had to be fixed *in one single way*. But what model would they follow? Animals. The Egyptians sought to achieve the maximum animalization of man. Not just making him resemble some species of animal in appearance and behavior, but training him to carry out a single gesture for each occasion. The certainty of the animal was their guide. The rigidity that they followed in images was certainly not due to an incapacity to represent movement, but to the obstinate wish to neutralize it as far as possible.

In relation to animals, humans were above all their protectors. This, for the Egyptians, was the rule. Those who broke it were sentenced to death. There were no fewer than thirty-four sacred animals. "Anyone who kills an ibis or a vulture, whether intentionally or unintentionally, must die." Of crucial significance was the death sentence reserved for *unintentional* killing.

But not everyone approved. Egypt, for some foreigners, was

the prime place for all that is monstrous. Juvenal wrote a vehement *incipit* about it: "Does anyone not know what monsters demented Egypt worships?" Cicero was appalled above all by this same aspect of Egyptian customs: "They would let themselves be slaughtered rather than harm the life of an ibis or an asp or a cat or a dog or a crocodile, even if they were to do so involuntarily." This was the dividing line: animals. And it was also the secret of Egypt, which made it inaccessible for a Westerner now convinced that man was supreme.

The unintentional killing of a cat was an act to be punished by death. This is what Herodotus writes, and it is often regarded as an exaggeration or an invention—a favorite view among many scholars. But Diodorus Siculus, four centuries later, states that he saw a group attack a Roman official who had inadvertently killed a cat. One day it would be described as a lynching. And Diodorus stated that this was still during the period when the Egyptians were endeavoring in every way to be well looked upon by the Romans: "Their king Ptolemy had not yet received the title of 'friend' of the Romans and the people were trying with the greatest zeal to earn the favor of the legation from Italy that in those days was visiting Egypt." And yet on that occasion "neither the guards sent by the king to beg for his release nor the fear of Rome, felt among everyone, were strong enough to save that man from punishment, even if he had acted unintentionally."

Cats and falcons were to be found among Egyptian troops returning from a military expedition. They were regarded as prisoners that had been "set free" and returned to liberty in places that gave them proper respect.

According to Diodorus Siculus, even during the Alexandrian period the Egyptians "are continually bathing the animals in warm water, anointing them with most precious ointments, and burning every kind of fragrant incense around them; they decorate them with the rarest and most splendid jewels and make sure they can have sexual relations as their nature requires; furthermore, for each animal they keep the most beautiful females of the same species as concubines and look after them with great expense and attention." Running parallel to human life, which was always imperfect, was the life of sacred animals, which was furnished with every pleasure and free of any impediment.

The Egyptian labyrinth, one of the seven wonders of the world, was to be found close to the City of the Crocodiles. There was a succession of courtyards, columns, crypts. Enormous blocks of stone. According to Strabo, who visited the site almost five centuries after Herodotus, "no stranger can find his way into a courtyard or leave it without a guide." From the roof of the labyrinth, a single story high, one saw "a valley of stones, made of immense stones."

After visiting the labyrinth, Strabo went on to the City of the Crocodiles, where he was greeted by a "mystagogue" of the locality. He was told that the sacred crocodile was called Suchos and was tame to the priests. It was fed with the food offered by foreigners. Suchos was in the water at the edge of the lake. "Some of the priests opened its mouth and another put a cake and then meat into it, and finally poured in a mixture with honey." The crocodile then swam off rapidly to the other side of the lake. The priests ran after it, "stopped it, and carried on feeding it in the same way with what had been brought."

However hard foreigners tried to understand the reasons for the Egyptian animal cult, holy crocodiles continued to be a mystery. And they asked why there was a City of the Crocodiles, and why the Labyrinth stood nearby, "celebrated by many." They didn't know how to explain it. One reasonable though inadequate argument was that the crocodiles acted as an obstacle against any invader who wanted to pass along the Nile. And so "the bandits that infest Arabia and Libya dare not cross the Nile, since they are afraid of the animals, which are very many." Alternatively, there was the story of one of the first kings, Menes, who had been chased by his own dogs and had thrown himself into Lake Moeris—and there a crocodile had taken him on its back and carried him across to the other bank. But could this story be enough for crocodiles to be treated as divine creatures?

The young bull chosen to succeed the sacred Api sailed toward the sanctuary of Memphis in a barge with a gilded cabin. It had been chosen after a careful study of its color and particular markings. It had to be black, with a white patch on its forehead. It had been born, just like the first Api, when a "generating light fell from the moon onto a cow in heat." For forty days, only women could look after it: "They stand before it and lift up their garments, showing their genitals, but afterward they are no longer allowed within sight of the god."

Embalming was a sacred procedure, discovered and passed down by the god Anubis, the dog-jackal. But the most attractive women were entrusted to the embalmers only several days after their death. This was "so that the embalmers cannot have carnal union with these women." One of them had been "caught having intercourse with the fresh corpse of a woman." He had been denounced by a fellow embalmer.

The gods bring the *ankh*—the *crux ansata*, image of life—toward the nose of the king and the people. They want to transmit the breath of life. But that breath is a hieroglyph, a fixed, recurrent, unmistakable image. There is nothing vague, ordinary, uncertain. The breath, from the very beginning, is *writing*. This is the profound legacy of Egypt, the *prisca Aegyptiorum sapientia*, which has ended up imprinted on the whole of later history and has become its seal.

There is a paradoxical closeness between the prohibition on killing and the institution of sacrifice. According to Hermes Trismegistus, when Isis and Osiris came to bring "help to the world which lacked everything" and "filled life with life," as a first gesture "they put an end to the cruelty of reciprocal killings." Immediately after, "to the ancestor gods, they consecrated temples and sacrifices": *thysías*, "blood sacrifices." As if, *in consequence* of the prohibition on indiscriminate killing, people had to learn to kill according to a ritual and by turning to the gods. The conversion of a criminal act into a holy act.

There is one mysterious and terrible point in which killing and the divine intersect. Certain cults circumscribe that point, elaborate it, comment on it. But they do not exhaust it. So the rituals have to be repeated.

Never was anywhere so studded with images of the gods as in Egypt, and not only those colossal granite monuments but the countless minuscule images that only the eyes of the dead could see, painted inside their sarcophagi. And yet, unlike the Olympians, the Egyptian gods did not allow themselves to be encountered on earth, either in disguise or openly. They invaded the space like a fragrance. This is what happened when Amun took the place of Thutmose I to give birth to Hatshepsut from Queen Ahmose. It anticipated the story of Zeus and Alcmene, but allowed no trace of comedy. Amun let his fragrance wake the queen and he immediately assumed his "true 'divine form.'" The Egyptians differed from the brazenness of the Greeks also in this way of revealing themselves.

Maat: goddess, substance, world order, right measure, the conception closest to the Vedic *ṛta* and Persian *aša*. In Egypt she becomes a small female figure crouched on a cup that rests on the king's left palm. On her head, an ostrich feather. In her hand, the *ankh*. Maat is that which should be offered to the god, since all that is offered is part of Maat. If man offers Maat, it has to be understood that he offers everything. If man offers Maat, the god is being told that order on earth is still undisturbed. The gods neither expect nor ask anything else. All they want is news from time to time that the earth, onto which Maat had once descended, is still there, silent, small, on the palm of the king's hand.

The magic exercised by the king is neither a trick nor an illusion. It is merely a faded copy of the powerful, all-effective magic exercised by the gods. This is what the Egyptians thought. If the magic practiced on earth always reached its target, the earth would be no different to the invisible world, to which access is never certain. Anyone able to get there can also obtain magic from the gods, as a weapon of defense, according to the *Teaching for Merikare* of around four thousand years ago. But it is a very delicate weapon to handle. It can be used even against the gods from whom it comes. And it can even become a blunt weapon. "The words that people speak are one thing; what the god does is another thing," warned the teaching of Amenemope. And also: "The language of man is the boat's rudder and the supreme Lord is its pilot." Man and god are literally in the same boat—and together they have to overcome the same trials. But never is the "tongue of man"—speech—separate from its pilot, who is divine. Vedic doctrine, which would be fully stated in the Upaniṣads, is no different, though less rigid in its form.

Formulas in enigmatic characters have been found on a number of stelae dating from the eighteenth Egyptian dynasty. In these cases, according to Étienne Drioton, "the intention of the cryptographer was to hinder the understanding of a text that had to remain secret." And yet these formulas, essential for the dead, were to be found in some of the least accessible areas of the tombs. Why then worry about secrecy? Drioton observes however that "their drafts circulated in the hands of painters and sculptors and were kept in libraries where they would go to obtain them." And so, if only the dead and the most faithful celebrants of their cult had to know a certain text, "it was strictly necessary for it to be written in cryptography, and that the secret was entrusted to its beneficiaries during their life so that they could benefit from it after their death." All was consequential—but only the Egyp-

tians had felt the need to draw such consequences. When hieroglyphs resurfaced in Europe, with the Corpus Hermeticum and
Horapollo, the Renaissance Neo-Platonists immediately realized
that if they wished to preserve a metaphysics of secrecy they had to
turn to Egypt. The fact that the hieroglyphs had still not been deciphered was secondary. But they were still the door—the "apparent
door"—to the secret itself.

The extreme image of hunting, which encapsulates all previous
images, is found in the *Cannibal Hymn*, discovered in the Pyramids of Unas and Teti. In life after death the king, an inveterate
hunter, slaughters the gods as though they were cattle that had to
be cooked and eaten.

The first revolution from above for which we have exact news
was that of Akhenaten. It was a revolution that occurred above
all through omission. The names of the gods were abandoned,
even the divine determinative *ntr* was abandoned. Animals were
abandoned. Even hymns that followed the ancient forms. They
were now more simple, no longer overloaded with names. What
Akhenaten sought to omit was nothing less than the world. Everything was flattened out and made equal under the radiant light of
Aten. There was no longer any need for mediators, but for sculptors, who defaced the effigies of the *others*. They even climbed to
the tips of obelisks to cancel out the name of Amun. They went
into the archives. Even today, the obliterated name of Amun is
used to give an exact date to a monument. But Akhenaten didn't
just want to cancel out the name of Amun. The plural "gods" had
to be eliminated as well.

It didn't last long. Aten continued as the main god for several decades after the death of Akhenaten. But the other gods
gradually returned. The temple of Tutankhamun at Faras was the
place that "gratifies the gods." Egypt could not accept life without
them. And there were many: ninety-four in some lists. Akhenaten

himself was canceled out, but he remained elsewhere, among the Hebrews and one day among the Arabs. He was a founder king for foreigners alone.

In Egypt, with the end of the eighteenth dynasty there is a proliferation of "books of the afterlife" (*Amduat, Book of Nut, Book of Gates*, and others), in radical opposition to the disruption of beliefs brought about by Akhenaten. All of these were works visible only in the decoration of certain tombs in the Valley of the Kings, in inaccessible areas, where no one was allowed to read them. It was the first war of doctrines. Every esoteric doctrine is related to that first secret, to those written works not to be seen and connected to death.

Shabaka reigned in Egypt at the end of the eighth century B.C.E. According to Diodorus Siculus, "he surpassed many of his predecessors for devotion and rectitude." He was Ethiopian, but had no hesitation about repealing an old law from those regions claiming to have the oldest laws: he abolished the death penalty, the first act of its kind so far as we know.

Shabaka must have had a particularly clear view about sovereignty, if we look at the way his reign ended. One night "the god of Thebes told him in a dream that he could not reign happily nor long unless he cut the bodies of all the priests into two and passed between them, accompanied by his escort." The dream was repeated several times. At that point Shabaka summoned the priests from every part of Egypt and "told them that his presence in the country offended the god, for otherwise he would not have been given such an order in a dream." He therefore preferred "to entrust his life to destiny." After which "he returned the kingdom to its people and went back to Ethiopia."

Greek sources, including Herodotus, Diodorus Siculus, and Plutarch, state as a well-known fact that the Greek Mysteries are of Egyptian origin. But European scholars didn't like this. Farnell spoke about the "fallacious generalizations of Herodotus," thus liquidating the question. With Herodotus it has always been an easy argument. But with Plutarch? This scholar among scholars, a priest at Delphi, was relying on Clea, who had been initiated into the Mysteries of Osiris. Both of them knew what they were talking about.

According to Diodorus Siculus, the *teleté*, the "initiation" of Osiris and Isis, was brought to Greece by Orpheus: "Only the names were altered." Osiris became Dionysus, Isis became Demeter. Plutarch wrote no differently, and with greater authority. And no Greek writer ever claimed the Mysteries were a purely Greek phenomenon. It was the moderns, especially the positivist scholars, who sought to distance Egypt from the origins of any Greek wisdom. They well knew that Egypt would have upset that image of classicism that dominated the German gymnasia at the time of Nietzsche. When Foucart published a book on Eleusis that carefully listed the sources affirming the links with Egypt, he was treated with condescension and a certain embarrassment.

In 1740 B.C.E., King Neferhotep, of the thirteenth dynasty, erected a sandstone stele along the wall beside the road to the temple of Osiris at Abydos. Though badly damaged, it would remain the most important testimony of that reign, about which little is known. Only one other stele has survived, which contained a short decree forbidding access to the cemetery at Tazoser, south of Abydos.

Neferhotep wanted to record in stone the account of one of his exploits, which was neither a war nor a conquest. And these were his words: "My heart hath desired to see the ancient writings of Atum [the god creator] . . . so that I may know the god [Osiris] in his form, that I may fashion him as he was in the beginning, when they [the gods] made the statues in their council, in order to establish their monuments upon earth." Then "the nobles and companions who were in his suite [of Neferhotep], the real scribes of the hieroglyphs, the masters of all secrets," said: "Let thy majesty proceed to the House of Writings, and let thy majesty see every hieroglyph." Neferhotep wanted to ascertain the measurements of the statue of Osiris as they had been originally established by the gods themselves. For he wanted to "fashion him, his limbs, his face, his fingers," exactly as he had read in the rolls. "May I make his monuments as at the beginning of the world," he said. On his return from the expedition, on the royal barge a priest with a mask of a jackal represented Wepwawet, the god that opens the ways. Neferhotep had the statue of Osiris made as he had wished. He commended vigilance over those monuments. And finally he added: "Behold, my majesty has made these monuments for my father, Osiris, First of the Westerners, Lord of Abydos, because I so much loved him, more than all gods."

Neferhotep knew that all decisions about statues of the gods had been taken by the council of the gods themselves. It was man's task simply to remember and apply them. But there could obviously be misunderstandings. So it was necessary to return to the House of Writings (which inevitably evokes, antiphrastically, the Writers' Building in Calcutta) and examine the texts. Only then would there be certainty about what, for example, the size and shape of Osiris's fingers should be. It was the king's task to ensure that proportions and measurements were respected. The making of the statues would then be entrusted to craftsmen. It was as though *orthótēs*, the justness invoked by Plato, was being impressed upon that which he found most insidious: the world of copies, simulacra, statues. Egypt was this, first of all.

In the Egyptian Thebes, at the entrance to the "sacred library" was this inscription: "Clinic of the Soul." Around it, statues of "all the gods of Egypt" and a circular building with many rooms. Everywhere there were paintings of animals worshipped in Egypt.

XIII

THE DIVINE BEFORE
THE GODS

"In those times everyone revered the divine," observes Pausanias. He doesn't need to refer to the gods. The divine itself is the origin of worship, "devotion," *eusébeia*. Every change in the nature of the times can be described as a diminishing or intensification of the relationship with the divine. All else follows.

It is perfectly possible to live without gods. This, according to the criteria of the scientific community, is the state that corresponds to *normality*. Gods are not accepted there, inasmuch as they are unverifiable. It is their privilege and a rule of their etiquette. If gods were verifiable, they wouldn't be gods. It is more difficult, however, to live without the divine. The gods, for the Greeks, had appeared not such a long time before: their epiphany coincided with the stories told in the epics. But *tò theîon*, "the divine"? The divine is perpetual, in that it is woven into all that appears. Within what appears, it is that which allows access to what does not appear. To the boundless world of the invisible. In Greece, there was no lack of people who mocked and deprecated the gods, but the divine remained unharmed, unreachable. The life of the gods sometimes intermingled with that of mortals, but they were never confused together. The gods "live easily."

For the Greeks, the divine was implicit. For thirteen centuries, from Homer to Nonnus, it appeared in almost every story, to save or to destroy. Or even just to bring wonder. A wonder mixed with apprehension, for which the Greeks had a word, *thámbos*, untranslatable in later languages. The divine could be opposed, but it was rash to ignore it. To omit it from that-which-is would have been an infringement of that "clear-sightedness," "*saphès skopeîn*," which was the purpose not only of Thucydides but of all that preceded and surrounded him. It was not a question of faith, but of evidence—and of the ability to recognize it.

The difference between the divine and the human, observed

Socrates in *Cratylus*, is also that between the "smooth," *leîon*, and the "rough," *trachý*. But the rough is also the "tragic," *tragikón*, whose original meaning was "goatish." This is the place where humans moved: the "tragic life," *tragikòs bíos*. In a few words, and with the light, mocking air that is typical of *Cratylus*, men have been isolated in their natural place: rough, bestial, tragic. Which is also the place where "myths and lies for the most part" dwell. Not many such essential ideas have been added after that.

In the beginning: there was no hunting without the divine; there was no divine without hunting. Then there was a time when hunting no longer had anything to do with the divine, and what was called divine had more or less nothing to do with the divine.

The gods were not a faith but something evident—a way of perceiving the fact of being alive. Homer established the strongest tension between what is alive and what is dead: someone alive is already a hero, a semi-god; a dead man is a carcass savaged by dogs and a simulacrum with no strength and no mind. Nor is there any prospect of a future mediation between the two states, there are no gleaming Elysian fields nor any salvation in heaven. Even Heracles, son of Zeus, and bestowed with all twelve merits for his enterprises, roams in the woods of Hades. Even the Dioscuri, also sons of Zeus and bearers of the mystery of Gemini, are buried like many others in Laconia. As for glory, the immortality that it transmits can be likened to unquenchable gossip. It is a rumor spread from mouth to mouth: *kléos*, "glory," was originally the anonymous voice that brings news, often false. Glory is a momentary flash, the splendor that radiates from the poet into the mind of the listener. This is the most beautiful moment of life, in the words of Odysseus, the only hero who for his skill as a storyteller is also a poet. And Alcinous immediately sees him as such. So that, when Odysseus shares a large chunk of meat with Demodocus, he is performing a gesture of kindness toward a fellow poet.

Regarding the gods, all the gods, the point is not a matter of belief but of recognition. There are places, moments, beings, combinations of circumstances, that make one say, as in Ovid: "*Numen inest*," "There is a *numen* here": that power that has no need for names, but from which names originate. The difference lies in recognizing and accepting it—or otherwise passing by.

The gods of Olympus were fairly new not only for Herodotus but also for Plato. But this didn't worry them. For Plato, the gods had inherited the name of their predecessors and were therefore called *theoí*, from *theîn*, "to move fast," because in ancient times they had been "the sun and the moon and the earth and the stars and the sky," in perpetual motion. For Herodotus, however, *theoí* were those who had "placed [*théntes*] all things in order and presided over all divisions." For once, Herodotus spoke as though he were Plato—and Plato replied as though he were Herodotus. Anyway, when men "recognized all the other [gods]," the name had already been given to describe them. And they therefore had to be content with it. It was a way of making it understood that the gods are part of those things that are discovered little by little, like various generations of a single family. And the gods worshipped by the barbarians had also once been part of that family. This was what brought a versatility and flexibility to the many gods, always capable of acquiring new and older names. The gods of Olympus were not offended when they heard talk about new gods, in the same way that the stars were not offended when the gods appeared.

There are various kinds of unknown—and two fundamental kinds. One differs from the known only because it is a known that is not yet proven. The other is an unknown that is destined to remain unknown: the *anirukta* of the Vedic texts, something indeterminate, indefinite, implicit that cannot ever become explicit. There lies the divine, of whatever origin. The first distinction is between those who recognize its presence (and power) and those who do not perceive it. Scientific knowledge, in expanding the area of the known, also expands that of the unknown. But there is another kind of knowledge that penetrates inside the unknown. Nonverbal by its nature, it can manifest itself through various forms, which may sometimes even be verbal. The unknown then appears.

The ethnographer cannot be asked to believe in the gods of the tribes he is studying in the field. Likewise, a Greek scholar cannot be asked to believe in the gods of Olympus. Those gods are figures of the unknown that surrounds us and anybody else on all sides, then and now. It is not a matter of comparing our known with their unknown, which can only be done with a certain degree of condescension. It is a matter of comparing their unknown with our unknown, like comparing two infinites. And as we know, when one moves to the transfinite, things often happen that don't accord with good sense.

Karl Reinhardt once asked W. F. Otto: "Do you believe in the reality of Zeus?" "Yes," replied Otto. Reinhardt then asked: "Do you pray to Zeus?" "Yes," replied Otto. "So you must also sacrifice bulls to Zeus," said Reinhardt. There is no record of Otto's reply.

For the Twelve, the earth is a place where they spend time, a place they go down to—or which they contemplate from above to follow the actions of certain favorites. Artemis uses the waters of the Parthenion to refresh herself after the hunt. Then she climbs back into the sky. In those places where the Twelve generally spend time, humans begin to notice something. Sanctuaries or altars are built there.

Those who look at ruins don't like to think of them intact. They are suspicious and impatient in front of the plaster models that museums put on display for visitors. All the pillars are upright, and there is a sudden sense of being on the set of a movie epic. Plutarch anticipated these concerns and gave a brisk response when he described the Acropolis enriched by the works commissioned by Pericles: "At that time each for its beauty was antique and yet so perfect that even to this day it appears fresh and only just finished; so that its newness is ever lush, and its appearance remains untarnished by time, as if these works had a spirit ever alive and a soul untouched by age."

With his innocent tone, Herodotus makes astonishing statements that sometimes go unnoticed. Among these: it was Homer and Hesiod who established "where each of the gods originated and whether all existed eternally and what appearance they had." A remarkable declaration, in every sense, about a literary origin not of the divine but of the specific nature of the divine. Surprising above all where he says that Homer and Hesiod established "what appearance" the gods had. He suggests that their indelible characteristics were fixed not by simulacra but by words. No longer heads of a ram or a dog, but glaucous eyes and slender ankles. And all because two poets—an itinerant bard and a Boeotian peasant—had pronounced the definitive words a few years before (four hundred, according to Herodotus himself—and that date is now considered not unlikely). Words that didn't come from high priests or prophetesses. Two poets, distant and opposite, had dared to say "what appearance" the gods had, in the same way they had presented other human, too human, characters: the greedy brother Perses and numerous warriors under the walls of Troy, who had no divine ancestry.

Not the gods, but "the divine," *tò theîon*, is "envious and tormenting," writes Herodotus at the beginning of his *Histories*, which speak of these torments. To transfer the "envy" (and "jealousy") of the gods into a neutral, faceless entity radically changes the nature of the phenomenon. The gods are no longer the origin, but are bearers of something created outside them and which at the same time forms them.

Just as they are blinded by *átē*, a deadly form of deceit, so too can the gods be bewitched by erotic desire. Iynx, daughter of Pan and Echo, made Zeus drink a love potion to make him fall in love with Io. Which had innumerable consequences. A question remains: if humans become possessed by gods, by whom do the gods themselves become possessed? There is no given answer, but it can be supposed that certain unnamed powers act vertically, at all the levels of that-which-is. Zeus himself is subject to it, just as much as he has to yield to Ananke. Perhaps this is the most intimate and unacknowledged characteristic that men and gods have in common.

Yielding to something that has no face, and could be called Ananke or Destiny, was not peculiar to Zeus. The gods of Akkad felt lost and defenseless if the Tablet of Destiny was stolen from them, as Anzû, the lion-headed eagle, had once managed to do. Was that clay tablet enough to throw the gods into panic? In their primordial courtliness, frozen by the fear of losing their power, firm on their fat calves, they knew above all that they were first among their subjects. They thought they would now no longer manage to hide it.

The goddesses of Mount Olympus are perfectly separated from nature. They appear as self-sufficient forms. But there are other goddesses, who sometimes move away and come down from Olympus, living mostly in an emanation of light. Daughters of Titans, they still recall primordial times, when the divine figures were hostile and scattered around the cosmos, nor did they trouble to assemble together and visit one another in their palaces. Eos guides the daylight from its first appearance; Selene shines from the moon and crosses the sky. They are daily companions for the eyes of men, an intimate presence for all. And yet their attachment to a visible light makes it more difficult to distinguish their womanly body. And they seem to free themselves from their natural appearance only on certain occasions, only for certain actions, which they continually repeat. Rather than souls, they are luminous waves.

According to Homer, Aphrodite was born from Zeus and Dione, daughter of Uranus, whereas according to Hesiod the goddess was born from the semen of Uranus himself, which rises as foam from the sea. She is "lover of the smile [*philommeidés*], because she appeared from the genitals [*médéōn*]" of her father, who had been castrated by his son Cronus. And she is a pure mixture of elements. If relatives had to be attributed to her, Aphrodite would be sister of the Titans and therefore precede Zeus. When she goes to join the gods on Olympus, she is the only one who represents an earlier generation. Even if the characteristics that Hesiod attributes to her ("the whispers of young girls and the smiles and tricks and the delight and sweet lovingness and gentleness") are features from the repertory of earthly women, there is something primordial in Aphrodite, the daughter of semen and of waves, which even eludes Zeus. The version of her birth from Dione is an attempt to conceal this. But Dione is also a sister of the Titans. When the divine draws close to erotic desire, it veils even itself, in that place where its figures have taken up residence, on Olympus. Love and Death: what holds them together? They are born without a need to resort to coitus, according to Hesiod. Aphrodite from sperm and seawater; Thanatos from Nyx, "who had no intercourse with any of the gods."

If by "enlightenment" we mean the *Aufklärung* that Adorno and Horkheimer wrote about, its foundation is a misunderstanding of the divine. Whereas in the *Śatapatha Brāhmaṇa* a ṛṣi says: "All the earth is divine." For a long time that sensation was like an element of the air. Different from the sacred and from the saint, as well as from the profane. Then what the Greeks called *tò theîon*, "the divine," was absorbed into sacraments and institutions, which carried and transmitted it. But it was no longer in the air.

Puppets, solstices, the incommensurability of the diagonal of the square: these are the three examples of "astonishing" things that Aristotle cites. And it is immediately clear that the diagonal is the most disturbing case, since it is the only one to which Aristotle refers in order to explain the difference between the *before* and the *after* of wisdom. In the beginning there has to be astonishment: in the end we would be astonished if everything were *not* as it is. In the end we think the diagonal of the square *must* be incommensurable—and it would be inconceivable if that were not so: "An expert in geometry would be astonished more than in any other case if the diameter were measurable."

With unparalleled swiftness, and with the same colloquial tone that he uses at the beginning of *Metaphysics*, Aristotle has tied down what happens during the *process* of knowledge. Which culminates in the statement that everything has to be as it is. The difference between the "lover of wisdom," *philósophos*, and the "lover of myths," *philómythos*, is reduced to this. Both start off from astonishment, but only lovers of myths remain astonished. Others, having reached the peak of wisdom, are astonished only in seeing that one can doubt the necessity of that which is. But Aristotle has nothing to say about the ultimate result of the two types of knowledge. Which could be identical, except for that difference between those who are amazed and those who are amazed that someone is amazed. As for Aristotle, he clearly preferred to stay on the side of the *philósophoi*.

According to Thales, the origin of everything was water. According to Homer, the father of everything was Oceanus. Thales was the first link in the chain of lovers of wisdom, who found in Aristotle the first historiographer and genealogist. They became the philosophers. Homer, on the other hand, belonged to the lovers of myths. A scattered and stateless tribe, which never had any historiographers. They came and went, like crests of waves, and recognized one another by allusions, from Pindar to Hölderlin.

Those powers with which the ancients associated the names of the gods continued to be alive and active, even if they had lost their names. And they act relentlessly, under false guises. A sober allusion by Erika Simon: "From the fate of Hölderlin we know that for a man of our times complications arise if he starts from the assumption that 'the gods exist.'" Complications: for Hölderlin the tower at Tübingen, for Nerval the clinic of Doctor Blanche.

But do other possibilities also exist? The world is not only indifferent but hostile to the divine. Remembering how much effort it took to break free from it, it is compelled to recognize that its own forms are still those that the divine had minted. A clandestine existence is reserved for those who follow the divine. Unless they declare themselves to belong to a religion. In that case they are afforded respect, along with a certain amount of deference. Religions are regarded much like big political parties, formidable because they can count on an excessive loyalty and devotion from their followers. Above all, believers are more prolific than nonbelievers. And population figures arouse increasing unease. Whereas anyone who recognizes the divine but does not identify with any social body remains outside. He is the ultimate stranger. Only in the sphere of literature can he express himself, since literature is the place where nothing is legally binding. Otherwise, he will have to observe the rules in force. And will be tolerated, so long as he doesn't meddle in any practical pursuit. In which case, he is suspected of promoting criteria unacceptable to the community.

"There is nothing in religious life that happens *only once*": an incisive and definitive phrase, hidden among Nietzsche's notes for his last course at Basel. Its implications are endless, but in this case they serve to explain the function of the priest. Why should the priest be necessary? To guarantee that something has happened. Something that, once it has happened, will always happen again: "Every priest is the means for perpetuating the story of the god which happened once in that place, to make something of it that always happens again." This is why there is only one priest for each temple: because he is the "temporary incarnation of the god." Or more precisely, of a single story of the god. The irreducible difference between divine events and all other events lies in their capacity to be imprinted on the elusive substance of time.

Once they have happened they cannot be suppressed, abandoned. Or rather: they can certainly be suppressed, but then the divine will be suppressed as well.

At a certain point the Olympians were no longer enough. A severe, turreted, often bronze, imposing woman was added: Tyche, Fortune. In her, the city—indeed society itself—assumed a shape, in its overwhelming and ever-changing power, which could certainly be no less than that of the Olympians. She was the last of the goddesses. She would be followed by allegories, which claim divinity in vain, and end up filling war memorials, chapels, and cemeteries. Whereas the last figure of the divine is embodied in a young dancing girl—perhaps a daughter of Tyche—poised on a golden globe, holding a sail that points the wind direction on the Punta della Dogana in Venice.

Strabo: "It has been rightly said that men more closely imitate the gods when they do good [*euergetôsin*]; but it would be even better to say they do it when they are happy [*eudaimonôsi*]; and this is rejoicing and celebrating and philosophizing and making music." Good deeds are not what bring men close to the gods; but something rarer and more difficult: the capacity to be happy. Which needs practice, training. And, says Strabo, it requires a "relaxation," *ánesis*, of the mind, which dissolves the rigidity of those who are burdened by "human cares." Only at that point can one turn "the mind-that-is [*tòn óntôs noûn*] toward the divine." This can happen in various ways: through intoxication or without; with music or without; secretly or openly: Strabo didn't wish to exclude any path. But he could not avoid adding that "the mystical secrecy of the holy ceremonies inspires reverence toward the divine, inasmuch as it imitates its nature, which escapes our notice."

The gods always return. Well accustomed to metamorphosis, they adapt to places, to times, to circumstances. By the time of

Canova they were a mere skin-deep whiteness, marble polished to avoid the coats of paint that had dressed them up in palaces, in forests, in alcoves, for more than three centuries. And they appeared to Borges as well, transmitting "stupor, exaltation, alarm, menace and jubilation." The place and time of the apparition was ominous: the School of Philosophy and Letters in Buenos Aires; the time, sundown, as if at an academic ceremony. For the first time, the gods were constrained to show themselves behind the platform of a lecture hall. A humiliating situation for them, worse than captivity. They had become objects of study, *bon sujet de thèse*. Observed by many eyes that would soon linger on other materials. This was how Borges recounted their appearance: "Four or five individuals emerged from the mob and occupied the platform of the main lecture hall. We all applauded, tearfully; these were the Gods returning after a centuries-long exile. Made larger by the platform, their heads thrown back and their chests thrust forward, they arrogantly received our homage. One held a branch which no doubt conformed to the simple botany of dreams; another, in a broad gesture, extended his hand which was a claw; one of the faces of Janus looked with distrust at the curved beak of Thoth. Perhaps aroused by our applause, one of them—I no longer know which— erupted in a victorious clatter, unbelievably harsh, with something of a gargle and of a whistle. From that moment, things changed.

"It all began with the suspicion (perhaps exaggerated) that the Gods did not know how to talk. Centuries of fell and fugitive life had atrophied the human element in them; the moon of Islam and the cross of Rome had been implacable with these outlaws. Very low foreheads, yellow teeth, stringy mulatto or Chinese mustaches and thick bestial lips showed the degeneracy of the Olympian lineage. Their clothing corresponded not to a decorous poverty but rather to the sinister luxury of the gambling houses and brothels of the Bajo. A carnation bled crimson in a lapel and the bulge of a knife was outlined beneath a close-fitting jacket. Suddenly we sensed that they were playing their last card, that they were cunning, ignorant and cruel like old beasts of prey and that, if we let ourselves be overcome by fear or pity, they would finally destroy us."

It was the moment to reach a temporary conclusion: "We took out our heavy revolvers [. . .] and joyfully killed the Gods." Who thought, even if Borges doesn't say so: "We have to die yet again."

The first poets, those we will never know about—and who are gathered together for us in one name: Homer—were those who invented epithets. In the shapeless continuity of reality, sharp splinters formed, which could be pieced together as parts of a story. Stray syllables of no further purpose detached themselves from the murmuring of ritual invocations, like photons. A frequent epithet for Zeus is *aigíochos*: he who, by shaking his aegis, stirs the waters of heaven. This is certainly practical—and each time it symbolizes the god as king of the rain. Likewise another epithet, *keraúnios*, will recall lightning, another highly practical symbol. But when Hera is accompanied by the epithet *leukólenos*, "with white arms," the word already strays from ceremonial observance and becomes elusive, incomprehensible. Why should the whiteness of Hera's arms be recorded? What do those white arms have to do with her plots and revenges? And why is it never said that Athena or Artemis have white arms, yet Hesiod says it of Persephone? And why, when Hector is anxiously searching for Andromache, does he have to tell the servant women that he wants to know where he can find Andromache "with the white arms"? The first web of relationships by affinity is formed, unnoticed, through epithets. Each time those syllables are repeated, and even more so if done casually and automatically, one characteristic stands out and shines among everything. Each epithet possesses the certainty of reality, held in a brief sound, a certainty unafraid of being worn out through repetition and associated with every gesture as its ineffaceable landscape.

Tanísphyros, "with slender ankles": in the papyrus that holds fragments of the *Catalogue of Women* this epithet describes Europa and Atalanta, as well as Helen. From Zeus, Europa gave birth to "leaders of many men, king Minos, Rhadamanthus the just, Sarpedon the divine, faultless and strong." Whereas Atalanta, who "possessed the radiance of the Charites," had decided to "escape marriage with the tribe of men." Who felt *thámbos*, a mixture of amazement and awe, as they saw her running and "the breeze of Zephyr fluttered the chiton over her tender breasts." Europa and Atalanta had very different stories, but at the moment they appeared in verse they both had "slender ankles." Which Helen, the epitome of beauty, could hardly lack.

In the *Iliad* the whole Mycenaean bureaucracy, the whole administrative structure, is canceled out. What remains is the king, *ánax andrôn*, "ruler of men," and the gods themselves. Set in verse, instead, are relics of a past that goes back even before Mycenae: the shield of Ajax and the helmet of Odysseus. Homer's memory is highly selective: of the lost kingdoms he has conserved as many talismans of sovereignty as he could, while eliminating the evidence of mediation, as though it interfered with the clash of naked forces. So that bargaining, when it appears in the demand by Agamemnon, who wants Briseis for Chryseis, is charged with a destructive power: it does not yet reflect the domestication and reverberation of social life, so that heroes of the same camp are induced to fight one another.

Plato makes this accusation against Homer: he *is not useful*, he hasn't even invented a "Homeric life" in the way that the Pythagoreans have invented a "Pythagorean life." Orpheus and Pythagoras teach a way of life that can save us from life. There is no trace of this in Homer. There is no salvation from life. Life is incurable—and has to be accepted whole.

Apollo's intervention is prompt, precise. He advances in the mist, cuts through the fray, approaches the hero from behind, "takes the armor from his shoulders." It is a clear and unforgiving act: in the same way, shortly after, he will take the breath from his bones. And so Patroclus dies. The world as it is: cruel, splendid, with no salvation: the *Iliad*.

In the Trojan War, the whole of Greece fights, but without the Mysteries. Dionysus and Demeter have no part in it. Life first had to be accepted with nothing more, in its luminous harshness. It had to be lived as self-sufficient. The Mysteries remained implicit and postponed for another occasion—or at least kept under silence. But wasn't this their prerogative?

"For men there is nothing without the gods," we read in a fragment of Euripides's *Thyestes*. The affirmation of the divine is so imperious, all-pervading, and all-embracing as to minimize and demolish all human responsibility. No one feels guilty, because no one feels himself as the "cause," *aítios*, of what happens. Helen is not guilty on the ramparts of Troy; Agamemnon is not guilty beside the ships of the Achaeans. The crucial and swiftest words come from Agamemnon: "The god passes through everything and brings everything to fulfillment." "*Theòs dià pánta teleutâ*": Homer needs just four words, but they have to be expanded to be understood. First of all, *theós*, "the god," indicates a certain indifference toward *the one* who acts. It may be "Zeus or Moira or the Erinyes who approach in the mist." The only essential aspect is their divine nature. What then is the role of men, these automatons operated by other beings? To recognize their powers. To be able to name them. Homer doesn't seem to concede much more. And can anything more be conceded?

But it was not enough to strip men of every claim to being a cause of something, and therefore of being responsible and guilty. Even the king of the gods, and consequently all the gods, could find themselves in the same situation. Ate is one of the first daughters of Zeus, and at his side from the earliest times. She often has glossy plaits of hair. Daughter of Eris, Strife. Before going with the nymphs, priestesses, princesses, who attracted him with their fragrant beauty, Zeus went with other female beings, whose physical features have not been described for us. Eris was one of these. Ever-present in human affairs, she allowed herself to be seen only when she hovered over the wedding feast of Peleus and Thetis and let the fateful apple fall on which a hand—her own—had carved the words: "To the most beautiful." It was an act of sharp revenge because they had not invited her, despite her being a goddess.

Crouched beside Zeus, Ate could even strike him, in the way she usually struck men. Then he became embroiled in the deception. Through the action of Ate, the sovereign god fell into a trap laid by Hera. She swore that a being of his blood—Heracles—was about to be born, and would reign over all neighbors. But before Heracles, Eurystheus was born, who was not a son but a great-grandson of Zeus—though of his blood. When he realized his error, Zeus took Ate by her flowing hair and hurled her from the sky onto the earth. She landed on the hill of Ilium, where the city of Troy would one day be built. And so it became the *hill of blindness*, the bewitched mirror in which the age of heroes would be observed and recounted one last time, before dissolving away.

A civilization founded on Homer instead of a canon of sacred texts must for this reason alone appear anomalous to its Mediterranean sisters. Many are accustomed to thinking that a civilization can end up in literature. But how can it have its beginnings in literature?

Rhapsodists were those who "stitch song together with new hymns." But for sung stories to be stitched together, they had to belong to the one same fabric, only partly visible, ridden with holes and frayed. This was myth, whose boundaries were always treacherous, uncertain, remote. But the rhapsodists—and mythographers who descended from them—knew that wherever a strip of that fabric was to be found, another would one day appear, and many others to be stitched to it. In the end, no one would know where that patient work had begun. But what can the mythographer do when the myths have become lost? According to Hermann

Usener, he should "eavesdrop on the strange language of myth and cult and learn to feel and think in the same way as his ancestors dormant for thousands of years."

Among the 680 fragments of Aristotle published by Valentin Rose at Leipzig in 1886, we find at no. 668 a single phrase that stirs the imagination: "The more isolated and alone I am, the more I have become a friend of myths [*philomythóteros*]."

Sallustius, with his usual readiness of mind, suggested the ultimate and insuperable explanation of myth: "In what is expressible and in what is inexpressible, in the unmanifest and in the manifest, in the clear and in the hidden, myths imitate the gods themselves." Myths are therefore not discourses on the gods, like all other discourses that people have; they are discourses *of* the gods, words that reach us mediated by the voice of an actor, the mythographer. But in them they repeat the approach and style of words spoken by the gods themselves. Thus knowing how to deal with the material of myth is not fundamentally different from knowing how to deal with the gods. And, just as the gods are to be tended through worship, so too mythical stories should be kept alive by repeating and lacing them together, each time in a different way, just as every ceremony addressed to the gods is different, though carried out repeatedly.

Of what does the material of Greek mythology consist? Three thousand six hundred seventy-three names that Harold and Jon O. Newman compiled over thirty-eight years, in seventy-two genealogical tables. Those names were "all related to each other within a single family of 20 generations." One who is brought up on Saint-Simon and Proust will find it easier than anyone to find their way around those tables. To become familiar with one of them, one has to attempt to become familiar with them all. Myth, as Burckhardt wrote, "is the true spiritual ocean of this world." Swimming around in that ocean, we will eventually be forced to give up—and at that moment we will be closer than ever to the mythical essence, all-enveloping and enveloped by nothing else.

Myths are stories that have no archetypal text. They exist as a sum of their variants, in words, images, deeds. Myth is that which is not lost in translation. The mythographer works within the gaps, between one episode and another, between one story and another. And, as he works, he creates new gaps, which will be of use to future mythographers.

"The Greeks had maintained the mythical eye for a long period still during the clear time of history," Nietzsche observed in his notes on the Greeks' divine worship. Between one civilization and another, the dividing line was this: whether the "mythical eye" existed there or not. Inhabitants of the twenty-first century can say they still retain that eye, though blurred. They grope about in search of powerful images and grab on to the first they find. They sometimes even call them "mythical." And they are definitely something else.

And yet in Nietzsche's *Birth of Tragedy* we read that mythical images exist as "a metaphysical supplement of natural reality" and "an abbreviation of appearance," and therefore cannot be extinguished except along with appearance itself. It is also thanks to these images that the Greeks did not become sanctimonious, unlike all the civilizations that surrounded them (every time, a different kind of sanctimoniousness exists in Egyptian, Mesopotamian, Hebrew, Persian, Vedic cultures, etc.). If ever there was a Greek *miracle*, this was a part of it.

Mythology, in Greece, is a late notion, if by late we include Plato, who speaks of "mythology" in relation to Homer. But we find a true dividing line only with Thucydides, who is not concerned about accusing "mythology" of falsity, but deprecates *tò mythôdes*, which is something else: the tendency to cloak the facts of the past with that mysterious and glamorous patina of myth itself—and this is enough to prevent "*tò saphès skopeîn*," "the clear vision" of human affairs, which is the specific task of the historian. Here Thucydides not only sees clearly but sees very far ahead, as far as to today. *Tò mythôdes*, which is an adulteration of myth, has had the function for centuries of gilding and decorating the past (and also the future), with disastrous effects. Very few historians have been content to "see clearly": Thucydides was the first, Burckhardt one of the last.

More than three hundred vases depict gods as they offer libations. They were there before the eyes of scholars for decades without the scenes they portray being thought worthy of any particular attention, until one young German archaeologist, Erika Simon, published her dissertation in 1953 with the title *Opfernde Götter*, "Gods Who Sacrifice." The title itself caused alarm to an august and parochial scholar like Martin P. Nilsson. Rather than *Opfernde Götter* it should have been *Spendende Götter*, "Gods Who Offer Libations," he thought. A difference of little importance, the libation being an integral and essential part of sacrificial rites. But what rankled was the very word *sacrifice*. To speak of a god who sacrifices went against every acceptable image of the Olympians. Whoever could they sacrifice to? Whyever would they have to worry about the ceremonial pouring of wine and water, especially when they drank only nectar? Corrosive questions.

"The libation performs a role favoring the events it inaugurates"—a preliminary observation by Jean Rudhardt. But why must that which is propitious—indeed that which *renders* the moment propitious—be connected to an irretrievable loss? Here the metaphysical noose of the libation—and of sacrifice in general—is tightened. Killing is none other than a specific case of something that disappears forever, in this case a life. But water or wine poured onto the ground in the libation also disappear. Essential in the act of libation is not so much the offering of something to a divinity who doesn't need it, but the voluntary dispersal of something that exists. It is as though the gods, about whom it is said that "they always exist," were demanding that whoever turns to them should acknowledge a submission to time. Only afterward—perhaps—will they listen to him. Gods, being cruel and metaphysical, ask every human being not only to accept his own impermanence, but to celebrate it with appropriate and festive gestures.

The libation celebrates the irreversible. No other gesture could demonstrate it so clearly. Apart from the sacrificial killing, concentrated into an instant. But which does not represent flux, a sign of the irreversible. Even before formulating a desire, the celebrant recognizes the dominion of impermanence, therefore of death. If a sacrifice has necessarily to be accompanied and preceded by the libation, this is because the desire, in order to reach the gods, must be preceded by an act of acceptance that is directed to the totality of that which exists.

In a blood sacrifice, libation would seem the most superfluous action. And yet it is the only action that makes the killing of an animal a sacrifice and not a slaughter. Telemachus and Athena, who is disguised as Mentor, arrive at Pylos while a sacrifice of nine black bulls is taking place. The victims have already been killed, the bones dedicated to the gods have already been burned. But the two strangers take part just the same in the sacrifice, even though the sacrificers don't yet know who these two strangers are. For them it is not essential to be present at the killing—nor at the division of the meat. But to take part they have to pour a libation. And pronounce a prayer. There is an obvious reason for this: "All men need the gods." A phrase that has a hint of Homeric paradox. Those words in fact are directed at Mentor, who is actually the goddess Athena. And the goddess immediately agrees and prays to another god: Poseidon. But before the accompanying prayer, it is essential to perform the libation, the simple act of pouring a liquid. An act that even the goddess performs, with the same naturalness with which she has prayed to a god who is a close relative—and occasionally a fierce adversary.

Plutarch offers a gloss that illuminates the whole history of sacrifice and libation: "It can be concluded, both from the words and
from the cults of the ancients, that they considered it an impious
act and contrary to the law not only to eat but to kill a living being
that causes no harm. But, compelled by the growing multitude and
because an oracle at Delphi, so it is said, ordered them to make up
for fruits that were becoming scarce, they began to sacrifice. And,
since this still tormented and terrified them, they called what they
were doing 'performing' [*érdein*] or 'doing' [*rhézein*], in that they
were performing a great thing sacrificing living beings, and people
even now are very careful not to kill the animal until a libation has
been poured over him and until the animal gives a sign of consent.
They took this precaution to avoid every unjust deed."

These words are enough to show how futile it is to deny the
inextricable nexus between sacrifice and guilt. But they are illuminating words also in regard to the libation. Without libation there
is no sacrifice. But at the same time the libation helps to treat and
mitigate the guilt of the sacrifice.

For those who traveled east and crossed the Khyber Pass it
was easy to recognize that there was nothing odd about the gods
constantly offering libations: it was an essential gesture. In the
Chāndogya Upaniṣad, which can be dated to around the time of
the early Athenian vases, it is said: "The world is Fire [Agni], the
sun is wood, its rays the smoke, the day the flame. The embers are
the moon, the sparks are the constellations. Into this Fire the gods
pour faith [*śraddhā*] as an oblation. From this oblation is born the
king Soma." A perpetual act that assures cosmic continuity.

In Vedic India, sacrifice and libation are the subjects of a vast
number of treatises that are concentrated in the Brahmaṇas and
culminate in their final part—the Upaniṣads. But the gesture is
never depicted. Everything happens in the word and in the liturgy.
In classical Greece, no one wrote a theory of libation. Not even
Plutarch, who would have found ideal material there for one of his
Moralia. Yet a large number of vases and carved monuments show

gods who offer libations. Even in their extreme diversity, the two forms—Vedic and Attic—share the same premise: the sacrificial attitude.

The libation is not just the sign of the irreversible—and therefore of disappearance—but of superabundance. In the theology of the Vedic seers the "waters," *āpas*, have a privilege in comparison with everything else: they are the only "all-pervasive" element. Every rite must therefore start off from contact with water. Only that which Nietzsche would call *Überfluss*, "overflowing superabundance," makes ordinary life possible. Excess lies at the origin.

The "vase, the jug of plenitude," *pūrṇakhumba*, *pūrṇakalaśa*, is a venerable object, but an object that has to be broken so that the liquid flows out, or tipped so that superabundance is poured out of it. There is no divine world without that which is *pūrṇa*, "full" and overflowing, without a plenitude that is poured out from itself. The liquid can be *amṛta*, on which the gods feed, or *soma*, which makes mortals rejoice, or ordinary water. However, it must flow, limitlessly, whatever it is.

In Greece there were certain acts of libation, *choaí*, where the sense of dispersal was clear, acute. The liquid was not poured onto the altar, but over the ground. And all of it had to be poured out. Sometimes it was water that was poured into a river. Liquid into liquid. Often the *choaí* were addressed to the dead. They presupposed a contamination, as when Oedipus offered them to the Eumenides; or at least an injury, which is death. It was necessary then just to pour out the liquid, disperse it. One could not hope to get to that premonitory symptom of communion which consisted of drinking what remained of the liquid spilled. Appeasing the dead is difficult, it requires harsh, sometimes convulsive gestures, like when the *choēphóri*, the libation bearers, bang their arms.

Athena had just emerged from the head of Zeus and was running holding a lance; her long, thin feet appeared beneath her peplos. With his left hand, Hephaestus had just struck Zeus's head with his ax and was raising his right arm in uncertainty and terror. The other gods who were watching the scene also seemed perplexed and afraid. But not Zeus: firm on his throne, in his right hand he held the *phiálē* of the libation. Not even at that moment, unique in the life of the Olympians, was there any delay in the gesture of pouring a liquid onto the ground.

When Sindbad met Utnapishtim, he asked him of what substance the gods were made. The old man replied: "All the gods who you have met and who you will meet, everywhere, beyond all the seas, are made of the same substance. There is a great shiny coil that rolls and it continually leaves some piece behind it. And those pieces are other shiny coils that continue to roll, and they in turn leave behind them other smaller shiny coils. This is the life of the gods."

RETURN TO ELEUSIS

When Athens had only just become Athens, it went to war with another city built thirteen miles away: Eleusis. Athens was a kingdom and Eleusis was a kingdom, neighbors too close to avoid conflict. It was a war usually described as *mythical*, since it has no date. And it was a theological war, since Athens belonged to Athena and Eleusis to Poseidon. Eumolpus and Erechtheus, the founding kings of the two cities, both died in it. Still at the time of Pausanias, on the Acropolis, close to the temple of Athena Polias, there was a small statue of Lysimache's maid, priestess to the goddess for sixty-four years, and beside it two large bronze statues of warriors facing each other: Erechtheus and Eumolpus. According to some, Erechtheus killed Eumolpus and was then stabbed by Poseidon's trident.

Euripides wrote *Erechtheus*, of which few fragments survive, during preparations in Athens for "the building that would reunite in a ritual unity the venerable statue of Athena Polias and the altar shared by Poseidon and Erechtheus." The killer god and the murdered king were worshipped there together, under the direction of Athena: "In memory of his killer, Erechtheus will take the name of august Poseidon, when the citizens will sacrifice oxen." This also bound Eleusis to Athens. The place can still be visited today and is called the Erechtheum.

Eumolpus, the fine singer with flowing curls, the man of the white swan, founding father of the hierophants of Eleusis, had a troubled life from the very beginning. As the son of her "illegitimate marriage" with Poseidon, his mother, the snow-white Chione, threw him straight into the sea, back to his father. Who saved him, transporting him from Thrace to Ethiopia, where he was left in the care of another daughter, Benthesikyme. Eumolpus had to escape from Ethiopia because he had raped his wife's sister.

He returned to Thrace, where he became king. His father ordered him to march an army against Athens, which had offended him. And so the dispute between the olive of Athena and Poseidon's trident, originally an argument between two gods, was transformed into a ceaseless war between men. Erechtheus, king of Athens, was told by the oracle of Delphi that if he wanted to save his city he would have to immolate one of his daughters. Erechtheus tried to avoid this with every excuse. He even thought of sacrificing an adopted son. But his wife, Praxithea, placed him in no doubt, relying on reasons of state: "As for me, I will offer my daughter to be killed. And for many reasons . . . The entire city has a single name, but it is inhabited by many. Ought I to let them die, if instead of all I can let just one die? . . . This daughter, who is mine only through nature, I will sacrifice for our land." And so Chthonia was immolated. Two of her sisters (it seems Procris at that time was in Crete) threw themselves at once from the walls of the Acropolis. They had made a pact to kill themselves together. This would remain part of the story between Athens and Eleusis. Demeter revealed the Mysteries to Eumolpus, who was their founder.

As often happens in myths, Eumolpus did not live just one life. He was the son of Poseidon, but also of Musaeus, a pale counterpart to Orpheus. As the son of Musaeus, Eumolpus composed the *Bacchics*, a work whose title is all that survives, which corresponds perfectly, at the other end of time, to that last esoteric work of the pagan age: the *Dionysiaca* by Nonnus.

But Eumolpus's double descent revealed a sense of bewilderment. As Johannes Toepffer wrote in his *Attische Genealogie*: "That a stranger, a *xénos* whose ancestors were wild barbarians of the north, could not be the founder of the most sacred divine service of the Greeks already seemed clear to the followers of the Eleusinian mystery devotion during its highest period as it does to modern-day scholars of mythology." And yet what seems a tardy, euphemistic camouflage is Eumolpus's descent from Musaeus.

Quite a number of historians felt it easy to dismiss the war between Athens and Eleusis as a legend. But Creuzer had refuted them in advance with a simple phrase: "Something historic is certainly at the base of this war, otherwise Thucydides would not have recorded it." After a human sacrifice and the death of the two enemy commanders, Eleusis and Athens "ended the war in these terms: that the Eleusinians were subject to the Athenians in everything except the Mysteries, which they would continue to perform for themselves [idía]." Ídion, the same word that would one day be used to accuse Alcibiades of celebrating the Mysteries "in private," was also used to describe the statute of the Mysteries: they were to be wholly independent, not attached to any society, extraterritorial by constitution.

The Eumolpids, high priests of Eleusis, lost their name at the moment in which they became hierophants. And the name sank into the Poseidonic flow from which their progenitor had been saved. On a stone at Eleusis there was this inscription of the hierophant Apollonius: "Do not ask my name, who I am. The law / of the Mysteries has driven it toward the deep purple sea." Philostratus records that Apollonius was buried on the road to Eleusis, "in that suburb that is called Sacred Fig, and when the sacred objects of Eleusis are brought in procession toward the city, they pause there."

There had been another Eleusis before the Eleusis that is visited today in a bay dotted with oil refineries. And also another Athens. Both, according to Pausanias, had been submerged by the waters of Lake Copais. Strabo adds: "These cities, it is said, were founded by Cecrops, when he ruled over Boeotia, which was then called Ogygia." But Ogygia is an adjective, as Wilamowitz pointed out, and it means "Primordial." It is the name of the island of Calypso and of everything in the world that belongs to something that precedes it. Ogygia is the shadow of history—it is the shadow that sank beneath the waters of a lake that resembled no other. A movable, indented lake, which each year flooded the neighboring areas and changed shape. J. G. Frazer had a chance to observe the landscape around Lake Copais when the drainage works had not yet been completed and, awestruck, he wrote a very detailed description of it—equivalent, for him, to a paean. He dwelt much on the peculiarity of those constantly changing places: "So well recognized were these vicissitudes of the seasons that places on the bank of the lake such as Orchomenus, Lebadea, and Copae had summer roads and winter roads by which they communicated with each other, the winter roads following the sides of the hills, while the summer roads struck across the plain." And the view changed totally. From autumn to the end of March, "viewed from a height such as the acropolis of Orchomenus it appeared as an immense fen, of a vivid green color, stretching away for miles and miles, overgrown with sedge, reeds, and canes." Whereas, in full summer, islands emerged and eventually joined together. On the abandoned water edges grew corn, rice, cotton. And herds of animals grazed in the lower parts. Beneath and around the lake, the ground was gashed by countless clefts, underground passageways and caverns called *katavothres*. Forty-one were marked on the maps. Lake Copais no longer exists today. Crossing the region of the Ethnikì Odòs, one has a feeling of slight hallucination, as though entering a parallel world, detached from everything. It is the mark of the lost landscape of primordial times.

The descendants of Eumolpus "formulated their exegeses" on the basis of unwritten laws. A noble task, cloaked in silence, detectable only through occasional testimonies, such as that of Pseudo-Lysias, who recalls how Pericles wanted to apply unwritten laws—*in addition to* those in writing—against anyone who had committed impiety.

"Unwritten laws," *ágraphoi nómoi*, are the only kind of laws that are unchallengeable because they are invisible. Otherwise every *nómos* is vulnerable for being *nómō*, established by convention and collective agreement, but also open to being revoked and repealed by convention and collective agreement. Whereas the *ágraphoi nómoi* are "laws which no one has ever had the power to repeal nor dared to challenge, and of which it is not known who has established them." It is not specified here whether they are natural or divine laws (even if unwritten laws alone give the opportunity to "pay the penalty [*díkēn didónai*] not merely to men but also to the gods"). Pseudo-Lysias seeks only to explain that these are laws of unknown origin, laws for which history cannot account.

It is not clear what prevented "unwritten laws" from being written down. What harm would result? And why did those laws have to be entrusted to the Eumolpids—and to no one else? Like the Mysteries, the unwritten laws could be revealed in another way. Instead of written words, they were based on *páthos*, "emotion." The unwritten laws did not stand in opposition to written laws like a hidden word to a stated word, but like a primordial recognition as opposed to a precept.

Eleusis marked the most serious crisis in the life of the Olympians from the beginning of the reign of Zeus to its prophesied downfall, brought about by a "son more powerful than the father," which was then neither Apollo nor Dionysus, but Jesus. And the origin of the crisis was due to the amorous forays of three sovereign brothers—Zeus, Poseidon, and Hades—among the women of the earth. A matter of enormous consequence, and not just *vaudeville*. The divine compulsion to venture onto the earth, spurred on by Eros, was part of the cosmic order, but could also upset it. The descents (or ascents) of Zeus and Poseidon onto the earth, brought about by a woman, were innumerable. But the women, for both of them, had to be searched out in their own surroundings: under a tree, in a pond, or in bed. Zeus managed to reach Danaë even though she was imprisoned. Hades, however, appeared only once. He stole a young girl from earth, and from that moment placed the whole earth in peril. She wasn't *a* girl, but *the* girl, Kore, who cannot have any other name because she is "the girl whose name cannot be spoken." That was the method chosen by the irreversible to send out its challenge to the Olympians—and therefore to men. If Kore vanished, it was implicit that everything vanished.

This was why Demeter rebelled. To accept that Kore had been assumed into the invisible, once and for all, meant accepting that
the gods themselves would vanish. Demeter demanded instead to
return to "see [her daughter] with her own eyes." If the Twelve had
not managed to achieve it, Demeter, by breaking away, would have
forced them to do so. This was the harshest indictment that any of
the Olympians had made against heaven, "for the intolerable action of the blessed gods." As a consequence, humans took part, as
always, under threat of extinction in a dispute that had arisen in
the heavens. A quarrel that was difficult to understand on earth.
But humans knew the gifts of the gods were also a yoke. With this
thought they approached Eleusis. They had to find a formula—and
a form—that would heal the rift opened by the disappearance of
Kore. That formula and that form were the Mysteries, necessary
for the gods no less than for men.

For those familiar with the stories of the gods, what led to Eleusis was not one of Zeus's many affairs, but the most scandalous affair of all, for a triple reason, as Emperor Julian sought to explain:
"Zeus had intercourse with his mother and, having had a daughter
by her, he married the daughter, or rather he didn't marry her
but had intercourse with her, then he simply passed her on to another." And that other was his brother Hades, uncle of Persephone,
king of the dead.

Prior to the pact between Demeter and men, the pact between
Zeus and Hades had been much more serious, much more radical. The "shrewd" Zeus (*mētíeta*, equipped with the Metis that he
had swallowed) handed his daughter Persephone to his brother
Hades, concealing this arrangement from her mother, Demeter.
Why did this happen? Zeus knew, after all, that he had beaten Hades at dice. His supremacy was as chancy as gaming. And, among
the gods, as then among men, the supreme game is the one played
out between presence and absence. Death was a part—even if
only one part—of that game. Zeus knew that he would have to
accept a compromise. He did it in silence, telling no one. This was

what Demeter considered scandalous and irremediable. Zeus had handed his daughter over in secret. And had handed her over to his brother. Only Helios, who sees everything, could witness it.

But why did Zeus want to come to an agreement with Hades? It wasn't a game this time, but a necessity. *Kore* means "pupil"— and the pupil is the only point of the body that holds a reflection. But, where the reflection is, there is also a gaze that looks at itself. For humans, there is no life without that gaze. And at the same time that gaze reveals the unshakable predominance of absence over presence.

Looking is the only physiological process that can be endlessly divided: in the one who looks there is also the one who is looking at himself while he is looking. And this one can be looked at by another. But who, then, is the subject? The one who is looking, or the one who looks at the one who is looking? The latter, one might say, because he includes the one who is looking. But the one who is looking is us. Then the one who is looking at the gaze becomes another in relation to us, who yet dwells inside us. We depend on him. But we cannot confuse ourselves with him, because at the moment in which we become that other, a gaze takes form that watches us becoming that other. The process can start all over again, ad infinitum. That which rules us while we are looking is that which always eludes us. But it is also that which is always with us. We can obscure it, ignore it. But, if the attention becomes fixed for a moment, then here it is again, to take hold of us, as Hades took hold of Kore. But the being that is looking at the one that is looking: where is it when we are not aware of it, which is a large part of our life? Is it absent or present? And where? It is absence itself, but—when it appears—it is a presence that captures every other presence.

With Hades who abducts Kore, the figure of the absolute Enemy reemerges: the predator, whom men had now driven away into the shadows, but only because they had succeeded in imitating him so well that they could occupy his place in the *machina rerum*, in the "mechanism of things." Claudian describes the king of the dead no longer as a powerful and lecherous abductor, but as a lion that has sunk its teeth into a heifer and has "ripped its entrails with its claws, raging over all its limbs." Then the lion "stands up stained with gouts of blood and shakes its tangled mane and scorns the feeble rage of the shepherds." Here is the mark of the irreversible. And Kore, at the moment she is abducted, has time to invoke the many other women who have gone before her, calling them "fortunate": "*O fortunatas alii quascumque tulere / raptores! saltem communi sole fruuntur,*" "O fortunate are those whom other abductors have taken! / at least they enjoy the shared light of the sun." Only through Eros does one approach the cleft of the irreversible. Then the whole framework of existence is at stake.

Persephone never spoke a word against her abductor once she had arrived in his kingdom. She sat beside him on the throne—and they soon began to look similar, like an elderly couple. In his name there was "the invisible," in her name "the killing." Together, they represented something ultimate. There was no beyond.

Sophocles—poet of the *deinón*, of the "tremendous," which is also the "stupendous," a word that continually recurs, a talisman and a torch in the labyrinth of his tragedies—is the poet who recognized in the firmest and clearest manner that "deception," *apátē*, is not just the prerogative of men, but rules the gods. If Ananke forces them to bow, Eros manages to treat them just like humans, luring them into traps. No one has managed to escape from the three sovereign brothers—Zeus, Hades, Poseidon—says the chorus in *Women of Trachis*. And it doesn't linger. "I will pass over the affairs of the gods. I won't tell how Cypris tricked the son of Cronus or the somber Hades or Poseidon who makes the earth shake." Bold litotes. But while we know that Zeus and Poseidon were occasionally deceived, the situation of the king of the dead is different. Here Sophocles suggests that Eros had also managed to trick Hades. But when? There are not as many stories about Hades as there are about his brothers. The only detailed story attributed to him is the abduction of Kore. That was the deception: the incursion of a predator who was forced by his abduction to introduce an everlasting life into his kingdom. A supreme deception carried out by Aphrodite. The chorus in *Women of Trachis* wants to move straight on to something else, as if content to have suggested something enough to upset the state of the world—and it doesn't wish to say any more.

We cannot live without the invisible, but included in the invisible is death. The Mysteries originated from this thought, this obsession. Hades the predator bears the invisible in his name and abducts the flower of appearance—Kore who is gazing at the narcissus, "wondrous for all to see, for the immortal gods and for mortal men," says the *Hymn to Demeter*—into the kingdom of the dead.

Kore is Demeter's only daughter, but they are often named as two, mother and daughter: "the two goddesses," Kore and Demeter, a roaming entity, where the two are never separated, not even when Demeter cries out along the magma of Etna, and Persephone is already smiling in silence, watching Hades, on the throne of the dead: from the deep crevice of the earth she hears her mother's call, but has chosen not to answer. Kore is the daughter of Zeus and Demeter—but she is also daughter of Poseidon and Demeter. Of the three brothers who divide up the universe, two are her fathers—Zeus and Poseidon—and one is her husband: and Kore is the only girl to whom all three sovereigns lay claim, and is sovereign with each (*Déspoina* is another of her names). The unique one is always split.

Demeter appeared at Eleusis disguised as an old woman. Now all she could do was to be a wet nurse, if there had been a small child to look after. Or the keeper of a dark storehouse. She was one of those beings who go unnoticed. She was sitting beside a well, like a silent beggar. Four sisters of dazzling beauty then approached: Callidice, Cleisidice, Demo, and Callithoe. They spoke to the old woman, then invited her to follow them to their house. The four sisters ran like fawns, their hair streaming in the wind, "like the crocus flower." Demeter followed them, in her long robe, with her head veiled. But as she also ran, "her dark peplos coiled itself around the slender ankles of the goddess," says the Homeric Hymn. It is a striking detail. The last sign of divinity, which cannot avoid being revealed.

Demeter sat on the stone of a well: it was the rock that obstructed the cosmic cavern from which the waters flow. Only laughter provoked by Baubo, only raucous, futile hilarity could loosen the stone that obstructed life. This is the most archaic aspect of Demeter. She corresponds to Amaterasu, in Japan, as recounted in the *Kojiki*.

The *"agélastos pétra,"* the "stone that does not laugh," on which the desperate Demeter had sat, was the stone that reflects no light. It indicated that the world had become opaque. To emerge from it, the only thing needed was laughter. But Demeter wasn't the only one to laugh. "The whole earth laughed," says the Homeric Hymn. How can the earth laugh? By becoming illuminated. The first meaning of the verb *geláō* is "to shine with reflected light." Homer says that beneath the walls of Troy the earth "laughed all around for the splendor of the bronze." Physicality and mind. At the time when Demeter was sitting at Eleusis on the "stone that does not laugh," a cosmic crisis had reached its peak. The world could not continue long without the reflection of light. So the Mysteries save the world, even before saving its individual inhabitants.

All that happens at Eleusis is metaphysical and sexual. And it is concentrated in Baubo, a figure that appears in five lines attributed to Orpheus, cited by Clement of Alexandria: "Having spoken thus, she lifted her peplos and showed all / the indecent part of her body. The young boy Iacchus was there / and moving his hand he laughed under Baubo's crotch; / then the goddess smiled, smiled in her mind / and accepted the variegated bowl that contained the potion." In the *Hymn of Demeter* and in Apollodorus, Baubo becomes the "old woman" Iambe, a servant at the palace of Celeus and Metaneira, whereas nothing is said about the age of Baubo born in the region of Eleusis. Iambe "with much jest" persuades Demeter "to smile, to laugh and to cheer her spirit"; the same happens when Baubo exposes her crotch, while the child Iacchus appeared between her legs.

With Baubo's gesture, the cosmic paralysis is ended. The display of the vagina wins over the "stone that does not laugh"; that which is hard and arid is released by that which is soft and moist. The same gesture had been made by Hathor, "lady of the southern sycamore," when her father, Ra, offended by the god Baba and exasperated by the dispute between Horus and Seth that had been going on for years, stretched out "on his back in his pavilion, and was much saddened and lonely." Then Hathor, after much reflection, "came and stood before her father, the Universal Lord, and exposed her vagina before his eyes. Then the great god laughed at her; he got up and went to sit with the Great Ennead, and said to Horus and Seth: 'Speak you!'"

If the course of events is interrupted, the only way of restoring fluidity is with laughter, along with erotic play. Together, they refloat the grounded cosmic ship. This, too, was an Eleusinian doctrine. The "unquenchable laughter" of the Olympians, on the one hand, was an insuperable barrier that separated them from humans, for whom laughter could be nothing more than an outburst, a brief spasm. On the other hand it offered the firmest guarantee that the universal machine was always in operation— boosted from time to time by erotic impulse.

The first to laugh is the boy Iacchus—and "*Íakchos*" was the cry repeated in the procession toward Eleusis. The Mysteries made shouting turn to laughter. Even Demeter was persuaded to follow the "sacred child."

Hesychius's *Lexicon*, under the heading "Baubo," states: "Demeter's wet nurse. Vagina, according to Heracleon." "Vagina" is connected to Baubo's gesture of exposing her crotch in front of Demeter. "Demeter's wet nurse" raises some doubt: in the Homeric Hymn it was in fact Demeter who offered herself as "wet nurse" for little Demophon, whom she would try to make immortal. How could Baubo have been "wet nurse" for the goddess who was mother of Persephone? Unless Baubo was born before Demeter and spanned the whole of her life. So Baubo's indecent gesture was thus maliciously attributed by Gregory of Nazianzus to Demeter herself, citing Orpheus: "He doesn't spare us this other fine phrase: 'Having said this, the goddess exposed her two thighs' to give her lovers the initiation that her postures still bestow today." Words that still reverberate in the Byzantium of Michael Psellos: "Then again Baubo who throws open her thighs and her female conch, for this is what they shamefully call the genital organ; and thus they end the mystery in obscenity [*en aischrô*]." As the Fathers of the Church had always sought to demonstrate.

About Eleusis, which means "place of the advent," Diodorus Siculus had first this to say: the Mysteries were notable for their "extreme antiquity and purity"; they were "magnificent for the splendor of their pomp"; they imitated "the ancient life." And he added that during the ten days of ceremonies the participants "use an obscene language [*aischrología*] when they meet together, because through such obscene language the goddess, grieving for the abduction of Kore, laughed."

When "Hermes the runner, swift messenger, / sent by his father, Cronides, and by the other gods," arrived in the underworld, Kore was seated on the throne, beside the sovereign Hades. According to a story passed on by Cicero, Hermes at that moment had an erection: "*Mercurius ... cuius obscenius excitata natura tra-ditur quod adspectu Proserpinae commotus sit,*" "Mercury, about whom it is said that on seeing Proserpine he became obscenely excited."

Greek life revolves around one pivot: the recognition of the gods. In the double sense of recognizing the gods and of being recognized by the gods. In this second case the recognition is also a gift, the origin of grace. "The gods are difficult for mortals to see," warns the *Hymn to Demeter*, demonstrating its consequences. Recognizing a strange old woman wandering, desperate, discovering that she is a powerful god: this will be the basis for the Eleusinian Mysteries and for a new system of life. Misunderstanding, intrigue, epiphany: these are the territory for every recognition.

In the *Hymn to Demeter* the revelation of the Mysteries is a series of scenes that take place on a single night, between women. At the end, there is a child abandoned on the ground. Even the mother "doesn't remember / her favorite son, to pick him up from the pavement." The four daughters of Metaneira will be the ones to look after him, though they are "poorer wet nurses" than Demeter. King Celeus will be told only "on the appearance of the dawn." And will then decide to build a temple for the goddess. But he will have seen nothing. It is as though the royal, male intervention were only a secondary consequence of something that has already happened in an obscurity streaked by "a great flame" and by a flash "as if by lightning," a drama for women only.

Demeter is a *gift* for mortals: the Mysteries. But she reveals this nature of hers within a *false* story that Demeter presents like this to the daughters of Celeus: "It is right that I answer your questions with the truth." She says she comes from Crete, that she has been abducted by pirates, and that her name is Dos, Gift. But the story is also wholly true: the initiation comes from Crete, her daughter Kore—a dual unity with her mother—was abducted by the pirate Hades, who broke the law of Zeus with the agreement of Zeus himself, father of the abducted girl. And Demeter herself was Gift. There was even a reference that offered a key to the story: the people of Crete were reputed to be "all liars."

Demeter's gift was not agriculture—contrary to what scholars of positivistic (but it would be more accurate to say *productivistic*) persuasion have claimed in countless publications—and for the simple reason that, when Demeter reached Eleusis, agriculture already existed. And cereal farming in particular. To remove all possible doubt, this is stated in the *Hymn to Demeter*, which is the first and most revealing source on Eleusis: "In the fields the oxen drew many curved plows in vain, / much white barley fell into the furrows to no avail." If cereal farming was already practiced, it couldn't be the gift of Demeter. The Mysteries themselves were her first gift, which people since then have been trying to discover. And with it she gave opium, as indicated by the poppy, which is her emblem, together with the ear of wheat, as it also appears in Theocritus.

According to the dictates of the *fertility cult*, a devotion that flourished in the Victorian era and still attracts followers today, fertility in the ancient world *had* to be of equivalent value to that of production in the industrial world: the only faith beyond discussion, the only reasonable basis for existence. And so the enigma of Eleusis continued to be protected and hidden in the university lecture halls, and still survives unscathed.

The theory about the agrarian significance of the Eleusinian Mysteries, so cherished by scholars, had already been disposed of by Plato in *Epinomis*: "The making of barley and wheat flour and their transformation into food is a good and noble thing indeed, but they will never produce a perfectly wise man." Words followed by a phrase of deadly sarcasm: "Indeed the very term 'making' would produce instead an aversion for such things."

Why were the Mysteries needed? Why was there a need to reach some hidden thing? The answer is in Hesiod: "The gods hold the life hidden to mortals." And this concealment was exactly what Zeus intended, in response to the trick that Prometheus "with his twisted mind" had played on him. What is hidden is life itself.

But Eleusis is not just the secret about hidden things. Eleusis is also the secret about things that are there before everyone's eyes. Every textbook says that Demeter is the goddess of "fertility." And immediately adds that wheat is her emblem. According to some, wheat *is* the secret of Eleusis. And yet on statues, reliefs, coins, as well as in the words of poets, Demeter is displaying not only wheat, but something else: the poppy, or rather, poppy capsules. Why the poppy, always the poppy—and not some other flower or plant? Several scholars, with supreme naïveté, have explained that the poppy was the image of fertility because it contains many seeds.

The ancients knew something more about the poppy. They knew about the "juice," *opós*, that drips from the vertical incisions in the capsules of the *Papaver nigrum*: from which comes *opium*, a word that appears for the first time in Pliny. In this respect, Pliny is as clear as he always was: "The black poppy is a narcotic that acts if the capsule is cut before the flowering, as Diagora suggests . . . The juice, as for every herb, is collected on wool or, if there is little of it, on the thumbnail, as is done for lettuce, it is collected even better the following morning, when it has dried; poppy juice, in abundant quantity, is thickened, ground and kneaded into small cakes and left to dry in the shade. It has not only soporific powers but, if taken in abundance, can also cause death in sleep." And then: "*Opium vocant*," "They call it opium."

Demeter discovered the poppy at Sicyon. And she transformed her lover Mekon into a poppy. We know nothing about Mekon, except that he was an Athenian who wandered the region around the gulf of Corinth, while Demeter roamed everywhere, desperately searching for Kore, her lost daughter. The place at that time was not called Sicyon: after Demeter had been there, it was called

Mekon, meaning Poppy. It was a prosperous region, rich in wheat, pumpkins, cucumbers, olives. One day it would become the setting for another discovery: painting. And there, even further back in time, the meat of the "great ox" had been shared out between Zeus and Prometheus. On that occasion gods and men had separated forever. Each had remained in their own part and with their own portion. Sicyon-Mekon was a place where events took place after which the whole of life became different.

Nothing is as alien to the gods as exclusivity. What belongs to Demeter can also belong to Aphrodite and what belongs to Aphrodite can also belong to Artemis. The chain continues without ever breaking. The poppy, which taught Demeter at Sicyon how to alleviate pain, also appeared, once again at Sicyon, in the hand of a gold-and-ivory Aphrodite, as her emblem. In her other hand the goddess was holding an apple. Some claim instead that it was a pomegranate. The pomegranate fruit and the poppy capsule contain the whole story of a mother and a daughter, of Demeter and Kore. But they also belonged to Aphrodite, whose nature was neither that of a mother or a daughter. The secret of one divinity was received through another. And it was to be found not in certain gestures, objects, words, but in certain plants: the pomegranate, the poppy, the myrtle. In the Heraion of Argus there was a statue of Hera enthroned, the work of Polykleitos: "imposing, of gold and ivory," the goddess "holds in one hand a pomegranate and in the other a scepter." Pausanias adds: "I can say nothing about the pomegranate, for its story cannot be told." According to Ovid, when Demeter reached Eleusis she collected and even tasted poppies "unknowingly, to ease her long hunger," some time before mixing the juice with warm milk to save the boy Triptolemus, who appeared to be dying. In early Corinthian ceramics, pomegranates and poppies are mixed together—and it is "interesting to observe to what extent they become interchangeable," noted Axel Seeberg. And the pomegranate that Persephone casually tasted in Hades, and which bound her forever to that kingdom, was grown from the blood of Dionysus. In the poppy and in the pomegranate there is a ceaseless circulation of the divine, permanently interwoven with the powers of eros and the underworld.

The poppy at Eleusis, the *soma* in Vedic rites: they were substances that procured intoxication. And intoxication was the requirement of the ceremonies. For Vedic ritualists, the *soma* allowed immensely complicated sequences of words and gestures; for the hierophants, there was no written canon of ritual gestures and the poppy wasn't even named in the rare texts to be handed down. But it was shown, between the fingers of Demeter and Kore—or plaited into their hair.

The image of the goddess of Gazi of around 1200 B.C.E., on whose head are three poppy stalks with their capsules cut in the manner used to extract opium, brings onto the Mediterranean scene a substance that can work its way into the mind and transform it. A fragment of world that modifies consciousness. On a Corinthian plate of the fifth century B.C.E., Demeter is shown sitting on a throne. In her left hand she holds two stalks of wheat and two capsules of poppy, in alternation. Bread and opium, equally apparent.

Epopteía, "vision," was the highest level attainable, one year after the first visit to Eleusis. For the *epóptēs* to be recognized, the priest who held the torches, *dadoûchos*, handed him a round lead token with a stalk of wheat and a poppy—the essential. Beneath were the letters *epops*, which stood for *epopteía*.

Four centuries after the *Hymn to Demeter*, the learned Callimachus—whose rule was "Don't sing of anything that is not testified"—wanted to write a hymn to the goddess. He didn't speak about Kore and the Mysteries. But he spoke about a place for which Demeter "went mad like for Eleusis." And yet it was a place that didn't even have a name. It was just a wood, thick with trees.

One day Erysichthon, leading twenty strong men armed with axes, approached this wood where pine, apple, pear, elm, and poplar trees grew into one another. But so thickly tangled that an arrow wouldn't have found its way in. It was a place untouched. For Demeter, a "sanctuary." But a "wicked will" took hold of Erysichthon and drove him to destroy it. The first tree they struck was a poplar, "so tall as to touch the sky." This alone might have held them back. But they struck it, and the trunk let out a groan that Demeter heard. She said: "Who is cutting down my beautiful trees?"

The goddess then assumed the appearance of Nicippe, her priestess. "In her hand she held garlands and poppies, on her shoulder the key." An impressive key: we are not told for what. Perhaps for her sanctuary. At first she spoke calmly to Erysichthon and his men. She warned them they were attracting the anger of Demeter. But something murderous was shining in Erysichthon's eye, as happens—it is said—to lionesses just after they have given birth. From his mouth came words that no one had ever uttered to the goddess: "Go away, or else I'll stick this great ax in your flesh. This wood will roof the hall where each day I will be pleased to offer celebrations to my companions, until sated." As he spoke, another goddess, Nemesis, inscribed his words on a tablet. Especially that *áden*, "until sated."

Demeter then decided to return to her appearance of a goddess. And divinities rouse terror. Those twenty strong men, with axes in their hands, ran away. Demeter ignored them and spoke only to Erysichthon. This time she didn't call him "son," but "dog." She said: "Yes, yes, build your hall and give your celebrations; you shall celebrate, indeed, endlessly." At that moment she introduced into Erysichthon "a terrible and fierce hunger, an enormous, burning hunger." It was insatiable desire, which exists in itself, independently of what is desired. Demeter knew that it was an extreme evil, in response to another extreme evil.

If Callimachus had chosen such an unusual way to celebrate Demeter, it must have been some erudite whim, as many thought.

And in doing so they were passing over the metaphysical implication of the story. Demeter had rebelled against the Olympians
because she didn't accept that something, that anything should
disappear. Her daughter was the thing itself. And what makes
something disappear, before anything else, is the act of eating.
This was the primordial guilt, shared by all the inhabitants of the
earth without exception. Erysichthon's insatiable hunger coincided
with the voracious work of death. "By Death this world was covered, by hunger, because Death is hunger," we read in *Śatapatha
Brāhmaṇa*. When Hades slipped a few pomegranate seeds—
"furtively"—between Persephone's fingers, he knew that his consort would eventually put at least one into her mouth. That would
be enough. And, like the seed in her mouth, Demeter's daughter
would periodically disappear from the earth, to join her husband
in the underworld.

Sophocles fragment no. 837 states with the greatest clarity
what the Mysteries offer: "O three times blessed / those mortals
who after having seen these [Mysteries] / go to Hades; only for
them down there / is there life, for the others there are all evils."
To keep life intact: this is something the Greeks, outside the
Mysteries, had never dared to promise. The soul was not canceled
out, but became an inert, torpid, volatile, maimed being. Only
the Mysteries granted whole, unscathed, life. It is not a good, vir-
tuous, pious life. But pure life—"only for them down there / is
there life."

For any living being, life at first is the normal state. With difficulty, following tortuous paths, which may even pass Eleusis, one
comes to understand that life is a state of exception, just like death
which accompanies it. The normal state is non-life, the inanimate,
the "stone that does not laugh": normal insofar as prevalent. Evidence of this is the cosmos—and also the constitution of matter,
which ignores the possibility of life except in some minuscule
fragment of itself.

Eros wafts onto the chariot drawn by four horses on which Hades is taking Kore—who has now become perfectly calm Persephone—to her mother, Demeter. In his hands, Eros has three objects that are indispensable at that moment, attached to a wire: an *íynx* (a wheel of erotic possession), a crown, and a *phiálē* for libations.

Perhaps Hades is *not* Dionysus, as Heraclitus states, but he looks very much like him. Sitting on the throne in the house of the dead is a male figure, bare-chested, with pointed beard and a crown in his hair. Dionysus, standing in front of him, seems to be his brother. His right foot touches the left foot of Persephone, queen of the underworld. She is sitting on the throne beside Hades, who is holding in one hand the *phiálē* for the libation, and in his left a pomegranate. His strategy for calling Persephone to his side is already prepared. A bunch of grapes hangs from above.

The gods of the underworld also pour libations. The word *Theós* (the Eleusinian name for Hades) appears in the inscription on a vase now in the Getty Museum at Malibu. And it is Persephone who pours the liquid from the jug into the *phiálē*, which is being held by Hades. The libation was therefore passing vertically through all the worlds, from Olympus to the underworld. It was not a gesture of devotion by men toward the gods. If anything, since the gods come before men, it was a gesture with which men were imitating the gods. If someone asks what the gods do—and in particular what the ruler of the kingdom of the dead does— one certain answer is this: they are pouring libations. That gesture was evidently necessary for the extension of life, both divine and human. Even in the realm of the dead.

On the last day of the Eleusinian celebrations, there was the rite of the Plemochoe, which means "fullness poured": they were two clay vessels, filled with an unspecified liquid. The liquid was poured into a cleft in the ground at the farthest point to the east and west in the sanctuary, while a "mystical formula" was pronounced. This brought the Mysteries to an end.

"The soul in search of pleasure encounters the divine beauty, which appears down here in the form of worldly beauty, like a trap for the soul. Thanks to this trap, God takes hold of the soul, against its will." This was the abduction of Kore according to Simone Weil.

Kore was not just abducted "while she was playing with the deep-bosomed daughters of Oceanus, / gathering flowers." Kore fell into a "trap," which was another flower: the narcissus. That flower, a "toy" from which "a hundred other flowers" sprouted, was the result of an agreement between the gods: Ge had made them grow because Zeus wished to please He Who Receives Many, his brother Hades. Heaven, earth, and underworld came together to make that flower appear. This itself indicated the wondrous nature of the event. In what do gods and humans meet? In the contemplation of a flower. The essence of the Mysteries is revealed in this first moment: in looking at something that even the gods view with the same rapture as humans. This was the supreme "vision," *epopteía*. All eyes, immortal and mortal, converged on a flower that had sprouted "in the plain of Nysa," on the Enna plateau. Divine and human eyes were drawn to a certain, clearly defined, point of the visible. Something familiar—and at the same time "a radiant wonder."

What do the Mysteries have to heal? What need is there for this irreducible addition to the cult of the gods in the *pólis*? Why leave the *pólis* in search of something that can play only a delegate role in the *pólis*—at the Eleusinion in Athens? Only vague answers can be given. But they will always have something to do with what Nietzsche called "the eternal wound of existence."

In the Derveni Papyrus, and also in a quotation from the orphic poems in the Pseudo-Aristotelian *De mundo*, it is said, in almost identical words, that Zeus brought beings to light "from his sacred [pure] heart, performing terrible acts," "*mérmera rhézōn*." These "terrible acts" are not specified, but imply an immense divine guilt, simultaneous with the appearance of life, and a precondition for all human guilt. The Mysteries rested on that base: for the initiate to free himself from personal guilt he had to become part of an anamnesis of divine guilt, which was hidden in the vicissitudes of the story of the *two goddesses*, Demeter and Kore. It was the very guilt of existence that had to be redeemed, something incommensurable in comparison with modest human vices. Eleusis was an introduction to that guilt and dissolved it, as though breaking apart the "stone that does not laugh" on which Demeter had sat during her grief. Only on that condition could the extension of life be guaranteed.

The initiate returned to Athens and stripped off the ragged garment he had worn at Eleusis, to resume his usual petty and litigious life. If the Eleusinian Mysteries promised something beyond death, this was a feature that all religions shared. And many would have considered it a pious enticement. The unique feature of Eleusis was another—and the chorus of Eleusinian initiates revealed it in Aristophanes's *The Frogs*: "For us alone are the sun / and light sacred." Light that is "sacred," *hierón*, or "joyous," *hilarón*, according to certain codes. The sun shines for everyone, but only those who have been to Eleusis know that its light is sacred (or joyous) and "they behave with reverence / toward strangers / and citizens." But it has to be remembered that those initiates, at the moment they are speaking, are in Hades.

The purpose of the Mysteries is not just to experience the afterlife differently. Their purpose is to experience life in life differently. Their purpose is to *see* what everyone sees, all the time. They were not changing anything in that which is. But they were changing everything in the perception of that which is. At this point the mystery became impenetrable by reason of being too clear.

He who has seen is saved: this is what the *Hymn of Demeter* says, having reached its culmination. He who is good or has seen good things is not saved, unless he has *seen*. Nor is he who has done bad things excluded, provided he has *seen*. Seen what? The *órgia*, an indissoluble mix of "*drṓmena, deiknýmena, legómena*," "things that are done, things that are shown, things that are said." This vision, the *epopteía*, goes beyond merit and guilt. This itself is the good—and so strong as to guarantee a future life for those who achieve it, as a single "happy," *ólbios*, being. The others are destined to "marcescent darkness."

Ólbios is a word that recurs in three fundamental texts (*Hymn to Demeter*, Pindar fragment 137, and Sophocles fragment 837) which speak about what happens to the initiate after death. And all three speak about something that has been *seen*, using different verbs (*ópōpen, idṓn, derchthéntes*). Sophocles is the only one to state that only for initiates "down there is there life," "*ekeî zên ésti*." If this was a secret of Eleusis, it is no surprise that it had to be guarded, among people who until then had imagined the afterlife to be a place of torment and languishing survival.

For the Greeks, Eleusis was the place where they underwent a mutation. It was the living record of a time when metamorphosis was still a part of what happens, before it was banished and expunged. Delphi was the place to which people went to be ruled and directed in the choices of everyday life and was based on the word, whereas at Eleusis there were no words, other than short formulas. The rule was silence, and metamorphosis was invisible, no longer perceivable from outside, but only to those who underwent it.

Even if, according to Walter Burkert, the Eleusinian Mysteries are "the best-documented cult in the ancient world," none of those who took part have described them. And yet the Mysteries were open to everyone, including children, slaves, hetaerae (though these were excluded from the Thesmophorias). Not admitted: only murderers and those who couldn't speak Greek. "Athenians and any other Greeks who wish it are initiated," says Herodotus. For more than eleven centuries—if the *Hymn of Demeter* is taken as an arbitrary starting date and the final destruction of Eleusis by the Visigoths as the end date—none of the followers wanted to break the secret. And yet, according to Aelius Aristides, what took place in Eleusis was "that which is most terrifying and most splendid among all that is divine for men."

One inescapable characteristic of the Mysteries ("To say many funny things and many serious things," according to Aristophanes) was also a characteristic of theater as performed in Athens. This itself has perplexed modern scholars. Arthur Pickard-Cambridge couldn't but recognize this: "The problem which is baffling to modern and Christian readers—how was it possible for the same audience, possibly even on the same day, to be absorbed in the noblest tragedy and pass immediately to the grossness which, along with the higher qualities of wit and humor, comedy displayed for at least a century and a half—would not have been appreciated by the Athenians of the fifth century, and is perhaps one which will never be completely solved."

In an inscription at Eleusis, datable to around 80 B.C.E., it is said that "the association of the artists of Dionysus" (as actors were called) had always worked to promote the cult of Demeter and Kore. They had built an altar and created an enclosure in which to offer libations and sing paeans during the Mysteries. The altar had been destroyed during certain riots and eventually rebuilt, once again by the artists of Dionysus.

Tertullian has to admit, with a certain irritation, that nothing is said in Scripture against theatrical entertainment, which for him is the epitome and ostentation of that supreme outrage: idolatry. But Tertullian was a man not easily discouraged. While reluctantly admitting that there is no commandment in the Bible that reads "Thou shall not go to the circus or to the theater," to be placed alongside "Thou shall not kill," nevertheless he found in the opening words of the book of Psalms the condemnation of any entertainment: "Happy is the man who does not walk in the counsel of the wicked." Those two lines, according to him, certainly prefigured the assembly of the Jews to decide on the killing of Jesus, yet they could also be applied to the prohibition on going to the theater. And here Tertullian formulated the fundamental principle of biblical interpretation: "*Late tamen semper scriptura divina dividitur*," "Yet Scripture is always applied broadly" and is not to be understood only "*secundum praesentis rei sensum*," "in relation to its immediate sense." And so the decision to kill Jesus and the decision to go to the theater "in order to see and be seen" come together in one single meaning, on different levels.

Indeed, if Scripture *late dividitur*, and is therefore accomplished, fulfilled in various ways and degrees, it is equally true that all these ways and degrees must be coherent and consistent: therefore the collective decision to kill Jesus and the act of going to the theater prove to be similar and each will sustain the other. This in fact is what happened throughout Christian history up to Bishop Bossuet—and beyond. And it was a dismal symptom when the Church, in very recent times, tried to turn the liturgy into more of a spectacle to attract a few more devotees.

But Tertullian was not prompted by a wish to encroach on secular life. For him, spectacle—*any* spectacle—originated from a god, whether it be Apollo or Mars or Diana. The theater was merely a late variant of the *templum*. And therefore to be condemned as bitterly as other Fathers of the Church condemned the Mysteries. Behind spectacle, behind the temple, behind the Mysteries, one and the same power was at work: the power of appearance. Wherever something appears, there demons lurk. This is the setting for the hopeless conflict between the godless and the faithful.

Aristotle writes that initiation is no different to philosophy, but is a "part" of it—and more exactly the last part, that part which affords possession of the "ultimate purpose" of philosophy. But of what does it consist? Of a sudden inspiration, which "crosses the mind flashing like lightning" and is "the thought of the intelligible": a "unique" occasion to "touch and contemplate." Speculation is not pure vision of that which is, but something that makes it possible to *touch* (*thigeîn*, a common and wholly physical verb) that which is. Yet exoteric thought makes no reference to such *contact*, as though it were precluded. Initiation is therefore necessary, if one wishes to reach that extremity where philosophy *ends*.

No linguist has ever managed to explain why the Greeks and the Latins have described the same event—the Mysteries—with two words that indicate, for one people, the end, and for the other, the beginning: *teleté* and *initia*. A verbal clamp that isolates the event in the amorphous flow of time.

Teleté, teleuté, teleiótēs: these three words, which have the same origin and mean "initiation," "death," and "perfection," ought to appear indispensable to Plato, as he played with them so ostentatiously, moving indifferently from one to another: "*Teléous aeì teletàs teloúmenos, téleos óntos mónos gígnetai*," "A man only becomes truly perfect if he is initiated into perfect initiations." One can hardly go much further in courting tautology, allowing a glimpse of death at the same time.

The silence required by the Mysteries has held. From Herodotus to Pausanias we often find sentences that stop at the threshold: "About this it is not pious to speak," "on these rituals writing is not permitted." Not once do we find a pagan author ready to break that silence. And yet the silence is not total. It is accompanied by a marginal chatter, coincidences in names and places, ceremonial parallels, as well as the quiet eloquence of inscriptions on monuments, until those tenuous voices are superimposed by the invectives of the Fathers of the Church. They of course wanted to *say everything*, like de Sade. But they did not succeed. The Mysteries haven't suffered much for it. They remain intact in the silence, helped by the pavid prudery of philologists.

The malevolent Christian August Lobeck observed that numerous pagan authors were said to have written about the Mysteries, but nothing has survived that could be used as accurate testimony ("*nullo testimonio uti licere, cui non auctor et locus et tempus nominatim sint praescripta*"). But this is no reason to rely on the Christian apologists, according to whom the Mysteries were celebrated "*helluandi et scortandi causa*," "to carouse and go with whores." One was left with the possibility, frustrating to every positivist spirit, of an event celebrated for more than ten centuries, always in the same place, but which had left no reliable evidence of itself. Lobeck added that much of what had been written about the Mysteries seemed the work of the Sabines, "about whom it has been said that they dreamed whatever they wished."

Much has been written about Eleusis, from Lobeck's *Aglaophamus* to Károly Kerényi and Kevin Clinton. On the Mysteries, for the Mysteries, against the Mysteries. But no account seems entirely persuasive. More than a thousand years have passed since the destruction of Eleusis, and yet it might be said that the prohibition on speaking about them has never been lifted. It is as though the Mysteries have defied any comprehensive description and have allowed mention of themselves only in fragments and hostile attacks, as in the case of the Christian Fathers. Or through allusions in passing references, as in Plato and Plotinus. Or in Plutarch. One searches in vain for a detailed account of the Mysteries in his *Moralia*, though their subjects are so variegated. But Plutarch was a priest at Delphi.

"Eleusis, excluding only those tainted with murder, initiates all Greeks of whatever kind, without inquiring into their actions, their life, or even their character": this is how Erwin Rohde described the singularity of Eleusis. This above all is what distinguishes Eleusis from every other sacred ritual: the suspension of all accountability for good or evil. Initiation was not a passport that offered certain rewards. The paradox of the Mysteries lay in their being a separate path, inaccessible through the practice of virtue. A paradox that was considered scandalous. Diogenes the Cynic, a caustic reasoner, didn't miss this point: "The thief Pataikion, having been initiated at Eleusis, will have a better fate after death than Agesilaus and Epaminondas." So virtue *served no purpose*—or at least it had no power equivalent to the revelations of Eleusis.

Eleusis was not a ritual passage from one stage in the life of society to another. It was the way out of society toward what lies before and what lies after society itself. Not even in their period of full decline did the Eleusinian Mysteries become part of a state religion. This is the point of distinction. The Mysteries were never at the service of a society but were the way of going beyond society. One of Simone Weil's last notes in London: "Under Augustus, indeed, the Eleusinian Mysteries, even if reduced to a wretched caricature, had never let themselves be turned into an official Roman religion." Something that instead would easily happen with the Christian liturgy.

Through the night, Achilles was still hugging the corpse of Patroclus. He was sobbing loudly. In a circle around him, various soldiers, "many comrades." The saffron peplos of Eos colors the sky and "brings daylight." A goddess, Thetis, appears laden with "beautiful weapons that no mortal has ever held on his shoulders." They were Hephaestus's gift for Achilles. There is no preparation for the appearance of the goddess, nor any comment. Just as a warrior can spend the night clinging to a corpse, so—all of a sudden—can a goddess appear. Neither of these facts require any explanation. This is the "precipitous," *aipýs*, life of which Homer speaks. Its extremes, high and low, go a long way, where few dare to venture.

Achilles now spoke to the goddess, who was his mother. He told her he was ready at once to wear those arms, a task that "no mortal could have assumed." But Achilles had something on his mind that he now confessed to Thetis: he feared that as soon as he armed himself, moving away from Patroclus's corpse, the flies would penetrate his friend's body, "through the wounds opened by the bronze."

What is the point of a goddess if not to chase away the flies? And Thetis, who, it was then recorded, has "silver feet," knew that this was her first task: "to keep away that wild breed, those flies, that devour men slain in battle." Thetis reassured her son: she would carry out this goddess's task to leave "untainted the flesh" of Patroclus. "Untainted," she adds, "or even better": Thetis doesn't explain what "better" might mean. But one has a sudden glimpse of what immense power the teaching of Jesus would have in Palestine: the resurrection of bodies, attainable only by one who eats a divine body, that of the Son of Man. "A hard teaching," "*Durus est hic sermo*," commented "many disciples" of Jesus. He immediately challenged them: "Does this offend you?" "*Hoc vos scandalizat?*" In fact, this is the very "stumbling block," the *skándalon*, of all of Jesus's teachings.

The most delicate and arduous point, for every survival, is not the soul, but the flesh. Only the Christians resolved it with the most potent weapon: literal interpretation. The flesh is resurrected: if this dogma of Christianity is taken away, much of its attraction is lost. The Greeks did not venture as far. Henri-Charles Puech summarized the difference with luminous simplicity: "For Christianity, that which is saved or the stake of Salvation is not, as in Hellenism and in Gnosis, just the *noûs*, the timeless "self" capable of assuming a multiplicity of temporal bodies through the course of a series of cycles of reincarnations, but a unique individual in its own flesh as in its own soul, wholly constituted by the union of a body, of a soul and of a spirit." Compared with this detailed and legalistic promise, those of the Mysteries and then of Gnosis were vague and uncertain. Reincarnation is a threat more than a promise. The individual has not only the terror of losing his soul through death. Even more, he fears losing his flesh. He wants his body, his own body, and none other, if he has to be certain about life: about a life undiminished, and not too different from the only one he knows.

As for salvation, part of the contract was the recognition that salvation had already happened, once and for all, in the *hápax* of the death and resurrection of Jesus. Salvation was not therefore something to be attained, in a laborious and agonizing process, where one moves forward in solitude. Salvation was already available for anyone. It was enough to acknowledge it, to commemorate it in the rite of the Mass. But it was something already existing and already happening. And anyone could be part of it.

None of the religious doctrines before Jesus had promised so much—and with so much attention to detail. Paul's overweening certainty is founded on this. Whereas the difficult point is the other side of the contract: not what the follower obtains, but what he has to give. And this was the observance of a paradoxical and extreme doctrine, preached by Jesus in the Gospels. That doctrine, if observed in its detail, would expose anyone to the hardest trials. But the Church, from the very beginning, would take steps to mitigate those trials, to make them more accessible and negotiable for everyone.

They went from Athens to Eleusis, walking thirteen miles along the Sacred Way. A march that was also an *agón*, a "contest," protected by a special god, Telesidromos, "He who helps to finish the race." The initiation was the end of a race. They left the city from the Dipylon Gate. Along the roadside were tombs, sacred enclosures, altars, small sanctuaries. Step by step one could reconstruct the history of Athens but also hear its gossip. And encounter various divine presences. As a prelude to Eleusis, Demeter and Kore were celebrated in the place where Phytalus had given hospitality to Demeter at his house. And where the goddess, as a reward, had given him "the sacred fig tree." That fig tree, covered by a roof, was an obligatory stopping point. Then a group of waifs, led by "some whore" or a masked man, waited for the procession of prospective initiates by a narrow bridge over the river Cephissus. As they approached, they mocked and jeered them. Making cruel jokes. This moment was an essential part of the Mysteries. There also had to be much laughter for the Mysteries to be performed. They continued on through Skiros, a disreputable haunt of charlatans, gamesters, and prostitutes. Conspicuous among them was the priest of Poseidon, with his white umbrella. At Rheitoi, only the Eleusinian priests could bathe in the two saltwater lakes. This marked the boundary between the territories of Athens and Eleusis. An inscription of 421/420 B.C.E. suggests that a bridge there, probably destroyed in war, must have been rebuilt. The decree ordered that the bridge be wide enough to allow passage for the priestesses with "sacred objects" and future initiates, who were referred to as "the walkers." Nothing else was needed to describe the candidates for initiation.

There was a point on the Sacred Way between Athens and Eleusis from which the Acropolis could be seen. It was marked by a funerary monument to Pythionice, a famous prostitute, originally slave of the flute-girl Bacchis, who in turn had been a slave of Sinope. Of her it was said: "Thrice slave and thrice whore." Pythionice also had another tomb, in Babylon. The cost of the monument was enormous, more than two hundred talents. Some were indignant about the expense. They said it looked like the tomb of Miltiades or Pericles or Cimon, built at the expense of the *pólis*.

An early commentary on Aristophanes's *Pluto* noted that those taking part in the Mysteries refused to take off their clothing "until it was in pieces." The very long, detailed inscription of the Treasurers of the Two Goddesses refers to a *himatiothékē*: this, according to Chrestos Tsountas, was the building that received the clothing dedicated by the initiates. Initiatory rags.

Beneath the Acropolis in Athens: the Eleusinion, a high-walled sanctuary, the isolated anchorage for the sanctuary of Eleusis, its outpost in the *pólis*. Its bricks had been made from the *agélastos pétra*, the "stone that does not laugh," in Eleusis. The record of the cost of transporting those bricks still survives. Evidently it was felt to be the only suitable material. The builders working at the Eleusinion were slaves who had undergone the *mýēsis*, the "pre-initiation." Otherwise they could not have trodden the ground of the sanctuary.

"Many are the amazing things to be seen or heard in Greece; but divine grace is bestowed most of all on the rites performed at Eleusis and the games at Olympia." This was the view of Pausanias, a native of Asia Minor, a stranger to Greece, in the second century B.C.E. But this was also the feeling that ran through the whole of Greek history. Eleusis and Olympia were the only two places that could impose the *sacred truce*, the suspension of all servitude, to blood, to labor, to trade, which corresponded to the Jewish Sabbath. They marked the times in which something had to be performed: certain actions and certain words. The concentration on racing and the display of sacred objects. Nothing else in Greek life could claim to be so close to that which comes "*ek theoû*," "from the god."

Spondế, spondaí: this means "treaty," "agreement," but it also means "libation." Lastly, *spondế* means "truce," the suspension of all conflict, which only Olympia and Eleusis had the authority to impose. There is a profound relationship between the act of pouring, of spilling a liquid on the one hand, and the temporary ceasing of all conflict on the other. These two gestures harked back to a primordial state prior to any secular existence, which is the ordinary and conflictual state of events. But, for this to happen, the preliminary act is the libation, that acceptance of losing and dispersing something that is the prerequisite of the sacrificial attitude. What distinguished the Persians from the Greeks, according to Herodotus, was firstly that in the sacrifices "they do not use libations nor flutes nor fillets nor grains of barley."

Hálade mýstai, "Initiands to the sea": under the eyes of the "supervisors," *epimelētaí*, of the Mysteries, the initiands were ordered to run to the sea and throw themselves into the water. They ran dragging with them the piglets they would have to sacrifice with their own hands. One for each. The seawater, the blood of the young pig: they served to purify them. No different, after all, from what happened in Athens before public assemblies: "Several pigs with slit throats were carried around by groups of citizens and, if we believe the scholiast of Aeschines, the freshly spilled blood of these victims attracted the demons who could have led people's minds astray and tainted the deliberations."

Before the initiation, the sacrifices. Three animals led by an ox, for Demeter, for Kore, for Pluto, for the mysterious Dolichos, "god of the Long Run." They were the *protéleia*, rites in preparation for the initiation, which took place between the pillars of the *telestérion*. Various gods had temples and altars around the *telestérion*, as though they were besieging it—or wanted to be protected by it. Iacchus had led the march of the initiands, but there was no temple for him.

During the procession for the Mysteries of Andania, described by Pausanias as "for venerability second only to those of Eleusis," the married women had to dress in a nontransparent tunic, with a colored hem no wider than half an inch; the girls wore a long tunic in the Egyptian style and a nontransparent cape. "No one wore gold jewelry, nor makeup with rouge or white powder, nor did they wear anything knotted or have their hair plaited, nor did they wear shoes that were not of felt or of the leather of the victims offered in sacrifice." If the clothing was not appropriate, the *gynaeconomos*, who was responsible for checking women's dress to ensure it was "suitable for the gods," *theoprepôs*, was entitled to tear it to shreds, consecrating it then to the gods. The initiands could not wear anything that drew attention. Equality begins with initiation.

There were two large stones, side by side. On one particular night they moved them apart. They extracted writings that related to the Mysteries. They read them to the initiands. Then they put them back behind the rocks, that same night. This happened at Feneos, in Arcadia. Demeter had been there. A grandson of Eumolpus had arrived there, on the instructions of the oracle of Delphi. And there alone was there mention of writings that were read out during the ceremonies. There alone did the priest wear the mask of

Demeter. Then he beat the ground with sticks. In that way it was thought the people underground would be hit. At Feneos, too, the stone was essential for the Mysteries, in the same way that Demeter had been induced to laugh while she was sitting on the "stone that does not laugh." The two stones side by side at Feneos were called *pétroma*, and people swore oaths in front of them "for the most important questions."

Epaminondas wanted to reestablish the Mysteries of Andania in Messenia. He had been presented with a bronze urn that had been unearthed as the result of a dream. Epaminondas, "once he had managed to open it, found a slender sheet of tin there, rolled up like a book. It contained in writing the initiation of the Great Goddesses." These are fateful words: it is stated for the first time that the Mysteries could be *written down*. In Plato's last years, this had already been done. And something linked it to the original rites: the bronze urn holding the slender sheet of tin inscribed with letters inherited its power from the basket of the Mysteries—which contained the sacred objects to be displayed, not to be read.

Ever cautious, careful not to say a word too many when it came to secret matters, Pausanias did at least once give himself away when he wrote: "Anyone who has seen the mystery rite at Eleusis or has read the so-called *Orphic Writings* [*Orphiká*] knows what I mean." Here he implies that the Eleusinian initiation and the reading of certain writings—and specifically the orphic writings, which various generations of scholars have tried in vain to keep well distinct from Eleusis—were in some respects equivalent. That initiation through the book would one day be practiced in fifteenth-century Florence by the group around Marsilio Ficino, in the Oricellari gardens.

Zarmaros came from India as part of the embassy sent by King Porus to Augustus. Nicolaus of Damascus met him at Antioch. There were three ambassadors but the king's letters indicated more. They had probably died during the journey. The gifts for

Augustus were offered by eight naked young men who wore a strip of cloth around their loins and were fragrant with oils. With them were various animals, "including tigers, and it was the first time that not only the Romans but I believe also the Greeks had seen them," noted Cassius Dio. There were also snakes and an impressive river turtle, as well as a young boy without arms ("like the herms that we have here," notes Cassius Dio again).

Zarmaros appeared before Augustus at Samos, then followed him to Athens. He was initiated into the Mysteries. Eleusis could have very different effects, but they all had something to do with happiness. Having returned to Athens, Zarmaros set fire to himself because he was happy. "He jumped onto the pyre laughing, naked, wearing a cloth over his loins, well covered with oils." On his tomb it was written that he had "immortalized himself following the ancestral custom of the Indians."

Vettius Agorius Praetextatus emerges in the last years of Eleusis. Proconsul in Greece, "a man bestowed with every virtue," like many educated Romans he wanted to be initiated at Eleusis. In the year 364, Emperor Valentinian had issued an edict that banned all nocturnal celebrations. Praetextatus immediately recognized that this edict had a specific aim: to stamp out the cult of Eleusis "beginning from the hearth"—an allusion to an unexplained character in the Mysteries: "the child at the hearth." So Praetextatus simply *said no* to his emperor. And, according to Zosimus, "he gave this explanation, that such a law would make life unlivable [*abíotos*] for the Greeks if they were prevented from following the established way of celebrating the sacred mysteries, which reunited the whole human race, and guaranteed, so long as the edict were not in force, that everything would continue to take place in the way transmitted from their fathers." The now-Christian Empire was not powerful enough, if the Mysteries needed to be suppressed. Thirty-two years later, Alaric and his troops would take care of that. They spared Athens, but razed Eleusis.

Attica was deserted. The Athenians had left—to Troezen, to
Aegina, to Salamis. The Parthenon, set on fire by the Persians.
The Athenian Dicaeus and the Spartan Demaratus were on the
Thriasian plain, alone. They saw "advancing from Eleusis a cloud
of dust, as if raised by thirty thousand men; amazed, they won-
dered what men had raised such a cloud, and immediately heard
a call, and that call seemed to be the mystical call of Iacchus." The
Spartan was not convinced. Dicaeus told him that "since Attica is
deserted, that divine sound was coming from Eleusis to help the
Athenians and their allies." The Battle of Salamis followed, and the
Athenians did not fall under Persian dominion. The Mysteries—
Dicaeus recognized—don't just bring people closer to salvation
after death, but can save during life.

Eleusis, the place where "people of the remotest regions are initiated," according to Cicero. It was the closest approximation to
universality. But it left no visible signs. The initiates left Eleusis in
the same condition as they entered: the poor with the poor, rich
with the rich, half-castes with half-castes, powerful with the powerful, strangers with strangers. And, since the others couldn't say
who had been truly initiated, not even the initiate would ever be
certain about himself. Eleusis was a place to which people therefore had to return.

"*Eleusin servat quod ostendat revisentibus*," "Eleusis holds
something to show to those who return there." Seneca's five words
say something essential about Eleusis, without compromising its
secret. The Mysteries are not something that can be owned, like
a thought; they are not something that can be applied, like a formula. They are a place that offers some further thing each time
people return. But in order to return, people have to go away from
it, go back to their ordinary life—and then leave it once again.

SOURCES

The first number refers to the page, the second to the line of text where the quotation ends.

4, 10   A. Irving Hallowell, "Bear Ceremonialism in the Northern Hemisphere," in *American Anthropologist*, n.s., XXVIII, 1, January–March 1926, pp. 49–50.

5, 7   Ibid., p. 123.

5, 17   John Batchelor, *The Ainu and Their Folk-Lore*, Religious Tract Society, London, 1901, p. 487.

8, 31   Clottes, *What Is Paleolithic Art?: Cave Paintings and the Dawn of Human Creativity* (trans. Oliver Y. Martin and Robert D. Martin), University of Chicago Press, 2016, p. 43.

11, 9   Éveline Lot-Falck, *Les Rites de chasse chez les peuples sibériens*, Gallimard, Paris, 1953, p. 115.

11, 17   Éveline Lot-Falck, "À propos du terme chamane," in *Études mongoles et sibériennes*, 8, 1977, p. 8.

11, 24   Ibid., p. 11.

11, 31   Ibid., p. 18.

12, 33   *Ṛgveda*, 10, 136, 2.

12, 33   Loc. cit.

16, 5   Simone Weil, "L'Enracinement" (1943), in *Œuvres complètes*, edited by F. de Lussy, Gallimard, Paris, vol. V, part ii, 2013, p. 150.

17, 5   K. Rasmussen, *Rasmussens Thulefahrt*, edited by F. Sieburg, Frankfurter Societäts-Druckerei, Frankfurt am Main, 1926, p. 240.

18, 31   Henry James, *The Notebooks*, edited by F. O. Matthiessen and K. B. Murdock, Oxford University Press, New York, 1947, p. 164.

18, 32   Loc. cit.

19, 3   Loc. cit.

20, 13   Éveline Lot-Falck, *Les Rites de chasse*, cit., pp. 110–16.

20, 26   Ibid., p. 185.

21, 17   A. Friedrich and G. Buddruss, *Schamanengeschichten aus Sibirien*, O. W. Barth, München-Planegg, 1955, p. 150.

21, 20   Ibid., p. 149.

21, 30   Régis Bóyer and Éveline Lot-Falck, *Les Religions de l'Europe du Nord*, Fayard/Denoël, Paris, 1974, p. 639.

22, 2   Ibid., p. 640.

22, 9   A. Friedrich and G. Buddruss, *Schamanengeschichten aus Sibirien*, cit., p. 187.

22, 13   Loc. cit.

24, 10   Valerio Valeri, "Wild Victims: Hunting as Sacrifice and Sacrifice as Hunting in Huaulu," in *History of Religions*, XXXIV, November 2, 1994, p. 117.

24, 26   Ibid., p. 118.

27, 7   Creophylus, *History of Ephesus*, in Athenaeus, *Deipnosophistae*, VIII, 62, 361 d.

27, 8   Ibid., VIII, 62, 361 e.

27, 26   Diodorus Siculus, *Bibliotheca historica*, I, 86, 4–5.

27, 26   Ibid., I, 86, 5.

28, 2   Loc. cit.

28, 5   Strabo, *Geographica*, V, 4, 2.

28, 6   R. Merkelbach, "Spechtfahne und Stammessage der Picentes," in *Studi in onore di Ugo Enrico Paoli*, Le Monnier, Florence, 1955, p. 518.

28, 12   Pliny, *Natural History*, 10, 16.

28, 29   *Cnutonis regis gesta*, 3, 9.

33, 3   Plato, *Symposium*, 203 d.

33, 5   Loc. cit.

33, 34   Giordano Bruno, *De gli eroici furori*, II, 2.

34, 23   Claudian, *De raptu Proserpinae*, II, 27.

36, 24   Aelius Donatus, commentary on Terence, *Eunuchus*, 424.

38, 14   Euripides, *Iphigenia in Tauris*, 380.

38, 17   Pausanias, *Description of Greece*, X, 12, 1.

38, 20   Ibid., X, 12, 2.

38, 21   Ibid., X, 12, 3.

38, 24   Ibid., X, 12, 2.

38, 28   Callimachus, *Hymn to Artemis*, 7.

39, 34   Ovid, *Metamorphoses*, II, 442.

40, 11   Jean Rudhardt, *Notions fondamentales de la pensée religieuse et actes constitutifs du culte dans la Grèce classique*, Droz, Geneva, 1958, pp. 39–40.

40, 15   Ibid., p. 172.

41, 13   *Thesaurus cultus et rituum antiquorum*, J. Paul Getty Museum, Los Angeles, vol. II, 2004, p. 431.

41, 23   Virgil, *Georgics*, IV, 383.

41, 27   Aeschylus, fr. 168 (Radt).

42, 24   Lewis Richard Farnell, *The Cults of the Greek States*, Clarendon Press, Oxford, vol. II, 1896, p. 427.

43, 11   Pausanias, *Description of Greece*, VII, 18, 12.

43, 11   Loc. cit.

43, 12   Loc. cit.

43, 14   Ibid., VII, 18, 13.

43, 16   Loc. cit.

44, 19   Leonard Susskind, *The Cosmic Landscape*, Little, Brown, New York and Boston, 2005, p. 287.

48, 4   Aristotle, *Politics*, 1253 a, 29.

48, 22   *Odyssey*, V, 118.

48, 28   *Iliad*, XXIV, 30.

48, 30   *Odyssey*, V, 118.

48, 31   Ibid., V, 119.

49, 9   Cicero, *Aratea*, 424.

49, 14   Corinna, fr. 673 (Page).

49, 16   Joseph Fontenrose, *Orion*, University of California Press, Berkeley, 1981, p. 22.

49, 19   Karl O. Müller, "Orion," in *Rheinisches Museum für Philologie*, II, 1, 1834, p. 18.

49, 24   Claude Lévi-Strauss, *Le Cru et le Cuit*, Plon, Paris, 1964, p. 233.

49, 27   Aeschylus, *Prometheus*, 151.

49, 32   *Odyssey*, XI, 309–10.

50, 3   Ibid., XI, 574.

50, 13   Joseph Fontenrose, *Orion*, cit., p. 5.

50, 24   Karl O. Müller, "Orion," cit., p. 29.

50, 27   Ovid, *Fasti*, V, 532.

50, 34   Ibid., V, 501–502.

51, 5   Ibid., V, 513–14.

51, 13   Ibid., V, 523–24.

51, 21   Otto Gruppe, *Griechische Mythologie und Religionsgeschichte*, Oskar Beck, München, 1906, vol. I, p. 68.

52, 13   *Ṛgveda*, 7, 33, 11.

52, 19   *Bhāgavata Purāṇa*, 6, 18, 6.

52, 31   Ovid, *Ars Amatoria*, I, 731.

53, 7   Ibid., I, 729.

53, 23   Christian August Lobeck, *Aglaophamus*, Borntraeger, Regimontii Prussorum, 1829, vol. I, p. 586.

54, 17   *Iliad*, XXII, 29.

67, 10   Porphyry, *De Abstinentia*, II, 54.

69, 2   Pausanias, *Description of Greece*, X, 29, 6.

70, 21   Strabo, *Geographica*, X, 2, 9.

75, 4   Eratosthenes, *Catasterismi*, 1, 35.

75, 24   Apollodorus, *Bibliotheca*, I, 9, 16.

76, 11   Apollonius of Rhodes, *Argonautica*, II, 1223.

76, 20   Ibid., I, 773.

76, 27   Diodorus Siculus, *Bibliotheca historica*, IV, 48, 5.

77, 22   Pindar, *Pythian Odes*, IV, 79.

77, 24   Ibid., IV, 82–83.

77, 26   Ibid., IV, 86.

78, 3   Apollonius of Rhodes, *Argonautica*, I, 427–29.

78, 11   Ibid., I, 870.

78, 18   Ibid., I, 902–903.

78, 25   Ibid., I, 899.

78, 33   Plato, *Timaeus*, 68 c.

79, 28   Apollonius of Rhodes, *Argonautica*, IV, 728–29.

79, 32   Ibid., III, 619–20.

79, 33   Ibid., III, 623.

80, 24   Ibid., III, 541.

80, 29   Ibid., III, 550.

80, 32   Ibid., III, 388.

81, 3   Ibid., III, 2–3.

81, 15   Ibid., III, 202–203.

81, 18   Ibid., III, 262.

81, 19   Loc. cit.

81, 30   Ibid., II, 181–82.

82, 8   Ibid., IV, 801.

83, 4   Ibid., IV, 1673.

83, 5   Ibid., IV, 1674–75.

83, 6   Ibid., IV, 1675.

83, 14   Ibid., IV, 1666–67.

83, 15   Ibid., IV, 1669.

83, 30   Ibid., IV, 1695.

83, 33   Ibid., IV, 1697.

84, 24   *Odyssey*, XII, 70.

85, 17   Hesiod, *Catalogue of Women*, fragment 5, 4 (Merkelbach-West).

85, 18   Loc. cit.

87, 31   Hesiod, *Works and Days*, 106.

87, 33   Martin L. West, *Commentary*, in Hesiod, *Works and Days*, Clarendon Press, Oxford, 1978, p. 177.

88, 6   Hesiod, *Works and Days*, 158.

88, 9   Ibid., 153–54.

89, 15   Plato, *Laws*, V, 739 d; VI, 771 d; VII, 815 d; XI, 934 c.

89, 17   Ibid., VII, 815 d.

89, 29   Plato, *Cratylus*, 398 d.

90, 13   Gaius Julius Hyginus, *Fabulae*, 127.

91, 27   Loc. cit.

92, 19   Ovid, *Tristia*, I, 1, 114.

92, 31   Pausanias, *Description of Greece*, VIII, 47, 2.

93, 2   Ibid., VIII, 46, 5.

93, 7   Ibid., VIII, 45, 5.

93, 16   Ibid., VIII, 46, 4.

94, 11   Ovid, *Metamorphoses*, VIII, 313.

98, 23   William James, *Memories and Studies*, Longmans, Green, and Co., New York, 1911, p. 301.

100, 7   Alexandre Kojève, *Introduction à la lecture de Hegel*, Gallimard, Paris, 1947, pp. 554–55.

100, 20   Oliver Sacks, "The Mental Life of Plants and Worms, Among Others," in *The New York Review of Books*, LXI, April 24–May 7, 2014, p. 6.

101, 9   Herodotus, *Histories*, III, 108, 1.

103, 5   *Etymologicon magnum*, Weigel, Lipsiae, 1816, col. 568, under "Zagreús."

106, 32   Friedrich Nietzsche, *Also sprach Zarathustra*, in *Sämtliche Werke. Kritische Studienausgabe*, edited by G. Colli and M. Montinari, dtv-de Gruyter, Berlin-München, second revised edition, 1988, vol. IV, p. 65.

107, 7   Tertullian, *Ad nationes*, II, 7, 5.

107, 16   Plato, *Epinomis*, 982 b.

107, 19   Loc. cit.

108, 9   Apollodorus, *Bibliotheca*, I, 7, 4.

110, 7   Alan Turing, "On Computable Numbers" (1936), in *The Essential Turing*, edited by B. J. Copeland, Oxford University Press, New York, 2004, p. 75.

110, 9   Loc. cit.

110, 12   Ibid., p. 76.

110, 25   Ibid., p. 79.

110, 28   Loc. cit.

111, 11   Alan Turing, "Computing Machinery and Intelligence" (1950), in *The Essential Turing*, cit., p. 446.

111, 15   Andrew Hodges, *Alan Turing*, new enlarged edition, Vintage, London, 2014, p. 364.

111, 30   Alan Turing, "Computing Machinery and Intelligence," cit., p. 446.

112, 4   Andrew Hodges, *Alan Turing*, cit., p. 528.

112, 23   Simone Weil, *Cahiers*, in *Œuvres complètes*, cit., vol. VI, part ii, 1997, p. 547.

112, 27   Loc. cit.

113, 31   Paul Valéry, *Mauvaises pensées*, in *Œuvres*, edited by J. Hytier, Gallimard, Paris, vol. II, 1960, p. 795.

114, 21   Eugene Wigner, "The Unreasonable Effectiveness of Mathematics in the Natural Sciences," in *Communications on Pure and Applied Mathematics*, XIII, February 1, 1960, p. 1.

116, 11   Colin McGinn, "Storm over the Brain," in *The New York Review of Books*, LXI, 7, April 24–May 7, 2014, p. 62.

116, 21   H. Allen Orr, "Awaiting a New Darwin," in *The New York Review of Books*, LX, 2, February 7, 2013, p. 28.

117, 23   Genesis, 1:28.

117, 27   Ibid., 1:29.

117, 33   Ibid., 1:30.

118, 12   Ibid., 3:21.

118, 29   Ibid., 9:2–4.

119, 16   Jacques Derrida, *L'Animal que donc je suis*, Galilée, Paris, 2006, p. 147.

119, 21   Ibid., p. 140.

119, 26   First Letter to the Corinthians, 9:9.

119, 29   Psalms, 35:7.

120, 1   Plutarch, *On Eating Meat*, 999 a.

120, 2   Diogenes Laërtius, *Lives of Eminent Philosophers*, VII, 129.

120, 10   Plutarch, *On Eating Meat*, 996 b.

120, 14   Bernard Le Bovier de Fontenelle, *Œuvres*, Libraires associés, Paris, 1766, vol. V, p. 390.

120, 21   Ibid., p. 392.

120, 22   Ibid., p. 422.

120, 24   Ibid., p. 400.

120, 26   Ibid., p. 399.

121, 8   Nicolas-Charles-Joseph Trublet, *Mémoires pour servir à l'histoire de la vie et des ouvrages de M. de Fontenelle*, Rey, Paris, 1761, p. 115.

121, 14   Malebranche, *De la recherche de la vérité* (1674–1675), in *Œuvres*, edited by G. Rodis-Lewis, Gallimard, Paris, vol. I, 1979, p. 467.

121, 24   Plutarch, *On Eating Meat*, 993 b.

121, 26   Loc. cit.

122, 22   Porphyry, *De Abstinentia*, II, 24.

122, 29   Ibid., II, 25.

122, 31   Loc. cit.

123, 1   Loc. cit.

123, 19   Plato, *Timaeus*, 33 c–d.

124, 30   Harpocration, Oration of Aeschines, *Against Timarchus*, 23.

124, 31   Loc. cit.

125, 14   Tertullian, *De spectaculis*, 12, 2.

125, 16   Ibid., 12, 3.

125, 20   Heraclitus, fr. A 21 (Colli).

126, 11   Euripides, *Iphigenia in Tauris*, 1223–24.

126, 14   Aeschylus, *Eumenides*, 448–50.

126, 17   Ibid., 280–83.

126, 22   Robert Parker, *Miasma*, Clarendon Press, Oxford, 1983, p. 19.

128, 10   Jean Rudhardt, *Notions fondamentales de la pensée religieuse*, cit., p. 249.

128, 26   Martin P. Nilsson, *Griechische Feste von religiöser Bedeutung*, Teubner, Leipzig, 1906, p. 112.

129, 13   Porphyry, *De Abstinentia*, II, 44.

129, 17   Loc. cit.

129, 18   Loc. cit.

129, 21   Ibid., II, 41.

129, 23   Ibid., II, 45.

129, 26   Loc. cit.

130, 1   Ibid., II, 34.

130, 6   Ibid., II, 35.

132, 3   Giuseppe Rotilio, "L'alimentazione degli ominini fino alla rivoluzione agropastorale del Neolitico," in G. Biondi, F. Martini, O. Rickards, and G. Rotilio, *In carne e ossa*, Laterza, Rome-Bari, 2006, p. 101.

132, 7   Euripides, *Cretans*, fr. 2 (Jouan-Van Looy).

132, 9   *Etymologicon magnum*, cit., col. 568, under "Zagreús."

132, 14   Euphorion, fragment 13 (Powell).

132, 16   Loc. cit.

132, 31   Lewis R. Binford, *Debating Archaeology*, Academic Press, San Diego, 1989, p. 288.

133, 2   Ibid., p. 321.

133, 27   Giuseppe Rotilio, *L'alimentazione degli ominini*, cit., p. 101.

134, 27   Ibid., p. 109.

135, 7   Robert J. Blumenschine and John A. Cavallo, "Scavenging and Human Evolution," in *Scientific American*, CCLXVII, October 4, 1992, p. 96.

135, 30   Lewis R. Binford, *In Pursuit of the Past*, Thames & Hudson, London and New York, 1983, p. 59.

137, 8   Lewis R. Binford, *Debating Archaeology*, cit., p. 290.

137, 27   Lewis R. Binford, *In Pursuit of the Past*, cit., p. 48.

138, 26   Lewis R. Binford, *Debating Archaeology*, cit., p. 353.

138, 31   Loc. cit.

139, 18   Giuseppe Rotilio, *L'alimentazione degli ominini*, cit., p. 117.

140, 16   *Maitrāyaṇī Saṃhitā*, 1, 10, 12; *Kāṭhaka Saṃhitā*, 8, 5.

140, 27 Stephanie W. Jamison, *The Ravenous Hyenas and the Wounded Sun*, Cornell University Press, Ithaca and London, 1991, p. 83.

140, 32 *Kāthaka Saṃhitā*, 25, 6.

141, 1 Loc. cit.

141, 6 Stephanie W. Jamison, *The Ravenous Hyenas and the Wounded Sun*, cit., p. 51.

141, 11 *Ṛgveda*, 10, 72, 7.

142, 7 *Śatapatha Brāhmaṇa*, 3, 7, 4, 2.

142, 16 *Kāthaka Saṃhitā*, 25, 6.

142, 20 Loc. cit.

142, 26 Stephanie W. Jamison, *The Ravenous Hyenas and the Wounded Sun*, cit., p. 128.

143, 28 *Maitrāyaṇi Saṃhitā*, 3, 8, 1–3.

144, 13 *Taittirīya Saṃhitā*, 6, 2, 4, 4.

146, 2 Lewis R. Binford, *In Pursuit of the Past*, cit., pp. 63–65.

146, 14 David Lewis-Williams, *The Mind in the Cave*, Thames & Hudson, London, 2002, p. 87.

146, 17 Ibid., p. 88.

147, 3 Simone Weil, *Cahiers*, in *Œuvres complètes*, cit., vol. VI, part iv, 2006, p. 319.

147, 20 Marylène Patou-Mathis, *Neanderthal*, Perrin, Paris, 2010, p. 7.

147, 24 Ibid., p. i.

149, 12 Klaus Schmidt, *Sie bauten die ersten Tempel*, dtv-Beck, München, 2008, p. 211.

149, 15 Loc. cit.

149, 31 Ian Hodder, *Çatalhöyük. The Leopard's Tale*, Thames & Hudson, London, 2006, p. 98.

150, 26 Giambattista Vico, *La scienza nuova*, III, 1, 5, 17.

150, 34 Erwin Rohde, *Psyche*, Mohr, Freiburg and Leipzig, 1894, p. 11.

151, 23 Henry James, *The Notebooks*, cit., p. 212.

151, 31 Ibid., p. 224.

152, 10 Loc. cit.

152, 29 Ibid., pp. 224–25.

152, 30 Ibid., p. 224.

153, 4 Loc. cit.

153, 8 Loc. cit.

154, 14 Ibid., p. 225.

154, 16 Ibid., p. 224.

154, 19 Ibid., p. 248.

154, 33 Ibid., p. 225.

155, 7 Loc. cit.

155, 10 Loc. cit.

155, 13 Loc. cit.

155, 18 Loc. cit.

155, 22 Loc. cit.

155, 27 Loc. cit.

155, 35 Loc. cit.

156, 6 Loc. cit.

156, 8 Loc. cit.

156, 9 Loc. cit.

156, 14 Ibid., p. 234.

159, 3 Plato, *Timaeus*, 22 a.

159, 5 Loc. cit.

159, 6 Ibid., 22 b.

159, 11 Virgil, *Georgics*, IV, 347.

160, 14 Pindar, *Isthmian Odes*, VII, 5.

160, 22 Hesiod, *Theogony*, 944.

160, 33 Diodorus Siculus, *Bibliotheca historica*, IV, 9, 3.

162, 2 Ibid., IV, 14, 4.

163, 33 Ibid., IV, 9, 2.

164, 15 Plautus, *Amphitryon*, 61.

164, 16 Ibid., 59.

167, 14 Nonnus, *Dionysiaca*, XXXII, 299.

167, 21 Ibid., XXXV, 303–304.

167, 23 Ibid., XXXV, 306–307.

168, 5 *Jaiminīya Brāhmaṇa*, 1, 85, 3.

168, 6 *Ṛgveda*, 9, 86, 3.

169, 29 Hesiod, *Catalogue of Women*, fragments 25, 30–33 (Merkelbach-West).

173, 11 Ovid, *Amores*, I, 1, 20.

173, 13 Ibid., I, 1, 26.

173, 18 Ovid, *Metamorphoses*, I, 589.

173, 21 Ibid., I, 595.

173, 26 Ibid., I, 173.

173, 27   Ibid., I, 176.

174, 11   Ovid, *Amores*, III, 6, 17–18.

174, 32   Ibid., I, 5, 1.

175, 11   Ibid., III, 9, 19.

175, 21   Ovid, *Ars Amatoria*, I, 637.

175, 28   Ovid, *Metamorphoses*, I, 4.

176, 2   Ovid, *Epistulae ex Ponto*, IV, 8, 55.

176, 18   Ezra Pound, *The Spirit of Romance*, J. M. Dent, London, 1910, p. 6.

176, 22   Ovid, *Ars Amatoria*, III, 54.

176, 25   Ibid., III, 55–56.

176, 27   Ibid., III, 167–68.

176, 29   Ibid., II, 552.

177, 1   Ibid., I, 56.

177, 3   Ibid., I, 99.

177, 6   Ibid., I, 76.

177, 6   Ibid., I, 77.

177, 9   Ibid., I, 80.

177, 33   Ibid., II, 552.

178, 1   Charles Baudelaire, *Fusées*, in *Œuvres complètes*, edited by C. Pichois, Gallimard, Paris, vol. I, 1975, p. 661.

178, 3   Ovid, *Ars Amatoria*, III, 436.

178, 5   Horace, *Carmen Saeculare*, 57–58.

178, 6   Ovid, *Ars Amatoria*, III, 128.

178, 7   Loc. cit.

178, 9   Ibid., III, 121–22.

178, 11   Ibid., III, 113.

178, 14   Ibid., III, 770.

178, 18   Ibid., III, 775.

178, 21   Ibid., II, 714.

178, 22   Ibid., II, 715.

179, 2   Propertius, *Elegiae*, II, 7, 19.

179, 10   Ovid, *Ars Amatoria*, I, 756.

179, 15   Ibid., I, 761–62.

179, 20   Ibid., I, 45.

180, 2   Ronald Syme, *The Roman Revolution*, Clarendon Press, Oxford, 1939, p. 467.

182, 12   Ovid, *Fasti*, II, 5.

180, 14   Ibid., II, 7.

180, 16   Ibid., II, 8.

180, 20   Georges Dumézil, *La Religion romaine archaïque*, Payot, Paris, 1974, p. 64.

180, 33   Ovid, *Fasti*, II, 309–10.

181, 20   Ibid., II, 346.

181, 25   Ibid., II, 358.

182, 1   J. G. Frazer, *Appendix*, in Ovid, *Fasti*, Harvard University Press, Cambridge, 1976, p. 390.

182, 3   Georges Dumézil, *La Religion romaine archaïque*, cit., p. 72.

182, 6   Plutarch, *Life of Romulus*, 21, 6.

182, 22   Georges Dumézil, *La Religion romaine archaïque*, cit., p. 352.

182, 34   J. G. Frazer, *Appendix*, cit., p. 392.

183, 1   Georges Dumézil, *La Religion romaine archaïque*, cit., p. 355.

183, 14   Ovid, *Fasti*, II, 304.

183, 18   Ibid., I, 7.

183, 19   Ovid, *Medicamina Faciei*, 7.

183, 24   Marcus Terentius Varro, *De lingua latina*, VI, 30.

183, 25   Ovid, *Fasti*, I, 47.

184, 7   Ibid., IV, 936.

184, 11   Ibid., IV, 941–42.

184, 20   Ibid., IV, 784.

184, 29   Ibid., IV, 709.

185, 25   Ovid, *Metamorphoses*, X, 554.

186, 2   Ibid., X, 689.

187, 12   Ibid., II, 398.

187, 34   Ibid., I, 452.

188, 7   Ibid., I, 456.

188, 10   Ibid., I, 463–64.

188, 12   Ibid., I, 464–65.

188, 14   Ibid., I, 473.

188, 34   Ibid., V, 369–72.

189, 7   Ibid., X, 527–28.

189, 9   Ibid., X, 532.

189, 31   Pindar, *Nemean Odes*, 6, 1.

190, 9   Ovid, *Metamorphoses*, I, 602–604.

190, 11   Ibid., I, 606.

190, 15   Ibid., I, 610–11.

190, 25   Ibid., I, 617.

190, 26   Ibid., I, 620.

190, 29   Ibid., I, 620–21.

191, 33   Ibid., II, 621–22.

192, 3   Ibid., II, 609.

192, 10   Ibid., II, 623–25.

192, 20   Johann Joachim Winckelmann, *Gedanken über die Nachahmung der griechischen Werke in der Malerei und Bildhauerkunst* (1755), G. J. Göschen, Stuttgart, 1885, p. 24.

192, 27   Ovid, *Metamorphoses*, II, 259.

193, 11   Ibid., XV, 72–73.

193, 15   Ibid., XV, 103.

193, 16   Ibid., XV, 104.

193, 19   Ibid., XV, 106.

193, 26   Ibid., XV, 127–29.

194, 4   Ibid., XV, 465.

194, 8   Ibid., XV, 468–69.

194, 19   Ibid., XV, 143.

194, 22   Ibid., XV, 483.

194, 24   Ibid., XV, 483–84.

194, 28   Ibid., XV, 74.

195, 13   Ibid., XV, 130–35.

195, 27   Plutarch, *Life of Numa Pompilius*, 14, 1.

195, 29   Ovid, *Fasti*, III, 276.

195, 31   Plutarch, *Life of Numa Pompilius*, 8, 6.

196, 1   Ibid., 15, 11.

196, 3   Loc. cit.

196, 6   Ovid, *Fasti*, III, 277.

196, 7   Ibid., III, 281.

196, 17   Ibid., III, 293.

196, 24   Ibid., III, 333.

196, 25   Ibid., III, 339.

196, 26   Ibid., III, 340.

196, 27 Ibid., III, 341.

196, 30 Ibid., III, 342.

197, 2 Ibid., III, 344.

197, 11 Plutarch, *Life of Marcellus*, 3, 6.

197, 17 Ovid, *Metamorphoses*, X, 233–34.

198, 2 Pausanias, *Description of Greece*, VIII, 2, 4–6.

198, 26 Hesiod, *Catalogue of Women*, fragments 5, 3; 17 a, 5; 64, 17; 165, 9; 235, 3; 253, 3 (Merkelbach-West).

199, 2 Ovid, *Metamorphoses*, IV, 538.

199, 17 Ovid, *Amores*, III, 12, 41.

199, 18 Ibid., III, 12, 42.

203, 3 Plato, *Laws*, 756 a–b.

203, 9 Ibid., 739 e.

203, 18 Ibid., 624 a.

203, 30 Ibid., 890 d.

204, 2 Ibid., 889 c.

204, 6 Ibid., 891 b.

204, 10 Ibid., 888 a.

204, 11 Ibid., 887 c.

204, 13 Ibid., 964 d.

204, 14 Loc. cit.

204, 25 Ibid., 803 b.

205, 10 Loc. cit.

205, 14 Ibid., 803 c.

205, 15 Ibid., 804 b.

205, 16 Loc. cit.

205, 18 Loc. cit.

205, 20 Ibid., 804 c.

205, 33 Plato, *Protagoras*, 337 d.

206, 12 Plato, *Laws*, 715 d.

206, 13 Loc. cit.

206, 24 Ibid., 716 c.

207, 2 Ibid., 853 c.

207, 17 Giorgio Pasquali, *Le lettere di Platone*, Le Monnier, Florence, 1938, p. 115.

207, 25 Plato, *Laws*, 709 b.

207, 27   Loc. cit.

207, 28   Ibid., 709 c.

208, 14   Loc. cit.

208, 18   Loc. cit.

208, 25   Ibid., 757 a.

208, 31   Loc. cit.

208, 34   Ibid., 756 e.

209, 23   Ibid., 951 b.

209, 26   Ibid., 734 e.

209, 33   Ibid., 739 a.

210, 11   Ibid., 739 c.

210, 14   Loc. cit.

210, 18   Loc. cit.

210, 26   Ibid., 739 d.

210, 33   Ibid., 739 e.

211, 12   Ibid., 739 d.

211, 30   Plato, *Republic*, 493 c.

212, 14   Plato, *Laws*, 788 a.

212, 16   Loc. cit.

212, 17   Ibid., 788 b.

212, 18   Loc. cit.

212, 19   Ibid., 788 c.

212, 23   Loc. cit.

212, 24   Ibid., 788 b.

212, 27   Ibid., 743 c.

213, 4   Ibid., 701 a.

213, 6   Ibid., 693 d.

213, 12   Ibid., 701 a.

213, 13   Loc. cit.

213, 16   Ibid., 701 b.

213, 17   Ibid., 700 e.

213, 25   Plato, *Epistles*, VII, 340 d.

214, 5   Plato, *Laws*, 660 c.

214, 13   Plato, *Phaedrus*, 244 c.

214, 19   Ibid., 244 b.

214, 27   Ibid., 244 e.

214, 30 Plato, *Laws*, 803 d–e.

214, 33 Ibid., 803 e.

215, 24 Ibid., 747 d.

215, 28 Ibid., 747 e.

216, 2   Loc. cit.

216, 4   Loc. cit.

216, 10 Ibid., 888 b.

216, 11 Loc. cit.

216, 19 Ibid., 891 b.

216, 23 Ibid., 887 b.

216, 26 Ibid., 891 c.

216, 26 Loc. cit.

216, 28 Loc. cit.

217, 5   Ibid., 892 b.

217, 6   Ibid., 897 a.

217, 10 Ibid., 896 e.

217, 15 Ibid., 897 b.

217, 23 Ibid., 897 d.

217, 28 Ibid., 897 c.

217, 30 Ibid., 896 c.

218, 7   Ibid., 899 b.

218, 10 Ibid., 908 b.

218, 19 Ibid., 907 a.

218, 22 Ibid., 900 c.

218, 33 Ibid., 908 d.

219, 9   Ibid., 964 e.

219, 10 Loc. cit.

219, 14 Ibid., 959 e.

219, 18 Ibid., 951 d.

219, 31 Ibid., 808 b.

219, 32 Ibid., 808 c.

219, 32 Ibid., 808 b.

220, 6   Ibid., 808 c.

220, 24 Ibid., 828 b.

220, 30 Loc. cit.

221, 14 Ibid., 758 e.

221, 19   Ibid., 934 c.

221, 21   Ibid., 941 b.

221, 23   Loc. cit.

221, 25   Loc. cit.

221, 27   Loc. cit.

222, 9   Ibid., 797 a.

222, 10   Ibid., 797 b.

222, 12   Ibid., 797 c.

222, 13   Loc. cit.

222, 15   Loc. cit.

222, 17   Ibid., 794 a.

222, 24   Loc. cit.

222, 28   Ibid., 796 d.

222, 29   Ibid., 799 a.

222, 32   Ibid., 799 b.

223, 4   Ibid., 799 c.

223, 7   Ibid., 800 b.

223, 14   Ibid., 815 d.

223, 18   Ibid., 815 c.

223, 19   Ibid., 815 d.

223, 20   Loc. cit.

223, 29   Ibid., 816 c.

223, 32   Ibid., 816 c–d.

224, 3   Ibid., 815 d.

224, 12   Ibid., 915 b.

224, 17   Ibid., 817 b.

224, 25   Ibid., 817 c.

224, 32   Aristophanes, *Tesmophoriazusae*, 38.

224, 33   Aristophanes, *The Frogs*, 959.

225, 1   Aristophanes, *Tesmophoriazusae*, 426.

225, 7   Ibid., 151–52.

225, 10   Ibid., 153.

225, 25   Plato, *Laws*, 801 b.

225, 34   Plato, *Republic*, 607 b.

226, 11   Plato, *Sophist*, 236 d.

226, 11   Ibid., 235 a.

226, 19   Plato, *Laws*, 765 e.

226, 21   Loc. cit.

226, 25   Loc. cit.

226, 30   Ibid., 766 a.

227, 8   Ibid., 782 c.

227, 9   Loc. cit.

227, 10   Loc. cit.

227, 11   Loc. cit.

227, 18   Ibid., 782 d.

227, 21   Ibid., 793 b.

227, 25   Ibid., 793 c.

227, 29   Ibid., 793 b.

228, 1   Ibid., 792 d.

228, 3   Ibid., 793 a.

228, 6   Ibid., 793 b.

228, 15   Pausanias, *Description of Greece*, X, 24, 4.

228, 22   Pindar, fr. 169 a, 1–4 (Snell-Maehler).

228, 25   Philemon, *Thebaioi*, fr. 31, 4–5 (Kassel-Austin).

228, 26   *Iliad*, XIX, 91.

228, 29   Herodotus, *Histories*, I, 91.

228, 31   Simonides of Ceos, *Ode for Scopas*, in Plato, *Protagoras*, 345 d.

229, 3   Plato, *Republic*, 493 c.

229, 4   Simone Weil, "Dieu dans Platon," in *Œuvres complètes*, cit., vol.
          IV, part ii, 2009, p. 86.

229, 10   Plato, *Laws*, 818 a.

229, 14   Ibid., 818 b.

229, 18   Loc. cit.

229, 23   Ibid., 818 b–c.

229, 27   Ibid., 818 c.

229, 34   Ibid., 818 e.

230, 4   Hesiod, *Works and Days*, 277–80.

230, 5   Ibid., 276.

230, 15   Pindar, fr. 169, 1 (Maehler).

230, 24   Heraclitus, fr. A 11 (Colli).

230, 30   Plato, *Laws*, 936 b.

231, 1   Loc. cit.

231, 6   Loc. cit.
231, 16   Ibid., 822 b.
231, 18   Ibid., 823 b.
231, 22   Loc. cit.
231, 24   Loc. cit.
232, 8   Loc. cit.
232, 12   Ibid., 823 c.
232, 13   Loc. cit.
232, 19   Ibid., 763 b.
232, 21   Ibid., 763 a–b.
232, 24   Ibid., 763 b.
233, 3   Plato, *Sophist*, 218 c.
233, 5   Ibid., 218 d.
233, 10   Ibid., 221 a.
233, 12   Plato, *Laws*, 823 d.
233, 19   Ibid., 823 e.
233, 21   Ibid., 824 a.
233, 22   Loc. cit.
233, 23   Loc. cit.
233, 25   Loc. cit.
234, 1   Plato, *Sophist*, 235 c.
234, 8   Ibid., 221 a.
234, 30   Plato, *Laws*, 920 a.
235, 1   Ibid., 918 c.
235, 2   Ibid., 920 b.
235, 3   Ibid., 919 c.
235, 4   Ibid., 918 b.
235, 21   Ibid., 873 d.
235, 21   Loc. cit.
235, 28   Loc. cit.
235, 31   Loc. cit.
235, 32   Ibid., 873 e.
236, 1   Loc. cit.
236, 3   Loc. cit.
236, 4   Loc. cit.
236, 8   Loc. cit.

236, 19   Ibid., 874 a.

236, 21   Ibid., 874 e–875 a.

236, 23   Ibid., 875 d.

236, 31   Ibid., 906 a.

237, 32   Diogenes Laërtius, *Lives of Eminent Philosophers*, III, 60.

238, 4   Plato, *Epinomis*, 973 b.

238, 5   Loc. cit.

238, 6   Loc. cit.

238, 13   Ibid., 974 c.

238, 16   Ibid., 975 d.

238, 18   Ibid., 977 c.

238, 20   Ibid., 977 d.

238, 23   Loc. cit.

238, 25   Ibid., 979 d.

238, 26   Ibid., 979 e.

238, 30   Ibid., 980 c.

238, 30   Loc. cit.

239, 1   Ibid., 992 a.

239, 6   Letter from S. Weil to A. Weil in March 1940, in *Œuvres complètes*, cit., vol. VII, part i, 2012, p. 448.

239, 10   Plato, *Epinomis*, 981 e.

239, 11   Simone Weil, "La Science et nous," in *Œuvres complètes*, cit., vol. IV, part i, 2008, p. 151.

239, 21   Iamblichus, *Life of Pythagoras*, 247.

239, 23   Loc. cit.

239, 28   Paolo Zellini, *Gnomon*, Adelphi, Milano, 1999, pp. 164–65.

239, 30   Letter from A. Weil to S. Weil on February 29, 1940, in Simone Weil, *Œuvres complètes*, vol. VII, part i, cit., p. 533.

239, 32   Letter from S. Weil to A. Weil of March 1940, ibid., p. 457.

240, 1   Draft letter from S. Weil to A. Weil of late March or early April 1940, ibid., p. 465.

240, 6   Plato, *Epinomis*, 992 d.

243, 20   Aristophanes, *Lysistrata*, 1093–94.

243, 25   Debra Hamel, *The Mutilation of the Herms*, n.p., 2013, p. 3.

243, 29   Aristophanes, *Lysistrata*, 138–39.

245, 15   Thucydides, *History of the Peloponnesian War*, VI, 60, 2.

246, 8   Plutarch, *Life of Alcibiades*, 34, 6.

246, 9   Loc. cit.

246, 10   Ibid., 19, 2; 22, 3.

246, 19   Pausanias, *Description of Greece*, I, 38, 2.

247, 23   Pseudo-Lysias, *Speeches*, VI, 10.

248, 2   Andocides, *On the Mysteries*, 85.

248, 8   *Hymn to Demeter*, 10.

248, 9   Ibid., 11.

248, 11   Ibid., 6.

248, 29   Aeschylus, *The Libation Bearers*, 55–60.

248, 32   Jacob Burckhardt, *Griechische Kulturgeschichte*, *I*, in *Gesammelte Werke*, Schwabe, Basel-Stuttgart, vol. V, 1978, p. 228.

249, 5   Loc. cit.

249, 9   Ibid., p. 242.

249, 9   Ovid, *Metamorphoses*, XIII, 191.

249, 21   Thucydides, *History of the Peloponnesian War*, VI, 60, 5.

249, 26   Ibid., VI, 27, 1.

249, 29   Ibid., VI, 28, 1.

249, 31   Loc. cit.

249, 33   Ibid., VI, 28, 2.

249, 34   Loc. cit.

250, 16   Aristophanes, *Tesmophoriazusae*, 850.

250, 28   Euripides, *Helen*, 1354.

251, 8   Letter from Jacob Burckhardt to J. Oeri, October 24, 1868, in Werner Kaegi, *Jacob Burckhardt*, Schae, Basel-Stuttgart, vol. VII, 1982, p. 6.

251, 14   Thucydides, *History of the Peloponnesian War*, VI, 28, 1.

251, 20   Euripides, *Helen*, 1368.

251, 23   Aristotle, *Poetics*, 1456 a, 28.

251, 27   Ibid., 1456 a, 30–32.

252, 8   Euripides, *Helen*, 1688–91.

252, 27   Isocrates, *Panatenaico*, 181.

255, 4   Diodorus Siculus, *Bibliotheca historica*, I, 88, 7.

255, 8   Porphyry, *Vita di Plotinus*, 3, 5.

255, 13   Ibid., 3, 15–17.

255, 17   Ibid., 3, 21–22.

255, 22   Henri-Charles Puech, *En quête de la Gnose*, Gallimard, Paris, 1978, vol. I, p. 61.

256, 4   Plotinus, *Enneads*, V, 1, 8, 9–10.

256, 6   Ibid., V, 1, 8, 12–13.

256, 7   Ibid., V, 1, 8, 11.

256, 13   Plato, *Laws*, 930 e.

257, 9   Plotinus, *Enneads*, V, 8, 8, 21–22.

257, 11   Ibid., V, 8, 7, 22–23.

257, 12   Ibid., II, 9, 8, 14.

257, 16   Ibid., II, 9, 8, 30–33.

257, 20   Ibid., II, 9, 7, 6–7.

257, 24   Ibid., II, 9, 7, 2–4.

257, 32   Ibid., II, 9, 8, 36.

257, 34   Ibid., II, 9, 8, 37.

258, 7   Ibid., II, 9, 16, 11–12.

258, 11   Ibid., II, 9, 16, 37–40.

258, 13   Ibid., II, 1, 4, 17; II, 9, 7, 11; II, 9, 7, 30.

258, 23   Ibid., II, 9, 16, 24–26.

259, 31   Ibid., II, 9, 14, 45.

260, 4   Ibid., II, 9, 10, 3–5.

260, 15   Ibid., II, 9, 9, 26–27.

260, 19   Ibid., II, 9, 13, 7–8.

260, 22   Ibid., II, 9, 13, 4–6.

260, 29   Ibid., II, 9, 4, 1–6.

260, 31   Ibid., II, 9, 5, 37.

260, 33   Ibid., II, 9, 6, 1–2.

260, 34   Ibid., II, 9, 6, 5.

261, 1   Loc. cit.

261, 3   Ibid., II, 9, 6, 7.

261, 9   Ibid., II, 9, 6, 11.

261, 9   Ibid., II, 9, 6, 12.

261, 12   Ibid., II, 9, 6, 30–32.

261, 17   Ibid., II, 9, 6, 58.

261, 31   Ibid., II, 9, 12, 42–43.

262, 1   Ibid., II, 9, 12, 44.

262, 7   Ibid., VI, 4, 14, 16.

262, 9   Ibid., VI, 4, 14, 3–4.

262, 10   Ibid., VI, 4, 14, 19–20.

262, 10   Ibid., VI, 4, 14, 18–19.

262, 12   Ibid., VI, 4, 14, 21.

262, 14   Ibid., VI, 4, 14, 23.

262, 16   Ibid., VI, 4, 14, 24.

262, 19   Ibid., VI, 4, 14, 25.

262, 22   Loc. cit.

262, 25   Ibid., VI, 4, 14, 29.

263, 6   Ibid., III, 2, 17, 4–8.

263, 9   Ibid., III, 2, 17, 16–18.

263, 13   Ibid., III, 2, 17, 35–37.

263, 14   Ibid., III, 2, 17, 39–41.

263, 16   Ibid., III, 2, 17, 73–74.

263, 24   Ibid., III, 2, 17, 86–89.

264, 21   Ibid., II, 9, 15, 27–32.

265, 24   Ibid., VI, 9, 11, 47.

265, 29   Ibid., VI, 9, 11, 50–51.

266, 4   Ibid., I, 2, 7, 2–3.

266, 5   Ibid., I, 2, 7, 24–25.

266, 7   Ibid., I, 2, 7, 20–21.

266, 9   Ibid., I, 2, 7, 26–28.

266, 29   Ibid., III, 8, 1, 1–8.

267, 2   Ibid., III, 8, 1, 8–10.

267, 12   Ibid., III, 8, 1, 11–18.

267, 17   Ibid., III, 8, 1, 18.

267, 19   Loc. cit.

267, 26   Ibid., III, 8, 1, 18–24.

268, 6   Aristotle, *Nicomachean Ethics*, X, 1, 1172 b, 9–10.

268, 33   Plotinus, *Enneads*, III, 8, 4, 3–14.

269, 4   Ibid., III, 8, 4, 17.

269, 7   Ibid., III, 8, 4, 21–22.

269, 8   Ibid., III, 8, 4, 27.

269, 14   Ibid., III, 8, 3, 20–22.

269, 32   Ibid., III, 8, 4, 27.

269, 33   Ibid., III, 8, 4, 28.

269, 34   Loc. cit.

270, 2   Ibid., III, 8, 4, 31–32.

270, 7   Ibid., III, 8, 4, 33–34.

270, 9   Ibid., III, 8, 4, 34–35.

270, 10   Ibid., III, 8, 4, 35–36.

270, 16   Ibid., III, 8, 4, 39–40.

270, 18   Aristotle, *Metaphysics*, 1074 b, 34.

270, 30   Plotinus, *Enneads*, V, 6, 4, 21–22.

270, 33   Ibid., V, 6, 4, 2.

271, 9   Ibid., V, 6, 6, 31–32.

271, 13   Ibid., V, 6, 6, 32–35.

272, 17   Ibid., III, 2, 14, 1–6.

272, 21   Ibid., III, 2, 14, 15–16.

272, 22   Ibid., III, 2, 15, 2.

272, 23   Ibid., III, 2, 14, 19.

272, 25   Plato, *Phaedrus*, 247 e.

272, 28   Plotinus, *Enneads*, V, 8, 5, 22.

272, 32   Ibid., V, 8, 5, 23.

273, 1   Ibid., V, 8, 5, 24.

273, 3   Ibid., V, 8, 5, 21.

273, 4   Ibid., V, 8, 4, 53.

273, 7   Ibid., V, 8, 5, 24–25.

273, 13   Ibid., V, 8, 4, 54.

273, 27   Meister Eckhart, *Cuius est imago haec et superscriptio?*, Sermon XLIX, n. 511, in *Die lateinischen Werke*, edited by E. Benz, B. Decker, and J. Koch, Kohlhammer, Stuttgart, vol. IV, 1956, pp. 425–26.

274, 6   Plotinus, *Enneads*, III, 8, 6, 40.

274, 12   Ibid., II, 9, 9, 3–6.

274, 28   Ibid., III, 8, 8, 24.

275, 1   Aristotle, *Metaphysics*, 1072 b, 24.

275, 10   Ibid., 1072 b, 24–30.

275, 20   Plotinus, *Enneads*, III, 8, 8, 2.

275, 21   Parmenides, fr. 3 (Diels-Kranz).

275, 26   Plotinus, *Enneads*, III, 8, 8, 17–18.

275, 28   Ibid., III, 8, 8, 18.

275, 29   Loc. cit.

275, 31   Ibid., III, 8, 8, 18–19.

275, 32   Ibid., III, 8, 8, 19–20.

275, 34   Ibid., III, 8, 8, 27–28.

276, 6   Ibid., III, 8, 8, 28–30.

276, 11   Ibid., III, 8, 9, 2.

276, 13   Ibid., III, 8, 9, 15.

276, 15   Ibid., III, 8, 9, 16.

276, 16   Ibid., III, 8, 9, 23.

276, 19   Ibid., III, 8, 9, 26–28.

276, 20   Ibid., III, 8, 9, 30.

276, 20   Ibid., III, 8, 9, 32.

276, 24   Ibid., III, 8, 9, 33.

276, 25   Ibid., III, 8, 9, 35–36.

276, 27   Ibid., III, 8, 9, 50–51.

276, 28   Ibid., III, 8, 10, 1.

276, 30   Ibid., III, 8, 10, 3.

276, 31   Ibid., III, 8, 10, 5.

276, 34   *Bṛhadāraṇyaka Upaniṣad,* 5, 1, 1.

277, 1   Plotinus, *Enneads*, III, 8, 10, 10.

277, 3   Ibid., III, 8, 10, 12.

277, 4   Ibid., III, 8, 10, 15.

277, 6   Ibid., III, 8, 10, 22.

277, 7   Ibid., III, 8, 10, 30–31.

277, 13   Ibid., III, 8, 11, 11–12.

277, 16   Ibid., III, 8, 11, 14–15.

277, 21   Ibid., III, 8, 11, 26–29.

277, 22   Ibid., III, 8, 11, 31–32.

277, 24   Ibid., III, 8, 11, 42–43.

277, 31   Ibid., V, 8, 5, 20–25.

278, 9   Ibid., V, 8, 6, 1–9.

278, 19   Ibid., IV, 8, 1, 1–11.

278, 26   Plato, *Phaedrus*, 247 b–c.

279, 12   Plato, *Timaeus*, 90 a.

279, 13   Loc. cit.

279, 16   Plotinus, *Enneads*, IV, 3, 12, 5.

279, 18   *Bhagavad Gītā*, 15, 1.

279, 24   *Iliad*, IV, 441–43.

280, 2   Plato, *Timaeus*, 34 b.

280, 10   Aristotle, *Metaphysics*, 1074 b, 3.

280, 22   Plotinus, *Enneads*, II, 9, 16, 46–47.

280, 24   Ibid., II, 9, 16, 48.

280, 27   Loc. cit.

280, 29   Ibid., II, 9, 16, 51.

280, 30   Ibid., II, 9, 16, 54.

280, 31   Ibid., II, 9, 16, 50.

281, 6   Ibid., V, 8, 9, 36–42.

281, 21   Ibid., V, 5, 12, 15.

281, 23   Ibid., V, 5, 12, 32–33.

281, 26   Ibid., V, 5, 12, 34–35.

281, 28   Ibid., V, 5, 12, 36–37.

281, 34   Plotin, *Ennéades*, edited by É. Bréhier, Les Belles Lettres, Paris,
          vol. V, 1931, p. 105.

282, 10   Plotinus, *Enneads*, V, 8, 10, 5.

282, 12   Ibid., V, 8, 10, 2–4.

282, 14   Ibid., V, 8, 10, 27–28.

282, 15   Ibid., V, 8, 10, 30.

282, 16   Ibid., V, 8, 10, 36.

282, 20   Ibid., V, 8, 10, 41–43.

282, 32   Ibid., V, 8, 11, 10.

283, 2   Ibid., V, 8, 11, 12–13.

283, 6   Ibid., V, 8, 11, 17–18.

283, 30   Ibid., I, 2, 5, 1–2.

284, 1   Ibid., I, 2, 6, 2–3.

284, 3   Ibid., I, 2, 6, 7.

284, 4   Ibid., I, 2, 6, 8–9.

284, 6   Ibid., I, 2, 6, 6.

284, 12   Ibid., I, 2, 4, 5–6.

284, 16   Ibid., I, 2, 4, 15–16.

284, 19   Ibid., I, 2, 4, 13–14.

284, 23   Ibid., I, 2, 4, 23–25.

284, 33   Ibid., V, 8, 7, 9.

284, 34 Ibid., V, 8, 7, 25.

285, 1   Ibid., V, 8, 7, 26.

285, 4   Ibid., V, 8, 7, 40–41.

285, 7   Ibid., V, 8, 7, 12–13.

285, 8   Ibid., V, 8, 7, 16–17.

285, 17 Ibid., VI, 9, 9, 15–16.

285, 20 Ibid., VI, 9, 9, 16–17.

285, 22 Plato, *Republic*, 509 b.

285, 26 Plotinus, *Enneads*, VI, 9, 11, 45.

285, 30 Ibid., VI, 9, 9, 1–2.

286, 2   Ibid., VI, 9, 6, 55–57.

286, 9   Ibid., VI, 9, 7, 3–5.

286, 12 Ibid., VI, 9, 7, 16.

286, 13 Ibid., VI, 9, 7, 12.

286, 22 Ibid., III, 2, 2, 17.

287, 1   Ibid., V, 3, 17, 19–20.

287, 8   Ibid., V, 3, 17, 18.

287, 15 Ibid., V, 3, 17, 38.

287, 32 Ibid., I, 4, 12, 1.

288, 1   Ibid., I, 4, 12, 4.

288, 2   Ibid., I, 4, 12, 4–5.

288, 5   Ibid., I, 4, 12, 7.

288, 5   Ibid., I, 4, 12, 8.

288, 6   Plotin, *Ennéades*, cit., vol. I, 1924, p. 82.

288, 7   Plotin, *Plotins Schriften*, edited by R. Harder, Meiner, Hamburg, vol. V, 1960, p. 31.

288, 12 Pierre Chantraine, *Dictionnaire étymologique de la langue grecque*, Klincksieck, Paris, 1968, vol. I, p. 462, under "hiláskomai."

288, 17 Loc. cit.

288, 19 Loc. cit.

288, 28 Plotinus, *Enneads*, I, 4, 12, 10–12.

288, 32 Ibid., I, 4, 11, 1–3.

288, 35 Ibid., I, 4, 11, 12–13.

289, 4   Ibid., I, 4, 14, 19–20.

289, 8   Ibid., III, 2, 15, 31–33.

289, 10 Ibid., III, 2, 15, 35–39.

289, 14   Ibid., III, 2, 15, 43–47.

289, 17   Ibid., III, 2, 15, 55–56.

289, 30   Ibid., III, 2, 16, 5–10.

290, 2   Ibid., III, 2, 16, 4.

290, 4   Ibid., III, 2, 16, 10–11.

290, 8   Ibid., III, 2, 16, 12–13.

290, 14   Ibid., III, 2, 16, 17–20.

290, 18   Ibid., III, 2, 16, 22–23.

290, 21   Ibid., III, 2, 16, 23–27.

290, 27   Friedrich Nietzsche, *Nachgelassene Fragmente (Herbst 1885–Herbst 1887)*, in *Sämtliche Werke. Kritische Studienausgabe*, cit., vol. XII, p. 119, fr. 2 [114].

290, 28   Plotinus, *Enneads*, III, 2, 16, 30–31.

290, 30   Ibid., III, 2, 16, 32–33.

290, 32   Ibid., III, 2, 16, 35–36.

291, 1   Ibid., III, 2, 16, 47–48.

291, 3   Ibid., III, 2, 16, 49.

291, 4   Ibid., III, 2, 16, 54.

291, 8   Ibid., III, 2, 16, 54–58.

291, 10   Ibid., III, 2, 5, 18–19.

291, 14   Ibid., III, 2, 5, 23–25.

291, 18   Letter from Ch. Baudelaire to Ch. Asselineau of March 13, 1856, in *Correspondance*, edited by C. Pichois with the collaboration of J. Ziegler, Gallimard, Paris, vol. I, 1973, p. 340.

291, 23   Plotinus, *Enneads*, VI, 9, 11, 45.

291, 25   Ibid., VI, 7, 34, 2.

291, 30   Ibid., VI, 7, 34, 17–18.

291, 33   Plato, *Republic*, 509 b.

292, 1   Plotinus, *Enneads*, VI, 7, 34, 17–18.

295, 4   Hugo von Hofmannsthal, *Augenblicke in Griechenland*, in *Gesammelte Werke*, edited by B. Schoeller with the collaboration of R. Hirsch, S. Fischer, Frankfurt am Main, vol. VI, 1979, p. 618.

295, 5   Loc. cit.

295, 5   Ibid., p. 619.

295, 6   Loc. cit.

295, 8   Loc. cit.

295, 12   Ibid., p. 620.

295, 18   Ibid., p. 624.

295, 21   Ibid., p. 626.

295, 23   Loc. cit.

296, 1   Ibid., p. 621.

296, 8   Hermann Usener, *Mythologie*, in *Vorträge und Aufsätze*, Teubner, Leipzig and Berlin, 1907, p. 61.

297, 1   Hermann Usener, *Götternamen*, Cohen, Bonn, 1896, pp. 276–80.

297, 14   Friedrich Creuzer, *Symbolik und Mythologie der alten Völker*, Leske, Leipzig and Darmstadt, vol. I, 1810, p. 75.

297, 16   Loc. cit.

297, 25   Ibid., vol. III, 1812, p. 350.

297, 34   Ibid., pp. 350–51.

298, 6   Letter from Jacob Burckhardt to Eduard Schauenburg of March 25, 1847, in Werner Kaegi, *Jacob Burckhardt*, cit., p. 4.

298, 13   Letter from Jacob Burckhardt to Jacob Oeri of October 24, 1868, ibid., p. 6.

299, 1   Inscription of *Nikandre, Daedelic kóre* in marble from the sanctuary of Artemis at Delos, 640–630 B.C.E., National Archaeological Museum, Athens.

299, 19   Herodotus, *Histories*, V, 87.

299, 22   Loc. cit.

300, 9   Gisela M. A. Richter, *Korai*, Phaidon, London, 1968, p. 3.

300, 31   Herodotus, *Histories*, VIII, 53.

301, 1   Ibid., I, 131.

301, 7   Ibid., I, 135.

301, 11   Ibid., I, 138.

301, 22   Ibid., I, 140.

301, 26   Loc. cit.

301, 35   Ibid., I, 132.

302, 11   Ibid., II, 158.

302, 13   Ibid., II, 152.

302, 16   Loc. cit.

302, 19   Loc. cit.

302, 22   Ibid., II, 154.

303, 2   Gisela M. A. Richter, *Korai*, cit., p. 21.

303, 5   Plotinus, *Enneads*, I, 6, 9, 13.

303, 14   Plato, *Phaedrus*, 252 d.

303, 15 Loc. cit.

303, 17 Loc. cit.

303, 23 Loc. cit.

303, 29 Jan Assmann, *Tod und Jenseits im Alten Ägypten*, Beck, München, 2003, p. 145.

304, 8   Clement of Alexandria, *Protrepticus*, IV, 58, 3.

304, 14 Ibid., IV, 52, 4.

304, 20 Tertullian, *De spectaculis*, 2, 9.

304, 27 Ibid., 2, 10.

304, 29 Simone Weil, *Cahiers*, in *Œuvres complètes*, vol. VI, part iv, cit., p. 320.

304, 32 Plotinus, *Enneads*, III, 2, 14, 26–28.

305, 2   Ibid., III, 2, 14, 28–30.

305, 6   Plato, *Laws*, 930 e.

305, 15 Philostratus, *Life of Apollonius*, V, 20.

305, 17 Loc. cit.

306, 13 Loc. cit.

306, 33 Pausanias, *Description of Greece*, III, 19, 2.

306, 33 Loc. cit.

306, 34 Loc. cit.

307, 27 Ibid., III, 15, 11.

307, 29 Loc. cit.

307, 34 Loc. cit.

308, 3   Friedrich Nietzsche, *Der Gottesdienst der Griechen*, in *Werke. Kritische Gesamtausgabe*, edited by G. Colli and M. Montanari, de Gruyter, Berlin and New York, vol. II, part v, 1999, p. 383.

308, 5   Friedrich Nietzsche, *Nachgelassene Fragmente (Frühling-Sommer 1875)*, in *Sämtliche Werke. Kritische Studienausgabe*, cit., vol. VIII, p. 59, fr. 5 [65].

308, 7   Pierre Chantraine, *Dictionnaire étymologique de la langue grecque*, vol. I, cit., p. 402, under "zôō."

308, 8   Loc. cit.

308, 21 Aristotle, *Politics*, 1255 a, 31–32.

308, 24 Ibid., 1255 a, 30.

308, 27 Ibid., 1254 b, 35.

308, 28 Ibid., 1254 b, 36–37.

308, 32   Ibid., 1254 b, 33–34.

309, 25   Jane Ellen Harrison, *Themis* (1912), Merlin Press, London, second edition, 1963, p. xi.

309, 30   Loc. cit.

310, 10   Friedrich Nietzsche, *Die fröhliche Wissenschaft*, in *Sämtliche Werke. Kritische Studienausgabe*, cit., vol. III, p. 352.

313, 9   Herodotus, *Histories*, II, 143.

313, 12   Loc. cit.

313, 15   Ibid., II, 142.

313, 18   Loc. cit.

313, 24   Ibid., II, 39, 3.

313, 25   Ibid., II, 37, 4.

314, 10   Diodorus Siculus, *Bibliotheca historica*, I, 96, 3.

314, 18   Herodotus, *Histories*, II, 3, 2.

315, 10   Plato, *Laws*, 656 d–657 a.

315, 18   Ibid., 641 e.

315, 22   Ibid., 657 a.

315, 23   Ibid., 657 b.

316, 5   Herodotus, *Histories*, I, 57.

316, 7   Diodorus Siculus, *Bibliotheca historica*, I, 95, 5.

316, 8   Ibid., I, 96, 5.

316, 13   Strabo, *Geographica*, XVII, 1, 29.

316, 17   Loc. cit.

316, 19   Loc. cit.

316, 21   Loc. cit.

316, 23   Loc. cit.

317, 5   Plato, *Epinomis*, 987 d.

317, 6   Ibid., 987 a.

317, 9   Ibid., 987 e.

317, 14   Ibid., 987 a.

317, 18   Ibid., 988 a.

318, 4   Friedrich Nietzsche, *Nachgelassene Fragmente (Sommer 1875)*, in *Sämtliche Werke. Kritische Studienausgabe*, cit., vol. VIII, p. 112, fr. 4 [36].

318, 22   Herodotus, *Histories*, II, 123, 1.

318, 24   Ibid., II, 123, 2.

318, 25   Ibid., II, 35.

319, 31   Diodorus Siculus, *Bibliotheca historica*, I, 63, 7.

320, 15   Jan Assmann, *Tod und Jenseits im Alten Ägypten*, cit., p. 302.

320, 23   Loc. cit.

321, 23   Samuel A. B. Mercer, *The Pyramid Texts*, Longmans, Green, and
          Co., New York, 1952, vol. I, p. 206, inscription 527, 1248 a–d.

322, 4   Herodotus, *Histories*, II, 35, 2.

322, 6   Ibid., II, 3, 2.

322, 27   Ibid., II, 65, 2.

323, 3   Diodorus Siculus, *Bibliotheca historica*, I, 86, 1.

323, 8   Ibid., I, 83, 1.

323, 9   Ibid., I, 83, 4.

323, 10   Loc. cit.

323, 14   Ibid., I, 12, 9.

323, 17   Henri Frankfort, *Ancient Egyptian Religion*, Harper & Row, New
          York, 1961, p. 8.

323, 19   Ibid., p. 9.

323, 30   Ibid., p. 13.

324, 17   Antoninus Liberalis, *Metamorphoses*, XXVIII, 3.

325, 5   Jacob Burckhardt, *Griechische Kulturgeschichte, II*, in *Gesammelte
          Werke*, cit., vol. VI, 1978, p. 10.

325, 15   Henri Frankfort, *Ancient Egyptian Religion*, cit., p. 24.

325, 31   Herodotus, *Histories*, II, 65, 5.

326, 3   Juvenal, *Satires*, XV, 1–2.

326, 6   Cicero, *Tusculanae*, V, 78.

326, 21   Diodorus Siculus, *Bibliotheca historica*, I, 83, 8.

326, 24   Ibid., I, 83, 8–9.

326, 27   Ibid., I, 83, 3.

327, 3   Ibid., I, 84, 6.

327, 11   Strabo, *Geographica*, XVII, 1, 37.

327, 12   Loc. cit.

327, 14   Ibid., XVII, 1, 38.

327, 19   Loc. cit.

327, 22   Loc. cit.

327, 26   Diodorus Siculus, *Bibliotheca historica*, I, 89, 3.

327, 31   Ibid., I, 89, 2.

328, 8   Plutarch, *Isis and Osiris*, 43, 368 c.

328, 11   Diodorus Siculus, *Bibliotheca historica*, I, 85, 3.

328, 16   Herodotus, *Histories*, II, 89, 2.

328, 17   Loc. cit.

328, 31   Hermes Trismegistus, *Kóre kósmou*, fr. 23, 64–65.

329, 2   Ibid., fr. 23, 65.

329, 20   Erik Hornung, *Der Eine und die Vielen*, WBG, Darmstadt, 1971, p. 123.

330, 11   Teaching of Amenemope, in Budge Papyrus, XVIII.

330, 13   Loc. cit.

330, 23   É. Drioton, "Un Chapitre sur l'écriture énigmatique," in A. Piankoff, *Le Livre du jour et de la nuit*, Institut français d'archéologie orientale, Le Caire, 1942, p. 120.

330, 27   Loc. cit.

330, 32   Ibid., p. 121.

331, 31   Erik Hornung, *Der Eine und die Vielen*, cit., p. 246.

332, 15   Diodorus Siculus, *Bibliotheca historica*, I, 65, 2.

332, 23   Ibid., I, 65, 6.

332, 27   Ibid., I, 65, 7.

332, 28   Ibid., I, 65, 8.

332, 29   Loc. cit.

332, 33   Lewis Richard Farnell, *The Cults of the Greek States*, Clarendon Press, Oxford, vol. V, 1909, p. 172.

333, 8   Diodorus Siculus, *Bibliotheca historica*, I, 96, 4.

333, 31   James Henry Breasted, *Ancient Records of Egypt*, University of Chicago Press, Chicago, vol. I, 1906, p. 333.

333, 33   Loc. cit.

334, 1   Ibid., p. 334.

334, 4   Loc. cit.

334, 5   Ibid., p. 335.

334, 12   Ibid., pp. 336–37.

334, 28   Diodorus Siculus, *Bibliotheca historica*, I, 49, 3.

337, 1   Pausanias, *Description of Greece*, X, 28, 6.

337, 20   *Iliad*, VI, 138.

337, 27   Thucydides, *History of the Peloponnesian War*, I, 22, 4.

338, 2   Plato, *Cratylus*, 408 c.

338, 2   Loc. cit.

338, 4   Loc. cit.

338, 7   Loc. cit.

339, 4   Ovid, *Fasti*, III, 296.

339, 12   Plato, *Cratylus*, 397 d.

339, 14   Herodotus, *Histories*, II, 52, 1.

339, 16   Plato, *Cratylus*, 397 d.

341, 4   Plutarch, *Life of Pericles*, 13, 5.

341, 8   Herodotus, *Histories*, II, 53, 1.

341, 24   Ibid., I, 32.

343, 3   Hesiod, *Theogony*, 200.

343, 10   Ibid., 205–206.

343, 19   Ibid., 213.

343, 23   *Śatapatha Brāhmaṇa*, 3, 1, 1, 4.

343, 30   Aristotle, *Metaphysics*, 983 a, 14.

344, 6   Ibid., 983 a, 19–21.

344, 12   Ibid., 982 b, 19.

345, 1   Erika Simon, *Die Götter der Griechen*, Hirmer, München, second
          enlarged edition, 1980, p. 11.

345, 21   Friedrich Nietzsche, *Der Gottesdienst der Griechen*, cit., p. 464.

345, 29   Loc. cit.

345, 31   Loc. cit.

346, 19   Strabo, *Geographica*, X, 3, 9.

346, 23   Loc. cit.

346, 25   Loc. cit.

346, 30   Loc. cit.

347, 5   Jorge Luis Borges, "Ragnarök," in *Labyrinths* (trans. James E.
          Irby), Penguin, London, 1970, p. 276.

348, 2   Ibid., pp. 183–84.

348, 4   Ibid., p. 184.

348, 24   *Iliad*, VI, 371; VI, 377.

349, 2   Hesiod, *Catalogue of Women*, fr. 141 (Merkelbach-West).

349, 4   Ibid., fr. 73.

349, 6   Ibid., fr. 75.

349, 25   Plato, *Republic*, 600 b.

349, 31   *Iliad*, XVI, 782.

350, 9   Euripides, *Thyestes*, fr. 391 (Nauck).

350, 17   *Iliad*, XIX, 90.

350, 21   *Ibid.*, XIX, 87.

351, 25   Hesiod, fr. 357 (Merkelbach-West).

352, 3   Hermann Usener, *Mythologie*, cit., p. 61.

352, 7   Aristotle, fr. 668 (Rose).

352, 12   Salutius, *On the Gods and the World*, 3, 3.

352, 27   Harold Newman and Jon O. Newman, *A Genealogical Chart of Greek Mythology*, University of North Carolina Press, Chapel Hill and London, 2003, reverse of title page.

352, 31   Jacob Burckhardt, *Griechische Kulturgeschichte, I*, cit., p. 7.

353, 10   Friedrich Nietzsche, *Der Gottesdienst der Griechen*, cit., p. 466.

353, 19   Friedrich Nietzsche, *Die Geburt der Tragödie*, in *Sämtliche Werke. Kritische Studienausgabe*, cit., vol. I, p. 151.

353, 20   Ibid., p. 145.

353, 28   Plato, *Laws*, 680 d.

353, 31   Thucydides, *History of the Peloponnesian War*, I, 21, 1.

353, 34   Ibid., I, 22, 4.

354, 23   Jean Rudhardt, *Notions fondamentales de la pensée religieuse*, cit., p. 245.

354, 33   Hesiod, *Theogony*, 21.

355, 26   *Odyssey*, III, 48.

356, 13   Plutarch, *Quaestiones conviviales*, 729 e–f.

356, 27   *Chāndogya Upaniṣad*, 5, 4, 1.

357, 7   *Śatapatha Brāhmaṇa*, 1, 1, 1, 14.

361, 16   François Jouan and Herman van Looy, commentary to *Erechtheus*, in Euripides, *Tragédies*, Les Belles Lettres, Paris, vol. VIII, part ii, 2000, p. 110.

361, 19   Euripides, *Erechtheus*, fr. 22, 92–94 (Jouan-Van Looy).

361, 25   Ibid., fr. 1 (Jouan-Van Looy).

362, 14   Ibid., fr. 14, 4–5, 16–18, 38–39 (Jouan-Van Looy).

362, 32   Johannes Toepffer, *Attische Genealogie*, Weidmannsche Buchhandlung, Berlin, 1889, p. 27.

363, 5   Friedrich Creuzer, *Symbolik und Mythologie der alten Völker*, cit., vol. IV, 1812, p. 367.

363, 9   Pausanias, *Description of Greece*, I, 38, 3.

363, 19   *Inscriptiones Graecae*, II, ii, 3811.

363, 22   Philostratus, *Lives of the Sophists*, II, 20.

363, 28   Strabo, *Geographica*, IX, 2, 18.

364, 9   J. G. Frazer, *Commentary* to *Pausanias's Description of Greece*, MacMillan, London, 1898, vol. V, p. 112.

364, 13   Loc. cit.

364, 23   Pseudo-Lysias, *Against Andocides*, 10.

365, 2   Loc. cit.

365, 5   Ibid., 11.

365, 17   Aeschylus, *Prometheus Bound*, 768.

365, 32   Euripides, *Helen*, 1307.

366, 4   *Hymn to Demeter*, 350.

366, 8   Ibid., 344–45.

366, 22   Emperor Julian, *Against the Galilaeans*, p. 167 (Neumann).

366, 26   Hesiod, *Theogony*, 914.

368, 1   Claudian, *De raptu Proserpinae*, II, 280.

368, 4   Ibid., II, 210–11.

368, 6   Ibid., II, 212–13.

368, 12   Ibid., II, 260–61.

368, 31   Sophocles, *Women of Trachis*, 498–502.

369, 15   *Hymn to Demeter*, 10–11.

370, 6   Ibid., 178.

370, 8   Ibid., 182–83.

370, 17   Apollodorus, *Bibliotheca*, I, 5, 1.

370, 21   *Hymn to Demeter*, 14.

370, 25   *Iliad*, XIX, 362–63.

371, 4   Clement of Alexandria, *Protrepticus*, II, 21, 1.

371, 5   Apollodorus, *Bibliotheca*, I, 5, 30.

371, 8   *Hymn to Demeter*, 203–204.

371, 15   Chester Beatty Papyrus I, in *Letteratura e poesia dell'antico Egitto*, edited by E. Bresciani, Einaudi, Torino, 1969, p. 346.

371, 18   Loc. cit.

371, 22   Loc. cit.

371, 26   *Iliad*, I, 599; *Odyssey*, VIII, 326.

372, 2   Hippolytus of Rome, *Refutation of All Heresies*, V, 8, 40.

372, 4   Hesychius of Alexandria, *Lexicon*, under "Baubo."

372, 15   Gregory of Nazianzus, *Orations*, 4, 115, 21–25.

372, 19   Michael Psellos, *Quaenam sunt Graecorum opiniones de daemoni-bus*, 4, in *Patrologia Graeca*, vol. CXXII, 880 A.

372, 23   Diodorus Siculus, *Bibliotheca historica*, V, 4, 4.

372, 24   Ibid., V, 4, 7.

372, 24   Loc. cit.

372, 28   Loc. cit.

372, 30   *Hymn to Demeter*, 407.

373, 4   Cicero, *On the Nature of the Gods*, III, 22, 56.

373, 9   *Hymn to Demeter*, 111.

373, 18   Ibid., 282–83.

373, 19   Ibid., 291.

373, 20   Ibid., 293.

373, 24   Ibid., 248.

373, 25   Ibid., 280.

373, 29   Ibid., 120–21.

374, 4   Epimenides, fr. B 1 (Diels-Kranz); Callimachus, *Hymn to Jupiter*, 8.

374, 13   *Hymn to Demeter*, 308–309.

374, 29   Plato, *Epinomis*, 975 b.

374, 31   Loc. cit.

375, 1   Hesiod, *Works and Days*, 42.

375, 3   Ibid., 48.

375, 27   Pliny, *Natural History*, XX, 198–99.

375, 28   Ibid., XX, 199.

376, 4   Hesiod, *Theogony*, 536.

376, 25   Pausanias, *Description of Greece*, II, 17, 4.

376, 26   Loc. cit.

376, 28   Ovid, *Fasti*, IV, 534.

376, 32   Axel Seeberg, "Poppies, Not Pomegranates," in *Acta ad archaeolo-giam et artium historiam pertinentia*, IV, 1969, p. 11.

377, 28   Callimachus, fr. 612 (Pfeiffer).

377, 30   Callimachus, *Hymn to Demeter*, 29–30.

378, 5   Ibid., 49.

378, 5   Ibid., 32.

378, 7   Ibid., 37.

378, 10   Ibid., 41.

378, 13   Ibid., 43–44.

378, 21 Ibid., 53–55.

378, 27 Ibid., 63.

378, 29 Ibid., 64.

378, 31 Ibid., 66–67.

379, 9 *Śatapatha Brāhmaṇa*, 10, 6, 5, 1.

379, 11 *Hymn to Demeter*, 372, 411.

379, 19 Sophocles, fr. 837 (Radt).

380, 33 Athenaeus of Naucratis, *Deipnosophistae*, XI, 93, 496 b.

381, 4 Simone Weil, "Intuitions pré-chrétiennes," in *Œuvres complètes*, vol. IV, part ii, cit., p. 152.

381, 7 *Hymn to Demeter*, 5–6.

381, 8 Ibid., 18.

381, 9 Ibid., 12.

381, 19 Ibid., 17.

381, 22 Ibid., 10.

381, 28 Friedrich Nietzsche, *Die Geburt der Tragödie*, cit., p. 115.

381, 32 *Derveni papyrus*, 31; Pseudo-Aristotle, *De mundo*, 401 b, 7.

382, 18 Aristophanes, *The Frogs*, 454–55.

382, 21 Ibid., 456–59.

383, 6 *Hymn to Demeter*, 482.

383, 12 Sophocles, fr. 837 (Radt).

383, 25 Walter Burkert, *Initiation*, in *Thesaurus cultus et rituum antiquorum*, cit., p. 92.

383, 30 Herodotus, *Histories*, VIII, 65, 4.

384, 3 Aelius Aristides, *Eleusinian Oration*, p. 256 (Jebb).

384, 5 Aristophanes, *The Frogs*, 391–92.

384, 15 Arthur W. Pickard-Cambridge, *The Dramatic Festivals of Athens*, Clarendon Press, Oxford, 1953, p. 285.

384, 17 *Inscriptiones Graecae*, I, ii, 628.

384, 29 Tertullian, *De spectaculis*, 3, 2–3.

384, 32 Psalms, 1:1.

385, 4 Tertullian, *De spectaculis*, 3, 4.

385, 6 Loc. cit.

385, 7 Ibid., 25, 3.

385, 32 Aristotle, *Eudemos*, fr. 10 (Ross).

386, 14 Plato, *Phaedrus*, 249 c.

386, 33 Christian August Lobeck, *Aglaophamus*, cit., p. 196.

387, 1 Loc. cit.

387, 7 Ibid., p. 3.

387, 23 Erwin Rohde, *Psyche*, cit., p. 287.

387, 32 Loc. cit.

388, 10 Simone Weil, "Notes de Londres," in *Œuvres complètes*, vol. IV, part ii, cit., p. 331.

388, 14 *Iliad*, XIX, 5.

388, 15 Ibid., XIX, 2.

388, 17 Ibid., XIX, 10–11.

388, 26 Ibid., XIX, 22.

388, 30 Ibid., XIX, 25.

388, 32 Ibid., XIX, 28.

389, 1 Ibid., XIX, 30.

389, 3 Ibid., XIX, 33.

389, 3 Loc. cit.

389, 8 Gospel of John, 6:60.

389, 10 Ibid., 6:61.

389, 23 Henri-Charles Puech, *En quête de la Gnose*, cit., p. 61.

390, 24 Pausanias, *Description of Greece*, I, 37, 2.

390, 26 Hesychius of Alexandria, *Lexicon*, under "Gephyrís."

391, 6 *Inscriptiones Graecae*, I, iii, 79.

391, 12 Letter from Theopompus to Alexander, in Athenaeus of Naucratis, *Deipnosophistae*, XIII, 67, 595 b.

391, 19 Commentary to Aristophanes, *Pluto*, 845.

392, 3 Pausanias, *Description of Greece*, V, 10, 1.

392, 13 Loc. cit.

392, 26 Herodotus, *Histories*, I, 132, 1.

393, 3 Paul Foucart, *Les Mystères d'Éleusis*, Picard, Paris, 1914, p. 294.

393, 6 Kevin Clinton, *Eleusis. The Inscriptions on Stone*, Archaeological Society at Athens, Athens, vol. II: *Commentary*, 2008, p. 36.

393, 13 Pausanias, *Description of Greece*, IV, 33, 5.

393, 20 *Inscriptiones Graecae*, V, i, 1390, 22–23.

393, 22 Loc. cit.

394, 7 Pausanias, *Description of Greece*, VIII, 15, 2.

394, 13 Ibid., IV, 26, 8.

394, 23   Ibid., I, 37, 4–5.

395, 5   Cassius Dio, *Roman History*, LIV, 9, 8.

395, 7   Ibid., LIV, 9, 9.

395, 13   Strabo, *Geographica*, XV, 1, 73.

395, 15   Loc. cit.

395, 17   Zosimus, *Historia Nova*, IV, 3, 3.

395, 22   Loc. cit.

395, 30   Ibid., IV, 3, 2.

396, 7   Herodotus, *Histories*, VIII, 65.

396, 10   Loc. cit.

396, 15   Cicero, *On the Nature of the Gods*, I, 119.

396, 24   Seneca, *Naturales quaestiones*, VII, 30, 6.

INDEX